Music: The Listener's Art

CLASSIC	ROMANTIC	MODERN	
ide variety of instru- ental and vocal onorities; brilliant sound, ansparent; much ontrast between light nd full; wide dynamic nge; exploration of gher registers	increase in fullness, richness, and denseness of sound; concern with special color effects; striking contrasts; widened range of pitch and dynamics	extremes of transparency and density; experiments in new sonority effects; sharp contrasts of color; tendency to reduce the "sweetness" of sound	QUALITIES OF SOUND
3 to many parts; nphasis on principal elody, with some olyphony, some ve-and-take	tendency toward amplification of lines by doublings; active part-writing, often with rich ornamentation; 3, 4 to many parts	1, 2 to many parts; prominent polyphonic action, also give-and-take; also use of baroque, classic, romantic textural layouts	TEXTURE
ame consonance values s preceding eras	same consonance values as before; lesser proportion of consonance than previously	consonance no longer a synonym for stability, although traditional ideas of consonance and dissonance still have considerable force	CONSONANCE
issonance used for armonic tension, for ramatic emphasis, often ithout preparation; any "tritone" issonances	greater saturation of dissonance, often without intervening consonance; dissonances make rich sounds, and represent instability; tritone, 7ths, 9ths, altered intervals	as a rule, considerable saturation of dissonance, with dissonances frequently at points of arrival; functional distinction between consonance and dissonance disappears frequently	DISSONANCE
aturation of cadential ction; long-range efinition, long-range ntrast of key; very trong harmonic drive	retention of classic cadence feeling with tendency toward deceptive and elided resolutions; rapid elusive shifts of tonal center; harmonic color an objective; weakened harmonic drives	partial abandonment of older chord types; substitutes for older cadences; rapid shifts of tonal areas; modal, atonal, polytonal, tone-row, microtonal systems; little harmonic drive	HARMONIC ACTION
ide range of pace and anner; strongly fluenced by typical ong and dance manners; teady, active pace, with trong accentuation	wide range of pace and manner; appearance of imbalanced, unsteady qualities of movement; preference for slower pace, less vigorous accent	emphasis on active, percussively accented pace, with cross-rhythms and imbalances, often in rapidly paced music; wide range of pace and manner; uncertain, shifting pace often found	MOVEMENT
ear, frequent, strong oints of arrival; omentum often carries eyond, aiming for mphatic cadential oints	obscured cadences, disguised points of arrival more frequent	in neo-classic and folkloric music well-defined points of arrival; in expressionistic music, uncertain sense of arrival	ARRIVAL
ell-defined period tructure in all forms and pes; extension of eriods	in small pieces, clear periodization in symmetrical structure; in larger works, tendency toward asymmetrical phrase structure	as a rule, asymmetrical phrase structure; some use of baroque continuous expansion and classic periodization	PHRASE STRUCTURE

Music: The Listener's Art

SECOND EDITION

Leonard G. Ratner

Professor of Music
Stanford University

McGRAW–HILL Book Company

New York · St. Louis · San Francisco · Toronto · London · Sydney

MUSIC: The Listener's Art

Library of Congress Catalog Card Number 65–27679

45678910 HD 1098

MC GRAW–HILL SERIES IN MUSIC
William J. Mitchell, Consulting Editor

Atkisson Basic Counterpoint
Chase America's Music
Crocker A History of Musical Style
Ratner Harmony: Structure and Style
Ratner Music: The Listener's Art
Wagner Band Scoring

Preface

Music is an art of listening. This book, therefore, is intended for the listener who wants to increase his understanding of music. It aims to provide him with tools, with means by which he can better analyze, evaluate, and appreciate the music he hears.

We start with the listener's reaction to music. First, we listen. What are the immediate impressions? Sound itself, its strength, its color, then the movement of sound, how it is set in motion, its pace, its regularity, how it reaches a point of arrival. These effects carry expressive values; they become our first criteria. Thus, at the very outset, the listener can interpret his impressions in nontechnical terms.

Afterwards, we discover how specific musical elements and processes —melody, rhythm, texture, harmony, phrase structure—help to create musical impressions. In this way we begin to see the relationship between musical techniques and expressive values in music. In order to show how fundamental musical procedures underlie various types of expression, we have drawn the material for the first section (Chapters 1 and 2) from a wide range of sources, from medieval to modern music, from folksong to symphony. This will enable the listener to make his way more confidently and quickly within the various areas of musical style and expression. The criteria established in the first chapters are used throughout the entire book to guide us in our listening.

The approach described above invites comparison for fuller understanding and greater satisfaction. For this reason, the historical framework is used. It enables us to illustrate systematically different kinds of music; it helps us to visualize the growth which, during history, has given rise to many and various musical styles. A perspective is developed and a sympathy awakened for perhaps unfamiliar modes of musical expression. At no time, however, does historical data take precedence over the actual experience of listening to the music itself. Throughout the second section of this book (Chapters 3 to 8) there is constant reference to the ideas explained in the first section—sound, movement, departure, arrival.

The second edition of *Music: The Listener's Art* has been prepared in order to facilitate instruction, especially in applying the basic criteria of music listening. Checklists for critical listening are provided at the end of each historical chapter; summaries of major topics have been added, as well as supplementary listening projects. Chapter 2 has been completely reorganized and expanded to include a section on orchestration. The reader will find a fuller treatment of phrase and period, and of opera, chamber music, choral music, nationalism, jazz, and new systems in twentieth-century music. A full analysis of Beethoven's Symphony No. 3 is provided as a means for summing up musical form in the classic era. New illustrative material has been included, as well as a number of new graphs that delineate various aspects of musical procedure and structure.

When the layman comes to a music-appreciation class or takes up a book on music, he wants to retain his musical experience, to have it illuminated; he wants the instruction to be organized around what he can hear, what he can grasp by listening. This need of the listener is psychologically justified and has been the guiding principle in organizing the entire presentation of this book. It has resulted in establishing the nontechnical criteria of the first chapter and, throughout the book, in offering the music first, and then discussing it. It is an approach that is sympathetic with the listener's already strong motivations for wanting to know music better.

The greatest organized demand for a book of this kind is in the courses offered in colleges and universities for the general student, courses which usually have such titles as "Music Appreciation," "Survey of Music," and "Introduction to Music." It is hoped that this book will help serve the needs of such instruction. But the musical needs and curiosities of students in such courses are no different from those of the layman who listens to music at home or at a concert. From the public at large there is perhaps an even greater demand for help in musical understanding. The approach adopted in this book—from impression to evaluation, and thence to some insight into the qualities and structures of music—will, we hope, appeal to all listeners.

Leonard G. Ratner

Contents

Music: The Listener's Art

chapter one

The Musical Experience

Why do you listen to music? If this question were asked of a number of people, they might answer: "I like the beat," "I like to dance," "I like a good tune," "I am moved by the sound of choral singing," "I like music for many reasons, but I couldn't begin to describe them clearly." Very few, if any, would reply that music has little or no meaning to them. To most of us music is precious. It evokes a response of pleasure and satisfaction in one way or another.

Many listeners sense that there is something beyond the immediate appeals of music. They wish to make closer contact with the materials of music to understand better the ways in which it is put together. They would like to explore the various areas of musical style, form, and expression to increase their satisfaction in the musical experience.

This book is intended for such listeners. It endeavors to explain how the techniques of musical composition are directed to expressive aims. It takes up various aspects of music to show how they are able to communicate and thereby contribute to the musical experience. Each composer has used the elements of music in a distinctive way; as we become conversant with some of the materials of musical composition, we shall gain greater insight into the composer's style and we shall better appreciate his expressive intentions.

Our point of departure is *sound.* Although everyone hears music differently, music could not exist were it not for the physical phenomenon of sound. It is the raw material of music and makes up the substance of all musical activity.

The kinds of sound that can be used for musical purposes are amazingly varied. Throughout the cultures of the world, East and West, a virtually limitless array of sounds appears in the service of musical expression. For example, Oriental theater music and an excerpt from an opera by Richard Wagner are worlds apart in their qualities of sound as well as in almost every other feature; yet each says something of importance to some listeners. All music, whether it be the pulsation of tribal drums or the rich combination of voices and instruments in an opera, has this feature: *It is based upon the power of sound to stir our senses and feelings.* A simple demonstration can illustrate this effect. Play a single tone on the piano, perhaps middle C, using the sustaining pedal. As the silence is broken, the tone takes the attention; concentration is further intensified by the effort to hear the fading tone. A simple effect such as this can be very compelling. The opening trumpet signal in the overture to Wagner's opera *Rienzi* is a striking instance of the use of a single tone to command the listener's attention.

Yet sound alone is not music. It must embody some kind of action. To do so, *it must move forward in time.* Everything that takes place musically involves the movement of sound. In a series of drumbeats, there is an impression of movement from one beat to the next. In a melody, the successive sounds line out a pattern of movement from one tone to the next. All music moves, and because it moves, it is associated with a fundamental kind of experience: the movement of life itself. We are stirred by impressions of movement because our very lives are constantly in movement. Breathing, growth, decay, the change of day to night—these all testify to the fundamental role that movement plays in our lives. Music appeals to our desire and need for movement.

Movement that gives a random impression, going on without purpose, control, or stop, leaves us somewhat baffled. In our way of thinking, feeling, and acting, movement must have an aim, a reason. For example, when we move our feet in walking, we expect each step to arrive at a point of contact with the earth; each breath reaches its point of arrival at the instant of maximum intake; every motion is made with the anticipation of arrival at a point of rest. Motion is not continuous; *it is marked off in phases or cycles by points of arrival.* Likewise, the movement of musical sound proceeds in phases directed to points of arrival. In drumbeats, the intervals of time between the strokes become phases of movement. In a melody, the progression from one tone to the next is a small phase of musical movement. The flow of music, pausing at each tone, gives us an impression of being continuous in time, very much like the spot of light that seems to move in space when lamps are lit successively in an electrical display.

Music is made up of sound moving in time to points of arrival; every musical gesture represents a special, perhaps unique way of combining these elements. Yet not all kinds of moving sound have made acceptable music. Composers and listeners pick and choose according to their taste and training. Certain procedures have been preferred to others; some have been generally accepted for centuries, while others appear only in connection with special styles and forms.

Our first step will be to learn how to use these basic attributes—sound, movement, and arrival—as criteria by which we can begin to evaluate and understand what is taking place in a piece of music. There is an advantage to using these criteria at first; we need not concern ourselves with the technical vocabulary of music. Definitions and explanations will appear later, to clarify further our initial impressions. Then we shall proceed to discover how each age created its own music, how various techniques related to the basic criteria were applied to achieve goals of musical expression at different times in history.

The First Criteria of Analysis

THE POINT OF DEPARTURE: SOUND

When a composer begins to write, he has some idea or image which moves him to set tones together so that they will suggest meaning to the listener. The solemnity of the Mass, the pathos of a tragic opera heroine, the gaiety of a country dance, the vigor of a bold instrumental flight, the wonderfully intricate yet beautiful interweaving of a motet, the sweet lyricism of a song—these may represent the composer's intentions for all or part of his composition. He begins to shape this image with the very first tones he assigns to the piece. These first tones can provide, for the listener, an important clue regarding the composer's expressive intentions. Indeed, this first impact is a critical factor in the musical experience, because it indicates what sort of events will very likely be taking place throughout the piece. Very often, this first impact is largely a question of the qualities of sound that are projected. In the following compositions, observe how the first few seconds of sound establish a mood or delineate a characteristic manner:

Stravinsky: *Les Noces* (contrast of effects)
Beethoven: Symphony No. 3, second movement (low, dark sound)
Bach: Toccata and Fugue in D minor (brilliant opening flourish)
Wagner: *Lohengrin,* Prelude to Act I (very high blended sounds)

Sound, then, is the first impression we receive as we listen to a piece, although a sound effect may not be the most important thing that the composer wishes to convey. We can draw our own conclusions about this as the piece moves on. But since sound reaches us *first,* we shall adopt it as the point of departure in our study of the basic elements and qualities of music.

QUALITIES OF SOUND

As we hear musical sound, we note the following attributes: (1) level or pitch, (2) amount, (3) strength, and (4) color.

Level or Pitch of Sound

The pitch or pitches at which a musical passage is set can create an impression of mood or attitude. We tend to associate levels of pitch with degrees of buoyancy or heaviness; composers will direct our attention to extremes of pitch in order to project special effects. Thus, the Scherzo from Felix Mendelssohn's *Midsummer Night's Dream,* which begins on a high level of pitch, gives the impression of lightness and agility. On the other hand, Franz Liszt's *Les Préludes* opens at a very low pitch to establish the mood of introspection and of portentous events that color the ideas bound up in this piece. The opening of Johannes Brahms's Symphony No. 1, Op. 68, covers the entire range of sound to create a massive, grandiose effect, proper for a piece in a heroic vein. Much music remains on a middle level of pitch, without reaching for extremes of low or high. In such cases, our attention is directed to other elements, such as movement or color. Most familiar songs and dances exemplify this. In a few striking instances, the musical effect rests upon the combining of extremes of pitch, without a "binder" in the middle. Such a passage was written by Béla Bartók to begin the third movement of his *Music for String Instruments, Percussion, and Celesta.* The disembodied tones, set at a great distance from each other, with nothing intervening, are evocative of a strange and elusive mood.

Changes in the pitch level in the course of a composition are also to be noted because such changes help to give a shape to the piece. The very slow, steady rise in pitch from the lowermost levels in the Prelude to Wagner's *Das Rheingold* (The Rhinegold) is suggestive of the increasingly full flow of the river Rhine.

Amount of Sound

In listening it is not difficult to determine whether few or many sounds are being produced. Yet consider the various effects that such differences create. Contrast a large mass of sound with the effect created when only a few performers are heard—that of thinness and transparency. The Mendelssohn and Brahms examples cited above illustrate these points. Again, try to imagine a piece such as the Hallelujah Chorus from Georg Friedrich Handel's *Messiah* being sung with but one voice or instrument to a part. The impression of majesty and grandeur would simply not be present. For each participant in the musical experience—the composer, the performer, the listener—the amount of sound employed is a critical factor in the proper projection of musical expression.

Strength of Sound

Strength of sound—the degree of loudness—is again a very obvious feature of musical action. Because of this, it has great power to convey expressive values. Loud music tends to affect us with direct and strong impact; soft music moves us with persuasion. We have heard examples of both values in the Brahms and Mendelssohn works cited above. Strength increases and decreases and thereby projects a continuity of feeling or expression. A marked increase in strength can give the impression of growing tension; there is no more celebrated example of this than Maurice Ravel's *Bolero.* The entire piece is built upon an unrelenting increase, in both strength and amount of sound, to convey the effect of an excitement that finally reaches the point of frenzy. A gradual decrease has the opposite effect, of relaxation or release. Tchaikovsky, by gradually decreasing the strength and amount of sound at the end of his Symphony No. 6, conveys a mood of utter despair and resignation.

Color of Sound

The *kinds* of sound that have been used effectively for musical purposes are limitless in number. Color of sound—*tone color* or *timbre,* as we shall later designate this element—is one of the principal concerns of the composer. It constitutes an important criterion by which a musical composition is judged. (Listen again to the examples listed under "The Point of Departure: Sound"; each has a distinctive quality of tone color.)

Unlike level, amount, and strength of sound, tone color is difficult to measure or to describe in specific terms. We might draw an analogy between taste and the perception of tone color. A taste can be sweet, salty, sour, bland, rich, or thin. But more specialized flavors cannot be so described; they must be experienced to be recognized. Tone color, like taste, has some general values. It may be *bright,* as in the Mendelssohn Scherzo; it may be *dark,* as at the beginning of Tchaikovsky's Symphony No. 6; it may be *rich,* as at the beginning of Brahms's Symphony No. 1; it may be *thin,* as in the opening number of Igor Stravinsky's *L'Histoire du soldat.* Often qualities of tone color invite more specific indications or descriptions; they also have special connotations. For example, the brilliant, clear, sharp-edged tone of trumpets has an air of command, authority, and decision. Nowhere is this effect more dramatically projected than in Ludwig van Beethoven's *Leonore* Overture No. 3. At the height of an agitated passage, there is a sudden break in movement and the clear, penetrating tone of the trumpet is heard, signaling the rescue of the hero and heroine. Horns have been used in hunting and in music suggesting the hunt because of their rich, somewhat muffled color of sound that seems to reverberate and carry great distances. Such is the case in the Hunting Chorus from Karl Maria von Weber's opera *Der Freischütz,* where the horns are in their full glory as instruments of the hunt. Another example of specific color linked to traditional usage is found in the opening of the Overture to Wolfgang Amadeus Mozart's opera *The Magic Flute,* where the heavy, lean sound of the trombones suggests the solemn, ceremonial aspect of the opera's plot.

Qualities of tone color can also be set against each other with telling effect, so that each value is highlighted and dramatized by contrast. In the opening of Mozart's *Prague* Symphony a kaleidoscopic variety of tone colors appear in quick succession when short musical fragments are passed back and forth among various instruments.

The following chart incorporates the criteria of musical sound explained above. It may be used to summarize qualities of sound and also to relate them to each other, so that we can perceive what the composer's governing idea of sound might have been in a given work. Since the criteria involve matters of judgment, the indications will be approximate, and a sliding scale is provided to accommodate individual variation in perception.

QUALITIES OF SOUND			CHANGE		
a. Pitch: low	______	high;	much	______	little
b. Amount: large	______	small;	"	______	"
c. Strength: loud	______	soft;	"	______	"
d. Color:					
Bright	______	dark;	"	______	"
Rich	______	thin;	"	______	"

In addition to the works mentioned above, the following are suggested for study in the evaluation of qualities of sound:

Stravinsky: *Le Sacre du printemps,* first section
Wagner: Overture to *Die Meistersinger,* opening section
Haydn: Symphony No. 103 in E♭ major (*Drumroll*), introduction
Debussy: *Nuages* (Clouds) from Nocturnes for Orchestra
Gabrieli: *In ecclesiis* (In the Congregation)
Varèse: *Ionization*

In musical expression, sound helps to establish an expressive climate, a mood, within which other elements of musical communication may operate. The next aspect we shall explore is musical *movement.*

QUALITIES OF MOVEMENT

Sound, no matter how evocative it may be, must progress forward in time in order to make a musical point. The progression of sound in time, its *movement,* has much in common with physical movement in time and space. This similarity has been used to advantage by composers from antiquity to the present day. Music has accompanied dances, ceremonies, dramatic performances, and many other kinds of presentation where its qualities might enhance other kinds of action. Also, musical movement has relation to a more subtle and elusive kind of experience, the *emotional experience;* this refers to the stirring or "moving" of the listener's feelings. The attributes of musical movement, underlying both physical and emotional connotations, are its pace, its regularity, its articulation, and its intensity.

Pace of Movement

Quick musical movement has generally been associated with vigorous physical action, excitement, or agitation; it rouses feelings quickly and leaves little time for reflection. *Slow* musical movement can give the impression of concentration, or reflection, of feelings stirred deeply and deliberately; it can also convey a sense of relaxation. Many nuances of musical expression are projected by various degrees of quick or slow movement, so much so that the exact pace of a composition is one of the critical factors in performing it properly and grasping its content clearly.

The Scherzo from Mendelssohn's *Midsummer Night's Dream* moves very quickly. When we associate this with its high, light, airy quality of sound, the image of disembodied magical spirits is very easy to picture. In the second movement of Beethoven's Symphony No. 3 a slow pace and the lowest, darkest tones of the string instruments are used to suggest the deliberate, measured step of a funeral march.

Regularity of Movement

When music begins at a given pace, quick, slow, or moderate, we may expect it to continue at that pace and thereby to give an impression of regularity. We accept the pace and adjust ourselves to it, very much as we accommodate ourselves to the flow of traffic while driving or as we keep step while marching. If the pace is changed, however, or the established flow of the music is interrupted (broken or halted) in a noticeable manner, we are surprised and perhaps even shocked. While this may be quite irritating in physical movement, it can increase interest and present a challenge in musical movement if handled properly. Disturbances in pace can build up a sense of excitement and importance in music.

Two highly contrasting examples illustrate *regularity* and *irregularity* in musical movement. The first movement of Johann Sebastian Bach's *Brandenburg* Concerto No. 5 has a quick, regular pace that gives an impression of vigorous and exuberant activity. Moreover, the quality of sound is brilliant, full, with the most salient action taking place on a rather high level. In the Sonata for Piano in B minor by Liszt, we hear many changes of pace. At the beginning of this work, the pace is slow and uncertain; then it becomes quick and vigorous; both the level and the color of sound change from moment to moment. A mood of dark introspection or brooding, broken by outbursts of passionate declamation, is created by these values of sound and movement.

Sometimes regularity and irregularity of movement are combined simultaneously, as in the *Soldier's March* from Stravinsky's *L'Histoire du soldat*. Observe the mechanical regularity of the low instrument, the string bass. Above this repeated figure, the upper instruments seem to have quite an irregular pattern of movement. The conflict of these two procedures has a humorous effect, especially in view of the thin, rather dry quality of sound and the matter-of-fact manner of performance.

Articulation of Movement

Articulation of musical movement refers to the manner in which the music flows or proceeds. It is comparable to various kinds of physical gesture. The music may flow smoothly, *continuously,* as in the Nocturne from Mendelssohn's *Midsummer Night's Dream.* Conversely, the gestures may incorporate well-marked separations, or breaks, regularly or irregularly spaced, to create an incisive, crisp effect. In the familiar principal strain of Johann Strauss, Jr.'s *Blue Danube Waltz,* for example, the frequently and regularly spaced instants of silence in the melody contribute to the buoyancy and brilliance of the music.

Very frequently, we hear changes in articulation from one passage to another. This represents a level of organization in which the composer creates contrast in the quality of movement over a larger part of his piece. In the first few moments of the finale of Beethoven's Symphony No. 3, the *Eroica,* we hear many changes in articulation, ranging from a maximum of separation to an unbroken flow.

Intensity of Movement

Intensity of movement refers to the impression of effort or energy which the music imparts. Is the manner gentle or vigorous? Does the level of intensity remain constant, or does it increase or decrease? A song such as *Drink to Me Only with Thine Eyes* maintains a steady level of rather gentle movement. The *Blue Danube Waltz* has a vigorous but steady movement, with incidental increase in tension. Beethoven, in the first movement of his Symphony No. 3, often begins a passage in a rather gentle manner and then builds up intensity of movement to the maximum at the end of the passage. In his familiar *Volkslied* (Folksong), *Songs without Words,* Op. 53, no. 5, Mendelssohn brings the piece to an end by a steady decrease in intensity. He accomplishes this principally by reducing the strength of sound, but he also incorporates a decrease in the amount of sound.

The following chart summarizes qualities of movement to the extent that we have examined them in this chapter.

QUALITIES OF MOVEMENT			FLUCTUATION	
a. Pace:	fast	slow;	much	little
b. Regularity:	regular	irregular;	much	little
c. Articulation:	continuous	separate;	much	little
d. Intensity:	gentle	vigorous;	much	little
	steady	increase		
	steady	decrease		

Generally speaking, when we listen for musical movement, we are responding to the impression of musical *action*—action which develops the mood value established by qualities of sound. Suggested works for further evaluation of musical movement:

Stravinsky: *L'Histoire du soldat,* finale
Bach: *Brandenburg* Concerto No. 3 in G major, finale
Gabrieli: *In ecclesiis*
Estampie from *Masterpieces of Music before 1750*
Varèse: *Ionization*
Bartók: *Music for Strings,* third movement
Tchaikovsky: Symphony No. 6 in B minor, second movement
Beethoven: Quartet in B♭ major, Op. 18, no. 6, third movement

POINTS OF ARRIVAL

Movement cannot be appreciated unless it is observed or felt in relation to points of arrival. In the first illustrations of sound and movement, there were moments or instants in the music which gave the impression of resting, stopping, or ending. These are *points of arrival* in music. Likewise they are points of departure for new phases of movement.

Arrival, in music, is a *relative* quality. Each new tone, each pause in the flow is a minute point of arrival. Indeed, this is how the composer's idea of musical movement is embodied—by points which articulate and control the flow of sound. In contrast to this small-scale relationship of movement and arrival, we have learned to expect and to recognize the end of a long section, of a movement, or of an entire piece as a point of arrival.

When we try to assess effects of arrival, we ask: *In what manner* has the music arrived at a given point? Arrive it must, because it is taking place in time. As with sound and movement, the manner provides important indications of the style and expressive values of the piece. We can assess the particular effects of arrival according to degrees of *clarity, finality,* and *emphasis.* The questions we ask are: To what extent does a certain instant in the musical action give the effect of arrival (clarity)? To what extent does the effect of arrival seem to bring musical action to an end (finality)? How pronounced, how strong, is the gesture which gives the effect of arrival (emphasis)?

Clarity of Arrival

As music moves along, its patterns of motion are controlled and guided by instants of rest (see page 2). Some of these may stand out more prominently than others. For example, in Strauss's *Blue Danube Waltz,* the instants of rest are very noticeable and they clearly act as points of arrival for the motion which precedes them. On the other hand, in Lassus' motet *Tristis est anima mea* (Sad Is My Soul), *Masterpieces,* no. 23, we should find it difficult to identify clear points of arrival. While one voice pauses, another moves, so that a continual feeling of action is maintained until the end of the piece. In the Mendelssohn Scherzo, we can sense quite clearly when points of arrival are reached, even though the general momentum carries beyond such points.

Finality of Arrival

As we listened for clarity, it was evident that points of arrival differ in the degree to which they represent the completion of a line of action. Relatively few of these points give an absolute sense of finality or completion, nor should they, lest the piece seem to end too quickly. An analogy of speech may prove helpful. Certain sentences come to a full close, yet the train of thought has not been completed and some continuation is indicated. Other sentences will finish an idea or a series of ideas with a full sense of completion or finality; the subject has been covered. In a similar manner, musical points of arrival will be so arranged that only the last in a composition is intended to provide complete finality. The others will give some impression of ending, but only partially so, and hence will invite continuation. Almost any composition will exemplify this range in the effect of finality, based upon the position of the successive points of arrival in the larger scheme. For example, the song *Drink to Me Only with Thine Eyes* has four clear points of arrival. The first, second, and fourth are identical in every respect, and each might be acceptable for final arrival. Only the third demands continuation. Yet we need the last point of arrival to reach a fully satisfying ending for the song. The first and second, although they seem final, appear too soon in the piece for the listener to accept the idea that the music can end at these points.

Much the same situation is found in compositions of great length. We may hear many points of arrival, perhaps some that might qualify as being final, but it is only at the very end that a complete effect of finality is achieved in relation to what has gone before. Sometimes to achieve an effect of final arrival may require considerable time; in such cases we have *areas* of arrival. One of the important skills in musical composition is to prepare for arrival in such a way that the listener anticipates it and is eventually satisfied. Because of its very marked articulations and contrasts in sound, the finale of Mozart's *Prague* Symphony is a clear example of the arrangement of points of arrival in a long piece.

Finality of arrival can be deliberately weakened or clouded at the end of a composition if the composer wishes to achieve an expressive effect of uncertainty or question. This takes place at the end of Franz Schubert's song *Die Stadt* (The City); the poem and the music create the picture of a city seen through clouds, appearing and disappearing; the uncertain fading effect at the end suggests the final vanishing of the poet's vision. At times, when a composer reaches the end of a long section but does not wish to wind matters up, he uses a less than final effect of arrival, as though to tell his listeners, "There is more to come." There is such a gesture at the end of the long slow section that opens the first movement of Brahms's Symphony No. 1.

Emphasis of Arrival

The degree of power, the breadth of gesture, with which a composer projects an effect of arrival is designated here as *emphasis*. After the headlong downward rush at the beginning of the last movement of Beethoven's Symphony No. 3, the music pulls to a halt with increasingly broad strokes. Very few effects of arrival could be more emphatic. In contrast, the points of arrival that articulate the opening passages of Mendelssohn's Scherzo represent little more than touching points and turns in a capricious and easy flight; here, emphasis is at a minimum. We can correlate emphasis with intensity of movement. A calm, flowing piece with gentle, steady movement cannot absorb emphatic points of arrival; a piece that has an intense quality of movement, perhaps vigorous or agitated, would very likely require more emphatic points of arrival, particularly at important divisions in its form.

By throwing the effect of arrival out of joint, displacing it, a composer can create quite a humorous effect. Johann Strauss, in his *Perpetuum mobile,* accomplishes this; in a similar manner Glenn Miller, in his excellent jazz composition *In the Mood,* makes several tries at a final ending; by continuing after these attempts, the piece makes explicit the humor we have already sensed in the jaunty principal idea of the piece.

Criteria for arrival are summarized as follows:

a. Clarity: clear________________unclear
b. Finality: final________________nonfinal
c. Emphasis: gentle________________strong

The following works are suggested for study in evaluating effects of arrival:

Mozart: Symphony No. 35 in D major (*Haffner*), Menuetto
Debussy: *Nuages* from Nocturnes for Orchestra
Beethoven: Symphony No. 8 in F major, first movement
Bach: *Brandenburg* Concerto No. 3 in G major, first movement
Wagner: *Parsifal,* Prelude to Act III
Stravinsky: *L'Histoire du soldat,* final movement
Palestrina: *Al rivo del Tebro* (On the Banks of the Tiber)

Generally speaking, arrival in music has the effect of *rounding off* musical movement or action; in this way it *limits* the extent to which a given mood or set of moods will be allowed to expand.

INTERACTION OF MOVEMENT AND ARRIVAL

When sound moves to a point of arrival, a *phase of musical movement* is created. Such phases are the units of musical structure; they differ greatly in length as well as in their internal construction. By noting the *length* of a phase of movement, and by sensing the manner in which the point of arrival is approached, we can learn much about musical structure.

Length of Phases of Movement

There is no absolute length for a phase of musical movement. Like speech, which is built up by word groups into sentences and paragraphs, musical structure is created by the combination of smaller phases of movement into larger ones. Possibly the smallest appreciable phase of movement would be two tones sounded in succession. This would be comparable to a pair of words, such as "to go."

The manner in which small phases of movement are joined to build up larger structures provides a significant clue to the nature of a musical composition. Two excerpts, equal in length, can serve to illustrate contrasting procedures. In the song *Drink to Me,* we have *four* short phases of movement, each coming to a clearly defined, rather emphatic point of arrival. In the first movement of Beethoven's Quartet in F, Op. 59, no. 1, the smaller phases of movement are run together and their points of arrival are much less emphatic than in the song; momentum continues unbroken until a very emphatic point of arrival is reached, and the impression we have is that there is but *one* long phase of movement in this passage. The style of the song is sweet, sentimental, and touching. The style of the Quartet is broad and soaring. Each has the form, with relation to phases of movement, that best suits the musical values expressed.

When phases of movement in a composition are equal to each other in length, and when they are sufficiently short for the listener to sense this equality of length, an impression of regularity and balance is created. We may also refer to this quality as *symmetry* in relation to length. Symmetry constitutes part of the appeal of songs and dances—this pleasant regular motion associated with equality in length. Our song *Drink to Me* illustrates this plan very nicely, as does most of the familiar song and dance music of our time. In other works, more complex and broad in their form, more ambitious and searching in their expressive values, phases of movement do not, as a rule, have such neat balance; some may be short, others long. This establishes an irregularity among various sections of the piece, creating questions for the listener and compelling his attention through the heightened intensity. In such works, matters are generally settled and balance is reestablished by strong effects of arrival. The first movement of Beethoven's Symphony No. 3 epitomizes these qualities.

Approach to the Point of Arrival

From the preceding examples it is clear that some correlation exists among the length of a phase of movement, the symmetry or asymmetry in respective phases of movement, and the approach to the point of arrival. In certain types of music, the point of arrival is a resting place, a breathing point. It is an incidental moment of relaxation or articulation. In such music, phases of movement are not greatly extended. Early Christian plainsong has many examples of this kind of structure; also, much dance music treats its points of arrival as instants of rest, as does our song *Drink to Me*. In other music, movement develops increasing intensity and excitement as it approaches the point of arrival. We have the idea of a *drive* to a goal, which extends the phase of movement with broad and sweeping action. We find ourselves anticipating the moment of arrival, which will come with dramatic and momentous effect. Music of the eighteenth and nineteenth century often shows this kind of structure, as we heard in the opening moments of the Beethoven Quartet, Op. 59, no. 1. Yet again, the approach to the point of arrival may exhibit a letting go, a relaxation or settling down, such as in the final measures of Beethoven's overture *Coriolanus* or the second movement of his Symphony No. 3. Schubert's songs *Die Stadt* (The City) and *Der Doppelgänger* (The Phantom Double) manage to sustain the eerie mood which is characteristic of both songs by tapering off toward the final point of arrival.

The following criteria summarize the interaction of movement and arrival:

a. Phases of movement:
   1. short________________________________long
   2. equal________________________________unequal
b. Approach: 1. steady________________________
   2. increasing in strength________________
   3. decreasing in strength________________

The works we listed on page 13 for the evaluation of arrival may be used to evaluate the interaction of movement and arrival. In addition, the following works are suggested:

Haydn: Symphony No. 94 in G major (*Surprise*), second movement
Wagner: *Meistersinger,* Prelude
Schönberg: Quartet No. 4, first movement
Bach: Mass in B minor, Kyrie I

The interaction between movement and arrival bears strongly upon musical *form,* insofar as it is concerned with the length of phases of movement and the strength of the arrival effect.

Use of the Basic Criteria

In listening for the qualities represented by the basic criteria discussed in this chapter, we have made substantial contact with a number of musical compositions; this has been done without recourse to technical or specialized vocabulary. These criteria are by no means exact, nor are they intended to stand as listening goals in themselves. One listener may well judge a quality of sound, of movement, or of arrival differently from other listeners; or he may sense a different relationship between these qualities. The value of these criteria is that they draw attention to features which require judgment to assess and which lead further into the character of the work of art itself. Using the criteria invites the listener to come to grips with essential qualities of action, feeling, and expression. Thus, on hearing a composition, he will not ask what story the piece tells, what key it is in, which the second theme is, or what instrument is playing. More searching queries will be made *from the first:* What kinds of sound has the composer imagined? How does this piece move forward? What will happen at the point of arrival? Moreover, this will lead to an even more important question: What has the composer chosen to stress in his music; which elements have the greater importance? Each observation along these lines leads to another until we have created for ourselves an idea of the complete composition.

By way of summing up we shall examine two compositions: the Ostinato from Book Six of Bartók's *Mikrokosmos* and the second movement of Beethoven's Symphony No. 5.

BARTÓK

1. Quality of Sound

a. Level of sound. Middle to high; occasional sections on low level for contrast; now and then abrupt shifts from high to low and vice versa, crossing over a steady middle-level flow.

b. Amount of sound. Relatively small at beginning, increasing gradually and dropping off several times; section of considerable fullness toward end serving as kind of climax.

c. Strength of sound. Contrasts between loud and soft, sometimes sharp, sometimes gradual; some soft, full-sounding places contrasted with thin, loud passages.

d. Color of sound. Wide range from dark to brilliant; sharp contrasts in color; use of many different special effects drawing upon the flexibility and the numerous resources of the piano.

2. Quality of Movement

a. Pace. Quick; one section in middle somewhat slower.

b. Regularity. Strict regularity within sections, except for one or two places that seem to be held back momentarily.

c. Articulation. Emphatic; occasional contrasting lyric manner.

d. Intensity. Basically a driving, energetic manner; sometimes a sense of easy, regular, somewhat relaxed movement; at other times a more intense, strained effect, generally when color is most brilliant and sound is at its strongest.

3. Effects of Arrival

a. Emphasis. Generally quite strong because of separation of passages; some intermediate points very light; final points of arrival extremely strong; effect of ending very emphatic owing to repetition of passages denoting arrival.

b. Clarity. Clarity tied up with emphasis in this generally well-marked piece.

4. Interaction of Movement and Arrival

a. Length of phases of movement. Rather short phases at the beginning; longer toward the end; no regular relationships of length; grouping into larger phases of movement very clearly defined.

b. Approach to points of arrival. Simple articulations at beginning of piece; toward the end a strong sense of drive to points of arrival.

The quick, energetic pace and the driving quality of movement in this piece suggest some kind of vigorous, well-patterned physical movement, probably a dance. Working against this steady basic flow, certain striking contrasts of color and pace increase interest and intensify movement. Toward the end a climax to the dance is suggested by strong and repeated effects of arrival.

BEETHOVEN

1. Quality of Sound

a. Level of sound. Wide range through the entire piece. Each section on a given level. Occasional sharp contrasts between sections. Very few sudden or rapid changes of level within a section. Low level at beginning to set the lyric, thoughtful mood of the piece.

b. Amount of sound. Wide variation in amount of sound. Often only a few instruments playing; occasionally full orchestra for substantial period of time. Consistent alternation between full and thin sound.

c. Strength of sound. Almost completely identified with amount of sound. Soft for few instruments, loud for many.

d. Color of sound. Wide range, from mellow to brilliant, from dark to light. Use of many different instrumental colors in salient passages. Sharp contrast of trumpet fanfares with all the rest of the orchestra.

2. Quality of Movement

a. Pace. Slow, but with a swinging sense of movement.

b. Regularity. Regular, except for occasional moments of pause.

c. Articulation. Continuously flowing, lyric, even. Deviations from this manner occasionally, associated with greater strength and amount of sound.

d. Intensity. Generally rather calm; at times a driving, bold manner; at other times a sense of hesitation or suspense.

3. Effects of Arrival

a. Emphasis. Rather large number of emphatic points of arrival. Final section of piece apparently concerned with giving a very strong impression of final arrival.

b. Clarity. Almost all points of arrival, gentle or emphatic, quite clear in this piece. Repetitions of passages denoting arrival to add emphasis and clarity to arrival effect.

4. Interaction of Movement and Arrival

a. Length of phases of movement. Well-defined, rather short phases of movement, marked by clear points of arrival. Some phases spun out to greater length.

b. Approach to points of arrival. Simple articulations and gentle rounding off contrasted with occasional strong and dramatic drives to important goals.

The slow yet easily moving pace of this composition, together with its rich, varied, and luminous qualities of tone color, suggest at first some kind of deliberate dance or song. The new element introduced by the fanfare, however, combined with the moments in which a suspension of movement seems to occur, raises the expressive level of this piece far above that of a dance or song. There is a long-range feeling of growth and expansion. Many different ideas and values are incorporated.

Musical Expression

Our study thus far has served two purposes: (1) the listener has been provided with a means for making first contact with a composition in order to evaluate it; (2) standards of reference have been established to which the listener can refer technical, historical, and aesthetic data. Throughout this chapter we suggested or indicated the expressive quality of a given passage or composition by means of the criteria of sound, movement, and arrival. In considering the expressive values of music we were pursuing a line of thought followed by many great writers on music from antiquity to the present day. The ability of music to convey ideas of emotion and feeling has been recognized for centuries.

Plato, in the third book of his *Republic,* made distinctions between music which provokes violence and that which promotes tranquillity. Gioseffe Zarlino, the most influential music theorist of the Renaissance, devoted the final sections of his *Istituzioni armoniche* to a careful consideration of the expressive effects of all the tone systems or scales available to the composers of his time. Writers of the seventeenth and eighteenth centuries constantly discussed the emotional effects of various kinds of movement, qualities of sound, and tone systems. The entire aesthetic philosophy of these two centuries was centered upon a system called the *doctrine of the affections* in which the methods by which music could stir the feelings were thoroughly investigated and described. Alfred Einstein, the modern writer on Mozart, devoted an entire chapter to Mozart's choice of keys. He showed how Mozart selected keys for their affective quality, in order to stir the listener's emotions in one way or another. Paul Hindemith, the contemporary composer, in his song cycle *Das Marienleben* (The Life of Mary), assigned emotional values of very specific nature to various tones.

In all these cases music seems to have been considered neither an intricate pattern of tones nor an exact description of emotions or objects. Rather these writers and composers dealt with the power of music to suggest and imply. We have adopted this approach and in this chapter have offered some criteria that may provide a way of making entry into the world of musical value and meaning.

chapter two

Musical Elements and their Relationships

Until now in our listening we have been evaluating general impressions. Music was loud or soft; it moved quickly, slowly, vigorously, or gently; it had brilliant or dark color; it arrived with a flourish, or perhaps it did not seem to arrive at all. Through these impressions we were stirred to various kinds of emotional reaction; this testified to the expressive power of the music. Now we ask how these effects and impressions were evoked by the music. Such questions as the following arise: Why does this passage move smoothly while another progresses with much effort? Why is one piece easy to follow while another seems to lead into strange bypaths? How are various qualities of sound created? In what ways does music move? These questions, and many others like them, deal with the structure of music. To find the answers, we must look at the musical resources that the composer has at his command. As we do so, more will come to light; we shall hear effects and perceive relationships that would ordinarily remain unnoticed in the general impressions we receive at first. Such insights can be very exciting, especially when they lead us toward an understanding of musical design.

We shall explore the ways in which musical sound, movement, and arrival are created by specific musical processes. In order to derive the maximum benefit from this investigation, the reader should have some familiarity with the basic principles of musical notation explained in Appendix I.

Musical elements are generally considered under four headings:

Rhythm—organization of musical time
Melody—musical line
Texture—interaction of musical lines
Harmony—specific relationships of musical tones

When we correlate these elements with the criteria of Chapter 1, we find that musical sound will include texture, insofar as the pitch, strength, amount, and tone color of individual lines and combinations of lines are concerned; and harmony, insofar as the characteristic sounds of various tone combinations are concerned.

Musical movement and arrival will include rhythm; melody; texture, insofar as the composite action of musical lines is concerned; and harmony, insofar as tonal organization is concerned.

Elements of Musical Sound

In Chapter 1 we considered the *level* of sound; this we shall amplify here by discussing the ranges or compasses of voices and instruments. The *amount* of sound will be treated more specifically by examining the size and composition of performing groups. *Color* will be examined through a survey of musical instruments and by a preliminary approach to harmony via the topic of harmonic color. The *strength* of sound will be treated under the topic of *dynamics*.

RANGES (LEVEL OF SOUND)

The total range of available musical sound covers more than seven octaves. Among the familiar instruments, only the piano, organ, and harp approach this total range in their compasses. The human voice and most musical instruments operate within a segment of this musical "space." We designate specific voices according to their placement within the total range. The average ranges of the human voice are given on the following page.

EXAMPLE 2·1 Voice ranges

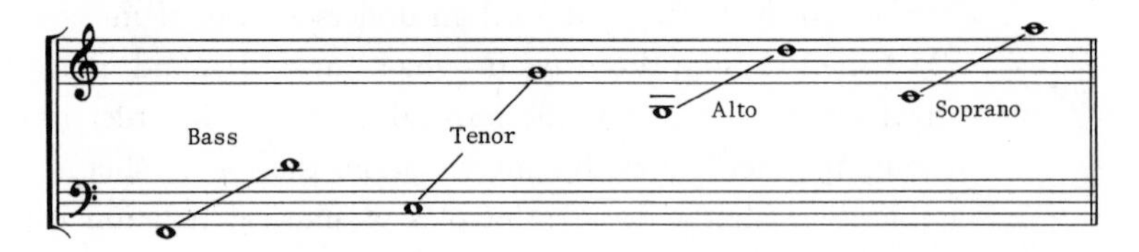

By way of illustration, the following works are suggested for listening, each is set for four voices within the ranges given above:

Deprès: *Ave Maria, Masterpieces,* no. 19
Stravinsky: *Symphonie des psaumes* (with orchestra)
Handel: *And the Glory* (with orchestra), from *The Messiah*

Instruments of the orchestra have considerably greater ranges than voices have, yet they are deployed within the orchestra quite like voices, i.e., as soprano, alto, tenor, and bass, in the following manner:

SOPRANO	ALTO	TENOR	BASS
Piccolo	Oboe	Clarinet	Bassoon and contrabassoon
Flute	Clarinet	Bassoon	Trombone and bass trombone
Oboe	Trumpet	Horn	Tuba
Clarinet	Violin	Trumpet	Cello
Trumpet	Viola	Bassoon	String bass
Violin		Cello	Timpani

Specific ranges of individual instruments are given in Appendix II.

Referring to the compositions given in Chapter 1 to illustrate levels of sound, we can now say that the Mendelssohn Scherzo emphasizes the soprano range, the Liszt example moves through the bass and tenor ranges as it begins, and the Brahms Symphony No. 1 covers all ranges, from deep bass to extreme soprano. In addition, we find that Berlioz's *Symphonie fantastique* is particularly striking in the manner in which it presents various instruments and instrumental groups in their characteristic ranges.

SCORING (AMOUNT OF SOUND)

Scoring refers to the number and the kinds of instruments or voices used in a piece of music. The word is derived from the term *score,* the musical notation used in writing a composition down on paper. *Orches-*

tration is the more familiar term; it means much the same as scoring but is more restricted in that it applies to instruments alone.

The composer has a wide choice when he considers which instruments he will use and how many performers may be involved. J. S. Bach's Sonatas for Solo Violin and Edgar Varèse's *Density 21.5* for flute alone represent one extreme, while Berlioz's Requiem is at the other extreme, calling for hundreds of instrumental and vocal performers. The amount of sound, then, can be classified as follows: (1) the number of separate parts represented and (2) the number of performers assigned to each part.

When there is but one performer for each part, we designate the type of scoring as follows:

NUMBER OF VOICES OR INSTRUMENTS	
1	Solo
2	Duet
3	Trio
4	Quartet
5	Quintet
6	Sextet

Listen to the following examples of scoring:

Solo:

Vocal: *Or la truix* (I Find It Too Difficult), *Masterpieces,* no. 4
Instrumental: see Varèse and Bach compositions above

Duet or duo:

Vocal: Britten: *Peter Grimes,* end of Prologue
Instrumental: Beethoven: Duos for Clarinet and Bassoon

Trio:

Vocal: Mendelssohn: *Elijah,* no. 28, *Lift Thine Eyes*
Instrumental: Poulenc: Sonata for Horn, Trumpet, and Trombone

Quartet:

Vocal: Deprès: *Ave Maria, Masterpieces,* no. 19
Instrumental: Beethoven: Quartet in F major, Op. 18, no. 1

Sextet:

Vocal: Weelkes: *As Vesta Was from Latmos Hill Descending*
Instrumental: Brahms: Sextet in B♭ major, Op. 18

Music that has a small number of performers, one to a part, is called *chamber music,* because traditionally it was intended to be performed in a room or in a relatively small theater. Music that has several performers to a part is designated as *orchestral* when musical instruments are performing; we do not have terms which differentiate vocal chamber music from large choral ensembles, yet the distinction exists and is critical for vocal as well as instrumental music. For example, in the plainsong *Laus Deo Patri* (Praise God the Father), *Masterpieces,* no. 1, we have but one actual part or line throughout the entire piece. Yet since some passages are sung by a single performer and others by a group, we obtain a feeling of musical perspective which adds an important dimension to the shape of the piece. Mozart's famous serenade *Eine kleine Nachtmusik* was originally written for four parts: two violins, viola, and bass. When it is played by a string quartet, one to a part, it has a light, intimate, sweet quality. When it is played by a string orchestra, in which we might find as many as six or more players to a part, the effect is much heavier, bolder, and more brilliant. Considerations of this nature are important for both the composer and the performer; they both must strike the proper balance between the amount of sound used and the kind of musical action that is to be projected.

SCORING (COLOR OF SOUND)

In Chapter 1 we gave some attention to the color of musical sound; in general terms we ascertained whether the sound had a bright or dark, rich or thin quality. Now we shall deal with some more specific aspects of tone color. Two areas will be explored: the characteristics of various instrumental timbres and the characteristic sounds of various tone combinations.

Instrumental Timbres

The instruments of the modern symphony orchestra constitute the principal subject matter of this section. Here we shall be concerned principally with the timbre of each instrument, listing passages in which the instrument is prominent. (For a description of the structure of each instrument, you may consult any current musical dictionary or book on orchestration. Several are listed in Recommended Readings.

WOODWIND INSTRUMENTS

Flute. The flute is the traditional soprano instrument of the woodwind family. It has a bright, round, and rather soft tone, with relatively little richness of color.

Examples: Tchaikovsky: *Nutcracker Suite, Danse des Mirlitons* (Dance of the Reed Flutes)
Mozart: Concerto for Flute in G major, K. 313

Piccolo. The piccolo is similar to the flute in construction but is much smaller and has a very high, shrill, and piercing quality. It is used to give an edge or bite to the uppermost level of musical action.

Examples: Beethoven, Overture to *Egmont,* Op. 84, final section
Sousa: March, *Stars and Stripes Forever*

Oboe. The oboe, because of its clear, thin, penetrating quality, which is sweet yet tends toward a slight edginess, is a solo instrument par excellence.

Examples: Berlioz: *Symphonie fantastique,* beginning of third movement
Stravinsky: *Symphonie des psaumes,* second movement

English horn. The English horn has a tone similar to that of the oboe, but much deeper, darker, and fuller, since it performs in the lower alto and tenor ranges. It has something of the penetrating quality of the oboe, but is less crisp.

Examples: Berlioz: *Symphonie fantastique,* beginning of third movement. Note the contrast of oboe and English horn in this duet.
Sibelius: *Swan of Tuonela*

Clarinet. The clarinet has a very wide range. In the lowest part of its range, called the *chalumeau* register, the tone is big, full, dark, and rich. In the middle register the clarinet has a warm, mellow quality, rather bright and rich. In the uppermost register this instrument displays a brilliant, piercing, powerful tone.

Examples: Mozart: Concerto for Clarinet in A, K. 622
Tchaikovsky: *Nutcracker Suite, Danse Arabe* (Arabian Dance)

Bass clarinet. This instrument has much the same quality as the lower register of the clarinet, with a darker tone, less rich and powerful.

Examples: Tchaikovsky: *Nutcracker Suite, Danse de la fée dragée* (Dance of the Sugarplum Fairy)
Wagner: *Tristan und Isolde,* Prelude, final measures

Bassoon. The bassoon has a rather dry, crisp tone, somewhat dark but quite penetrating. In its low register the tone is very powerful, with a kind of percussive attack; in higher registers the tone tends to be thin and penetrating, although not bright.

Examples: Mozart: Concerto for Bassoon in B♭ major, K. 191
Stravinsky: *Le Sacre du printemps* (The Rite of Spring), beginning

Double bassoon (contrabassoon). The contrabassoon has a tone quality which represents an amplification of the lower registers of the bassoon. It is very heavy, quite dark but not mellow; it retains some of the edginess that we find in the bassoon's tone.

Examples: Dukas: *L'Apprenti sorcier* (The Sorcerer's Apprentice), slow section toward end of piece

Mahler: Symphony No. 9 in D minor, second movement (near end)

A very attractive and characteristic use of wind instruments as a group is found in the second movement of Mozart's Concerto for Piano and Orchestra in C minor, K. 491.

BRASS INSTRUMENTS

Trumpet. The trumpet has a bright, clear, penetrating tone, rather rich yet a bit edgy. It is used for military signals as well as for salient melodic material.

Examples: Beethoven: *Leonore* Overture No. 3, Op. 72a (about two-thirds through the overture there are two trumpet signals)

Shostakovitch: Symphony No. 1, first movement

Horn (French horn). The horn has a very rich, somewhat muffled and dark tone. It often plays military and hunting signals but is also an excellent instrument for a salient melody. It blends well, singly or in groups, with other orchestral instruments.

Examples: Mozart: Concerto in E♭ for Horn and Orchestra, K. 447

Beethoven: Symphony No. 3 in E♭ major, third movement, middle section

Trombone. The trombone has a dark, lean, rather heavy tone. It is quite penetrating, but it lacks somewhat in fullness or body.

Examples: Beethoven: Symphony No. 9 in D minor, finale (*Seid umschlungen*)

Rimsky-Korsakov: Overture, *La Grande Pâque russe* (Russian Easter)

Tuba. The tuba has a very heavy, full, dark tone, very strong in supporting a body of sound.

Examples: Moussorgsky-Ravel: *Pictures at an Exhibition,* Bydlo

Berlioz: *Symphonie fantastique,* finale

In the first movement of Bartók's Concerto for Orchestra, about two-thirds through the movement, an extended passage for a group of brass instruments occurs; this passage gives the brass the opportunity to perform in an idiomatic fanfare style. The second movement of this piece is based entirely upon a "game" in which wind and brass instruments take turns playing the principal material, which consists of a dancelike idea. We hear, in turn, bassoons, oboes, clarinets, flutes, trumpets, and horns. In the last two "turns," the trumpets and horns take up a slower idea, in the manner of a chorale.

STRING INSTRUMENTS

Violin. One need hardly describe the violin's tone. Its bright, light, clear, and sweet quality is familiar to anyone who has heard music. Virtually every orchestral work in the repertory gives the violin the most prominent position in the tonal spectrum.

Examples: Brahms: Symphony No. 4 in E minor, first movement
Mozart: Symphony in G minor, K. 550, first movement

Viola. The tone of the viola has much in common with that of the violin, but it is less clear, darker, perhaps somewhat richer and decidedly heavier in quality.

Examples: Berlioz: Symphony, *Harold in Italy*
Bach: *Brandenburg,* Concerto No. 6 in B♭ major

Cello. The cello has a very rich tone, strong and heavy in the lowest register, brilliant and intense in the upper register. The cello is an excellent solo instrument.

Examples: Tchaikovsky: Symphony No. 6 in B minor, second movement
Haydn: Concerto in D major for Cello and Orchestra

Bass (contrabass). The contrabass has a heavy, dark, rather muffled tone, lacking in the richness of the cello. In the lower register the effect is powerful, capable of supporting a body of sound above it. In the higher register the tone has a rather thin and strained quality. As a matter of general orchestral practice this instrument is most often assigned to play along with the cello, except for special effects.

Examples: Verdi: *Otello,* Act IV, scene 3
Mahler: Symphony No. 1 in D major, third movement
Haydn: Symphony No. 103 in E♭ major, introduction (coupled with cello and bassoon)

As with woodwinds and brass, the string group in an orchestra constitutes a complete ensemble. Several examples of characteristic treatment of the strings as a group are listed below:

Beethoven: Concerto No. 5 for Piano and Orchestra in E♭ major, second movement

Smetana: Overture to *The Bartered Bride,* opening section

Harp. The harp is a string instrument, but its structure, sound, and function are very different from those of the string instruments listed above. Its tone is bright, rather light and sweet, pervasive but not penetrating or dominant in an ensemble. In the higher registers its tone is quite rich and colorful—sparkling, one might say; in the lower register the tone tends to fade a bit, to grow weaker and darker.

Examples: Tchaikovsky: *Nutcracker Suite, Waltz of the Flowers*
Berlioz: *Symphonie fantastique,* second movement

PERCUSSION INSTRUMENTS

If we were to list the percussion instruments used in orchestral music in the past two centuries, there would be dozens, of widely different kinds of sound and structure. In most orchestral scores, however, only one kind of percussion instrument is used, the kettledrum, or as it is usually designated by the plural in Italian, *timpani*. Most scores use two or perhaps three or four of these instruments. The pitch of the timpani is fixed, but because of its heaviness, darkness, fullness, and low level, this pitch may be difficult to hear precisely. It is used principally to reinforce lower-register instruments, to give additional emphasis and body to significant tones in the bass register. It is occasionally heard alone, as in the following examples:

Examples: Beethoven: Symphony No. 9, second movement
Berlioz: *Symphonie fantastique,* third movement, final section

In the third movement of Bartók's *Music for Strings, Percussion, and Celesta,* a number of percussion instruments are used in characteristic ways. These include xylophone, timpani, celesta, tam-tam, cymbals, bass drum, and side drum.

From the foregoing study of orchestral instruments, it is clear that the composer has a virtually limitless palette from which to draw his preferred orchestral tone color. We can often recognize a composer or a style of music simply by the quality of orchestral sound. Among late nineteenth-century composers, Wagner, Anton Bruckner, and Brahms tend toward a heavy quality, rich and full; Gustav Mahler seeks a thinner, brighter, more edgy effect; Richard Strauss achieves a very special quality of opulent brilliance and sweetness. Earlier, Mendelssohn's orchestral sound is much more balanced and sweet than that of Robert Schumann; Beethoven's music has a heavier and perhaps less evenly distributed sound than the orchestral works of Haydn and Mozart.

The instruments whose tone color we have described represent only the present traditional orchestral group. Throughout history and at the present time, much experimentation and variation has taken place in musical sound and in the structure of musical instruments.

HARMONY (COLOR OF SOUND)

Another area of special or characteristic effects, often associated with instrumental tone color, is *harmonic color*. While this topic belongs properly to the study of harmony itself, we shall examine at this time some examples of music in which harmonic color has especial importance for the expressive values in the music.

In Schubert's Quintet in C major, Op. 163, we hear three sustained sounds (chords) at the onset. The first and third of these are sweet and rich, and they provide a feeling of repose. In contrast, the middle chord is less sweet and perhaps even richer in effect, but principally it has a restless quality. Here, Schubert uses harmonic color, first to establish a basic mood for the piece, and second to give the impression of a minute cycle of departure, movement, and arrival, as represented respectively by the three successive chords.

Many compositions depend for their expressive qualities on special effects of harmonic color. Some examples are listed below.

Schubert: *Wohin* (Whither) (major triad; see page 75)

Debussy: *Voiles* (Sails) from *Preludes,* Book I (whole-tone scale, later pentatonic scale; see pages 74 and 356)

Wagner: Prelude to *Tristan* (chromaticism; see pages 74 and 283)

Perotinus: Measured organum, *Masterpieces,* no. 9 (fourths, fifths, octaves; see page 49)

DYNAMICS (STRENGTH OF SOUND)

Much of the general expressive quality we perceive in a musical passage is created by the sheer strength of sound being produced. This aspect of music is called *dynamics.*

The dynamic range of musical sound is indicated by certain conventional signs and terms, as given below:

ppp	pianississimo	extremely soft
pp	pianissimo	very soft
p	piano	soft
mp	mezzo piano	moderately soft
mf	mezzo forte	moderately full or loud
f	forte	strong or loud
ff	fortissimo	very loud
fff	fortississimo	extremely loud

Sometimes, to dramatize their point, composers have written pppp or ffff to indicate the utter extremes of soft or loud in their music.

One extremely important aspect of dynamics in music is the gradual increase or decrease of loudness. These changes, called *crescendo* and *decrescendo,* are directed to the ebb and flow of emotional tension and excitement in music. Tension is particularly strong when the dynamic range is great and the amount of time occupied in the rise or fall is considerable. Ravel's *Bolero,* which we mentioned in Chapter 1, is built on a huge crescendo.

Dynamic changes can be minute and subtle, and thus they add expressive nuances to musical performance. Very often the difference between a moving performance and a dull one is the degree of shading which the master artist uses to shape a passage, the slight swellings and taperings of sound which place the musical effects in clear and meaningful perspective. This can be overdone; nevertheless, when projected with subtlety and taste, it is one of the delights of the musical experience.

Dynamic strength can vary sharply between sections of a piece. This was frequently so in music of Bach's time and earlier. A change of registration from a full to a light quality in an organ piece, as if the music were ascending or descending the levels of a terrace, is called *terrace dynamics.* Alternation between a single or a few instruments and a full body of performers also creates a terracing in the dynamics.

Dynamics can give contour to a section of music, heightening expressive values by contrast. For example, consider the dynamic events in the first few moments of Beethoven's *Leonore* Overture No. 3, and observe how each reacts upon the other to provide a kind of "relief" effect: (1) *fortissimo* at the beginning, immediately fading to (2) *piano,* thence to (3) *pianissimo,* disturbed by minute crescendos and decrescendos, and (4) *sforzando* a moment later, followed by another pianissimo. Beethoven was extremely conscious of the expressive value of dynamics and meticulous in his instructions to the performer. Unlike the music of Bach, which unfolds its designs with relatively few changes in dynamics, Beethoven's music frequently seems to have been composed to express a certain electrifying dynamic value. In contrast, the disembodied, airy quality of much of Debussy's music depends on a minimum degree of strength or loudness.

The following questions may be used in evaluating elements of musical sound (see also page 7).

In a given passage:

1. How many parts are performing: one, two, three, or more?
2. Is there one performer to a part or more?
3. What ranges are represented?
4. What instruments or voices are heard?
5. Which instruments or voices are prominent?
6. Is the sound characterized by special types of tone combinations?
7. What is the approximate dynamic level?
8. In what way do the characteristics of musical sound relate to what is being expressed?

Suggestions for additional listening projects:

1. Stravinsky: *Le Sacre du printemps,* opening

2. Mozart: Divertimento in E♭ major, K. 563
3. Bach: Cantata *Christ lag in Todesbanden* (Christ Lay in the Bonds of Death), No. 2
4. Weber: Overture to *Oberon*
5. Melismatic organum, *Benedicamus Domino* (Let Us Bless the Lord), *Masterpieces,* no. 8
6. Arthuys, *The Veil of Orpheus,* from *Panorama of Musique Concrète*

Elements of Musical Movement and Arrival

In the elements we are now about to investigate—rhythm, melody, and additional aspects of texture and harmony—some procedures embody musical movement, while others represent arrival. As each procedure is explained, its contribution to effects of movement and arrival are pointed out.

RHYTHM

Everyone has found himself at one time or another tapping his foot to music. The beat of a march is most persuasive. When you keep time to music by tapping your foot, by dancing, walking, or marching, you are responding to the *rhythm* of the music.

Rhythm deals with the control of musical time. It *measures* it by determining when successive musical events are to take place. Naturally, this measurement takes place according to an idea or plan in the composer's mind; thus, the act of measuring musical time also *generates* and *maintains* musical movement in one manner or another.

Beat; Tempo

In tapping your foot, you have created a *beat* or a pulse. Musical movement in time arises from a basic beat, pulse, or stroke that is felt continuously throughout a piece. In music the beat is a sign of life; it not only gives evidence of vitality, but also provides a clue to the kind of life there is in the music. Pulse or beat establishes the fundamental quality of movement, its *pace* and its emphasis or *accent.* For example, in *Drink to Me,* we hear a steady, moderately slow beat, with little emphasis; this creates a gently flowing quality of movement. In the Scherzo from Mendelssohn's *Midsummer Night's Dream,* we hear a rather quick, light, but crisp beat, which contributes to the gay, buoyant sense of movement. The majestic quality of the *Star-Spangled Banner* owes much to its vigorous, rather quick, and heavy beat.

Although we are sensitive to the presence of a beat in music, we cannot always define or determine the extent of the beat in exact terms. The beat sometimes appears to fluctuate in pace, quickening or slowing down. Perhaps it may be subdivided into smaller beats; perhaps it may at times coalesce into longer beats. Sometimes it may not be present at all, or it may be so irregular that there is difficulty in finding it. In the opening of Wagner's Prelude to *Tristan* a beat is not easily detected. Only when the piece is well under way does the beat come forward sufficiently to be recognized in its pace, its emphasis, and its groupings.

We tend to associate physical or emotional states with various qualities of beat. If the pulse is strong, regular, and active, as in a dance or march, the connotation is physical action. If the pulse is doubtful, irregular, gentle, or changing, we tend to associate the music with emotional states or moods. Compare *The Stars and Stripes Forever* with the Prelude to *Tristan*. The first strikes the earth with each beat; the other seems to glide forward uncertainly.

The *pace* at which a series of beats moves along is called the *tempo*. Tempo has generally been indicated by terms which describe the general rate of speed and which may also give some idea of the quality of movement. Here are some examples of tempo indications, along with compositions which bear them:

presto—very quickly	Beethoven: Symphony No. 7, third movement
vivace—lively	Beethoven: Symphony No. 7, first movement
allegro—quickly	Mozart: Symphony in E♭ major, K. 549, finale
andante—moderately slow and moving	Mozart: *Don Giovanni* Overture, opening
adagio—slowly	Berlioz: *Symphonie fantastique,* third movement
largo—broad and slow	Berlioz: *Symphonie fantastique,* opening of first movement

Some terms that qualify the manner of pace and give some indication of the expressive value are:

con anima—with life	maestoso—majestically
con spirito—with spirit	dolce—softly or sweetly
grazioso—gracefully	con fuoco—with fire

There is no fixed value for tempo terms. The performer has the task of determining the exact pace of the music for himself. Within the general limits set by the composer, the performer must find a pace that will project the musical movement effectively and yet allow the nuances and details to be heard. This is not easy, and there is possibly no single correct answer. In two recorded performances of the same work by eminent artists, there may be several minutes' difference in the duration of the two readings. One may appeal to one listener but not to another. If nothing else, this makes for a great deal of critical commentary.

Gradual change in pace or tempo, by going either faster or slower, has a marked effect upon the expressive quality of the music. We have all heard performances in which greater excitement and brilliance were sought by a quickening of tempo; conversely, many an artist hopes to make a greater expressive impact upon his audience by slowing down at critical points. Composers may write such indications into their music: *accelerando* and *ritardando*. They will also compose the music so that it seems to lose or gain speed of tempo. Listen to the slowdown after the headlong rush at the beginning of the finale of Beethoven's Symphony No. 3. These rapid changes of pace certainly provide an effective foil for the precise, regular dance music to follow.

EXAMPLE 2·2 Beethoven: Symphony No. 3, last movement

Meter

Listening for beats, we find ourselves organizing their steady flow into small groups. Sometimes this is very easy to do, as in the *Blue Danube Waltz*. We find ourselves counting 1, 2, 3—1, 2, 3—1, 2, 3, etc. In other music, such as the Prelude to *Tristan,* the grouping seems uncertain and difficult to hear. In any case, there seems to be a strong tendency to listen for groups of beats as music moves along.

Groups of beats appear to us as small phases of movement. The first beat in each group generates fresh movement, while serving at the same time as a point of arrival for the previous group. A link is thus established between groups. *This link by which groups are joined is one of the bases of musical structure.*

The simplest of all such groups are those which contain two or three beats. *These simple groups combine into larger groups in multiples of two or three.* The larger groups are described as *compound.*

EXAMPLE 2·3 Linking groups of beats

Groups of beats

a. Simple two (duple). Beethoven: Quartet in G major, Op. 18, no. 2, finale

b. Simple three (triple). Mozart: *Se vuol ballare* from *Marriage of Figaro*

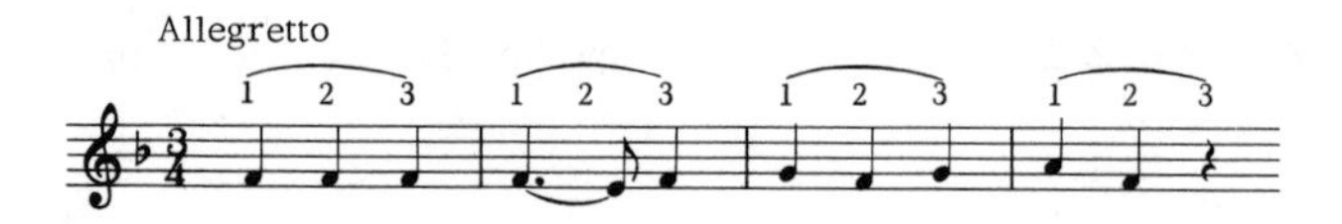

c. Compound two in multiples of three. Mendelssohn: Symphony No. 3 in A minor (*Scotch*), first movement

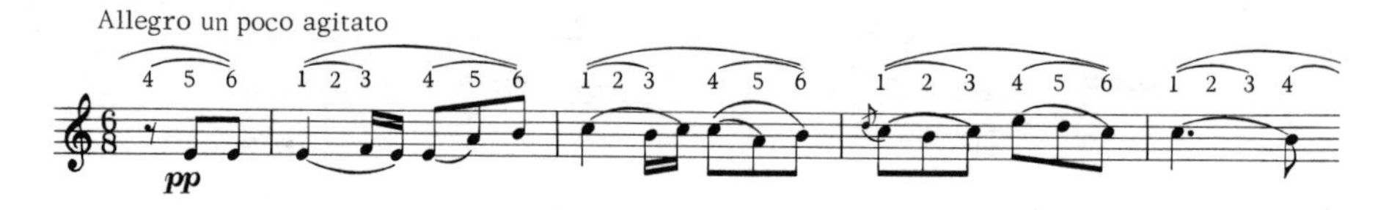

In compound groups we feel the strongest beat at the beginning of each large group. Sometimes groups that appear on the page as simple are heard as compound; thus we might find ourselves tapping the *Blue Danube* as:

EXAMPLE 2·4 Strauss: the *Blue Danube Waltz*

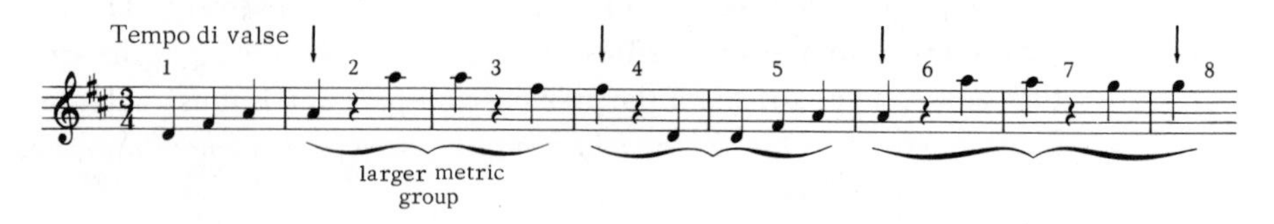

Meter is the term used to refer to grouping of beats. We designate specific types as duple, triple, simple, or compound meters, as illustrated in Example 2·3.

Each grouping, taken together with a given pace, has a characteristic quality of movement. For example, a simple grouping in quick tempo, in duple meter, has a vigorous, straightforward quality, as in the final movement of Beethoven's Symphony No. 1. A compound group in slow tempo, built up from triple meter, has a deliberate and somewhat swinging motion. Both are illustrated in Example 2·5, as well as a fairly quick simple triple meter:

EXAMPLE 2·5 Types of meter

a. Beethoven: Symphony No. 1, final movement (duple)

b. *Drink to Me* (compound triple)

c. *Star-Spangled Banner* (triple)

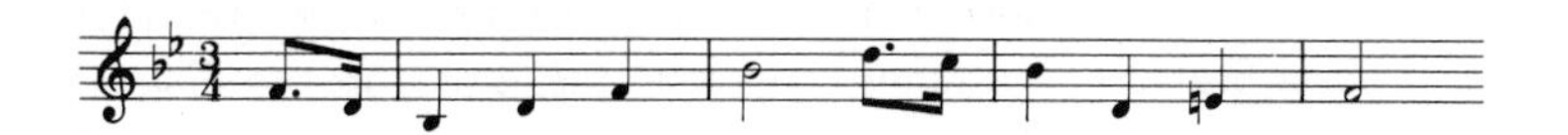

Musical metric groups were first based on dance patterns and on poetic rhythms, to which the music had to accommodate. As we all know, traditional dances and poetry move in a series of equal time groups known as *feet*. The more familiar poetic rhythms are illustrated in Example 2·6.

Music, particularly from the seventeenth century to the present time, has borrowed this type of organization; the term *measure* is applied to its metrical time groups.

Much can be learned about a musical style by examining the relationship between its metric groups and the tempo and emphasis of its beat. In early Christian church song there was a characteristic beat of moderate tempo that did not change markedly. The size of metric groups varied freely, however. In this music, the beat was not emphasized strongly. The result was a poised, smoothly flowing quality of movement, as illustrated in the antiphon *Laus Deo Patri* (Praise God the

EXAMPLE 2·6 Poetic meters

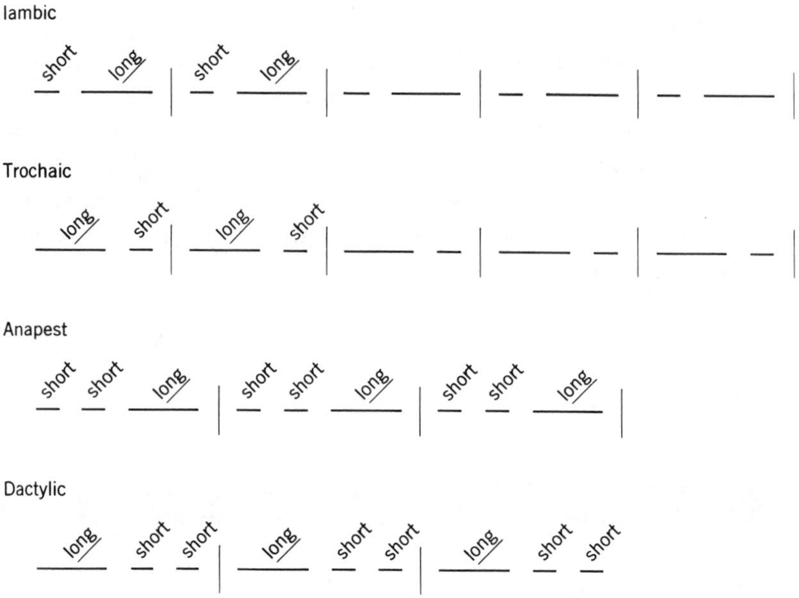

Iambic

short long | short long | | | |

Trochaic

long short | long short | | | |

Anapest

short short long | short short long | short short long |

Dactylic

long short short | long short short | long short short

Father), *Masterpieces,* no. 1. The metrical procedures of early Christian church song apply also to sacred music of the late Renaissance period (sixteenth century).

Music written in the seventeenth and eighteenth centuries had a regular quality of movement based on equal metric groups and well-emphasized beats. The listener can easily make out, in the first movement of Beethoven's Symphony No. 3, a metric group of three quick and light beats. This goes on so regularly that we begin to feel that the first beat in each group of three is the important one and that these stronger, more widely spaced beats themselves form groups of two and four. There is thus an *accent,* or stress, returning periodically to help organize the flow of steady, quick beats. This sort of accent has come from dance music and from simpler types of poetry, in which a marked stress was made regularly either by the foot, as in dancing, or by a strong syllable, as in poetry.

In twentieth-century music, we find passages with changes in the tempo and the length of the beat, as well as in the size of the metric group. Such procedure creates a subtle, somewhat imbalanced, often uneasy quality of movement. Properly handled, it can intensify movement effectively and make a very strong impact upon the emotions. A striking example is the *Dance of the Adolescents* from Stravinsky's work *Le Sacre du printemps.* Part of the curious, fantastic, primitive effect of this music is due to its metric unevenness.

Note Values

You have heard that notes have different lengths, or *values* in time. In the written examples these values corresponded to certain written symbols, which represent relative durations (see Appendix I). The composer decides how long a certain type of note will be; the others then are played in a fixed ratio, as we have indicated above. Since about 1820, instructions for note lengths have been communicated by indicating how many notes of a given value should occupy a minute of time.

We not only receive impressions of length or quantity from note values; we also sense a difference in the *weight* or accent of short or long notes. Short notes move quickly; they give an impression of buoyancy. Long notes move slowly; they give a sense of greater weight; they carry accent. Therefore, when long and short notes are combined in a passage, we assign the effect of arrival to long notes, the effect of movement to short notes. This can take place within the smallest rhythmic unit, the measure or the *foot*. Probably the most convincing effect takes place when the second of two notes is the longer. This is a universally familiar pattern; it corresponds to the iambic or the trochaic foot, the two most widely employed of poetic meters. Carried out regularly, it produces an easy, balanced, and virtually automatic quality of movement. A line from the song *The Jolly Miller* illustrates iambic meter in the poetry and trochaic in the music.

EXAMPLE 2·7 *The Jolly Miller*

The short notes in *The Jolly Miller* are called *upbeats;* the long notes are *downbeats*. Ordinarily, upbeats precede an accent; they carry a sense of movement. Downbeats coincide with accent; they represent arrival, as well as new points of departure.

When a long note is the first tone in a passage, it becomes a point of departure. Frequently, the last sound in a composition will seem to continue beyond its actual duration, taking on added power of length; hence, it will give a stronger impression of arrival.

We tend to expect a long note at the beginning of a measure, reckoning simply on the basis of weight, accent, and arrival. Suppose we shift the long note out of its normal position. The point of arrival in the measure changes momentarily, the metric groups around that note shift their positions, and a conflict arises in the flow of the music. This is called *syncopation.* See for yourself what effect syncopation has. In the example given below, count four equal beats to each measure; tap each note out. In the third measure, the displacement of the long note throws the music momentarily off balance, but in the fourth measure things are once again set to rights. In this example, as in many passages which use syncopation, the imbalance creates a stronger push toward the point of arrival at the end of the phrase than would be the case with completely regular rhythm. Syncopation can be thus used to create musical climaxes.

EXAMPLE 2·8 Syncopation

In the following example, from the opening movement of Beethoven's Symphony No. 3, a series of syncopations and changes in metric groups builds up a tremendous accumulation of rhythmic momentum. These imbalances finally discharge their energy at a climactic point of arrival. It is typical of eighteenth- and nineteenth-century composers to build such a growing sense of rhythmic urgency. Rhythmic balance and imbalance played against each other constitute the chief resource in such rhythmic progression.

EXAMPLE 2·9 Beethoven: Symphony No. 3, first movement

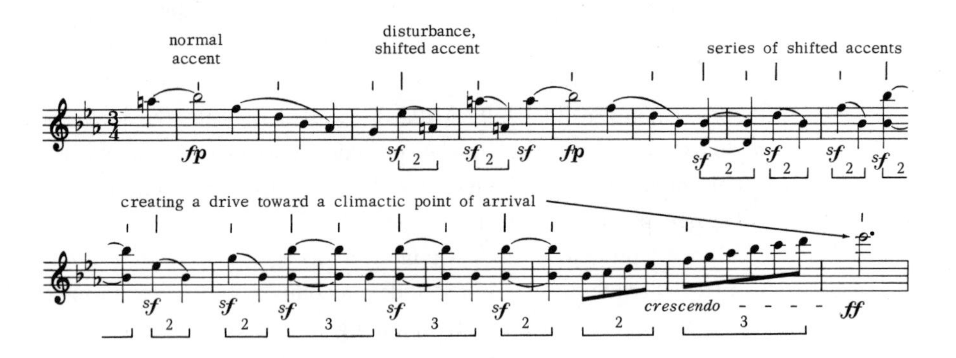

Syncopation can also create a buoyant, jazzy effect of movement. It is the very trade-mark of jazz itself and is the only way that this kind of music can escape from the perfectly regular rhythm which dance music requires.

EXAMPLE 2·10 Syncopation

a. Melody in even quarter notes

b. Same melody with syncopations creating a jazzy bounce

Rhythmic Motives

The measurement of musical time does more than set a pace, organize beats into groups, and create types of movement. It forms distinctive patterns, called *rhythmic motives*. The rhythmic motive at the beginning of Beethoven's Symphony No. 5 is a very famous one. Four notes establish the main rhythmic pattern of the entire first movement; we hear them hundreds of times. Characteristic dances, such as the rhumba, the tango, the mazurka, the gavotte, and the minuet, all have special rhythmic patterns or motives that set the quality of movement which distinguishes each dance. Here are some typical patterns:

EXAMPLE 2·11 Characteristic rhythmic patterns of dances

a. Tango—rather slow (see Albéniz: Tango)

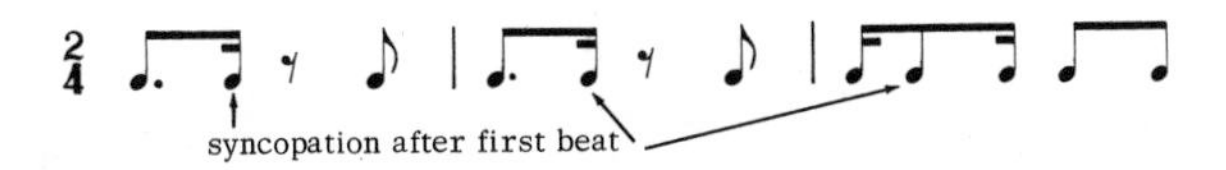

b. Gavotte—moderate tempo (see Mozart: Quintet in E♭, K. 614, second movement)

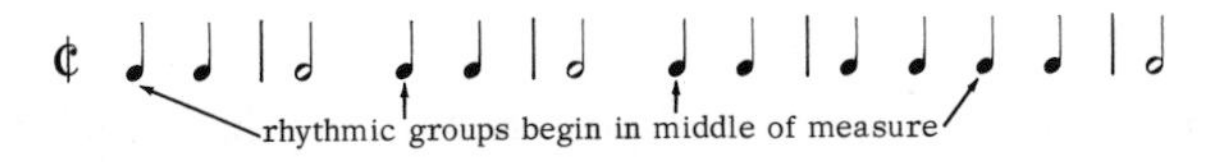

c. Polonaise—moderate (see Chopin: *Polonaise militaire*)

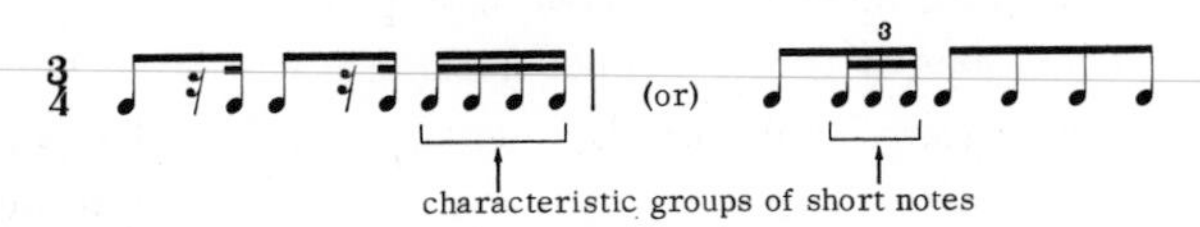

d. Mazurka—fairly quick (see Chopin: Mazurka in B♭)

e. Minuet (late eighteenth century)—rather fast (see Haydn: *London* Symphony, third movement)

Some minuets are performed in slower tempo and begin immediately with a downbeat. The Minuet from Mozart's *Don Giovanni* is a familiar example of this type.

Larger Rhythmic Groups: Phrase, Period

Beats tend to be grouped in twos, threes, or multiples thereof. The units thus formed are in turn gathered into larger structures—"doubled up." This is one of the important aspects of musical form. In many familiar songs and in music used for dancing, the formation of larger groupings is often carried out to the extent that the entire piece represents multiples of two, as in the following example:

EXAMPLE 2·12 Old Folks at Home

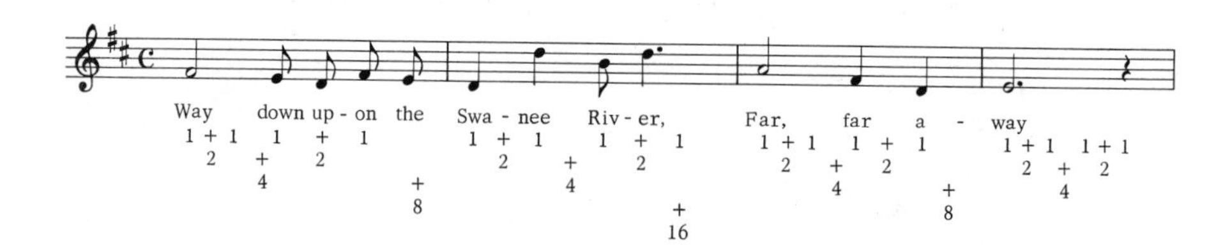

When we multiply the above pattern by 4, we have the entire piece, which consists of 64 beats. As a listener hears music that is built up in such a manner, he receives an impression of balance, of symmetry, of regularity; everything seems to be neatly in place.

In compositions of greater scope, the music will often begin by pairing rhythmic groups, but then frequently something happens to upset the "squareness"; we can no longer mark off equal units by multiples of two. This creates an imbalance, representing syncopation on a higher level; tension grows; we are somewhat disoriented rhythmically; we become more strongly involved in the movement of the music. Eventually, this tension may be resolved and balance reestablished. When this happens, we are relieved and satisfied. The following example illustrates this kind of rhythmic organization:

EXAMPLE 2·13 Mozart: Sonata in G major, K. 283

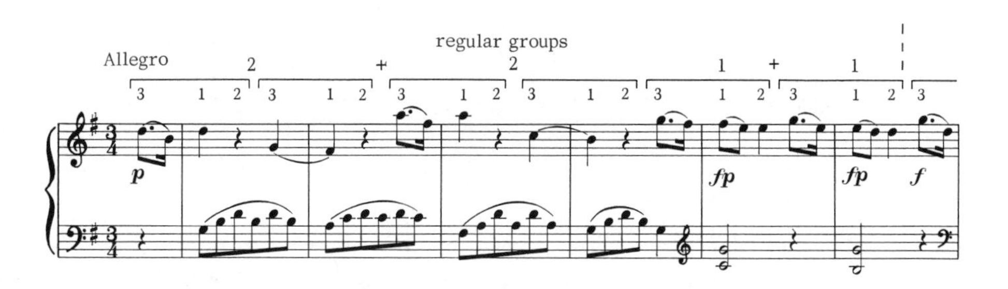

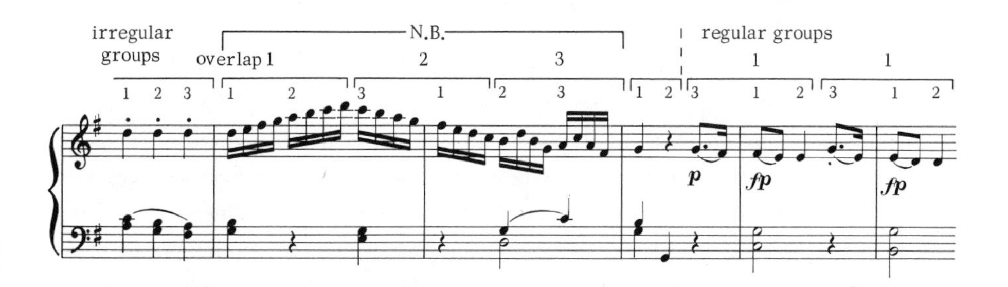

The larger rhythmic units in music are designated by the terms *phrase* and *period*. That these are borrowed from language gives evidence of the close similarities between music and language in matters of punctuation. In music, punctuation takes the form of various kinds of arrival, corresponding to commas, semicolons, question marks, and periods. These points of arrival (we might call them points of musical punctuation) enclose sections of various lengths and of differing degrees of completeness, again analogous to linguistic structures.

The phrase. While a musical phrase has no prescribed length, it is a fairly short section that has a clearly defined point of arrival. It contains material that is well delineated in style, yet it lacks something in form or sense to give the listener the impression that it is a complete musical statement. Example 2·14 on the following page gives two phrases of different length.

EXAMPLE 2·14

a. Mozart: *Jupiter* Symphony, second movement (quite short)

b. Brahms: *Variations on a Theme by Haydn* (rather long)

The period. A feeling of completion is experienced only when one or more phrases follow the first, to finish the musical thought at a point of arrival that gives a convincing impression of finality. A group of phrases with such a point of arrival is called a musical period. *In language, the sign of the period is the strong point of arrival in a sentence.*

Musical periods differ greatly in length; a period may contain but two phrases, or it may encompass a dozen phrases or more. The length and grouping of phrases give rise to differences in period structure. In songs and dances and in concert music of small scope we find that phrases tend to be of equal length, creating a sense of inner balance in the form of the piece. Periods also tend to equal each other in length in such music. In the example from *Old Folks at Home* (Example 2·12) we have two short phrases, each eight beats (two measures) in length, forming what might be called a larger phrase or, even better, a *phrase group.* The next group of phrases is exactly the same length, and it reaches the point of arrival which tells us that we have completed a period. We are at the halfway point; another period, of the same length as the first, finishes the piece. Thus we can say that *Old Folks at Home* consists of two periods which give an impression of perfect symmetry and total balance. If we listen to the continuation of the phrase from the Brahms *Variations* (Example 2·14 *b*), we should hear that the period is complete after the second phrase, which is equal in length to the first. Again we have a balanced construction. On the other hand, in the Mozart example (Example 2·13) only the first two short phrases balance each other and are well defined by points of arrival. What follows is a much broader, less clearly articulated phrase group in which the punctuation must wait for the period; this is an example of the *drive to the point of arrival.*

As you listen for the rhythmic quality of a phrase or period, note whether it maintains a sense of even flow, whether it seems to settle or relax, or whether it gathers strength and intensity as it approaches its point of arrival. Each phrase has a sense of *rhythmic progression,* as illustrated in the example below:

EXAMPLE 2·15 Tchaikovsky: *Nutcracker Suite,* Russian Dance

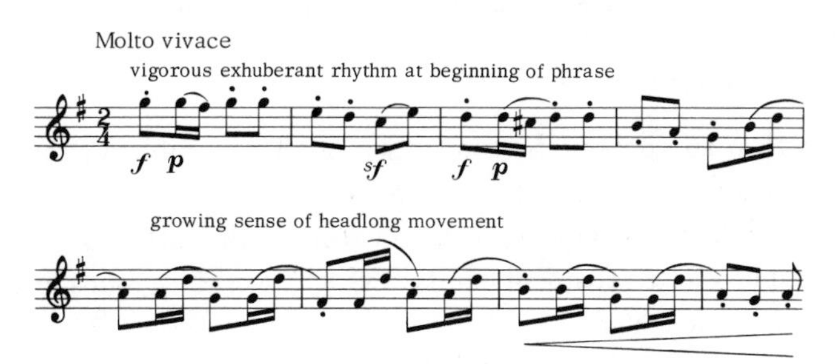

Rhythmic action ebbs and flows within a piece. We can sense a growing excitement as motives become shorter and more densely packed. When motives are sharply contrasted, a feeling of conflict may develop. The sense of rhythmic action in a phrase, a period, or an entire composition is a clue to the very life of the music. Like the general rise and fall of melody, rhythmic action, as it increases and decreases, can organize extended phases of musical movement.

All elements participate in the rhythmic life of a musical composition. Later, when we consider melody and harmony, we shall return to rhythm. An entire musical composition is an expression of rhythm on the broadest scale; it is a measurement and an organization of musical time over perhaps many minutes.

The following may be used in questions evaluating rhythmic elements (see also page 9).

Movement

1. How regular, how clear, how strong is the beat?
2. What is the approximate tempo?
3. Are beats grouped by two or by three?
4. What correlation is achieved through beat, meter, tempo? For example: light, steady beat in simple triple meter, quick tempo—buoyant movement of a waltz.
5. What is the characteristic style or styles of the salient rhythmic motives? Approximately how many motives are there?
6. Is rhythmic movement maintained, increased, or diminished throughout a phrase or period?

Arrival

1. How frequently do clear stops or points of arrival appear?
2. How do points of arrival vary in strength or emphasis?
3. How long are the phrases and periods? Are they balanced in their mutual relationship?

As we apply these criteria to the first movement of Beethoven's Symphony No. 3, our answers should touch on these points:

Movement

1. A clear and definite beat or pulse, sometimes emphatic, sometimes gentle; regular beat throughout the piece.
2. Quick tempo, energetic, with a deliberate, almost heavy effect.
3. Triple meter; frequent shifts and changes in groups overlying the basic triple meter.
4. A firm, steady beat in triple time, moving quickly, with sudden interruptions and displacements of the regular movement; a sense of vigorous, purposeful movement, intensified by the characteristic use of syncopation.
5. A great variety of motives handled so that they contrast with each other very boldly.
6. Almost every phrase or period has a sense of intensification as it progresses; much of this is due to the disturbances in regularity caused by syncopation and shifts of grouping; very long periods.

Arrival (rhythmic)

1. Many clear points of arrival, not regularly spaced.
2. Some points of arrival extremely emphatic.
3. Movement generally maintained over lighter points of arrival so that a great deal of drive is generated toward the more important points; very few periods that give an impression of inner balance.

Summarizing the rhythmic qualities of this movement, we note that the steady vigorous pulse sets the piece going with great assurance. Rhythmic displacements and contrasts set up striking conflicts which are settled with grand flourishes at widely spaced and emphatic points of arrival. Rhythmic interest is maintained and intensified by rhythmic contrasts. All these factors combine to create a tremendously broad and powerful rhythmic structure.

Rhythm serves a number of purposes in music. Most obviously it creates the basic quality of movement by the delineation of small time units, such as tones, measures, and motives. It sets our foot tapping; it quickens our spirit. Rhythm also has a long-range action, one which is felt strongly but not so easily recognized or described. To the composer, this long-range action suggests what should be done and when. It guides him in shaping periods and phrase groups; it tells him how long he can go on doing one sort of thing, when some contrast or fresh gesture is necessary, and when to arrive. We, as listeners and critics, are also governed by this long-range time sense in music, which is like the mental time clock that tells us when to eat, to work, to arise in the morning. Thus, rhythm, in the broadest sense, is a basic factor in the overall structure of music, even though we cannot set specific rules for its operation on this large scale.

The following works are suggested for evaluation of rhythmic elements:

Beethoven: Quartet in E minor, Op. 59, no. 2, first movement
Stravinsky: *Les Noces* (The Wedding)
Tchaikovsky: Symphony No. 6 in B minor, second movement
Brahms: *Variations on a Theme by Haydn*
Morley: *Sing We and Chant It*

MELODY

The memorable moments in music, its highlights, are often furnished by melody. Take, for instance, the *Blue Danube Waltz,* Tchaikovsky's Piano Concerto No. 1, Gershwin's *Rhapsody in Blue,* or *America;* if you were asked what it is that you recall about such a familiar composition, apart from its general impression, you would no doubt answer, "Its melody, its tune." In many works the melodies, tunes, or themes are the most salient features; composers have constantly used striking melodies to point up important moments in a piece or to give in concentrated form an impression of the general style.

Listed below are some notable melodies to be found in familiar concert literature:

Bach: Aria from Suite in D major, No. 3
Dvorak: Theme from second movement of *From the New World* Symphony (Goin' Home)
Mozart: *Non più andrai* (You'll No Longer Strut) from *The Marriage of Figaro*
Ravel: *Pavane pour une infante défunte* (Pavane for a Dead Princess)

It is difficult to say what is distinctive about a melody, what it is that gives it personality. Like emotion, the melodic gift is something that can be observed, its results described, its effect upon the listener suggested, but its secret never thoroughly explored. Some composers, such as Mozart and Tchaikovsky, seem to overflow with melodic riches. Others address themselves to different, though no less important, musical values. Nevertheless, all music, whether it be frankly songlike or complex and involved, is concerned with melody.

Melodic Contour

Melody gives us an impression of outline or contour. When we listen to a melody, we might imagine observing an artist sketching a figure. The path of his pencil gradually delineates a meaningful pattern. Likewise, the line of tones in a melody gradually forms and completes a meaningful musical shape. When a melodic line rises steadily, it may connote increasing tension or greater energy of movement. Conversely, a melody that drops steadily may convey a sense of relaxation or settling. A melody that is more or less level or works around a given tone may suggest steadiness and evenness of movement. Abrupt rise or fall, involving widely different levels, indicates a bold, emphatic, and perhaps strenuous quality of movement. The song *Drink to Me Only with Thine Eyes* has an even, level quality of melodic movement, with somewhat more expansiveness in the third phrase. On the other hand, the first strain of the *Blue Danube Waltz* owes much of its sense of exuberant physical movement to the bold upward drive of its melodic phrases.

The following examples illustrate various patterns of melodic movement.

EXAMPLE 2·16 Melodic movement

a. Rising

b. Falling. Beethoven: Sonata in F minor, Op. 2, no. 1, first movement

c. Remaining on a level. Beethoven: Symphony No. 5, third movement

d. Turning around one or two points: Schubert: Symphony in B minor, first movement

e. Connected or *conjunct*. Beethoven: Symphony No. 9, Hymn to Joy

f. Disconnected or *disjunct*. Bach: Concerto for Two Violins in D minor, first movement

g. Directly to a point. Beethoven: Sonata in F minor, Op. 2, no. 1, first movement

Note, in the above examples, how the changes in direction, the rise and fall, tend to compensate for each other. Such motion contributes to the sense of balance in the melody, in addition to its primary role in creating the melodic contour. If we were to listen further in most of these examples (beyond the points quoted), we should hear that these smaller turns are controlled by a general rise or fall to one farthest point, at which the line may end or else settle back in the direction of the starting point. This large-scale contour is very important as a means of directing musical movement and giving shape to a passage of some length. It may involve a few measures, as in the example quoted below, or it may organize an entire composition. For example, in the Fugue in C minor by Bach (*Well-Tempered Clavier,* Book I), the uppermost voice has a broad rise and fall over the entire piece, conveying the impression of an enormous melodic arc. This sweeping rise and fall of the melodic line is also an important factor in the Prelude to Wagner's

Tristan. The term *apex* (plural, *apices*) is used to designate the peak of the melodic contour.

EXAMPLE 2·17 Melodic apices. Beethoven: Symphony No. 5, Op. 67

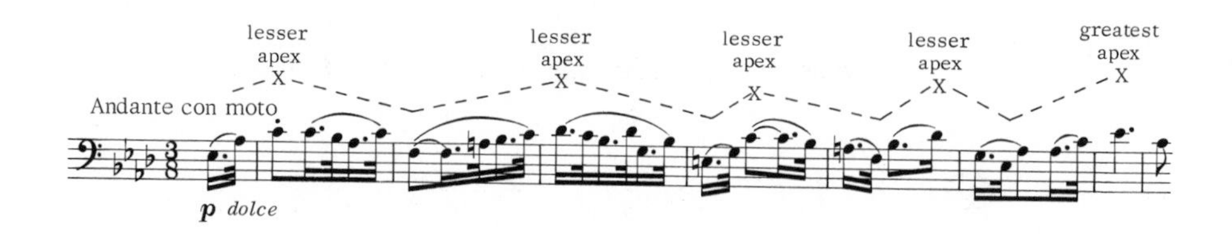

Melodic contour is built through a succession of *melodic intervals.* An interval is the *distance in pitch* between two tones, or a *quality of sound* created by these two tones. An interval or a series of intervals can become a motive when endowed with musical vitality.

Intervals differ in size; therefore, they differ in the impression of movement which they can give in a motive. For example, listen to the beginning of Mozart's *Haffner* Symphony:

EXAMPLE 2·18 Mozart: *Haffner* Symphony

The bold effect of this music is created by extremely large intervals in the melody. Certainly this is a most arresting way of introducing the brilliant and festive piece to follow.

Quite different is the effect at the beginning of *Drink to Me,* where there is actually no melodic movement up or down at first, and then only a gentle rise and fall. The melodic intervals here are proper to an elegant, persuasive, and fanciful love song.

The keyboard is useful for getting acquainted with the more common intervals. At the piano, play the note C as indicated on the diagram following. The white note immediately to the right of C is D; the interval connecting these two tones is called a *second.* Each interval is named according to the number of degrees on the musical staff which it includes.

EXAMPLE 2·19 Common musical intervals

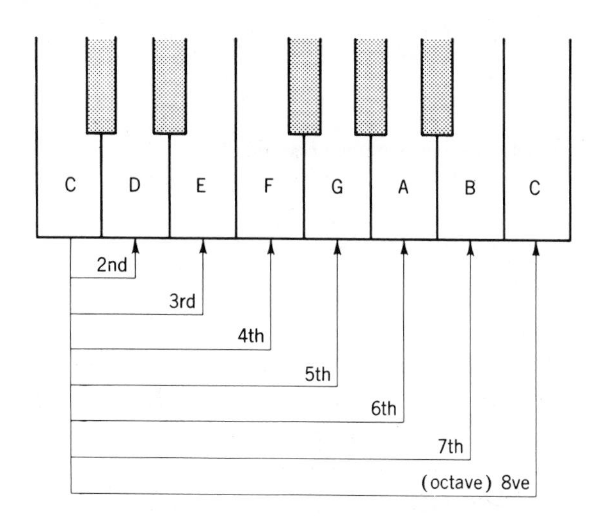

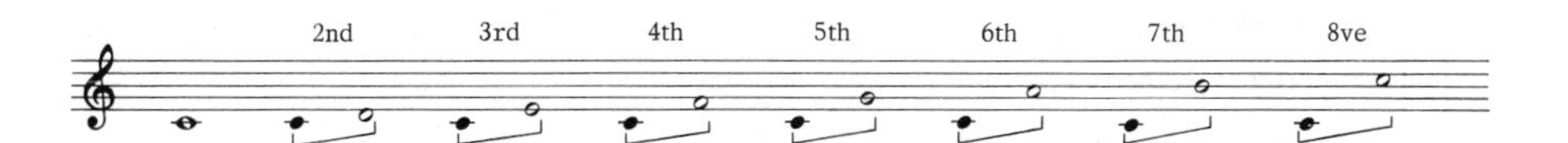

Listen carefully to each interval: you will notice that each has a characteristic quality of sound. Thirds and sixths sound full and rich; fourths and fifths have a rather open feeling; sevenths and ninths seem unsteady and tense; seconds are rather smooth and neutral in effect. These values will affect the nature of the melodies of which they are part. Here are some examples of melodies built with concentrations of a certain kind of interval:

EXAMPLE 2·20

a. Thirds and sixths

b. Fourths and fifths

c. Sevenths

d. Seconds. Mozart: *Jupiter* Symphony, Menuetto

As an example of the importance that every interval has within a melody, let us try the first phrase of *Drink to Me* with a slight alteration. Starting on C instead of the proper note E, play the melody using only white keys. The change in the position of the first tone with relation to the rest of the melody changes the effect of the passage.

Of all the intervals you have heard above, only one kind gives the impression of gradual melodic movement, of conjunct movement. This is the *second*. All others are disjunct, and give the impression of taking a leap. The bold, arresting melodic manner of the *Star-Spangled Banner* is due to the disjunct intervals which separate the first six notes (see Example 2·16 *f* and g for further examples of disjunct melodic movement).

Melodic Motives

Melodic contour combines with rhythmic patterns or motives to create *melodic motives*. In this way, distinctive musical figures are formed, which are then used as basic structural materials in musical composition. The following example shows how melody provides the *shape* and how rhythm provides the *style* or *manner* in the structure of motives:

EXAMPLE 2·21

Line of tones

Rhythmic motives incorporated

Melodic motives are put together to form phrases and periods. As this happens, the motives may have the following relationships with each other:

Repetition—exact restatement of a preceding motive
Variation—some change, but not enough to disguise the similarity to a preceding motive
Contrast—decided difference from the preceding motive

In Examples 2·22 and 2·23 we have illustrations of these three aspects of motive relationship. Example 2·22 is concerned entirely with *repetition* and *variation*. Beethoven states the motive of four notes, *repeats* it at lower pitch, then restates it eleven times in *varied* forms to build a period which rises steadily to a point of climax. The one motive has been used exclusively here to "spearhead" the direction of the larger melodic line.

EXAMPLE 2·22 Beethoven: Symphony No. 5, first movement

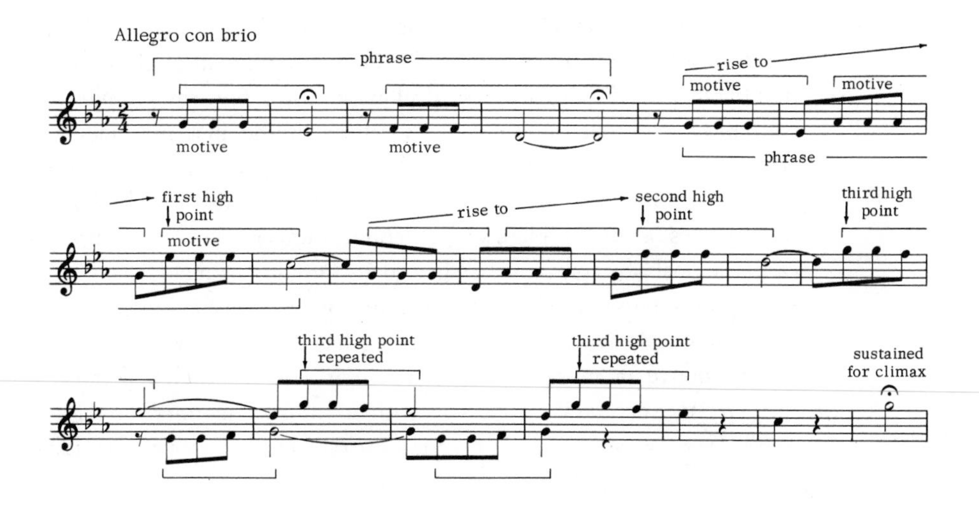

Contrast between melodic motives is illustrated in the following example:

EXAMPLE 2·23 Mozart: *Jupiter* Symphony, beginning

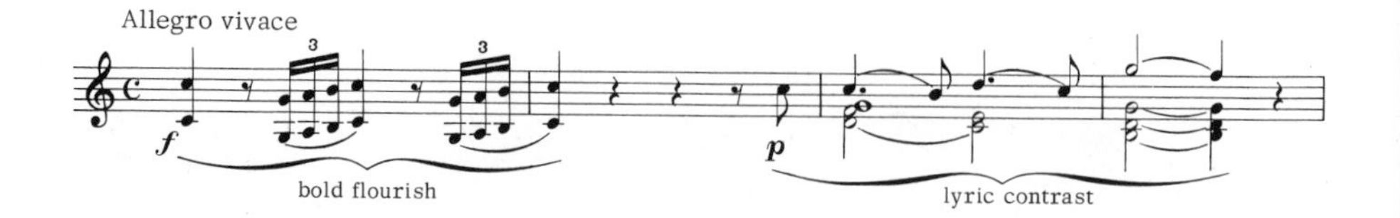

The whole orchestra begins with a flourish of three bold strokes; this is followed immediately by a reply, which offers, in contrast, the merest fragment of a soft lyric melody. Once again there is the alternation of bold and lyric motives, this time at a different pitch. Mozart continues the piece in the bold manner with fresh motives to reach the point of arrival of his first large period. In this example, Mozart has made effective use of contrast of motives in a very striking manner.

Repetition, variation, and contrast of motives convey different ideas of musical movement. Repetition and variation spin out or extend a single idea; therefore, they will tend to suggest a steadiness or unbroken continuity of musical thought. Contrast, particularly when it is sharp, introduces a fresh element, often a conflicting one. While it may interrupt the continuity of musical thought, the impact of contrasting motives may intensify the quality of movement.

Repetition, variation, and contrast are aspects of large-scale musical form; we shall return to these relationships for further consideration when we deal with form.

In listening for melodic motives, direct your attention to the *number* and the *variety* of figures. Some compositions use a great many different and contrasted motives, as we hear in the first movement of Beethoven's Symphony No. 3. Other works deal with just a few similar motives, constantly manipulating them, as we hear in the first movement of Bach's *Brandenburg* Concerto No. 2. Still again, the melodic material may be so consistent and continuous that we can hardly speak of separate motives, as in the plainsong *Alleluia, Masterpieces,* no. 2. In each case, the goal of expression is reflected in the play of melodic motives: Beethoven's music is charged with tremendous tension and conflict; Bach's has a playful vigor; the plainsong has a floating, remote quality.

The motive in music does not represent a fully developed musical idea, yet its very brevity, coupled with its distinct manner, enables it to fill a very powerful role in carrying forward musical movement. Each time we hear a familiar motive reappear or encounter a new motive, we sense that the music has gained fresh melodic momentum.

Treatment of Melodic Material

The role of melodic material in a musical composition is of particular interest to the listener, because it is frequently by means of melody that he is able to follow the action of a piece. Melodic material provides a thread of continuity that gives the clue to musical meaning. To understand the various forms melody takes, we shall examine its different uses in musical composition.

TUNE

The most familiar kind of melody is that which we call a tune. A tune may be characterized as follows:

1. It is generally complete in itself.
2. It is generally built symmetrically, with phrases and periods that balance each other.
3. It has a distinctive contour.
4. It has distinctive rhythmic motives, with some alternation between long and short notes.
5. It does not generally involve extreme contrasts in style or among its motives.
6. It has a relatively small range and thus can be sung easily.

Of these characteristics, the sense of completeness is probably the most important. Tunes can exist by themselves, as small, independent pieces. *Old Folks at Home, Drink to Me, America*—all well-known songs are independent tunes. Tunes may also be part of larger works. *The Hymn to Joy* from Beethoven's Symphony No. 9, the opening of the second movement of Dvorak's Symphony No. 5 (the "Goin' Home" melody), the opening of the second movement of Mozart's Quintet in E♭ major, K. 614—these are also well-rounded complete tunes.

In a tune, the arrangement of figures and motives contributes to the sense of completeness of the piece. It is very easy to recognize repetitions, variations, and contrasts as they complement each other. In the song *Drink to Me,* the first phrase is repeated to become the second and fourth phrases, while the third provides a contrast. These phrase relationships can be charted as: AABA. (It is useful to employ letters to designate the melodic components of a musical passage. For repetition, the letter is repeated; for variation, a prime sign is added to the original letter, A′; for contrast, a new letter is used.)

SUBJECT, THEME

The terms subject and theme are generally used to refer to melodic material that is part of a larger composition, whether it be a fully formed tune or a section consisting of one or more distinctive phrases *without* the completeness that characterizes a tune. *Subject* is a very broad term. It may refer to the opening few notes of a fugue, which form the principal material for the piece; it may also refer to a large group of melodic figures and phrases put together to make a single extended part of a composition. The implication is that a subject is an important topic, a subject for discourse. *Theme* has something of the same meaning; we use the term to refer to a melodic statement that indicates the style or manner of a section. A theme is a salient melodic phrase, a period, or a group of periods that generally has something of tunefulness about it, but need not have the rounded structure of a tune. Thus, the opening theme of Beethoven's Symphony No. 3 has a striking character, but it does not become a tune until almost the very end of the movement (see pages 85 and 252). The theme of the second movement of this work, on the other hand, is a fully formed tune. The opening of the third movement is so neutral in its melodic contour at first that it is properly designated a subject, which, as the listener learns, becomes the topic for an extended discourse.

We should also refer here to important melodic materials that do not have strong character or profile, but are used to carry musical movement forward through patterns of short tones of equal value. Often these alternate with melodic material that has strong profile. Example 2·25 from the Invention in G major by Bach illustrates this kind of melodic material; you can also hear this in studies, exercises, any solo concerto, and most concert music from the eighteenth and nineteenth centuries. This we shall designate as *figuration*. Listening to the opening movement of Mozart's Sonata in C major, K. 545, we hear the following scheme of melodic action:

1. Salient theme
2. Patterned figuration
3. New salient theme
4. New pattern of figuration
5. Melodic fragments with distinctive profile

This takes us to a very strong and conclusive point of arrival, not quite halfway through the movement. The remainder carries out much the same alternation.

DEVELOPMENT

Melodic motives can act as binding factors in a piece of music. We hear a melody with its distinctive motives. Later on this melody returns. We connect and relate the various appearances; the melody thus becomes a point of reference, a landmark in the flow of the music. As a matter of fact, melodies can retain their identities even when they are altered or broken up in different ways. Certain parts or features of a theme are immediately recognizable, although they may undergo a number of changes. These changes are aspects of *development* and occur extensively in all styles of Western music. Here is an example from a contemporary work.

EXAMPLE 2·24 Bartók: String Quartet No. 6, first movement *

a. Original motive group—nine notes

b. Shortened—seven notes, four notes

c. Extended

Development represents an evolution in the life of the melody itself; therefore it is another way movement in music is made manifest.

SEQUENCE

One special way of organizing motives that has been very useful for centuries is the *sequence*. In a sequence, a single motive is restated several times in succession at a higher or lower pitch. This is one of the most valuable techniques for broadening and extending a musical phrase. The effect of the sequence is to carry the entire level of the music gradually upward or downward; it creates a longer line of melodic movement, and it governs and guides the play of intervals and motives.

EXAMPLE 2·25 Bach: Two-part Invention in G major

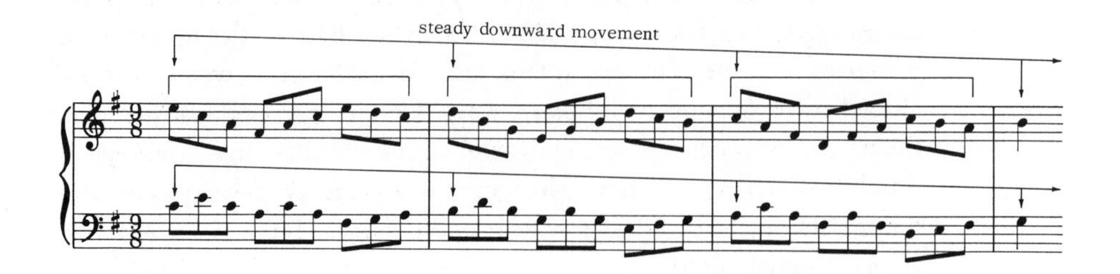

Sequences are frequently used in the process of development.

Both development and sequence make use of melodic variations; they constitute methods by which variation can achieve rather extensive scope.

PICTORIALISM

Composers have often taken advantage of the adaptability of musical sounds, rhythms, and melodic figures to suggest literary ideas, emotional states, or various kinds of action or locale. Such musical pictorialism is illustrated in Example 2·26, where rage is expressed by a grand melodic flourish.

EXAMPLE 2·26 Musical pictorialism. Handel: *The Messiah,* Why do the nations rage?

Pictorialism can also be humorous. Saint-Saëns managed to imitate "personages with long ears" very effectively in *The Carnival of the Animals.* We receive a most realistic picture of the hee-haws of their conversation in the extremely abrupt and wide skips in the violins.

When the composer tells us to make such specific connections by associating the text with the music, we are on safe ground. This kind of association is also possible when the musical indications are unmistakable, as, for example, when we hear a march, a trumpet call, a shepherd's pipe, or any strikingly characteristic effect. But we must guard against reading *exact* meanings into music that has no direct *literary* counterpart. Pictorialism is simply a demonstration of music's ability to adapt itself to other media of expression.

Aspects of Melodic Movement and Arrival

In relating melody to the basic criteria, movement and arrival, we have two points to consider: (1) the contour of the melody itself and (2) the treatment of the melody in relation to the overall play of movement and arrival in the piece.

With respect to the contour, we find a number of points of arrival; in fact, each time the melody changes direction, the point of change acts as a point of arrival for the melodic line which leads to it. Among these, the upper or lower limit stands out as the most important, serving as a goal in the delineation of the melody. Then again, the last tone of the melody is a point of arrival, providing the final repose or sense of completion. Thus we can say (concerning *many,* not necessarily *all* melodies) that we have one point of arrival representing the *maximum of action* and another representing the *completion of the thought.* Example 2·27 (see also Example 2·17) illustrates movement and arrival with respect to melodic contour.

EXAMPLE 2·27 Mozart: Quartet in G major, K. 387
Andante cantabile

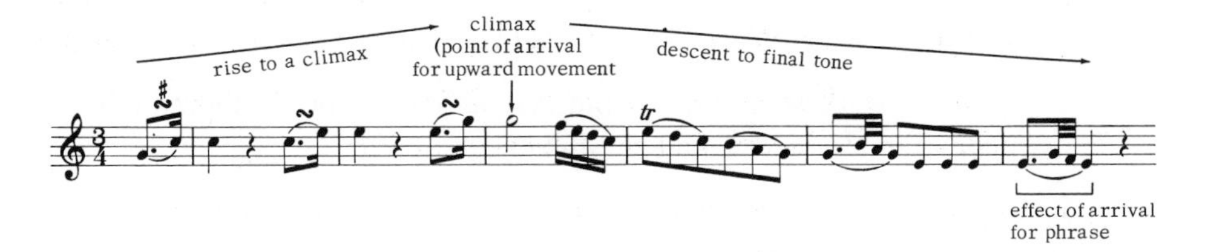

Judging a melody in this way, we can determine whether the composer has visualized the melody as a *grand sweep,* rising to a *climax* and covering a considerable period of time; or whether he has preferred to limit the melodic line to a *specific range,* through which the rise and fall will take place several times as a *play* among the melodic motives. The former process is embodied in the opening of Beethoven's Quartet in F, Op. 59, no. 1, first movement; the latter in the Scherzo from Mendelssohn's *Midsummer Night's Dream.* Few melodies can be said to embody in a pure fashion either the rise to a climax or the play of motives; the two procedures intermingle and reinforce each other.

The use of different kinds of melodic material provides a clue to the general interplay of movement and arrival in a composition. In an extended work, a section which presents a distinctive theme or tune is felts as a relatively stable moment in the work, a kind of plateau in the contour of the action. When we hear melodic motives undergoing development, we sense greater intensity of movement. In works of large proportion, these processes tend to alternate; the extent to which one leads over the other also tells us something about the degree of intensity in movement. Thus, in the first movement of Beethoven's Symphony No. 5, development seems to be taking place most of the time. In the second movement of the same work, the converse is true; the composer appears to be concerned mostly with presenting and returning to salient thematic material.

The following questions may be used in evaluating the melodic content of a composition.

1. What is the general contour of the melody? Does it have wide or narrow range? Where are the apices?
2. How are motives distributed according to repetition, variation, and contrast? Are there few or many different motives? What are the characteristic intervals?
3. How is the melody formed? Is it a complete tune? Is it formed by motive groups without sense of completeness? Is there sequence, development, pictorialism?
4. How is the melodic material distributed in the piece? What is the relation, if any, of complete tune to fragments, and to development? When, and how frequently, are themes and other melodic materials restated?

Applying these criteria to the first movement of Beethoven's Symphony No. 3, we can find the following answers:

1. Individual melodies differ from each other in contour; some have gradual, rounded movement; others are angular; in general, there is a rise to an important melodic goal following the appearance of each salient theme.
2. There is a great profusion of melodic material; striking contrasts are frequent; all relationships are exploited.
3. Very few, if any, of the salient themes have a sense of completeness: they begin with striking profile material and tend to break forward into developmental processes.
4. In spite of the many salient themes, development is paramount in this work; *all* melodic materials are restated, some many times.
5. The opening theme, heard many times throughout the movement, appears as a real tune only toward the end; before this point, it always moves off in some digressive or asymmetrical fashion (see pages 85 and 251–252).

Suggested works for melodic evaluation:

Mendelssohn: Symphony No. 4 in A major, third movement
Haydn: Symphony No. 103 in E♭ major, finale
Mozart: Sinfonia Concertante in E♭ major, K. 364, first movement
Schönberg: Quartet No. 4, first movement
Bach: *Brandenburg* Concerto No. 3 in G major, first movement
Stravinsky: *Le Sacre du printemps,* opening

TEXTURE

When we studied rhythm and melody, we were concerned principally with a single important line of musical action. Still, the total effect of movement in nearly all music is the result of a number of lines working together. This aspect of music is called *texture,* and it refers to the *action of the component parts or voices.* We shall consider three kinds of texture: homophonic, polyphonic, and give-and-take (combining homophonic and polyphonic procedures).

The terms *voice* and *part* as they are used in the discussion of texture refer to a single line, whether it is heard alone or among other lines. Both terms may apply to vocal and instrumental performance.

Homophonic Texture

When there is (1) *one principal part* taking a featured melody or (2) *one procedure* governing the entire texture, the texture is called *homophonic.* The following examples show these two kinds of homophonic texture. Example 2·28 comprises a melody and its *accompaniment.* The accompaniment furnishes a steady rhythmic background by means of a simple figure. This creates a light and flowing sense of movement.

EXAMPLE 2·28 Mozart: Sonata in C major, K. 545, second movement

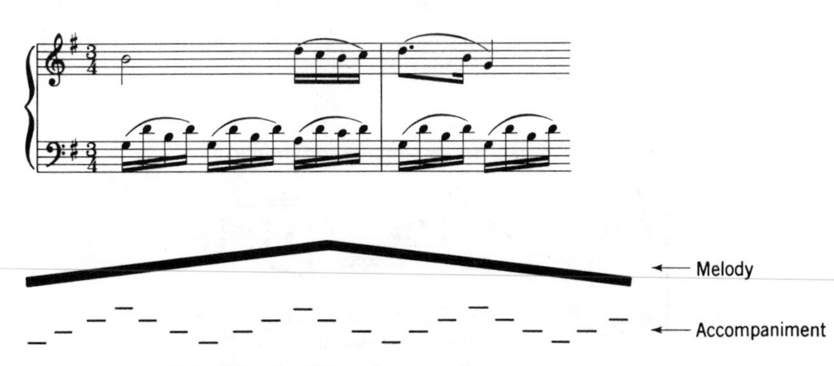

(Note different patterns of movement in melody and accompaniment.)

In the second kind of homophonic texture (Example 2·29) one procedure dominates, although the melody is carried by the uppermost part. There is a massive, forthright, and vigorous quality to the movement. This kind of texture may be called *isometric,* from the terms

EXAMPLE 2·29 Beethoven: Symphony No. 5, last movement

The accompanying voices carry out the same rhythmic action as the uppermost voice, the melody.

iso, meaning "the same," and *metric,* meaning "measured." In an isometric texture all voices are governed by the same rhythmic pattern.

Another kind of texture, that in which but *one* line of music is being performed, is designated as *monophonic.* Examples of this texture will be given in Chapter 3, Medieval Music.

Polyphonic Texture

When several voices play clearly separate and independent lines, with all appearing to be equal in importance, the texture is called *polyphonic.* The terms *counterpoint* and *contrapuntal* also describe this kind of texture. In Example 2·30, polyphonic texture creates a tightly knit and intense kind of movement; many musical events seem to take place in a short time.

EXAMPLE 2·30 Bach: Sinfonia in D minor

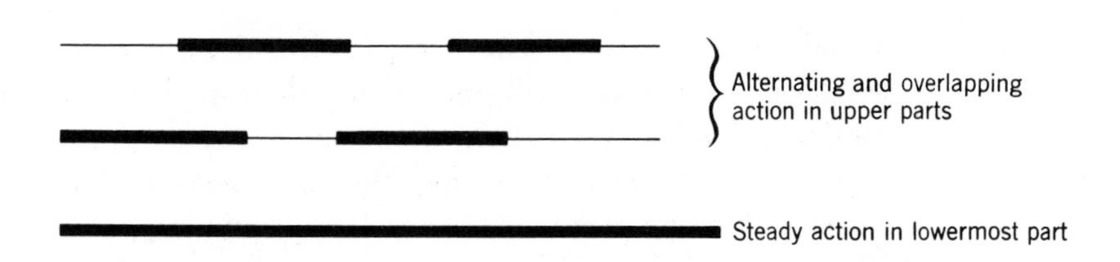

If the voices take up the same melody or *subject* in turn, the procedure is called *imitation.* The use of the same subject binds the voices together even more tightly than in nonimitative counterpoint. Example 2·31 illustrates imitation, which is a form of polyphony.

EXAMPLE 2·31 Bach: Prelude in E♭ major, *Well-Tempered Clavier,* Book I

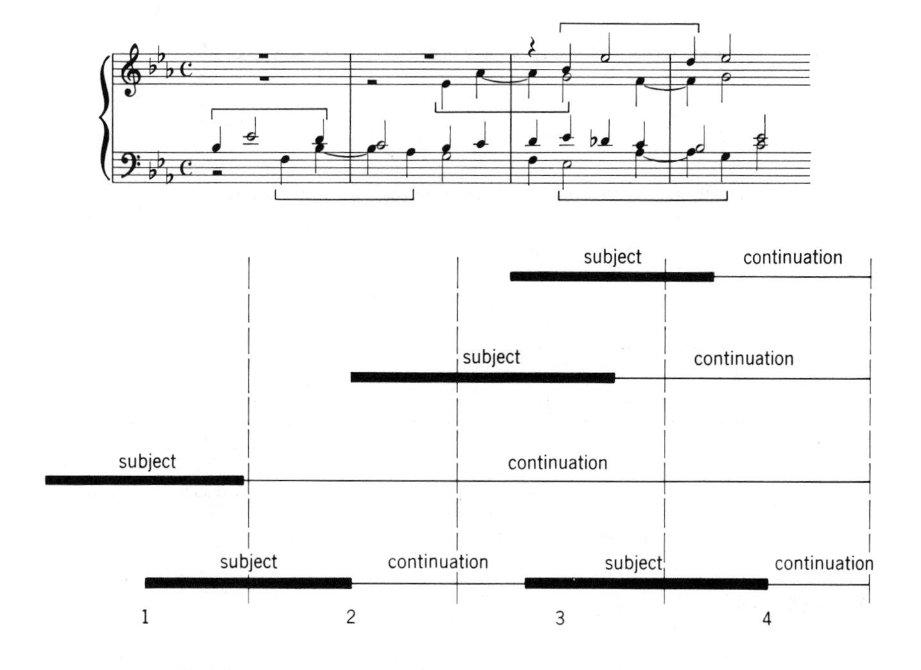

A familiar, simple type of imitative polyphony is the *round,* such as *Row, Row Your Boat.* In singing such a piece, each performer feels that his part works against the others in a neatly fitted texture; he thus gains a vivid satisfaction in musical participation. Indeed, much polyphonic music was written originally with this purpose in mind; in such music, the values are sensed most keenly from the inside out, rather than by the nonparticipating listener.

With regard to *phrase structure,* homophonic and polyphonic textures tell completely different stories. When there is but one salient idea, the progress of the music is relatively easy to follow and points of arrival tend to be clear. The line pauses, and we have a caesura. In polyphonic music, especially imitation, different phases of movement overlap each other. The caesura of one part is covered by the movement of another. Polyphonic music, for this reason, tends to flow along continuously for long periods of time and frequently to give an impressive effect of accumulation. The diagram below illustrates the two different procedures in relation to phrase structure:

EXAMPLE 2·32

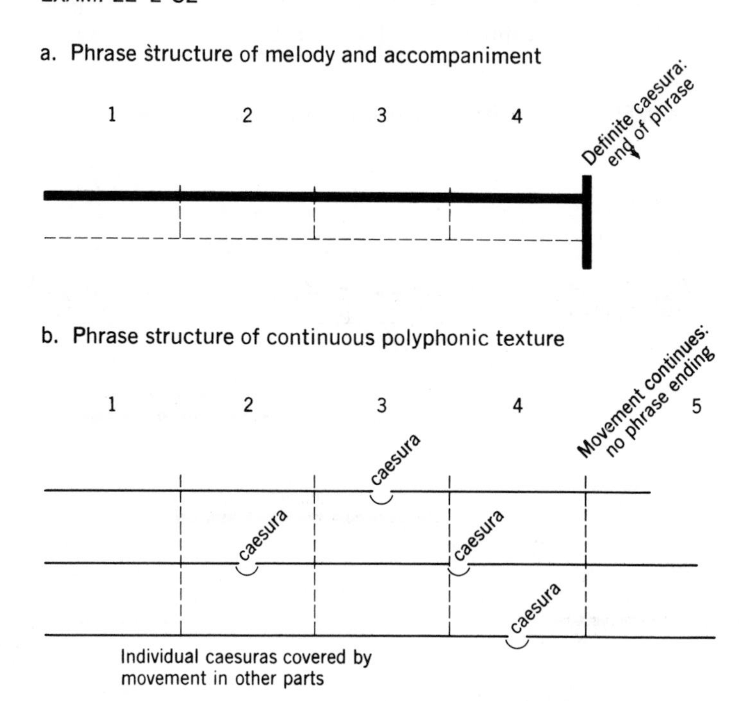

Give-and-Take

A great deal of music that is basically homophonic in texture shows elements of contrapuntal treatment. Perhaps the accompaniment will take on some personality of its own by means of a distinctive melodic figure; perhaps the principal melody will be shared by different voices; sometimes incidental and short-lived imitations will appear to give a bit more interest and momentum to the music. This kind of texture, designated in this book as give-and-take, is illustrated in Example 2·33. The principal melody is in the uppermost part, yet the bass voice is important and at one point suggests an imitation of the melody.

Throughout the first movement of Beethoven's Symphony No. 3, we hear a wide variety of textures, covering the categories we have

EXAMPLE 2·33 Beethoven: Sonata for Piano in B♭ major, Op. 22, second movement

just described. (This variety, of course, corresponds to the rich melodic content and the wide range of rhythmic procedures we have found in this piece.) Here is a list of the textural layouts in the first eighty-two measures of the movement:

1–2: full orchestra, full chords (*isometric*)
3–15: *melody* in cello, *accompaniment,* melody taken over by violins, light texture
15–23: *melody and accompaniment,* handled in give-and-take fashion, light texture
23–37: a moment of *counterpoint* at beginning, superseded by *one procedure* dominating the entire texture, heavier sound
38–45: *melody and accompaniment* in full orchestra
45–57: *give-and-take* with some *contrapuntal* action, light texture; heavy texture, full orchestra, *one procedure* at end of period
58–65: *melody* with *contrapuntal* line in basses, light texture increasing in heaviness
65–82: *melody and accompaniment,* heavy texture

As we listen for textural values, it becomes apparent that we must take into account the relationship of tone qualities within the texture. Tones will be blended when the instruments are similar in quality; tones will be set off sharply from each other if the instruments are contrasted in tone quality. In some kinds of music, such as the Lassus motet *Tristis est anima mea* (Sad Is My Soul) or a composition for string quartet, all the voices and instruments have similar qualities of tone. In other music, sharp contrasts in tone color will cause even a melody-and-accompaniment texture to sound contrapuntal. This we heard from time to time in Beethoven's Symphony No. 3.

Hector Berlioz elevated this principle of contrast between instrumental qualities of sound to a very important position in his scheme of composition, and it is the basis of much of his contrapuntal writing. His *Symphonie fantastique* is typical in this respect. To use an analogy of painting, the boldness of contrast in line can be intensified frequently by sharp contrasts in color or shade. On the other hand, when many colors are run together, the result may be a rich blend in which no single value dominates. This would be comparable to a massive effect for the full orchestra, in which all instruments blend but partially cancel each other's specific qualities of sound. It is obvious that in evaluating texture the listener must take qualities of sound into consideration; it would be well to apply the criteria for musical sound which were discussed earlier in this chapter.

Each conscientious performer or conductor makes a special study of the textural values in a piece. He must have a clear idea of the action of the component voices and the degree of blend or separation. This is necessary so that the composer's idea appears clear and undistorted. How often in a performance do we miss an important figure or voice because of a poorly projected texture and thereby lose the thread of movement and the meaning of the music itself for a time.

The two most important voices or parts in a musical texture have traditionally been the outer, that is, the lowermost and uppermost, parts. This is simply because we can hear better what goes on in these parts than we can hear inner parts. Example 2·34 shows how the outer parts assume textural leadership. At various times, the lowermost part has been called a *bass, pedal, tenor,* or *basso continuo.* In vocal music, the uppermost voice, which sang the most important melodic part, was called a *discant, superius, soprano, duplum,* or *treble,* at different times. To this day, outer voices form the skeleton of most musical textures, with other voices filling in for richer sound.

As we might expect, textural values provide important clues in the analysis of different musical styles. We shall find perhaps the greatest

EXAMPLE 2·34 Haydn: Quartet in D major, Op. 64, no. 5, first movement

Allegro moderato
Violin I
Violin II
Viola
Cello
lowermost part divided between Viola and Cello

contrasts in comparing a vocal piece of the Renaissance period, such as the Lassus motet, with a modern work for a small group of instruments, such as Stravinsky's *L'Histoire du soldat.* The Renaissance piece would have the following textural features:

1. A blending of voices; homogeneity of sound
2. Limited range of sound
3. Much contrapuntal activity, but because of (1) and (2), not a very strong impression of the independence of voices

The texture of the modern piece would show:

1. Sharp contrasts of sound; heterogeneity of sound
2. Wide range of sound; wide separation in the pitches of different instruments
3. Strong impression of contrapuntal activity, even when a melodic line with accompaniment is used, due to the extreme independence of the voices, their lack of blend in sonority

The following questions may be used for summarizing textural values:

1. What is the predominant type of action: melody-accompaniment, isometric, imitation, nonimitative polyphony, or give-and-take? To what extent, if any, are these procedures combined?
2. Is the texture varied: within phrases, between phrases, from period to period?
3. To what extent does textural action affect the structure by emphasizing or obscuring points of arrival?
4. To what extent does tone color affect the action of the component parts?
5. To what extent does texture highlight the melodic or rhythmic effects?

Suggested works for textural evaluation:

Mozart: *Eine kleine Nachtmusik,* second movement
Bartók: *Music for Strings,* first movement
Berlioz: *Symphonie fantastique,* finale
Palestrina: *Stabat Mater*
Bach: Chorale, *Wachet auf* (Sleepers, Awake) from cantata *Wachet auf*

HARMONY

As we listened for qualities of sound, for rhythmic patterns, for melodic design, and for texture—the elements thus far discussed in this chapter—it was apparent that another factor was a part of the total picture. That was the effect created by tones sounding together or in close proximity to each other. We heard that each interval had a special quality of its own; some groups of tones sounded "sweet," blended, with an effect of stability; others were less sweet, harsher, unstable in effect. A composition could acquire a special quality from the use of certain tone combinations. These qualities, and the relationships they create, form the basis of *harmony*.

Among the many combinations that are available, each musical style has chosen those which can best support its general ideas of structure and expression. Western music, from the medieval period to the end of the nineteenth century, has been fairly consistent in its choice of tone combinations. While there has been much change and growth in Western harmony since its beginnings, these modifications represent "dialects" of a language, rather than a fundamental change in vocabulary or grammar. This is the harmony we shall study.

The elements of harmonic language are closely related to general effects of movement and arrival; this will be explained as each harmonic procedure is taken up, in order to add harmony to the basic criteria which constitute the musical viewpoint of this book.

Tonal Center

When tones are sounded, whether simultaneously or in succession, there seems to be a tendency for *one tone to assert itself* in our hearing more strongly than others, to establish itself as a point of reference. This can be illustrated simply. Hum to yourself a familiar song as *My Old Kentucky Home* or *America*. Stop humming just before the last note. In this case the song is halted short of its goal. No matter what you do rhythmically or melodically, the sense of arrival necessary to round off the piece is missing unless you sing the last note; this tone, thus, is a point of reference for the whole piece. It has established itself as a *tonal center*.

Listen now to *Laus Deo Patri* (Praise God the Father), *Masterpieces*, no. 1. In this piece, can you hear one tone, one pitch that seems more prominent than any other? The answer is yes; the tone is E. It is more prominent because (1) we hear it first, (2) we hear it frequently, (3) it is often longer than its neighboring tones, and (4) it ends almost every phrase—it is the last tone in the piece. The prominence of this tone, arising from *first impression, frequency, length,* and *final impression,* gives it a central position among all the different pitches used in the piece; therefore, it acts as a *tonal center* and is designated a *tonic note.*

In terms of our general criteria, a tonal center represents *departure* and *arrival*. Movement takes place *away* from the point of departure and *toward* the point of arrival; in the plainsong *Laus Deo,* these movements were represented by melodic rise and fall, which used the tonal center as a point of reference.

In our musical language there is another means for communicating the impression of a tonal center: by making use of the distinctive qualities which intervals and combinations of intervals possess. Tones are like chemical substances which have an affinity for each other. When elements are put together, they can combine to form new and distinctive compounds; similarly, musical tones, combined, form distinctive combinations which can be organized in many ways.

In order to understand how these combinations can act to give an impression of tonal center, we first examine some of their distinctive qualities. The first point to be considered is the impression of stability or instability that tone combinations create.

Stability and Instability

Stability and instability are relative qualities. Some intervals are strongly stable; others have a marked effect of instability. Still others range between these two limits. The two qualities may be described as follows:

1. A stable interval gives a feeling of rest, of poise; it is *consonant,* which means that the tones seem to have a blend, an "agreement" with each other. Stable intervals express arrival in harmony.
2. An unstable interval gives a feeling of motion, of restlessness; it seems *dissonant,* which means that the tones do not "agree" with each other as well as in a stable interval. Unstable intervals seem to have an inherent capacity for movement.

We can classify familiar intervals according to their degree of stability or instability as follows:

STABLE	RELATIVELY STABLE	UNSTABLE
Octave	Major and minor thirds	Seconds
Unison	Major and minor sixths	Sevenths
Perfect fifth		Augmented and diminished intervals

The perfect fourth has a stable quality in some cases, an unstable one in others.

General qualities of stability and instability contribute to the expressive values in a composition. For example, in *Drink to Me* the combinations of tones, the *chords,* appear fairly stable throughout. The simple, sweet lyricism of the song is supported by sounds that have a gratifying, consonant quality. In the Prelude to *Tristan* by Wagner, the first chord and most of those which follow have a striking effect of instability; these harmonies make the most important contribution to the restlessness and tension which characterize this piece.

We may reasonably expect to find effects of harmonic stability at important points of arrival, at the ends of phrases and periods. Conversely, harmonic effects of lesser stability are suitable for maintaining musical movement. We have only to listen once more to our song *Drink to Me* in order to see how this relationship of stability and instability operates in the phrase structure of familiar music. At the end of the first, second, and fourth phrases a satisfying effect of harmonic stability has been created. Although the entire song does not venture into harmonic problem areas, the chord that ends each of these phrases is considerably more stable than the chords within the phrases. You may have noticed that in order to secure an effect of harmonic stability, it is necessary to reach a strong rhythmic point of arrival, a marked caesura. Thus, rhythm and harmony work together to build the outlines of phrase structure.

EXAMPLE 2·35 Rhythm and harmony in phrase structure

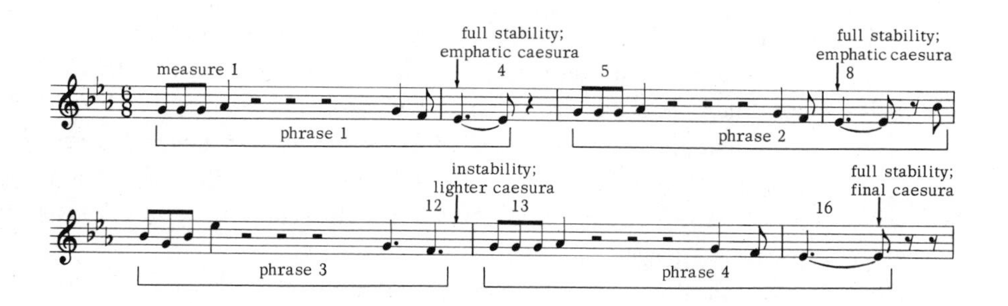

Wagner, in the Prelude to *Tristan,* seems to have tried deliberately to counteract this feeling for harmonic arrival. There is hardly one chord in the entire piece that would satisfy a need for arrival. The listener has to depend partly on texture, partly on the rhythmic caesuras to tell him that a point of arrival has been reached.

In the first period of the opening movement of Beethoven's Quartet in F major, Op. 59, no. 1, we can hear a tremendously strong point of rhythmic and harmonic arrival, settling the problem of harmonic instability which the preceding measures have created.

The fact that some tonal relationships convey a sense of movement while others act for arrival is evidence of the presence of order within harmony. Within this order, the interval of the perfect fifth plays a vital role. The ear accepts this interval as the embodiment of stability, with the lower note acting to secure the effect of stability. At the piano play first C, then G above; immediately after, play G, then C below. The first interval will pose a question; the second provides a fitting answer. When we hear C, we are satisfied that a complete effect of arrival has been achieved. This relationship between the two notes of the perfect fifth is so strong and pervasive that it can be felt over long stretches of musical action. It has been used to organize phrases, periods, and even longer sections of musical compositions.

In the demonstration just described, the effect of the perfect fifth was embodied in a melodic progression. When the two notes are sounded simultaneously, as a *harmonic* interval, the effect is also that of stability and we take the lower member to the tonal center. In the Estampie, *Masterpieces,* no. 12, observe how the interval of the perfect fifth is used at points of arrival in most of the phrases. Other phrases end with a single prominent tone, doubled in the octave. Both effects act for arrival for their respective phrases. Bartók's *Ostinato* exploits the stability of the perfect fifth to establish a tonal center and then to shift to another. The perfect fifth with which it begins is repeated many times in the lower register of the piano (the register adds solidity to the effect), and we have a strong sense of D as the tonic. When the perfect fifth changes in pitch, the tonal center changes and we have a strong kinesthetic effect, as if we had moved up or down a floor in an elevator.

The stability and consonance values of intervals have been linked with their positions in the *harmonic series.* To understand the harmonic series, we start with the fact that a sounding body—a string, a pipe, a membrane, or any other medium that gives out a fixed pitch—vibrates not only in its full length but also in segments of one-half, one-third, one-fourth, and so on, presumably to infinity. The tone we hear is produced by the length of the entire body; all the other vibrations, unheard yet present, influence the color of the tone we hear. Were the fractional vibrations to be heard, they would sound at pitches that have fixed relationships with each other—a series of relationships known as the harmonic series. The lowest six members, including the sounded tone (also designated as the *fundamental*), give us a widely spaced combination, the notes of which create a most agreeable consonance. Very likely, through millennia of adaptation to this *chord of nature,* we have come to accept it as a pleasant and thoroughly stable sound. Therefore, the intervals comprising this chord (octaves, fifths, fourths, thirds, and also sixths) seem to embody consonance more convincingly than any other other intervals. Example 2·36 shows the harmonic series of C.

EXAMPLE 2·36

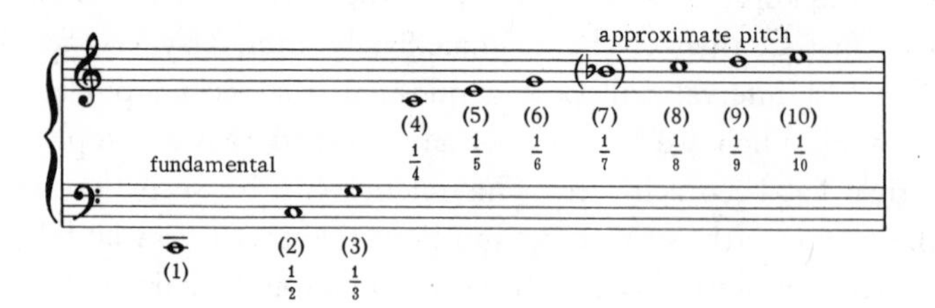

It now remains to answer the most important question regarding stability and instability: In what specific ways can they be related? The answer to this question provides the clue to the nature of Western harmony.

An unstable interval can be heard in two ways: (1) as an *effect,* separate and distinct, so that its particular color is the principal value; (2) as a *question* that calls for an answer.

When an unstable interval is treated as a question, it is linked to the interval which provides the answer. We have a pairing off, a phase of movement and arrival. The following example illustrates this relationship; each unstable or dissonant interval proceeds to a stable or consonant interval which is an acceptable answer to the question asked.

EXAMPLE 2·37 Relationship of stability and instability

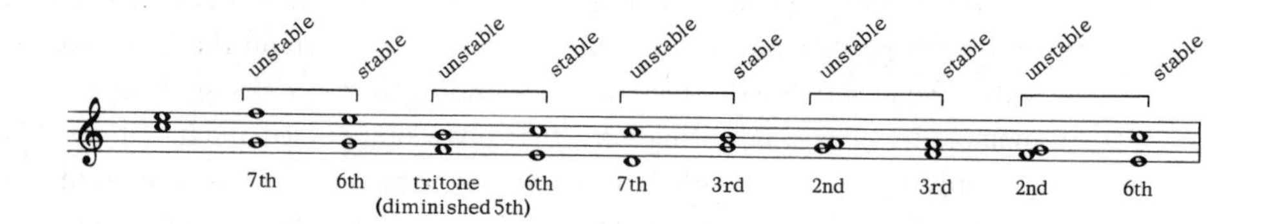

Our familiar Western music is built as an unbroken chain of action in which the relationships demonstrated above have virtually complete control as far as harmony is concerned.

Among the instability-stability pairings, there is one that has preeminence. It is illustrated in Example 2·38. Among the four tones in this progression, there is one that acts in the capacity of a tonal center; it is the more important tone in the interval of resolution and best represents arrival. It is the focus of stability for the action that takes place in this progression. That note is C.

If you take the first member of this progression, the interval of tension, you will find that one tone resolves upward, the other downward.

EXAMPLE 2·38 Tritone and its resolution (harmonic question and answer)

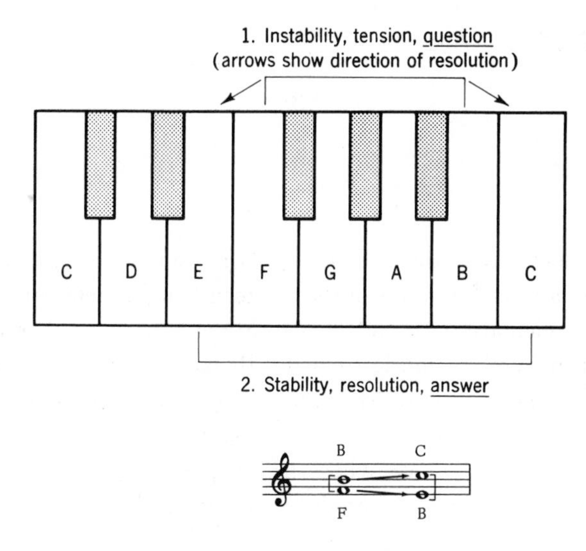

Experiment further with this first interval; this time place F on top, B at the bottom. F will move down; B will move up. No matter what position this combination assumes, the tones will resolve in opposite directions if their natural tendency is realized. This tendency governs this interval very strongly. F–B, or any other interval of the same size, is called the *tritone,* meaning an interval of three whole tones or steps. B–F, which creates the same effect, is called the *false fifth* or diminished fifth.

We usually designate the rising member of the tritone or the false fifth as the *leading tone,* since it leads to the *tonic* note. By extension, harmonies which contain the leading tone, and which thereby contain an element of tension, are called *leading-tone harmonies.* Leading-tone harmonies are the strongest embodiments of movement in harmony and occupy a vital position in the movement-arrival formulas which govern music.

We now have three ways in which a tonal center may be defined: (1) by prominence; (2) by the lower note of the perfect fifth; (3) by its position in a *tension-resolution* formula. Putting these all together, we create an extremely powerful definition of tonal center. In the following example:

1. C is prominent by virtue of its being in the outer voices and at the end of the progression.
2. C is the lower note of the perfect fifth.
3. C is the resolution of the tension created by B sounding against F.

EXAMPLE 2·39 Tonal center defined by tension and resolution

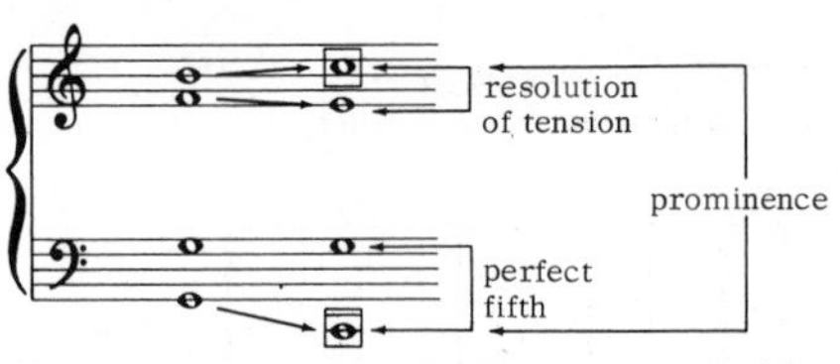

(note descending perfect fifth in bass; see pp. 68-69)

You will hear this particular kind of progression at almost every important point of arrival in music of the eighteenth and nineteenth centuries. The tonal relationships it embodies form the basis of the harmonic system used in Western music from the Renaissance to the present day. This progression can be varied infinitely in color and weight, but when it is present, it always acts to focus the harmony upon a tonal center. Also, as we shall see later, when the composer wishes to move to another tonal center, he will introduce the tritone that is paired with his new objective.

By way of illustration, listen to the beginning of the finale of Beethoven's Symphony No. 5 (Example 2·29). In this passage, nine chords are notated. Tonic and tritone harmonies are used exclusively, in the order cited below:

1	2	/3	4	/5	6	7	8	/9
ton.	ton.	ton.	trit.	ton.	trit.	ton.	trit.	ton.

The impression of the tonal center C is extremely strong as a result of this powerful progression. Other examples include:

Schubert: Song *Wohin* (Whither)
Mozart: *Eine kleine Nachtmusik,* first movement, beginning
Bach: *Brandenburg* Concerto No. 2, first movement, beginning

When a tonal center is defined by the tension-resolution method, as described above, it is generally referred to as a *key*. We speak of the key of C, of E♭, of A; by this we imply that the harmony has much to do with tritone-to-tonic progressions. In the next section we shall have a closer look at the relationships of tones in a key.

Key, Scale

The tonic note of a key is the center of a group of tones which interact with each other to make it clear that the tonic is the point of reference. This is illustrated by playing or singing the *scale* of a key. A scale is a series of notes that proceeds stepwise in one direction, up or down. Example 2·40 is the scale of the key of C.

EXAMPLE 2·40

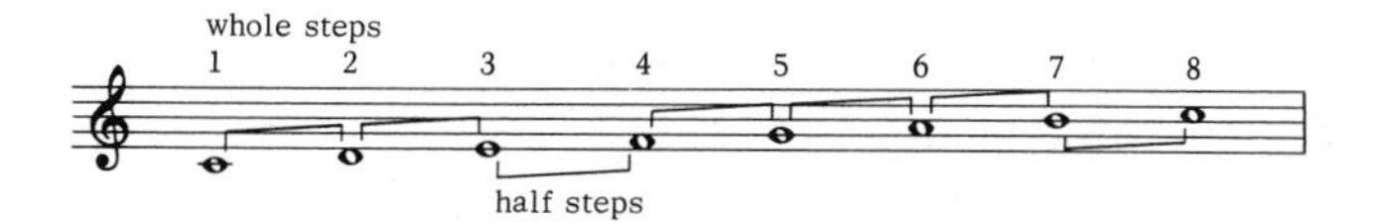

As we sing this scale, we accept the first note, the lower C, as the point of departure; we do not have a satisfactory sense of arrival until we reach the upper C. The two C's represent a tonic; all the other notes depend upon C for their relative positions. Conversely, C needs the other notes for clarification and support. We have, in this example, the scale of a *major key;* other tones can become tonic notes of major keys if the intervals between the members of the scale duplicate the arrangement of whole steps and half steps given above. Of particular importance are the half steps 3–4 and 7–8. Note that the tritone appears as 4–7, while the tonic effect is represented by 3–8. In the major scale the tritone occurs "naturally" between 4 and 7. In other scales this is not the case; for this reason, the major scale or key has a stronger power for defining its tonic than any other scale. The melodies in Examples 2·16 *a, d,* and *e* use the major scale.

A companion scale to the major, more colorful in sound perhaps, but less strong in its ability to define its tonic, is the *minor scale.* (The terms major and minor refer to the size of the interval between 1 and 3; in the major scale the interval is a major third; in the minor it is a minor third. This third, in each case, gives the characteristic color of the key.) In Example 2·41 a minor scale is shown first *without* a leading tone; next, a leading tone is provided; finally, accommodation is made for the rather awkward interval that otherwise occurs between 6 and 7 when a leading tone is used. The first is called the *natural* minor, because it is diatonic. (The term *diatonic* refers to scales that have two half steps, placed three or four notes distant from each other; a feeling of evenness and coherence results from this kind of arrangement.) The second is called *harmonic,* because it uses the leading tone for a tension-resolution effect. The third is called *melodic* because it differs from the harmonic minor in being easier to sing.

EXAMPLE 2·41 Minor scales

Natural

Harmonic

Melodic

Examples 2·16 *f* and 2·16 *g* use the minor scale.

The major and minor keys were used almost exclusively in music of the eighteenth and early nineteenth centuries; other scales were virtually ignored. Before this time, especially in the medieval and Renaissance periods, scales designated as modes were used. During the past century, modal scales have come again into use from time to time. We shall describe these scales in Chapter 3, Medieval Music.

Two other scales are of importance in providing a system of tones for musical composition. These are the *chromatic scale,* which has half steps throughout, and the *whole-tone scale,* which has whole steps throughout. Since all intervals are equal in these scales, we cannot find a tonal center by means of whole-step and half-step interaction. Any impression of tonic will be arbitrary and probably not clear, being based on prominence rather than tension and resolution. These scales are illustrated below:

EXAMPLE 2·42 Chromatic and whole-tone scales

a. Chromatic scale

Passage using chromatic scale

b. Whole-tone scale

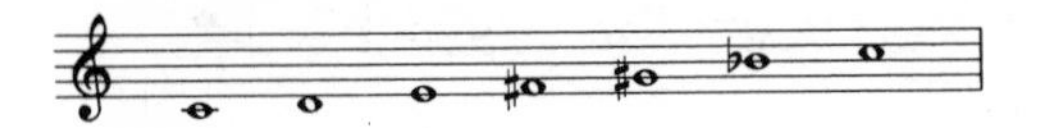

Passage using whole-tone scale

Chords

In discussing stability and instability we referred to chords, which were described as combinations of tones. Generally, the term is used when three or more tones are involved as a group.

In Western music, certain combinations were evolved and became standardized. This took place because (1) the actual sounds of some combinations were felt to be more satisfactory than those of other combinations, and (2) it was possible to create effective harmonic progressions with certain chords; this led eventually to the system of key definition we have been describing. Thus, qualities of *sound* and *movement* (*progression*) have been important factors in the building of our familiar chord vocabulary. It must be stressed that this took place, by trial and error, over several centuries; our present chord system is not a "natural" phenomenon, although, as we have seen, it does draw upon some aspects of the physical properties of sound. Chords originally came into being when composers wished to amplify the sound of a single line to create a fuller sonority or a more active texture. As this took place, the possibilities for harmonic action began to make themselves felt, and gradually our familiar harmonic language was evolved.

We reckon chords by labeling the *different* notes in a given combination; all duplications, such as octaves or unisons, are canceled. Thus, in the six-note chord A, A, C, E, A, C, we count only A, C, and E.

The most familiar chord of all is the *major triad*. It is called *triad* because it contains three notes; it is called *major* because the middle note is a major third above the lowermost note. The two outer notes form a perfect fifth. The diagram in Example 2·43 on the following page shows you how to obtain triads.

The major triad presents a compact, well-blended, sonorous, and sweet sound, the most perfect embodiment of harmonic balance, coherence, and fullness. Indeed, this combination was called the *armonia perfetta,* the perfect harmony, by musicians of the seventeenth and eighteenth centuries.

Other kinds of triads are like the major in that they are built from a third and a fifth. They include the minor, diminished, and augmented triads.

The *minor* triad has a small or *minor* third above its lowermost note. Try D, F, and A on the piano, using our diagram as a guide. The sound

EXAMPLE 2·43 Triads

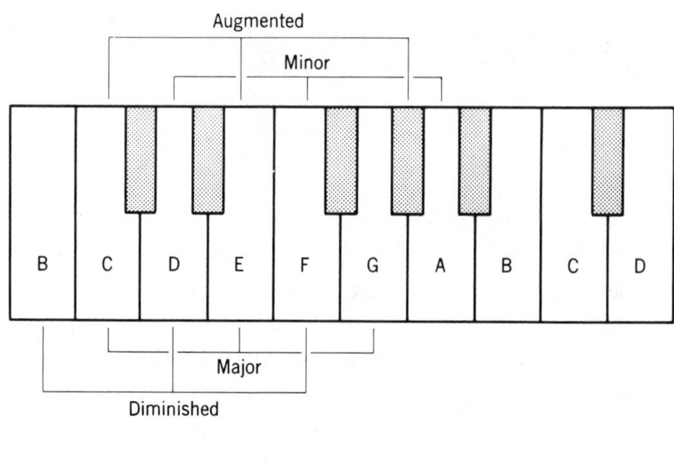

of the minor triad is not as bold and bright as that of the major triad; it is somewhat darker and rather clouded in effect. The second movement of Beethoven's Symphony No. 3 has a great concentration of minor-triad sounds; in this piece, as in many others, the minor triad lends itself to tragic qualities of expression.

Both the major and minor triads, since they are consonant sounds and contain the perfect fifth, can stand as harmonic points of arrival; they can represent the tonic note if they are approached by the tritone.

The triad B–D–F is called *diminished* because its fifth is smaller than the perfect fifth. The diminished triad has a hard, compact kind of dissonant quality. Since it contains the tritone, it is a most useful harmonic device to carry movement forward. We can hear it frequently, either by itself or in combination with one or two other tones, in the harmonic progressions of eighteenth- and nineteenth-century music.

A much less familiar kind of triad is the *augmented triad;* here the fifth is larger than the perfect fifth. Try C, E, and the middle black key next to G. The sound is rich, perhaps a bit oversweet, suggesting nostalgia or a poignant turn of feeling. The sound is also unstable, but not strongly dissonant. Late nineteenth-century music often uses the augmented triad for special effects of color.

Chords that contain more than three different tones are named according to their distinguishing interval. Thus, if we place the note B above the triad C–E–G, we obtain a four-note chord in which there is an interval of a *seventh*. Such a chord is called a *seventh chord*. In traditional harmony, additions are generally made by piling thirds on top of each other. We can go on to ninth chords, eleventh chords, and thirteenth chords. By the time we arrive at the fifteenth, we find ourselves duplicating the root, or first note of the chord, and so we have reached a limit. For practical purposes, the sevenths are useful; the others appear but occasionally. All these chords are dissonant in sound and will therefore serve specifically for musical movement.

The chords heard in *Drink to Me* are mostly major triads; the chords in the Prelude to *Tristan* include many seventh chords and ninth chords, most of them with a tritone among their component tones. We can easily link this particular aspect of each piece to what we already know about its expressive qualities. *Drink to Me* is gentle, sweet, and stable in its effect; the Prelude to *Tristan* is very restless and unsettling.

Triads are identified according to the position which their lowermost tones, called *roots,* take in relation to a given tonal center. The following example illustrates the position of the triads that have relation to the tonal center in the key of C major. (Their usual names are also given; often the scale degrees themselves are referred to by these names.)

EXAMPLE 2·44 Triad relationships

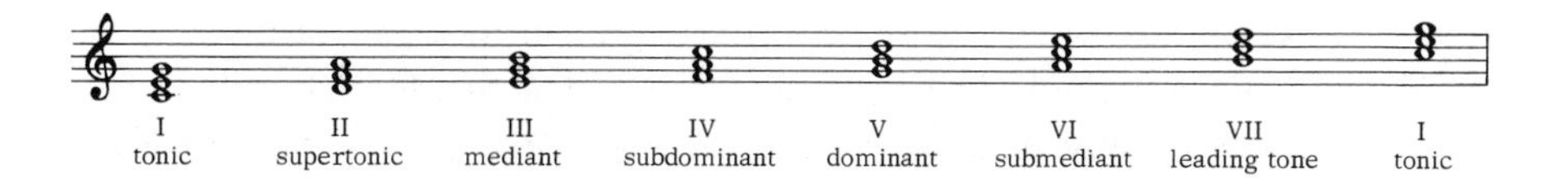

The sound combinations heard in modern music do not often fit into the picture we have given above. There seems to be little agreement about chord types; each combination has a special, perhaps unique sound. Most of the chords in modern music are unstable, yet many of them give no clear indication of where they will lead. Sometimes the vertical combinations appear to be the accidental meeting of tones within several energetic contrapuntal lines; at other times, a very special evocative effect is projected by a freshly devised mélange of tones and textures. In listening for chordal values, we should not judge these works by what we expect from earlier music. On the other hand, the modern age should not underrate the power and the logic of key-centered harmony.

Cadences

We can discover many different progressions among the chords in a musical composition of some scope. Most of these, if the composition was written in the eighteenth or nineteenth century, play some sort of part in defining a key. As a rule, we expect to receive a strong statement of key, a clear and definitive impression at the beginnings and ends of phrases and periods, especially at the ends of periods, where the harmonic sense of arrival reinforces other aspects of arrival. The chord progressions which are used to create these harmonic effects of arrival are called *cadences;* they correspond in language to effects of punctuation. (See page 40 for a discussion of phrase and period; also page 68 for the relation of rhythm and harmony.)

There are four standard cadences in harmony: authentic, half, deceptive, and plagal cadences.

Authentic cadence. This is the progression heard in Example 2·39. It has the effect of a period in a sentence, giving a positive impression of completion. It ends many periods in music and is the preferred harmonic ending for an entire movement or composition. The first, second, and fourth phrases of *Drink to Me* end with authentic cadences. In a grandiose manner the last twelve measures of the first movement of Beethoven's Symphony No. 3 make an authentic cadence. The authentic cadence involves a progression from a dominant to a tonic chord.

Half cadence. This is a partial ending, a point of rest within a musical period, like the effect of a comma or semicolon in language. It leaves a harmonic statement to be completed; this pause is generally represented by the chord built up from the fifth degree of the key, the *dominant* chord. The third phrase of *Drink to Me* ends with a half cadence. Most of the harmonic caesuras in the Prelude to *Tristan* are types of half cadence in that they offer us an incomplete harmonic statement.

Deceptive cadence. Sometimes the composer does not want to bring a period to an end even though the harmony may call for an authentic cadence. Then, in place of the tonic which the listener expects, he introduces a chord which is not anticipated. He deceives the listener; therefore, such a progression is called a *deceptive cadence.* Such a progression has two principal effects: (1) the surprise and freshness of an unexpected sound; (2) the maintenance and increase of musical momentum by the avoidance of arrival. When a composer has used a deceptive cadence, it often gives greater point to an authentic cadence that will appear somewhat later. The composer has been using harmonic suspense. Listen for the cadences at the beginning of Mozart's *Prague* Symphony. Again and again Mozart seems to promise an authentic cadence, a fully satisfying point of harmonic arrival, only to thwart us at the last moment. Not until the slow introduction of this piece joins to the quick part of the movement do we hear what we have been waiting for during four minutes of music: the authentic cadence.

Plagal cadence. In literature, we shall sometimes find, after the main problem of a poem, essay, play, or novel has been settled, an epilogue that brings movement finally to a state of quiet. This is an afterthought which helps to provide a transition from our artistic experience to the realities of life itself. In music we also find such afterthoughts. (The Amen at the end of a hymn is an example.) Here we are likely to find the *plagal cadence,* a rather quiet progression. The settling, calming effect of the plagal cadence was used by Wagner to bring some of his great music dramas to a close. *Götterdämmerung* (The Twilight of the Gods), the last of the four operas of the *Ring* cycle, ends with a plagal cadence, suggesting the end of the struggle for the treasure when it is returned to the Rhine maidens, the original and rightful owners. We sense, in this last cadence, a final resignation and reconciliation to destiny. At the end of *Tristan,* as the lovers find fulfillment in death, very much the same harmonic effect occurs. Generally, the plagal cadence progresses from the subdominant chord to the tonic chord.

Briefly, we shall list the progressions which make up these four main cadences:

1. Authentic cadence: V to I, with both chords in root (lower note of perfect fifth in bass) position
2. Half cadence: a pause upon a dominant chord
3. Deceptive cadence: V to VI, or possibly some other chord
4. Plagal cadence: IV to I, the latter generally in root position

EXAMPLE 2·45 Cadences within a phrase

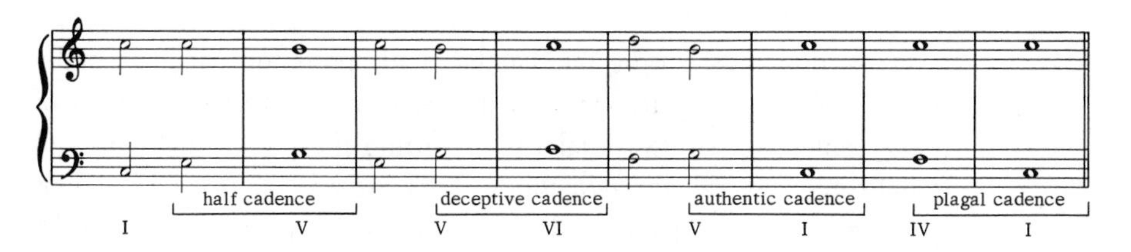

We can illustrate cadential action by showing its relationship to phrase structure. In Example 2·46, the first phrase ends with a half cadence; it leaves a question to be answered. The second phrase ends with an authentic cadence; it answers the question. The phrases and the cadences complement each other in a completely satisfying balance. Many dance and song periods are built this way harmonically; *Old Folks at Home, Turkey in the Straw,* and *Yankee Doodle* are examples.

Within phrases, we find progressions that are similar to these cadences.

EXAMPLE 2·46 Mozart: Sonata in A major, K. 331, first movement

Such cadencelike progressions keep the sense of the tonal center well in mind, but, at the same time, keep the music moving. Music of the eighteenth century is saturated with such progressions; this is one of the main reasons that the music of Mozart is so easy to follow and to grasp. The brackets in Example 2·46 all mark off cadencelike progressions. You can find no cadencelike progressions, *cadential formulas,* in much modern music, for example, in Schönberg's *Pierrot lunaire.*

Distribution of Tonal Centers, Modulation

A piece of music using familiar harmonic procedures will generally begin and end with the same tonal center or *key.* However, shifts of tonal center almost always take place during the piece. Such shifts of tonal center are called *modulations.* They are accomplished in various ways, sometimes by making a new tone so prominent that it takes on the aspect of a tonal center, but generally by making cadences in the new key. When a piece begins in one key, shifts in turn to several other keys, and ends in the original key, it is like setting out from home, visiting various other places, and returning home again. Sit-at-home music can be very boring! A harmonic plan involving modulations gives some large-scale contour to the form of any piece of music. We could not bear to listen to the extremely long first movement of Beethoven's Symphony No. 3 unless it had the freshness and new interest that comes with well-planned shifts of tonal center.

Example 2·47, illustrating three shifts of tonal center, presents in miniature a plan that could sustain a composition several hundred measures in length. (Play the example also without the altered tones; note the lesser interest, milder effect.)

EXAMPLE 2·47 Shifts in tonal center

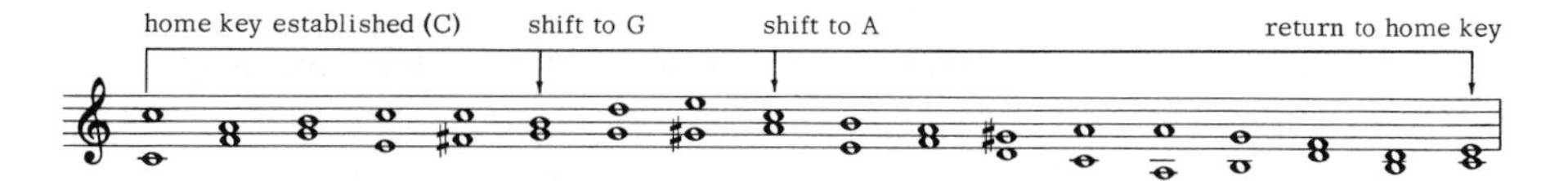

In the example, you will note that the fifth, eighth, and twelfth intervals introduce an altered tone; in each case, the tone is the leading tone of the new key. When such an alteration is made, it points to the new key by arranging the tones in the scale of the new key. To hear such a change in a large-scale composition, listen to the final movement of Beethoven's Symphony No. 5. Shortly after the authentic cadence that ends the first period of the movement (about thirty to thirty-five seconds after the beginning), you should hear a tone that does not belong to the key of C major; that tone is F♯, the leading tone of G. The harmony arranges itself to point to the key of G and shortly thereafter makes a strong cadence in G. This change, from C to G, organizes the first two large sections of this movement. The process is gradual and deliberate, but nonetheless powerful and total, for it represents an important change of tonal center within the piece. In other cases, modulation takes place abruptly, often with brilliant contrast of color. The purpose of such changes is to create a striking and bold effect, as in the first part of the second movement of Beethoven's Symphony No. 5. In this example, the contrasts in key and color are associated with a contrast between a smooth, singing melody and a martial fanfare.

EXAMPLE 2·48 Beethoven: Symphony No. 5, second movement

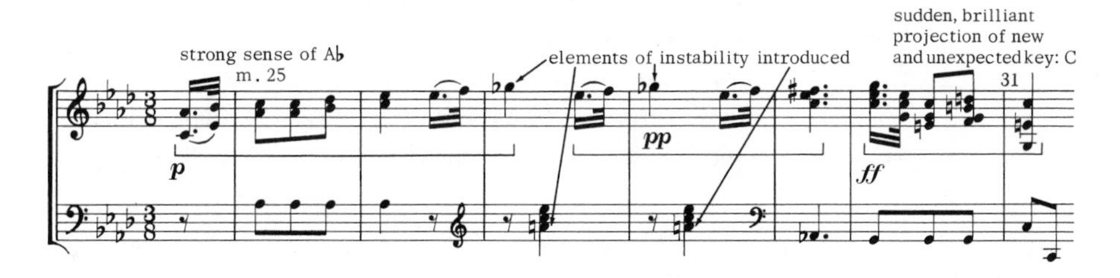

The following questions may be used in evaluating the harmonic aspects of a composition:

1. How is the tonal center defined: by prominent tone, perfect fifth, cadential progressions, or combinations of these processes?

2. What degree of stability or instability appears?
3. Is the piece in a major or minor key? Are traditional chord types used? Is the key defined clearly? Does there seem to be much chromaticism?
4. What kind of cadences are heard: authentic, half, deceptive, plagal? How frequent are the cadences?
5. Does modulation take place? If so, are the modulations gradual or abrupt?
6. How do these harmonic values relate to the expressive qualities in the piece?

Applying these questions to the first movement of Beethoven's Symphony No. 3, we can observe the following:

1. Tonal center defined by strong cadential action, supported by prominence of the tonic, especially at points of arrival.
2. Sharp conflict between stability and instability; some sections strongly stable, others entirely unstable.
3. Major key, some sections in minor. Traditional chord types used, triads, sevenths. Very clear sense of key. Some chromaticism, but not highly colored.
4. Authentic, half, deceptive cadences. Strong cadences widely spaced, acting as goals for long sections of directed instability. Arrival generally accomplished by emphatic cadences.
5. Many shifts of tonal center, some gradual, some abrupt.
6. These harmonic values, combined with a richly varied motivic content, constant play between rhythmic balance and imbalance, and bold contrasts of texture, present the impression of a work in which a strong, purposeful conflict is taking place.

Other works suggested for harmonic evaluation:

Haydn: Symphony No. 94 in G major (*Surprise*), second movement
Stravinsky: *Les Noces* (The Wedding), beginning
Chopin: Prelude in E minor
Morley: *Sing We and Chant It*
Rimsky-Korsakov: Overture *La Grande Pâque russe* (Russian Easter)
Wagner: Magic Fire Music from *Die Walküre* (The Valkyrie)

Perceiving Musical Form

By this time we have some idea of what takes place in a musical composition with respect to those elements which embody musical sound, movement, and arrival—sonority, rhythm, melody, texture, and harmony. As we observed these in operation within a phrase or period, noting how the shape of the passage was brought to being by their interaction, we were making an entry into the realm of musical form.

Musical form can mean different things. It can be understood as a sort of blueprint, telling where things are to be placed. This theme appears here, that theme follows it; the keys, sections, and movements are placed in a certain order, according to conventional usage. This aspect of form is general; it is a kind of framework available to anyone who wishes to put together a piece of music. It is part of the basic vocabulary of music.

Another aspect of form is individual in that it applies to a single work. The composer has innumerable choices within a general framework, or he may choose to organize his piece according to a plan which he himself has invented, one that accommodates best his ideas, his feeling for design. He alone has the power to decide how much variation and contrast to use, where to make repetitions, if any, where to digress, where to remain, and how to begin and end. For example, in the first movement of his *Prague* Symphony, Mozart composed the slow introduction according to an individual plan, while the allegro that follows represents Mozart's own treatment of a widely used "blueprint."

No one grasps the full meaning of the form of a piece upon first hearing. Musical form unfolds on various levels. At first the attention may focus on interesting details and striking effects. As the piece moves on, a series of impressions will be stored up. Among these, some will strike the listener as being more salient or important than others. He will take these to be landmarks along the way. Listening again and more closely, he will recognize that more and more of these impressions are interrelated; and further, he will see that the composer has employed some plan, pattern, or formula in order to organize the effects of movement and arrival on a large scale. When these patterns become clear, much of the detail work will acquire a greater significance. It will no longer consist of one interesting effect following another; rather, the function of each gesture in the overall scheme will make itself felt. Thus, by understanding the plan of a piece and the working out of its larger sections, the listener can be more comfortable and sure in the evaluation and appreciation of specific effects and qualities.

Listening for musical form in this way is very much like watching a play. At first we are impressed by the setting, the appearance of the players, or striking moments and lines; these are immediate impacts upon our senses. Then we follow incident upon incident, watching the unfolding of the plot, in order to grasp the step-by-step continuity. In a well-constructed play we are led to important points of climax in an effective manner; perhaps these will balance or match each other. Finally, our experience is brought to some recognizable point of completion as the play ends. Later we relive certain moments and reflect upon the various issues presented in the play; we evaluate the author's, director's, and actors' skill or lack of skill in moving our emotions or delighting us with their offering.

Specifically, the listener should ask these questions as he gives his attention to the form of a piece:

1. What is taking place now?
2. What will happen next?
3. How does the present material relate to what has gone before?

The composer must also take these matters into account as he creates the successive phrases of his music; he must consider what has happened in one phrase in order to proceed effectively to the next. He must assess each gesture or section in relation to what precedes and follows it. The flow of music is carried on by such action, which can be expressed in the formula:

STATEMENT answered by COUNTERSTATEMENT

Statements and counterstatements are linked in a continuous chain. Each link is separate; yet the entire length and shape of the chain gives the observer a single impression of the outline or form of the whole. In order to find our way through the form of a piece, we shall make use of the statement-counterstatement formula. It will enable us to relate motives, phrases, cadences, and other effects to each other.

Here are some ways in which statement and counterstatement relationships are manifested in musical structure:

STATEMENT	POSSIBLE COUNTERSTATEMENTS
Motive	1. Repetition, or 2. Variation, or 3. Contrast
Melody	1. Repetition of melody, or 2. Contrasting melody
Half cadence	Authentic cadence
Tonal center or key	1. Contrasting key, or 2. Return to home key as counterstatement to contrasting key
Phrase	1. Answering phrase of comparable length, giving rise to symmetrical construction, or 2. Answering phrase or phrases of markedly different length, giving rise to nonsymmetrical construction

By way of illustration, consider the relationship between (1) the two arresting chords that begin the first movement of Beethoven's Symphony No. 3 and (2) the singing melody that follows. The two chords represent a bold statement; the melody comes then as a somewhat surprising but extremely effective counterstatement based on contrast. This relationship exists in the *smallest possible structural unit.* In the *largest possible way,* a final counterstatement to this first melody appears as it returns for the last time near the end of the movement and is heard again and again, reiterating the principal melodic idea of the whole piece. As listeners, we make a connection, establish a link between the *first* statement and the *last* counterstatement. This *repetition* is one more item of rational organization that helps us acquire a perspective of the form of this movement.

EXAMPLE 2·49 Sketch of first movement, Beethoven's Symphony No. 3. Statement and counterstatement

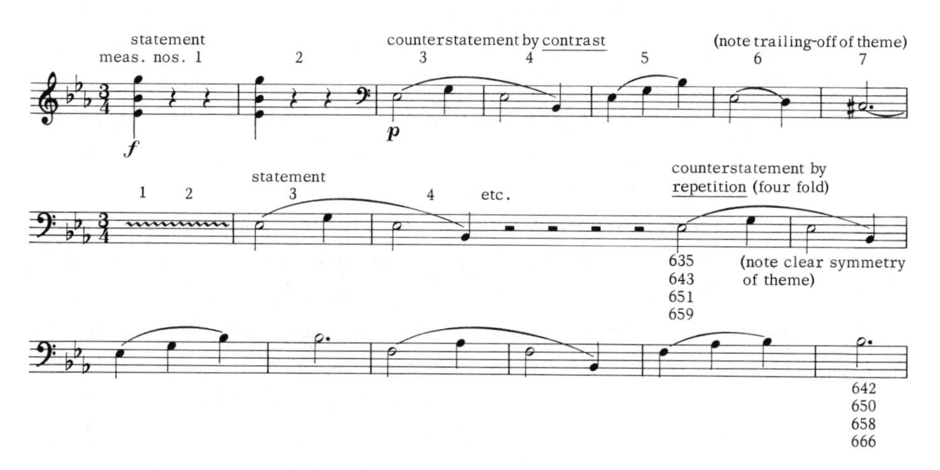

Of all the types of counterstatement, repetition provides the strongest and most convincing kind of binding action in musical form, as it does in the process of learning and in other kinds of experience. Repetition in a musical form helps us to *know* the music better. As a matter of fact, this applies not only to restatements of material within a given piece, but even more tellingly, to rehearings of the entire piece itself.

Musical forms run to type. Recognizing a type of musical form will be of great assistance in developing better acquaintance with the piece itself. Basically, there are two ways in which a piece of music extends itself in time: (1) by adding well-defined phrases and periods to the original statement; (2) by spinning out movement continuously without clearly marked articulations. The first of these we designate as *sectional,* the second as *continuous.*

You will recall that we touched upon this matter when we discussed larger rhythmic units, time, and polyphonic texture. In sectional structure, the phrases and periods are quite clearly marked; the points of arrival are well defined; the phases of movement tend to be of approximately the same length. Generally, there is a sense of balance, of trim, clear-cut outlines. Since the principal musical interest lies *within* these fixed limits, we expect that very pleasing, strongly melodic material will be used, material that is valuable for itself, not for what will happen to it. Thus, we find dances (*Blue Danube Waltz*), marches (*The Stars and Stripes Forever*), songs (*Old Folks at Home*), theme and variations (Mozart: Sonata in A major, K. 331)—all neatly organized in distinct sections, with each section offering something special. Music of this sort gains length by having sections added, as in the *Blue Danube Waltz*.

Certain typical sectional forms are found. Of these the simplest is the *two-part structure*. Essentially, two-part structure rests on perfect symmetry and balance. It may consist of nothing more than a phrase answered by another phrase, a half cadence answered by an authentic cadence, as in Example 2·45. Two periods may be joined in such a form, as in *Drink to Me* or in the first half of the march *The Stars and Stripes Forever*. Later we shall see how the most monumental form in all music history, the sonata form, makes use of the statement and counterstatement plan of two-part structure.

Frequently, the first part of a piece will be brought back at the end in order to round off the form more completely. This return is usually signaled by a restatement of the original melody. In such cases, a *three-part structure* has been created with the plan ABA. Here the binding effect of melodic repetition is desired. Many dances and marches go through this cycle. The Menuetto of Mozart's *Eine kleine Nachtmusik* has such a layout. Three-part form also can be realized on a broad scale, as in the Scherzo of Beethoven's Symphony No. 9.

Music that is organized in continuous structure shows much less uniformity than we find in sectional music. It has fewer strong points of arrival, and they are not evenly spaced. Such a piece may be organized according to the rise and fall of dynamic intensity or strength; it may involve a subtle and complex interweaving of motives in relationships of statement and counterstatement which change every few measures; it may be concerned simply with maintaining a steady and unbroken flow of sound for a given period of time. We shall find such forms in the preludes and fantasias of seventeenth- and eighteenth-century music and in music written contrapuntally, such as the fugues of the Baroque period and the motets of the Renaissance. At first such forms may be puzzling to the listener, but the musical content that gives them their continuous flow is very challenging. The first fugue, in C major, from the *Well-Tempered Clavier* of Bach illustrates this kind of structure; likewise, we find such continuous flow in the Prelude to *Tristan.*

Sectional and continuous structures also intermingle. Thus, in the first movement of Beethoven's Symphony No. 3, some sections have a clearly marked balance and a tunelike manner. Others spin out into long periods of increasing momentum. In the first movement of Bach's *Brandenburg* Concerto No. 2, phrases are grouped in pairs to provide an effect of balance; yet the total action is such that a continuous drive is maintained over the relatively light points of arrival. The interplay between sectional and continuous action that may occur in extended pieces may be heard as another embodiment of movement and arrival; the following diagram illustrates this relationship:

Departure	Movement	Arrival	Movement	Arrival
sectional	continuous	sectional	continuous	sectional

The finale of Mozart's *Prague* Symphony alternates these procedures quite clearly.

The following chart summarizes the relations of the elements of music to sound, movement, and arrival. In some instances, we can only indi-

ELEMENT	SOUND	MOVEMENT	ARRIVAL
Texture	Range Scoring Dynamics Tone color	Changes in tone color Composite action of lines	Changes in tone color
Rhythm		Upbeat Tempo Beat Motives Syncopation	Caesuras at the end of motives, phrases, periods Downbeat Regularity
Melody		Contour Motive play Variation Contrast	Apex Final tone Restatement or repetition Tune
Harmony	Chord color	Instability Dissonance—tension Tritone Modulation—movement away from tonal center	Stability Consonance—resolution Tonic Arrival at tonal center Cadences

cate which is the principal effect; obviously, in context, a composer can cause any effect to act for movement or arrival, but he will then have to be aware of the usual value or effect which is assigned by the listener to a specific element and somehow cause its unusual application to seem convincing.

Musical Performance

At this point we should be able to recognize and understand many of the procedures and relationships that are encompassed in a musical composition. We are able to appreciate the composer's decisions more clearly than before by using the criteria that have been explained. These criteria can be useful, as well, in the evaluation of a musical performance.

As a matter of fact, when we hear a musical composition, we hear only what the performer thinks the composer has heard. The composer's conception can never be fully known. The performer incorporates his ideas, style, and experience into the act of bringing a musical composition to life. The notation which the composer set down is by no means precise; it is only some form of instruction for organizing a flow of sound, an instruction that the composer felt to be adequate, within the tradition of his own times. For example, in the seventeenth and early eighteenth centuries, the performer was expected to add many ornamental notes to a melody, when feasible, and to fill in the chords if he was a keyboard player. Nowadays, on the other hand, some composers are so exacting in their instructions that whatever variation in performance does occur takes place only because of human error. This has been eliminated in some instances by turning the performance duties over to such machines as computers and tape recorders.

Assuming we are dealing with the more familiar aspect of performance, that in which the composer has been quite explicit (as Beethoven was in his music), we discover that performers read the music in very different ways. We have only to take the matter of tempo. One recording of a movement may require several minutes more than another. Consider what this does to the qualities of movement in the piece. In poetry, a quick reading of a stanza might convey an impression of nervous haste; a slower reading might drag and make the listener impatient. The performer must try to sense the suitable tempo, so that the music is "pronounced" clearly and at the same time maintains its motion. The listener can quickly train himself to evaluate this aspect of musical performance.

In performance, sound and movement have a reciprocal action, as a rule. That is, rich, full, striking musical sound tends to require slower movement, so that the listener's attention will be fixed upon sonority more than upon action. Conversely, active music tends to ask for lighter sonorities. When a conductor takes up a piece that has an inherent briskness of action and tries to clothe it with very "luscious" sounds, he is at best recomposing the piece and at worst distorting it, perhaps to the point of its being unrecognizable. There are no rules here, only common sense and taste.

Tempo and sonority are two of the principal areas in which the performer comes into his own. Further, he, as well as the listener, must decide which elements in the piece seem to be salient, which have the greatest meaning. These he must then delineate without obscuring the supporting action if he is to re-create the composition with clarity. He should regard each piece as having a narrative value—not as telling a specific story, but as providing him the opportunity to take the role of the narrator; the story itself will be the movement from one action to another; it will consist of statements and counterstatements, of tensions and resolutions, of variations, contrasts, repetitions, and developments—in short, of all the procedures which combine to give a sense of consequence and design in music. If he is successful in shaping this action by his performance, the sensitive listener will have no difficulty in perceiving it.

chapter three

Medieval Music

Until quite recently, most of the music available for listening, either in concert or on recordings, was written after the year 1700. Lately, thanks to music historians, we have become acquainted with music composed during the Middle Ages and the Renaissance and have discovered much of it to be interesting and appealing. Today, a great deal of early music is being published; many concerts of this music are being given, and many fine recordings are available. A new craft, the construction of older types of instruments such as recorders, lutes, viols, and harpsichords, has been developed to respond to the ever-growing demand by amateurs for the proper means of performing medieval and Renaissance music. In some ways, this music is more accessible to listener and performer than the music of later eras. Many delightful pieces from earlier times are shorter, simpler, and easier to perform than comparable pieces of the classic or romantic periods.

Unlike most of the concert music which is familiar to us, medieval and Renaissance music was not written expressly for a large audience of listeners who were expected to give all their attention to the music. Rather, music of these two eras made its appearance in connection with events of a religious or social nature. Many of the services and devotions of the church called for music; the entertainments of the court centered around singing and dancing, both of which made special demands upon music. Moreover, most of the music that has been discovered in musical manuscripts of the Middle Ages and Renaissance was intended for the highest social classes, the nobility and the clergy. We have few relics of popular or lower-class music, although it is quite clear that common folk and peasants had a vigorous musical culture. Thus, in any evaluation of music from these earlier times, we must recognize the limited size of the audience, the special background of the participants and observers, and the division of interest between music and some other form of activity. Try to imagine a scene at court or a service in a great cathedral as you hear this music.

In our sampling of medieval music, we have chosen works for two reasons: (1) to illustrate the wide range of style and expression embodied in the musical literature of this era, and (2) to trace, step by step, the growth of the musical art. We begin at the point at which the musical materials were simple, and we follow the process of elaboration in melody, rhythm, harmony, and texture until we have reached the stage at which the musical language approaches the familiar idiom of our present concert literature.

The wellspring of Western music is *plainsong.*

PLAINSONG

Listen to the first three numbers in the recorded collection, *Masterpieces of Music before 1750,* the antiphon *Laus Deo Patri* (Praise God the Father), the Alleluia *Vidimus stellam* (We Have Seen the Star), and the sequence *Victimae Paschali* (The Paschal Victim).

These three pieces are taken from a vast body of music called *plainsong,* or *Gregorian chant.* From the sixth century until the end of the sixteenth, plainsong was the most important kind of music in the Christian world. (Gregorian chant as well as other single-voiced music of the medieval period represents *monophonic* texture, music for one part. The term *monody* is also applied to single-voice performance.)

Pay attention first to the quality of sound in this music. Voices are singing in unison, simply and in a straightforward manner; the music is deeply felt, intimate, and strongly evocative. Music set to a sacred text was intended to emphasize and intensify the emotional qualities and meanings of the sacred words. The steady, continuous intonation of the text on definite pitches certainly reaches the emotions of the hearer more surely and strongly than if the text were recited. The full effect of voices singing this music is felt only in a cathedral, where the echoes and reverberations intensify and amplify the sound, creating an all-pervasive effect.

In general these songs resemble each other. The quality of sound is the same. Movement is moderately slow, rather gentle, even, and flowing. Melodic shapes are rounded, using small, generally conjunct intervals. Points of arrival give the singers breathing spaces; they are not emphatic breaks in the flow of the music. Such qualities suggest calmness, security, and reflectiveness rather than extremes of emotion. Church song is music of the cloister, of retreat. Its features are not as bold and striking as those of latter-day music. Its distinctions are subtle, even elusive.

Yet plainsong has a wide range of expressive values, and we can discover this in the songs we have heard. Listen for differences between *Vidimus* and *Victimae. Vidimus* moves much more smoothly, lightly, and freely than *Victimae. Vidimus* is a song of jubilation. The star of Bethlehem has been seen in the East; it is a time for joy. Alleluias are sung; the music breaks away from the text, giving many notes to a single syllable. Such melodic flights were called *melismas;* and the term *melismatic* now refers to music that has elaborate melodic ornamentation beyond its text.

In *Victimae* we are told a story about the sacrifice of Christ, His death, and His resurrection. The words occupy the worshiper's attention. Since the words are declaimed one tone to each syllable, that is, in a *syllabic style,* the music has a much heavier quality of movement than the Alleluia. The narrative is told in poetry; the poetic meter brings about an even and regular pace in the music. In contrast, our Alleluia seems irregular and improvisatory in its quality of movement. *Victimae* gives a very comfortable feeling of balance in phrase structure, because its caesuras are regularly spaced and quite strong. Statement and counterstatement complement each other clearly and firmly. This strong impression of balance is missing in *Vidimus,* because we cannot detect the caesuras as clearly nor sense a balance of phrases.

Differences in style and structure in these two songs grew from their expressive values and aims; in one case, the emotion of joy gives impetus to a flight of melody; in the other, the solemn, tragic emotion calls for a deliberate manner and form.

Example 3·1 illustrates graphically the relationship between music and text in syllabic and melismatic styles.

EXAMPLE 3·1 Syllabic and melismatic settings

Syllabic

music ____ ____ ____ ____ ____ one note for each

text ____ ____ ____ ____ ____ syllable

Melismatic many notes
music — — — — — — — — — — — — on one
text —. . . . .— syllable

Now, for a closer look at the structure of plainsong, we shall examine the *Laus Deo Patri* (Praise God the Father). In this plainsong, neither the syllabic nor the melismatic style dominates. This combination of the two, where syllabic style is broken up by short melismas, is called the *neumatic style.*

Qualities of *Laus Deo Patri:*

1. *Sound and texture*
   a. Middle to low range; rather limited range.
   b. Dynamic range narrow, centering around mezzo piano.
   c. Contrast between single voice and group.
2. *Movement: rhythmic aspects*
   a. Gentle but steady pulse of moderate pace.
   b. Size of pulse or beat groups changes between two and three; less clear organization in the recitation section.
   c. Two kinds of note value: longer equals two of shorter.
   d. Phrases comparable but not equal in length.
   e. No salient rhythmic motives; rhythmic patterns reflect declamation of the text.
   f. Legato performance.
   g. At important caesuras, long notes used to give the effect of arrival; otherwise, short notes predominate.
3. *Melody*
   a. Conjunct lines, some few small leaps.
   b. Range of less than an octave.
   c. Gentle rise and fall, with melodic phrases tending to turn around one or two points; repetitions of a pitch in the recitation section.
   d. Little or no differentiation among the various figures; consistency of melodic behavior except for the contrast of the recitation section.
   e. The phrase beginning *et tibi* (And to Thee) distinguished by its start on a higher pitch.
4. *Harmony*
   a. Clear sense of arrival at the tonal center at each caesura.
   b. Tonal center defined by prominence, especially at caesuras.
   c. Shift of tonal center in recitation section and between the caesuras of the first and second lines.
   d. Position of half steps constant, between 1 and 2, 5 and 6 of the scale; Phrygian mode (see page 95).

5. *Form*
   a. Large three-part form, set up as antiphon, psalm tone, antiphon. (The term *antiphon* refers to alternation of performers and is applied to music so performed; a *psalm tone* is a melodic formula used for the recitation of a psalm.)
   b. Considerable extension due to many repetitions of the psalm tone.
   c. Statements and counterstatements balanced in relative length; counterstatements tend to continue, vary, and extend melodic material of preceding statements.
   d. Several areas of gentle contrast, i.e., (1) *et tibi,* (2) recitation tone, giving large contour to the song.

After noting the specific characteristics of the antiphon as indicated above, listen to the piece once more as a complete, unified selection without making an effort to put every detail into place. You should find that you can follow the music much more easily, that you know where you are, and that many of the details *do* fit into place as the music flows onward. You will have returned to the first general impression of the work, but this impression will have become much firmer, broader, and richer as a result of the better acquaintance which our study has developed. Not only will the idea of this song become more vivid, but its similarities to and differences from other kinds of plainsong will loom larger and more important. It will not be difficult, then, to understand why musicians, musical theorists, priests, and worshipers in the Middle Ages were concerned with these distinctions, since plainsong was the only organized body of music in Western civilization at that time.

Plainsong was evolved from the cantillations, the chanting of verses, of Hebrew and Greek antiquity. In the early Christian era, a tremendous literature of church song developed. Each cathedral and religious center had its own repertoire, and the numerous variations in the music of the prescribed liturgy resulted in much confusion. Led by Pope Gregory I (590–604), a reform which aimed at codification took place. Various songs were grouped according to certain of their characteristics, such as range, style, typical melodic formulas, and final tone or tonal center. Thus the medieval *system of modes* was evolved. Each mode was distinguished by its range and final tone; with each were associated typical melodic formulas.

There were eight of these modes, and to the trained listener and student the distinctions between music in one mode and that in another were very important, although, to us, accustomed to much bolder contrast in music, the differences are at first hard to detect. So strong was this feeling about different values and effects residing in the various modes that theorists assigned different emotional and moral qualities to them. They considered some modes proper for the expression of joy, others for sadness, solemnity, gaiety, etc. Whether or not these connotations seem valid to us, the important idea is the evidence they give of the power of music to stir men's feelings.

THE MODAL SYSTEM

We can easily demonstrate some of the distinctions that exist among the medieval modes. The following examples show first the eight modes of medieval music and then the four modes added by sixteenth-century theorists. In these examples, note the following points:

1. The *range,* which in each case is a diatonic scale of eight tones.
2. The *final tone* or *tonic* and its place in the scale. In an *authentic mode,* the final is 1 and 8; in a *plagal mode,* the final is in the middle of the scale.
3. The characteristic *order of whole steps and half steps.*

EXAMPLE 3·2 Medieval and Renaissance modes

a. Medieval modes

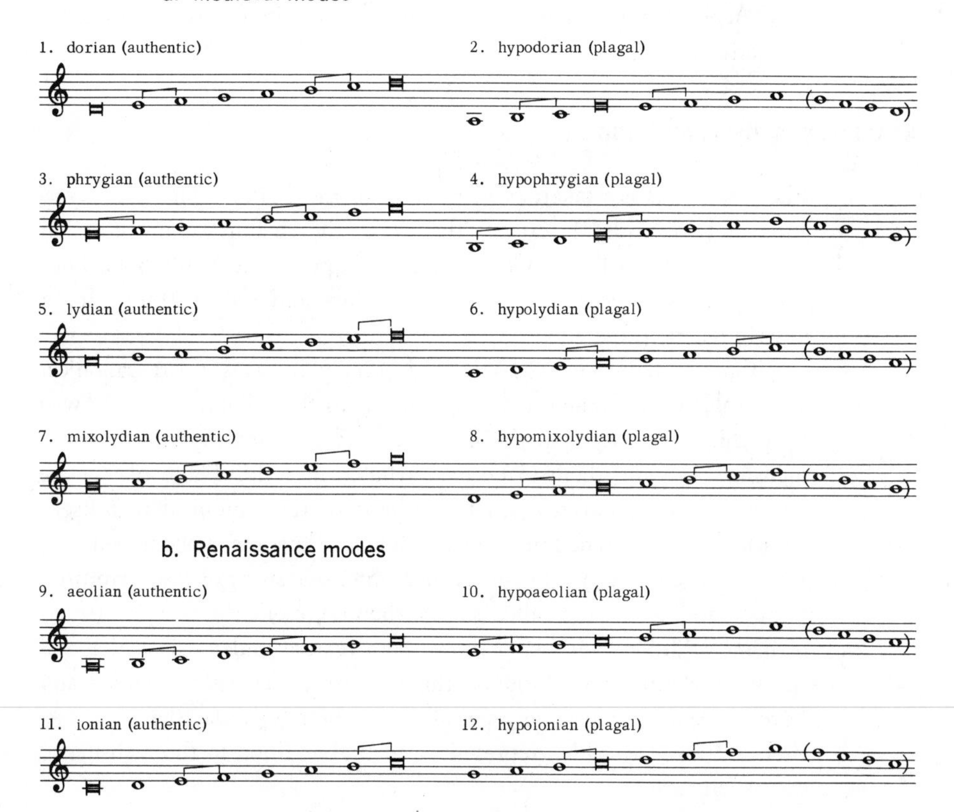

The modes also controlled the range of melodies. Thus, a melody in the Dorian mode would have an approximate range from D to D, while Hypodorian melodies would move between A and A.

In order to savor the effect of each mode, sing the scales given above. Pause for a moment upon reaching the final, and in the plagal modes, add the final four notes to reach a point of arrival. In the authentic modes, the sense of position and arrival is more definite than in the plagal modes. Each mode has a characteristic quality. For example, the Phrygian modes lend themselves to darker expressive values, the Lydian and Ionian modes to brighter effects. Thus, melodies based upon specific modes will reflect something of their characteristic qualities. Later, when we examine Renaissance music, we shall refer to the expressive values of the twelve modes as described by the theorist Gioseffe Zarlino.

The modal system was evolved in order to codify music that was monophonic in texture; it was a way of cataloging melodies. When several voices are singing together, the clearness of the modal effect is clouded. Yet the classification and procedures of the modal scales continued to have value for musical composition in later style periods, and even to the present day. Two modes in particular were to receive special emphasis and widespread use; these two modes, the ninth and eleventh (the Aeolian and Ionian), correspond to our minor and major scales, respectively.

BACKGROUNDS OF PLAINSONG

Plainsong texts are taken principally from the Psalms. The music was sung at two kinds of service: the *Mass,* the solemn commemoration service of the sacrifice of Christ, and the *Office.* (See Willi Apel, *Harvard Dictionary of Music,* articles on Mass and Office Hours, for a description of these services.)

Although plainsong was intended principally to support canonical (Biblical) texts, its melismatic sections, as in the Alleluia, moved away from this strict usage. In the ninth century new texts were set to the melismas, causing them to become syllabic in style. These texts were generally commentaries upon the subject of the canonical text itself. Charlemagne, crowned in 800 as Roman Emperor, encouraged this practice; it reflected his support of more intensive study of the Scriptures.

Such additions were called *tropes;* they represent the first in a series of many additions and elaborations, both textual and musical, that tell the story of musical evolution to the end of the Renaissance period and beyond. Among tropes, an especially important type was the *sequence,* such as *Victimae,* which represents a textual addition to the melisma of the Alleluia.

Troping led to independent compositions. An offshoot of the practice, one which brought Biblical events to the worshiper's attention in a vivid way, was the *liturgical drama.* This was a play whose dramatized text was sung throughout with plainsong and original music. Action thus was added to the troped text. The *Play of Daniel,* recently recorded and frequently performed in the past several years, represents this early genre of stage presentation. The music for another liturgical drama, *Infantem vidimus* (We Have Seen the Child) (ca. 1100), is to be heard in the collection *A Treasury of Early Music,* no. 5. Within a small framework the liturgical drama was a multidimensional medium of expression and must have been moving and impressive to viewers and listeners of its era.

During the fifteen hundred years and more of its existence, plainsong has been the most significant musical factor in the life of the Roman church. Today it is the authorized musical language of that church. Throughout its history, plainsong has been a rich source for musical materials, an inexhaustible fund from which composers have borrowed continuously. As an art form, it was highly polished, subtle, full of delicate shadings and nuances, and within its own realm, a complete and well-rounded mode of musical expression.

The Evolution of Polyphony

Although life is short and art is long, the life of an art form undergoes growth, flower, and decay very much as living beings do. Some time before the year 1000 a drastic change in the history of plainsong occurred. *Another voice or part was added* at times. Consider the implications of this practice, called *polyphony,* for the history of Western music. It caused changes in every aspect of musical art, and indeed it is responsible for music as we know it today.

1. It created a *new sonority value,* giving a new dimension to musical sound and increasing thereby the range of its evocative power.
2. Potentially, although not at first, it carried the promise of *countermovement* between the different voices, both melodically and rhythmically; therefore, it led to the development of a greater intensity of movement.
3. It contributed to the evolution of *harmony;* some order in the distribution of intervals was necessary; conversely, preferences for certain types of intervals between the polyphonic voices were codified into systems which we call *harmony.*
4. It enforced *rhythmic order.* Thus, it required the development of a system of *notation* which would enable the performers and composers to communicate with each other and would give the performers some

way of singing the right notes at the right time in order to stay together properly.

5. It set the text aside as the principal item of interest and the principal means for controlling the form. *Musical relationships* became more and more the central concern and interest.
6. It pointed the way continually to new and fresh ways of *extending* and *elaborating* music.

Polyphony began as an addition to an established melody. This should not be unfamiliar to us as a process nor hard to understand. When musicians perform, they have a natural, almost irrepressible tendency to add a few touches of their own to the established musical text. Only under the strictest control do they toe the line. Today many conductors and performers take liberties with the printed score. Addition and elaboration in music are part of the art itself.

From the tenth to the seventeenth century we shall follow the history of music largely through the additions that composers have made either to specific musical compositions or to established musical techniques. Music grew during this period through elaborations upon preexisting models.

THE CANTUS FIRMUS

Throughout the Middle Ages the Gregorian chant was the most important type of preexisting material. Much if not most of the music written and performed during the Middle Ages and the Renaissance was used in connection with sacred ceremonies. The text and its proper music, the plainsong, were of prime importance during the proceedings; therefore, whatever elaborations took place had to be built upon an appropriate plainsong. Such a plainsong was called a *cantus firmus,* meaning a "fixed melody." Thousands of complete, independent compositions used part or all of a plainsong as the basic framework. During the Renaissance composers frequently turned to secular music, to songs and dances, for their cantus firmi, even when music for the church was involved. Addition first grew as an extension of liturgical procedures; later, elaborations upon a cantus firmus broke away and became independent of liturgical associations. Eventually much music for social occasions was written upon a preexisting melody.

Once the trend of polyphony was set in motion, it developed and grew in many directions over a period of five hundred years and more. The main path from plainsong to Renaissance music progresses in phases that are fairly well defined; each of these is an elaboration or refinement upon a preceding phase. Like all growth, the development of Western music is an exciting thing to observe. Some of the important stages in this evolution are diagramed below, with particular reference to the qualities of movement created by each style.

PARALLEL ORGANUM

Organum is the term applied to polyphony from the ninth to the thirteenth centuries. It probably refers to the fact that the voices were *organized* or fitted together. The plainsong voice was the *principal* voice; the added voices were *organal* voices. In this first phase of polyphony in Western music, the added voices were dependent both rhythmically and harmonically upon the principal voice. They mirrored the melodic contour of the principal voice, remaining at the same distance from it. The new feature in this music is its sound, the *richness of sonority* that comes about when the added voices move in the resonant intervals of the fourth, fifth, and octave. Because of this fuller sonority, parallel organum has a heavier quality of movement than plainsong, which it otherwise resembles in its melodic shapes and patterns. The parallelism also creates the impression of a rather rigid type of action, as if a squad of three or four men were marching perfectly in step. This kind of music flourished during the ninth and tenth centuries. Listen to *Masterpieces*, no. 6, for a famous example of parallel organum, *Rex caeli, Domine* (King of Heaven, ca. 800).

EXAMPLE 3·3 Diagram of parallel organum

FREE ORGANUM

We could hardly expect the added voices to submit for very long to the melodic and harmonic conditions established by a particular plainsong. The first signs of growing independence appear when the added voice or voices create their own melodic patterns against the plainsong. This procedure is called *free organum*, in which interest is provided by two different melodic lines moving against each other. The effect of movement is somewhat smoother and lighter than in parallel organum. A play of different sonorities is created as the music progresses. The different melodic patterns create fourths, fifths, octaves, and unisons in a well-mixed variety. In addition, we hear a few thirds, which provide a "sweeter" harmonic touch. Harmonically, points of arrival are indicated by the standard medieval intervals: fourths, fifths, unisons, or octaves.

Here and there we notice that the added voice sings several notes to a single note of the plainsong, suggesting the first move toward rhythmic independence. A feeling of melodic ornamentation is coming to life, something like the melismatic style we heard in the Alleluia. Still, free organum is *rhythmically* dependent upon the plainsong, even though it has asserted its melodic autonomy. You may hear an example of free organum in *Masterpieces,* no. 7, the trope *Agnus Dei* (Lamb of God, ca. 1100).

EXAMPLE 3·4 Diagram of free organum

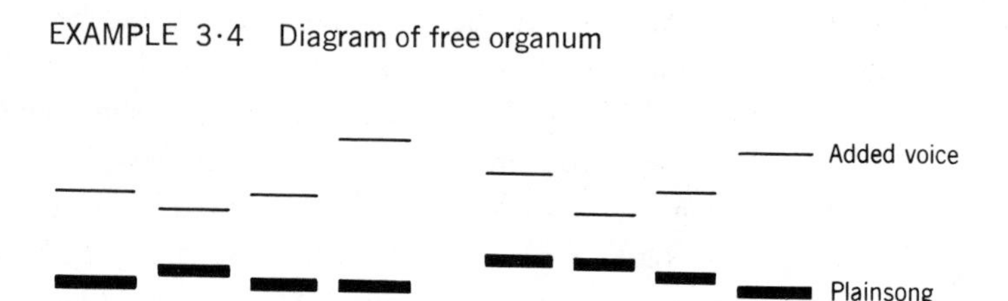

MELISMATIC ORGANUM

We are still moving in the direction of freedom. In *melismatic organum,* the rhythmic and melodic independence of the organal voice comes into full flower. It sings many notes to each one of the cantus firmus. To accommodate these melismas, the cantus firmus must move much more slowly than it did in parallel or free organum. The organal voice sings long notes, and since it holds its notes for a considerable time, it came to be designated as the *tenor,* meaning "that which holds." The combined movement of the two voices suggests a flight which is not quite free, which is controlled by the deliberate changes of tone in the cantus firmus. When the cantus firmus moves, the impression of arrival becomes strong by contrast with the phase of movement in the melismatic sections. There is a great deal of florid ornamentation in the organal voice. Still, its shapes and patterns continue along the lines established in plainsong; there is gentle rise and fall with smooth, even, and small intervals characterizing the movement of the melody.

Harmonically, the sound of open intervals, fourths, fifths, and octaves, dominates. Yet it was inevitable that the melodic voice would touch upon tones that were dissonant with the cantus firmus during phases of movement. Now and then we can clearly hear some clashing dissonances. Melismatic organum flourished in the twelfth century. *Masterpieces,* no. 8, provides an example: a *Benedicamus Domino* (Let Us Bless the Lord, ca. 1100–1150).

EXAMPLE 3·5 Diagram of melismatic organum

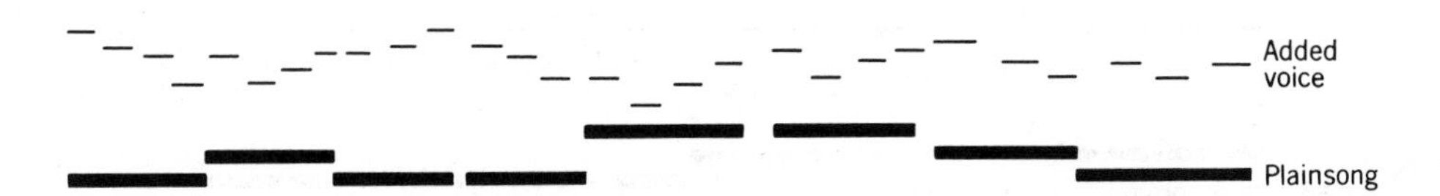

MEASURED ORGANUM: ARS ANTIQUA

In measured organum we have turned a corner. The freedom of the added voice has been curtailed. This, too, was inevitable. Two voices singing together on completely different rhythmic planes need some method by which they can cooperate efficiently. At first the notes of the melisma were measured into short, self-contained rhythmic patterns based on the modes of poetry, which distribute syllables according to alternations of long and short in a triple meter (see page 36). These rhythmic patterns in measured organum gave prominence to short, melodic figures which began to sound like motives. When there were two or more organal voices, they would often exchange motives in successive phrases, so that a simple kind of imitation resulted. This all signifies a tighter internal organization of the music, a centripetal pull rather than a centrifugal flight. The continual statement and restatement of these short motives, piling up momentum, give a vigorous, driving quality to this music.

The quality of sound differs but slightly from that of previous polyphonic styles: open, sonorous, capable of much reverberation. One difference is very important: because of the regular, accented rhythm, dissonance and consonance are more strictly controlled. Accented points call for consonance, which in medieval music amounts to the usual open intervals. Unaccented points can accommodate dissonance. Still, here and there we hear the impact of a dissonance upon an accented tone; this but adds to the impression of strength which this style gives.

Measured organum appeared around the year 1200; it was the first important stage in the development of meter in music. The *Alleluya (Nativitas)*, *Masterpieces,* no. 9, illustrates two kinds of measured organum: (1) one in which the principal voice sustains one note of the plainsong for a long time, while the upper voice moves actively in modal, that is poetic, rhythmic patterns (see Example 3·6 on page 102); and (2) one in which the plainsong voice changes its tone with each *foot* of the upper voices. The cantus firmus becomes part of the entire pattern of movement in this style, abandoning its role as a tenor. It has its own rhythmic patterns (see Example 3·7).

EXAMPLE 3·6 Diagram of measured organum (1)

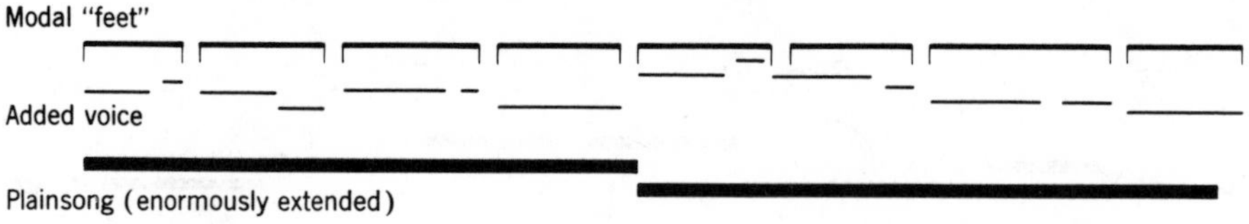

Modal "feet"

Added voice

Plainsong (enormously extended)

EXAMPLE 3·7 Diagram of measured organum (2)

Modal
Added voice

Active
Plainsong

ARS NOVA

In the music of the fourteenth century in Italy and France one fundamental change developed in the quality of movement. Heretofore the rhythm had been measured by the rhythmic modes, which were basically triple in meter. The divisions allowed for two kinds of note value—longs and shorts. In the soloistic music of measured organum, however, many ornamental passages of very short notes were introduced. Again the impulse toward ornamentation asserted itself. In order to account for these shorter notes when the music was written down, it was necessary to invent symbols and assign values to them. A system of *proportional* or *mensural notation* grew up as a result of this more florid and complex music. Composers began to use proportional values in many subtle ways; this undermined the regularity and driving momentum of the Ars Antiqua style and substituted a highly refined rhythmic imbalance. It was music for experts in performance and listening.

Another result of this rhythmic revolution was the establishment of *duple meter* as an important rhythmic factor. Still, not all the music of the fourteenth century is complex and subtle in its rhythms. The *Agnus Dei* (Lamb of God) from Guillaume de Machaut's Mass, *Masterpieces,* no. 13, shows a vigorous, straightforward quality of movement, based principally on duple meter, particularly in the shorter note values. There are four different parts here, some sung, some played by instruments. Again, the sounds are predominantly the open intervals characteristic of medieval music. We can hear them reinforced by doublings and duplications, creating a larger amount of sound.

One special feature of Machaut's *Agnus Dei* is the well-delineated contrast between movement and arrival, harmonically speaking. Points of arrival are clear and emphatic. There is leading-tone action preceding the chords which act for arrival. We have no difficulty in hearing the difference between the clear resonance of the heavy caesuras and the somewhat edgy, frequently dissonant sound within the phases of movement. The structural role of harmony in this music is well defined because of the distinctions between consonance and dissonance, assisted by the careful distribution of rhythmic motion and rest. The total effect of this composition by Machaut is very impressive; his Mass is one of the monuments of fourteenth-century music.

In the development described above, the plainsong melody, the central point of reference, is analogous to a scriptural text to be expanded upon in a sermon. You will notice, however, that the plainsong is far from being the musical support to a text that speaks directly to the worshiper. The plainsong is lost in the web of added voices; moreover, in many liturgical compositions, we hear but a fragment of the chant. Plainsong often alternated with the elaborate compositions we have been hearing; the entire music of a given chant might be divided between original and elaborated presentations.

Secular Music

Catholic church music, represented by plainsong and its progeny, ranked first in importance in the music of the medieval period. Still, not all medieval music was solemn, serious, or sacred. In the later Middle Ages an important secular art of music developed in connection with the rise of chivalry.

Poetry, music, and dancing were cultivated by the nobility, with the assistance of minstrels of low birth. This age is the source for many romantic stories about *troubadours* and *trouvères,* the poet-musicians of France, and the *minnesingers,* their counterparts in Germany. Blondel, the faithful servant of Richard I, was said to have helped rescue his master from Leopold of Austria, discovering him by means of a minstrel song. Tannhäuser, the hero of Richard Wagner's opera, is a minstrel who vacillates between the unholy love of Venus and the pure, holy love of Elizabeth. This is a curious combination of pagan and Christian ideas, a mixture quite frequently encountered in medieval culture.

The subject matter of medieval secular music had to do with stories of love, war, adventure, good living, fair weather, disappointment, jealousy, perhaps a bit of thinly disguised scandal—in short, the subjects that you might find in an opera or musical comedy today. Often the tone of these songs was moralizing or cynical. Naturally, the principal interest was in the text. The Crusades (First Crusade, 1095) and the code of chivalry and courtly love, which came into being during the early part of the twelfth century, provided much topical material for these songs.

Musically, the solo songs, the *monophonic* pieces, have much in common with plainsong, as we can hear in the trouvère song *Or la truix* (I Find It Difficult) and the minnesinger song (or minnelied) *Willekommen Mayenschein* (Welcome, May's Sun), *Masterpieces,* nos. 4 and 5. *Polyphonic* secular songs reflect the style of sacred music with which they are contemporaneous, i.e., organum; they are set in the rhythmic modes, and they have well-defined phrase structure marked by clear and rather evenly spaced points of arrival.

Composers of secular music, often clerics, used the polyphonic techniques of sacred composition. One important form, the *motet,* derived from *mot,* or "word," involved adding texts to the upper parts of measured organum. These added texts might be comments on the text of the plainsong, or they might be secular, even amorous, in content (see *Masterpieces,* no. 10). Such polytextuality suggests that the full flavor of this music was appreciated only by those to whom all the texts were familiar; it would appear to be a kind of connoisseur's music.

Many purely secular pieces in polyphonic style were composed during the fourteenth century. Of these, one of the most spectacular was the *caccia,* meaning "chase." In the caccia, one voice or part "chases" the other, singing exactly what the first voice has sung. In other words, the second voice imitates the first exactly. This is called a *canonic* type of imitation. Caccias deal with scenes of the hunt, of fishing, and of the market. Composers managed to include many descriptive and pictorial effects; they imitated the barking of dogs, the sound of hunting horns, and the cries of hunters and street vendors.

In the caccia of Ghirardellus, *Tosto che l'alba* (Since the Dawn), *L'Anthologie Sonore,* no. 59, note the brilliant, sonorous, sparkling manner and lively, vigorous rhythm. Dogs bark, hunters sound their horns from the mountaintop, the excitement of the chase is caught and maintained by the clearly projected imitative figures. All this takes place within a transparent textural layout: two upper voices and a supporting lower voice, illustrating the three-voice music of the fourteenth century. This layout represents a scheme which will become standard for musical composition in future centuries.

Dancing as well as singing was an important form of diversion at court. The music produced for dancing has well-defined accents in modal rhythm; because of the patterns of the dance, musical phrases must balance each other in length. These phrases tend to have an even number of measures, often eight, conforming to symmetrical patterns in the dance. In the Estampie, *Masterpieces,* no. 12, you can easily make out the eight-measure phrases from the beginning of the piece to the end. If you listen closely, you will hear that the lower voice repeats its melody, and states each phrase twice. The ending of each first phrase is *open,* which corresponds to a half cadence in later music. The ending of each second phrase is *closed,* which corresponds to an authentic cadence in later music. Each closed cadence, with the exception of one, ends upon the same tonal center. We have then the impression of a *harmonic digression* and a return with each pair of phrases. Such a pairing represents a very clear relationship of *statement and counterstatement.*

EXAMPLE 3·8 Diagram of estampie

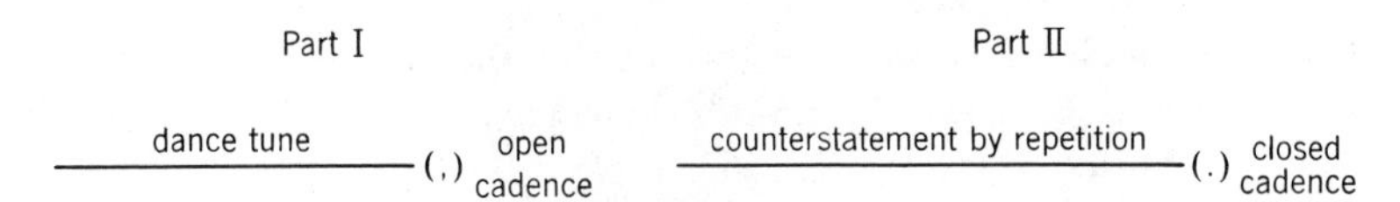

Performance of Medieval Music

The performance of medieval music involved voices, instruments, and combinations of voices and instruments. It was quite in order to substitute a voice for an instrument or vice versa in many kinds of music. Thus, in one manuscript from the thirteenth century, there are motets expressly indicated for instrumental performance. We are still investigating the performance practices of medieval times, but we do know that it was considered adequate if each part had a representative performer of some kind. Therefore, contrasts and variations in tone quality, not only in different pieces but in different performances of the same piece, could very well have occurred. Indeed, in view of the general transparency of the texture and the consistency of style, such variations in performance may have been quite welcome.

Early instruments included plucked and bowed string instruments, wind instruments, keyboard instruments, and percussion. There was a tremendous variety within these groups; they were not at all standardized as at present. Recordings made recently of early instruments, including those in *Masterpieces,* show that the tone quality of these instruments was far less rich and full than that of present-day instruments. Still, there is a freshness and lightness of tone quality that well suits the performance of one-, two-, or three-voice music.

Summary

Sacred music in the medieval period was based on plainsong, which in turn was developed from the cantillations of Hebrew and Greek music. Addition and elaboration were the processes by which the art of musical composition grew during this age. Briefly, the stages were as follows:

1. ***Addition*** of text to the melismatic sections of plainsong; tropes and sequences; liturgical drama
2. ***Parallel organum:*** Addition of voices moving in parallel fourths, fifths, or octaves
3. ***Free organum:*** Development of melodic independence in the added voices
4. ***Melismatic organum:*** Slowing down of the cantus firmus; extensive elaboration in the added voice
5. ***Measured organum, known as the Ars antiqua:*** Control of the melismatic voice by modal rhythms; rhythmic patterns in parts of the plainsong
6. ***Motet:*** Texts set to the added voices
7. ***Ars nova:*** Rhythmic elaborations and complications; duple as well as triple meter; proportional relationships; and mensural notation

Throughout medieval music, from the time that voices began to sing together, the general harmonic quality of sound remained constant. Points of arrival, for both large and small phases of movement, were characterized by the sound of open intervals, principally the fifth and the octave. These gave a maximum impression of stability. Open intervals also fairly saturated the entire harmonic language. Between points of arrival, mixed in with the fourths, fifths, and octaves, there was a considerable amount of dissonance, brought about by the incidental clashes of melodic lines. Medieval harmony is thus characterized by rather sharp contrasts between the stable sounds of arrival and the active dissonances heard frequently between points of arrival.

Later medieval music, particularly that cultivated in France during the thirteenth and fourteenth centuries, has been called *Gothic* by analogy to other phases of culture at that time. Parallels between music and Gothic architecture have frequently been drawn. If we consider how each of these, Gothic music and the Gothic cathedral, took shape, that is, by the addition and juxtaposition of separate, distinct, and often clashing elements, and that these elements were focused on the central idea of the worship of God, then the analogy seems quite valid. Indeed, throughout the history of Europe from A.D. 400 to 1400, the period we have been considering musically, the force of a central, all-powerful authority makes itself felt in every aspect of religion, politics, and art. Feudalism and the hierarchy of the church dominated men's thoughts and, indeed, their very lives. As we have seen, music reflected this state of affairs; the only music of which we have record is that performed in church or court.

FIGURE 1. Strassburg Cathedral (from an 18th century engraving). An example of the Gothic style in architecture. (Courtesy of the Stanford University Libraries.)

Genres and Compositions Discussed in This Chapter

Plainsong
Laus Deo Patri (Praise God the Father), *Masterpieces,* no. 1
Vidimus Stellam (We Have Seen the Star), *Masterpieces,* no. 2
Victimae Paschali (The Paschali Victim), *Masterpieces,* no. 3
Liturgical drama
Infantem Vidimus (We Have Seen the Child), *Treasury,* no. 5
Organum (Ars antiqua)
Parallel: *Rex caeli domine* (King of Heaven), *Masterpieces,* no. 6
Free: *Agnus Dei* (Lamb of God), *Masterpieces,* no. 7
Melismatic: *Benedicamus Domino* (Let us Bless the Lord), *Masterpieces,* no. 8
Measured: *Alleluya (Nativitas), Masterpieces,* no. 9
Ars nova
Machaut: Mass, *Agnus Dei, Masterpieces,* no. 13
Secular monody
Or la truix (I Find It Difficult), *Masterpieces,* no. 4
Willekommen Mayenschein (Welcome, May's Sun), *Masterpieces,* no. 5
Caccia
Tosto che l'alba (Since the Dawn), *L'Anthologie Sonore,* no. 59
Motet
Eius in Oriente, Masterpieces, no. 10
Dance
Estampie, *Masterpieces,* no. 12

Suggestions for Critical Listening

1. Sound
   a. Range: wide, moderate, narrow
   b. Amount: number of voices
2. Movement; meter and rhythm
   a. Pace: slow, moderate, quick
   b. Groupings: by two, by three, shifting; clear, unclear
   c. Rhythm: free, modal
3. Arrival
   a. Clear, unclear; emphatic, light; final, nonfinal (closed, open)
   b. Approach to arrival: strong, light
4. Melody
   a. Type of contour; position of apex, if present

   b. Motives: clearly defined, not clearly defined; repeated, varied, contrasted
5. Texture
   a. Medium of performance: solo, group; instruments, voices, both instruments and voices
   b. Monophonic, melody-accompaniment, single-action, polyphonic, imitative
6. Harmony
   a. Final: easy, difficult to identify
   b. Mode: plagal, authentic
   c. Cadences: open, closed
   d. Intervals predominating: open (unisons, fourths, fifths, octaves), some thirds, sixths, dissonances
7. Structure; statement and counterstatement
   a. Phrases: long, short; equal, unequal in length
   b. Principal sections: repeated, varied, contrasted
8. Relation of music to text
   a. Syllabic, neumatic, melismatic, modal setting
   b. Expression: pictorialism, general mood of piece
9. Type of piece: syllabic, neumatic, melismatic plainsong; parallel, free, melismatic, measured organum; motet; dance; caccia; secular song

Suggested Listening Projects

1. **Easter Alleluia *Pascha Nostrum*, *L'Anthologie Sonore*, Vol. 1**

   Listen for: Melismatic melody; long phases of movement; repetition of phrases and melodic turns; manner in which melody winds around a given tone; narrow melodic range, sense of shifting points of arrival within a single mode; use of larger intervals, particularly the fifth, to create a dramatic contrast with usual melodic procedure; floating effect of entire piece suggesting the jubilation of the Alleluia.

2. **English Gymel, *L'Anthologie Sonore*, Vol. 1**

   Listen for: Short phrases; repetition of motives; prevalence of thirds in harmony; dancelike rhythms (trochaic rhythmic mode); cadential effect at end; the down-to-earth effect of the entire piece; compare with the estampie in *Masterpieces*.

3. **French secular song, fourteenth century, *L'Anthologie Sonore*, Vol. 1**

   Listen for: Intimate manner; graceful, supple melodic lines; fluid rhythm; short phrases; repetition of refrainlike phrases; open harmony (few thirds); transparency of the texture, especially the separation of solo and accompaniment; the syllabic setting.

4. **Organum duplum, *Viderunt omnes* (They All Saw), *Treasury of Early Music*, no. 9**

Listen for: Modal rhythm in upper voice; three-part structure in the tenor on the following plan: (A) sustained tones, (B) modal rhythm, (A) sustained tones; some melismatic action in upper voice; repetition and variation of rhythmic motives; generally narrow range; some incidental dissonances; broad final cadence.

5. **Motet, *Ave gloriosa mater* (Hail, Glorious Mother), *Treasury*, no. 10**

Listen for: All voices in modal rhythm; polytextual setting; clearly defined Dorian mode; different rhythmic pattern in each voice; short, relatively balanced phrases, with frequent caesuras in one or more parts; prominence of fifths and octaves; occasionally fuller harmony; repetition of figures and motives; change in rhythmic mode of tenor about halfway through.

chapter four

Renaissance Music

The Renaissance is considered one of the greatest ages in the history of man. From our present-day point of vantage we can see the amazing richness with which science, letters, art, and discovery flowered in the fifteenth and sixteenth centuries. We feel a strong kinship with this age because many modern concepts were first developed during it.

Renaissance music, too, strikes a warm and familiar note. Anyone who has sung in a choral group knows the style of Renaissance music, possibly through singing Roman motets, English madrigals, French chansons, or chorales dating from the Reformation. The importance and vitality of Renaissance music is shown by the influence it has had upon composers of succeeding generations; it has created an unbroken tradition to this very day and is the basis of an important branch of music instruction, that is, strict counterpoint.

Josquin Deprès's motet *Ave Maria* (ca. 1500), *Masterpieces,* no. 19, illustrates the Renaissance style of composition. We can note the following characteristics in this work:

1. A new quality of sound, different from that of medieval music; drastic reduction in the amount and the impact of dissonance; harmony based upon thirds and sixths, rather than fourths and fifths

2. Many changes in the amount of sound
3. Very clear and distinct separation of voices with respect to range
4. Sustained quality of movement; moderately slow beat; avoidance of extremes of brevity or length in note values (compare melismatic organum); overlapping voice parts; joining of phases of movement; gracefully turned melodic material; imitation
5. Several very strong points of harmonic arrival

As an overall impression, we can say that this music seems to have a balance, a control, an evenness, a sense of parts fitted together in a perfectly integrated and smooth manner.

These are general comments on this piece; yet they can well apply to much music written during Josquin's time (ca. 1500). He was a great figure in the development of Renaissance music, representing the final crystallization of Renaissance techniques of musical composition, an embodiment of the unity of style which is characteristic of the era. Before his time, Renaissance music was moving toward clarification; after Josquin, music, like art, began to develop special mannerisms.

Now, we shall look more closely at the various component qualities and procedures of Renaissance music, those elements which comprise its unity.

Qualities of Sound

TRIADS

Around the year 1425, a new kind of sound began to filter into Western European music. The music has a fuller, richer, sweeter, and more thoroughly blended quality of sound. We hear many thirds and sixths in addition to the fifths and octaves which were the standbys of medieval music. Dissonances have receded to an unassuming position; instead of clashing head on at times, the melodic lines make way for each other. In Guillaume Dufay's Kyrie (1), *Masterpieces,* no. 15, from his Mass based on the secular song *Se la face ay pâle* (If My Face Is Pale), an early manifestation of this new style is illustrated. This music has none of the strident, bold dissonances and little of the open sounds of Machaut's music.

The important fact about this new sound is that it is composed almost entirely of major and minor triads. This is the moment in history when the traditional harmonic system of Western music began to take definite shape. The establishment of the triad as the basic harmonic unit was almost as important as the beginnings of polyphony itself. Each note in a chord had to be a member of a triad; if not, it had to be led gently to a tone which was a member. In this new style, the sense of harmonic movement from one triad to another, based on the play of different triad colors, was the principal harmonic interest. For an exceptional demonstration of the fondness of fifteenth-century composers for triad sounds, listen to Dufay's *Gloria in excelsis* (Glory to God in the Highest) *ad modem tubae* ("in the manner of trumpets"). Actually, the entire piece alternates between tonic and dominant harmony. The trumpets have a simple fanfare figure, while the voices decorate the harmonies with intertwining imitations. The incorporation of fanfares into highly elaborated musical compositions will become a favorite procedure of composers in later times. This is an early example and can be heard on the *2000 Years of Music* set, no. 7.

The impetus toward the new harmonic language probably came from England. During the Middle Ages the English seem to have had a preference for singing in thirds instead of fourths and fifths (see Example 2, gymel, on page 109). As a result of the Hundred Years' War (1337–1453), which was fought in France, English ways became known to Continental musicians, and they began to use the sonorities they heard in English music. The sweetness of this new style was so captivating that frequently whole chains of such chords were sung, decorating the plainsong in parallel movement.

You can discover for yourselves the effect of this technique, called *fauxbourdon* in the fifteenth century. At the piano select any white note. Play along with it the third above, and add to these the fourth above the upper note. You now have a chord in which the interval between the outer voices is a sixth; also, the middle voice forms a third with the lowest voice. Such a chord is called a *sixth chord*. Keeping the voices strictly parallel, move up and down the keyboard. The effect is pleasant on the piano, but in voices its sweetness is much greater. Indeed, many popular singing teams today rely heavily upon the sixth-chord progression to give body and color to a simple melody. In fauxbourdon, we receive the impression that a single melodic line has widened into a consonant, rich, and sonorous stream of sound.

Musicians of the fifteenth century themselves were aware of this new sound. Johannes Tinctoris, the leading musical theorist of that period, said in the introduction to his book *The Art of Counterpoint* (1477): "There does not exist a single piece of music, not composed within the last forty years, that is regarded by the learned as worth hearing." In this, he was referring to the new idea of sound based upon the use of thirds and sixths.

FIGURE 2. Hartmann Schedel: Landscape from *Liber Cronicarum,* 1493 (The Nuremberg Chronicle). The architecture illustrates Romanesque and Gothic styles while the overall design demonstrates the Renaissance treatment of perspective. (Courtesy of the Stanford University Libraries.)

RANGE OF SOUND; TIMBRE

Renaissance music has a wider range of sound and a generally fuller quality than we have heard in medieval music. Medieval music was written principally in two or three parts, fairly close in range. Renaissance music was written typically in four or more parts, with a wider range than medieval music. Note in Josquin's motet the compactness and fullness when all four voices are singing. Observe also how Josquin took advantage of range differences to set pairs of voices against each other in textural contrasts. It is as if he were creating a third dimension, a sense of aural perspective in the contrasts of high and low. In later Renaissance music, the blend of five or more voices, full, rich, sonorous, and vibrant, becomes a principal appeal, as we can hear in sections of Orlandus Lassus' motet, *Tristis est anima mea* (Sad Is My Soul), *Masterpieces*, no. 23.

The range of tone quality is quite broad in Renaissance music. Within Luca Marenzio's madrigal *S'io parto* (If I Leave), *Masterpieces*, no. 27, the first ten measures encompass ten changes in the amount of sound, from one to five voices being involved. The element of *contrast* in texture becomes very important. Toward the end of the sixteenth century, contrasts in quality of sound were exploited more and more; such contrasts represent one of the forces that eventually destroyed the consistencies of Renaissance music and ushered in the Baroque era. Indeed, contrast was the watchword among certain Venetian composers, who made a practice of alternating phrases between choruses placed at different positions in the church. Instrumental groups, adding their sonorities to multiply the contrast, also participated in this type of performance, which depended largely upon the effects of reverberation in the great cathedral of St. Mark's in Venice. Giovanni Gabrieli's *Sacrae Symphoniae* are magnificent examples of this impressive style of composition (see page 147).

Before we leave the matter of sonority values, a subject which is fascinating and absorbing in any age or style of music, we should refer to another aspect of Renaissance music, namely, the use of instruments. During the period, interest in instrumental performance appears to have expanded and flourished tremendously. Many compositions required a virtuoso command of the instrument. Treatises on instrumental performance were written. Music was composed to develop and exploit the special sonorities and agilities of different kinds of instruments, such as organ, harpsichord, strings, lute, and brass.

Musical instruments were used for many purposes. In the home and at court they provided entertainment, furnishing the music for songs and dances. In the church the organ was the chief musical instrument, either as a solo instrument or to support and augment voices. Often, at the option of the composer or performer, instruments might replace one or more voices in a vocal ensemble or play along with the voices. Characteristic techniques of performance for keyboard, bowed, and plucked instruments were developed; meanwhile, the instruments themselves had been improved over the models of earlier times. All this bespeaks a lively and widespread interest in instrumental performance—an interest that was to grow prodigiously in the centuries to come.

Qualities of Movement: Rhythm; Melody

Renaissance music has a steady momentum. We sense, in the works we have heard, a *moderate* pace that controls all movement. Josquin's motet provides an excellent example. As it proceeds, we feel a gentle strength in the quality of movement, a deliberate pulse, even and regular, without the emphatic accent that invites foot-tapping in a dance or march. Yet the movement has vitality. The interplay of voices, each with its own action to contribute to the composite movement, creates the impression of a reserved but undeniably purposeful pace. As a rule, we can say that Renaissance music moves deliberately.

Indeed, this moderate and regular pace was recognized at the time as a basic stylistic feature. Musical theorists of the Renaissance called the unit of beat a *tactus*. The tactus corresponds to the half note in a present-day andante tempo, approximately one second in length. The pulse we heard in Josquin's motet as a steady undercurrent represented the tactus.

The steadiness of movement in Josquin's motet does accommodate some differences in grouping; at other times in Renaissance music we hear stronger accents; still again, in some pieces, florid melodic elaborations give rise to an impression of greater speed. Thus, change of grouping, variation in accentuation, and a range of tempo can modify the underlying moderate and regular quality of movement that governs the music of this period.

Grouping is illustrated in Josquin's motet by a shift from duple to triple and then back to duple; these changes take place in the latter half of the piece. Often, in Renaissance music, such changes call for a quickening or slowing of the pace, since three notes are then expected to be sung in the time previously allotted to two; the converse also holds: two for three.

Differences in *accentuation* often arise from the manner of performance. Two selections from *Masterpieces,* the lute dances, no. 22, and Lassus' motet, no. 23, exemplify this contrast. In the vocal piece, the familiar smoothness of movement associated with Renaissance music is apparent; the voices virtually glide from one tone to another. On the other hand, the very manner in which the lute produces its tone by plucking tends to create a highly articulated flow of sound. Each note makes a tiny accent, while the chords furnish strong accents. This ability to establish accent made the lute an ideal instrument for the accompaniment to dancing; its crisp utterance enabled it to give a stress to each touching or turning point in the dance. To this very day, dance music relies upon a plucked string instrument. Consider the effect that a string bass provides in a dance orchestra. It helps to set the beat and the pace; at the same time, it furnishes harmonic support as a bass instrument. The lute also served this function in many ensemble pieces of the sixteenth century, as well as in later music; thus, the lutenist of the Renaissance and the jazz bass player of today are counterparts to each other, notwithstanding the centuries that separate them.

In the lute dances and Lassus' motet, the basic tempos are about the same. Yet the motet has a broad and deliberate quality of movement, while the dances have a lively quality. This difference arises from the fact that in the dances the tactus is divided into many small notes—four, six, or eight—while the motet rarely uses more than one or two per tactus.

Polyphonic action also contributes to the sense of musical movement in Renaissance style. You will remember, from our study of polyphony, what its effect is upon the overall sense of movement: how it creates overlaps, how it covers cadences and caesuras with fresh movement (see page 62). This is also true of Renaissance music, particularly choral music. Many times you will hear the harmony focusing upon a cadence, yet the sense of arrival will be blurred by some melodic or rhythmic action in one or more voices. For this reason more than any other, Renaissance music has been described as a "long-drawn-out sweetness."

Melodic movement in Renaissance music contributes to the sense of moderate pace, balance, control, and subtle play. Renaissance melodic action seems to describe a rounded pattern, in which the melody dips and rises gradually with respect to a fulcrum that keeps it in comfortable balance. The Renaissance composer made his melody move so that it neither displayed too sharp a profile nor lost its momentum by insufficient action. In particular, you will hear very few large or striking leaps.

The opening of Josquin's motet serves well as an example of this melodic style. The subject begins with a small downward leap; as a counterstatement, the melody rises gradually beyond the pitch of the beginning, turns around the high point several times, and makes its way downward gradually. In this melody, as the music moves upward, rhythmic action becomes more lively with the appearance of shorter notes; with the descent, action quiets and longer notes again predominate. One can hardly find anywhere a more exquisite example of a melodic period that creates, out of the gentle ebb and flow of movement, such a perfect inner balance.

The final flowering and the utmost concentration of the Renaissance melodic style (latter half of the sixteenth century) is found in the music of Giovanni Palestrina, which moves with the greatest suavity and smoothness. This style is exemplified in the *Agnus Dei* from the Mass *Veni sponsa Christi* (Come, Bride of Christ), *Masterpieces,* no. 24. If you have had occasion to study counterpoint based on sixteenth-century styles, you are well aware that one of the basic criteria is a melody that moves sweetly, gently, and yet with a clear sense of direction.

Harmony

Renaissance harmony consists principally of triads and sixth chords, set in three to six or more voices. The following characteristics are evident:

1. The appearance and the increasing use of progressions that we can recognize as our familiar cadences
2. A sharply defined and tightly controlled interaction between consonance and dissonance
3. The appearance and increasing use of chromatic progressions
4. The beginnings of a codification of chord progression
5. The idea that musical expression is linked to the size and structure of intervals and scales, i.e., *proportion*

THE AUTHENTIC CADENCE

We have heard harmonic points of arrival in medieval music. The leading-tone action in Machaut's Mass definitely points to a resolution. In most medieval cadences the action of the voices leading to the chord of arrival was stepwise:

EXAMPLE 4·1 Stepwise cadence

Thus, the idea of the cadence had already become important for indicating arrival. However, in music of the Renaissance, it was discovered that a much stronger, emphatic, and clearer sense of harmonic arrival could be projected if a leap in the bass voice from the *fifth* tone of the mode to the *tonic* were added below the stepwise movement from 7 to 8. Example 4·2 illustrates the effect of adding the bass part in such a manner.

You will recall the strong effect of arrival that is created when the bass moves from 5 to 1, down a fifth (or up a fourth). This is the *authentic cadence* (see page 78).

EXAMPLE 4·2 Bass cadence

It was only in music of the Renaissance that a genuine bass voice appeared in the harmony, acting as a support and harmonic guide. Previously voices in a texture were equal in harmonic action, differing only in range. Now the bass behaved in its own fashion; it created a new kind of cadence. This distinctive action of the bass developed a new harmonic dimension, somewhat like the sense of visual perspective that was created in Renaissance painting in the fifteenth century.

Note, in the illustration (Figure 2), the feeling of distance; the eye is drawn by the vanishing point into the engraving, so to speak, so that we have a greater sense of depth and position than in the somewhat flat representations of medieval painting. This was a new *horizontal* dimension. In music a new feeling of space distribution was developed in which voices were organized on a *vertical* dimension. This contributed an effect of musical *depth,* analogous to the depth in space that we sense in the engraving. Both perspective in painting and the bass part in music represent the incorporation of new areas into the theater of action. The bass and the upper voices had their own levels of action, and they performed distinctly different roles—the bass supported; the upper voices elaborated.

Throughout the Renaissance and during the seventeenth century, the feeling for organizing harmony around cadences guided by the bass grew continually stronger, until, in the eighteenth century, the cadential feeling saturated the entire harmonic language. Josquin's motet has several cadences of this kind. The strongest and most obvious cadence is the one we hear at the end; it creates a very convincing impression of finality. Such cadences thus serve important structural roles.

OTHER CADENCES

We have already studied the other cadences of traditional harmony —the half cadence, the deceptive cadence, and the plagal cadence. These cadences all made their appearance as basic harmonic procedures during the Renaissance; each is guided by the bass part. The half cadence comes to rest on the fifth degree of the scale; the deceptive cadence substitutes some note other than the tonic in the bass (generally the sixth) as a resolution for the dominant; the plagal cadence, in its most typical form, takes the bass from the fourth to the tonic. In each case, the voices above the bass are singing the triad of which the bass is the root.

The half cadence is used in Josquin's motet *Ave Maria* at the point where the duple meter is resumed, shortly before the end, on the word *regum* (king). A plagal cadence is heard as the final arrival point in the keyboard canzona, *Masterpieces,* no. 26. We hear a deceptive cadence in Lassus' motet *Tristis* upon the entry of the soprano near the beginning on the word *tristis.* Much attention was given to the art of using nonfinal and deceptive cadences. Gioseffe Zarlino, in his *Istituzioni,* devoted considerable space to methods by which the cadence may be avoided. His purpose was to demonstrate that the music should not come to a close until the sense of the text was complete. He used the term *period* to apply to both types of arrival, musical and poetic. Still another kind of cadence, carried over from medieval music, is that which is used in the Phrygian mode. It is called the Phrygian cadence and is characterized by the lowermost voice moving one half step downward, from 2 to 1 in the Phrygian mode, while an upper voice moves from 7 to 8. Here the leading tone descends. This cadence is illustrated in Example 4·3.

DISSONANCE TREATMENT

As we heard in Josquin's motet, Renaissance music deals mainly with consonances, triads, thirds, and sixths as the basic raw material of its sound; nevertheless, it does not disregard dissonance. The limitation of dissonance and its careful control opened new possibilities for musical expression. With fewer dissonances, each one became more important. The Renaissance approach to dissonance is very special. One of the principal procedures is as follows: A dissonant tone is introduced as a temporary *suspension,* i.e., *replacement* of a consonant tone, and it must move to, or resolve into, that consonant tone.

EXAMPLE 4·3 Dissonance treatment (suspension and resolution)

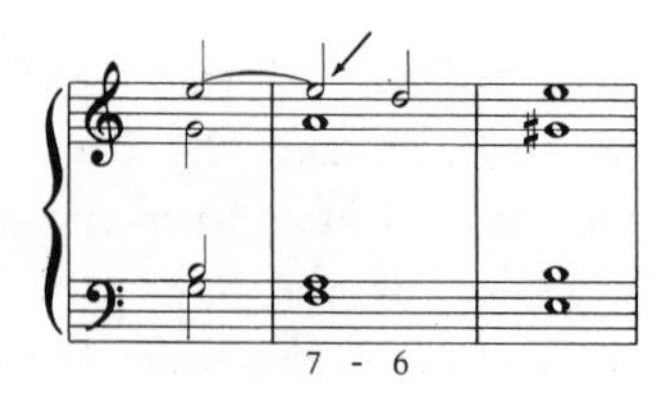

The dissonance thus creates a special kind of tension calling for a specified resolution. This, in fact, is the basis of the consonance and dissonance relationship that will have a profound effect upon harmony for four centuries to come. Dissonance, in traditional harmony, is not a special effect on its own; it has an obligation to its resolution.

In the final few chords of Josquin's motet we can hear such a suspension dissonance and the intensification of expressive quality which it creates. Listen to the topmost voice. Note that just before the end it holds back before moving to the leading tone, while the other voices go to their appointed positions in the chord. The suspension is the most thoroughly exploited technique of dissonance in all Renaissance music. It binds, and at the same time, by its contrast with the predominantly consonant sound, it creates a strongly expressive accent.

Later composers turned this quality of the suspension to use in expressing especially poignant or touching moments in their music. Dissonance was used for dramatic accent; it created a focus upon a critically important word or phrase of the text. Sixteenth-century composers took delight in working out such relationships between music and poetry. An especially effective example of dissonance used pictorially can be heard in Marenzio's madrigal *S'io parto, i'moro* (If I Leave, I Die), *Masterpieces,* no. 27, at the word *moro,* meaning "I die." Marenzio and some of his contemporaries represent a late and rather highly mannered aspect of Renaissance music, particularly in this respect.

CHROMATICISM

Another technique for creating special effects against the even flow of Renaissance harmony was chromaticism. In this technique chords belonging to different scales were placed either next to each other or very close to each other, giving the impression of a colorful, somewhat unstable shift of harmonic meaning. In the Marenzio madrigal, at the words "and yet I must still leave thee," there is a chromatic relationship between the chords that begin and end the passage. This movement from one scale to another cleverly underscores the idea of departure. Such expressive and pictorial play upon music and words bespeaks the flexibility and richness of musical resources in the Renaissance. Chromaticism, as well as dissonance, increased from rather restrained, moderate use in Josquin's time to a high point of concentration in some very late sixteenth-century Italian composers, particularly Carlo Gesualdo. It was used so much that a sense of tonal center was almost entirely lost.

CHORD PROGRESSION

We should be overstating the case were we to say that in Renaissance harmony a system of chord progression had been developed. To a great extent, the choice of chord is controlled by part writing, that is, by the circumstances which allow the various tones of a chord to move most smoothly to the next chord; also, the general effect of the mode tends to be emphasized by chord progressions. Still, in much music of this time, we can hear certain kinds of progressions that occur frequently, often repeated one or more times. In John Bennet's madrigal *Thyrsis, Sleepest Thou? Masterpieces,* no. 28, the music which accompanies the opening words, "Thyrsis, sleepest thou, Holla," contains just two different harmonies; these stand in the relationship of a dominant to a tonic, and we hear eight alternations, in a flexible metric scheme, of these two chords. This passage illustrates one of the typical chord progressions for which composers began to display a marked preference. We find such crystallizations through repetition in secular music particularly—popular Italian songs, French chansons, and English madrigals. The progressions themselves have a strong cadential effect, which the listener can easily sense by paying attention to the bass part.

HARMONIC PROPORTION

Very early in the history of Western man, it was discovered that numbers and musical intervals had exact relationships with each other. For example, if a string is divided in half, the sound produced by each half will be one octave higher than the sound of the entire string. The proportion of this relationship is then expressed as 1 to 2. All musical intervals can be thus expressed as two numbers, in varying degrees of complexity. The simpler intervals, after the octave, have the following proportions:

Perfect fifth	2 to 3
Perfect fourth	3 to 4
Major third	4 to 5
Minor third	5 to 6

These can be heard when a string is divided in two, three, four, five, or six parts. Intervals occur naturally in increasingly smaller size as the pitch rises (see pages 69, 70).

Musical theorists of the Renaissance were especially concerned with these proportions, inasmuch as the first six numbers represented the harmony that they considered "perfect," i.e., the major triad. They associated harmonic proportions with musical expression. As a rule, when a chord or a mode is built on the "natural" series, with the larger units representing the lower pitches, the effect is strong and sweet, suited to brighter effects of expression. Thus, the major triad represented the Ionian mode, which was called the *modo lascivio* and was considered suitable for dances and gay songs by Zarlino, who gave much space in his *Istituzioni armoniche* (1558) to characterizing intervals and modes by their various proportions. The minor triad, with the major third above, contradicts the "natural" system and was considered proper for sadder, darker expressive values. The minor triad is the basis of the Dorian, Phrygian, and Aeolian modes.

Following are Zarlino's recommendations for the use of the modes in musical expression:

MODE	RANGE AND FINAL	EXPRESSIVE QUALITY
Dorian	D-D	partly sad, partly gay
Hypodorian	a-D-a	severe, grave, humble
Phrygian	E-E	moves one to tears
Hypophrygian	b-E-b	for lamentations, supplications
Lydian	F-F	cheerful, modest, entertaining, victorious
Hypolydian	c-F-c	grave, devout
Mixolydian	G-G	for allegro, threats, anger
Hypomixolydian	d-G-d	smooth, sweet, for speculation
Aeolian	A-A	open, lyrical, gay, sonorous
Hypoaeolian	e-A-e	liturgical music, offertories, graduals
Ionian	C-C	dances, *balli, modo lascivio*
Hypoionian	g-C-g	for sad love

Measurement of intervals involves a highly complex set of problems; it is a science in its own right and forms the basis by which the tuning of instruments is accomplished. Here, we have introduced the topic only to show that it has a direct relationship to qualities of sound and expression and that these matters were dealt with in a systematic manner by musicians of the Renaissance.

Rhetoric in Renaissance Music

The various aspects of harmony in Renaissance music—triads, cadences, modes, consonance and dissonance, chromaticism, progression, proportion—provided the Renaissance composer with a well-organized "language" with which to express his ideas. This language had its own grammar (rules for harmonic construction) and its own rhetoric (means for achieving a persuasive and eloquent effect). Many of the composer's decisions were controlled by the words he chose to set; the rhetoric of language was intimately linked with the rhetoric of music. With all the categories and distinctions that were made among the parts of both musical and linguistic speech, it was possible to compose in highly characteristic, individual, and very often subtle ways. A composer might have asked himself the following questions involving rhetorical and grammatical judgment: Should a mode with major or minor third be used? Does the text call for a cadence at a certain point? Does a certain word or phrase call for dissonance? Does a change in meaning suggest a chromatic inflection? Is repetition of a progression in order?

As the listener becomes more familiar with this musical language, as, indeed, with any musical language, he will be able to note such decisions and will applaud the aptness and persuasiveness of the composer's treatment of his material. Many of the specific illustrations in this chapter represent samplings of rhetorical skill on the part of composers of this era. When a Renaissance composer decided to mirror the expression of the words in his music, he did it carefully so as not to disturb the coherence and continuity of his music. The nuance was subtle, in contrast to the ideas of expression that arose in the early seventeenth century, when intense, explosive expression became an aesthetic goal and individual turns of figure and phrase stood out boldly in order to underscore the feeling value of the poetry. In Renaissance style, the music tended to control the expression of the text; in early baroque music, the intense expression of the text broke through the highly refined musical technique and gave rise to striking new gestures (see page 145).

In reflecting the meaning of his text, the Renaissance composer often introduced musical analogies. A figure or a progression would imitate a particular idea or action in the words. This was called *pictorialism.* The analysis of Lassus' motet *Tristis* (see page 130) points out a number of musical pictorial effects. Pictorialism is even more vivid in Thomas Weelkes's madrigal *As Vesta Was from Latmos Hill Descending* (see page 135).

Aspects of Form

After the initial evaluation of impressions received from a Renaissance composition—its characteristic sonorities, its qualities of movement and arrival—attention might well turn to the entire piece itself. How does it take shape? What can be grasped about its structure?

ADDITION, ELABORATION, IMPROVISATION

As we studied medieval music, we saw how it evolved through addition and elaboration. One part was added to another; and the resulting patterns were expanded as elaborations were introduced between tones: rhythmic patterns were superimposed. Some of the most important types of music took shape by such accretions. In the Renaissance these procedures were still at work in many different ways. Josquin's motet illustrates one important method.

Its very title provides the clue: *Ave Maria, Gratia Plena* (Hail Mary, Full of Grace). This is the title of a plainsong. Josquin "borrowed" the plainsong and elaborated it so that each phrase in turn became the melodic basis of a section or period of his motet. The preexisting material was completely assimilated insofar as style is concerned. We no longer deal with the declamatory free style of plainsong but discover that the chant is altered rhythmically so that it assumes the typical quality of movement found in Renaissance music—a steady, continuous flow, governed by the beat or tactus.

At other times the Renaissance composer would borrow a popular song, as Dufay did in his Mass *Se la face ay pâle* (If My Face Is Pale). Sometimes, as a play on words, the composer would invent his own "borrowed" material, by fashioning a motive from some motto—a phrase or name. Thus, in a Mass written to honor the Duke of Ferrara, Josquin employed a subject he had created from the tones whose vowels correspond to those in the Duke's name and title. This is how it was worked out:

EXAMPLE 4·4 Motto for the *Missa Hercules*

When a Mass was composed upon a cantus firmus, each of its five major sections, as a rule, used the same preexisting material. In this way, the Mass achieved unity as a musical composition.

In *Ave Maria,* as in many other works, Josquin used a limited amount of precomposed material. But in the later sixteenth century, borrowing was carried so far that entire compositions were reworked into more extended or more highly decorated pieces. About three-quarters of the Masses of Lassus and Palestrina, the two most important composers of sacred music in the later Renaissance, are *parody masses;* they are elaborated from smaller sacred pieces or from secular polyphonic compositions. The parody mass represents the ultimate stage in the evolution that began during the early Middle Ages, that is, *the evolution of musical structure and texture by additions to preexisting material.*

Another striking example of borrowing is the *canzona francese,* in which Italian composers transcribed and reworked French secular songs, *chansons,* into instrumental compositions. We can hear what changes took place when this was done by contrasting nos. 20 and 21 in *Masterpieces.* These are two versions of the same song, *Pour un plaisir* (For a Pleasure). The vocal piece is quite straightforward, brisk, and declamatory in manner. The keyboard piece derived from the chanson is florid, and its movement is less straightforward and vigorous. The florid effects in Andrea Gabrieli's piece arise from the process of *ornamentation;* in this proces the composer or performer *breaks up a long tone into a number of shorter tones* which describe a pattern centering around the original tones. Later, independent pieces were composed in the style of the canzona francese.

Written and improvised ornamentation, both in instrumental and vocal music, was an important aspect of musical performance from the fifteenth to the middle of the eighteenth century. As we have heard, it made a profound difference in the musical effect, melodically, rhythmically, and harmonically. Ornamentation was extensively used in the numerous sets of *variations* written during the sixteenth century. In these, the basic melody or the harmonic plan of a preexisting model was given new treatment in the variations, of which there might be five, ten, twenty, or even more. Giles Farnaby's Variation for Virginals on the tune *Loth to Depart, Masterpieces,* no. 29, shows how ornamental figures were used in variations of the late sixteenth century. The appeal of such pieces, then as now, is the fresh quality of texture, movement, and expression given to a familiar musical idea.

Another type of elaboration in Renaissance music is found in the *intonations, preludes,* and *toccatas,* principally for organ, which preceded the singing of motets and other church music. These may originally have served to give the singers the *tone* on which they were to begin or to make the tonic note of the mode clear to them. From a few simple chords and running passages that occupied a moment or two of time, these studies gradually became more and more elaborate until works of monumental scope were produced. As befits the situation wherein the performer is at liberty to improvise freely, these studies began to display brilliant virtuoso passages, making use of all the coloristic potentialities of the instrument. The great organ toccatas and preludes of Johann Sebastian Bach are direct descendants of these early organ intonations, themselves expanded from a single tone! Ponder this when next you hear Bach's Toccata and Fugue in D minor. A longer work which exemplifies this procedure in Renaissance music is Claudio Merulo's Toccata, *Treasury*, no. 29.

Lute and string players also liked to exercise themselves upon their instruments, possibly before launching into the principal musical business, a dance, a song, or a set of variations. These exercises, called *ricercare,* from the verb meaning "to search," or possibly designated as *tastar de corde,* "touching of the strings," exhibited the distinctive sonorities of the instruments and their special capacities for brilliant technical display. *Full chords,* to emphasize rich resonance, and *rapid passages,* to show off agility, alternated in such pieces. Thus, the form was built on bold contrasts. The term "ricercar" also applies to the sacred counterpart of the canzona francese; such ricercare were based on the motet either through transcription of a motet or through imitation of the motet style.

Addition, elaboration, and improvisation represent typical attitudes toward the use of musical material, not only in Renaissance and medieval music, but also throughout the history of Western music to the present day. Here the emphasis is not so much upon originality or discovery as upon taste, distinction, and the resourcefulness of the composer to create an individual work. In the Renaissance the amount of borrowing ranged from entire compositions, such as motets or chansons, down to small melodic fragments; the borrowed material helped either to create a framework for the new piece or to establish points of structural reference.

IMITATION

Returning to Josquin's motet, we recall that the treatment of the plainsong as a cantus firmus differs considerably from the medieval procedure. Here, the plainsong is no longer an underpinning but becomes the melodic source for a series of *imitations* which carry throughout the entire piece. Imitation, then, is one of the principal structural features of this piece, as it is in a great deal of Renaissance music.

Earlier we saw how melodic and rhythmic motives began to take shape in measured organum; frequently these motives were traded off between the upper voices. These voices were thus imitating each other from time to time; thereby, they created a clearly recognized kind of melodic statement and counterstatement. But the kind of imitation that began to permeate the music of the mid-fifteenth century is not the casual exchange of voices we heard in measured organum. In Renaissance imitation the texture is cumulative, for as each voice enters, those already singing continue to spin out their figures. A set of entries of this kind is called an *exposition* or *point of imitation*. Eventually, a cadence is made and a new exposition may follow. In fact, the entire form of a composition may be made up from a series of expositions. In Renaissance compositions based upon points of imitation, the composer would tend to invent or use new material for each succeeding section. (Baroque fugues generally used the same theme for all entries.) One procedure frequently employed was to draw the subjects of the points of imitation from the plainsong on which a motet was based, as Josquin did in his *Ave Maria, Masterpieces,* no. 19. In Example 4·5 one point of imitation is shown; the imitated material in it is marked by brackets.

EXAMPLE 4·5 Josquin Deprès: *Absalon fili mihi*

Most of the imitation you will hear in Renaissance music is *free imitation,* in which the successive entries sing the same basic motive yet do not repeat exactly what the preceding voices have sung. Much freedom could be attained without losing the sense of imitation which is all-important in this technique of composition. For example, in the Lassus motet, *Masterpieces,* no. 23, each voice enters with the characteristic three-note motive which is the subject of the first phase of imitation; yet some of the voices sing a different version of the motive, and the first voice sings it upside down! Still we have no trouble in recognizing the basic motive in each entry. Working with such short flexible motives, the composer could handle his part writing very freely and constantly discover opportunities for fresh movement. Not only was free imitation by far the most useful and prevalent type in the Renaissance, but it has dominated contrapuntal composition from that time to the present day. It is an ideal vehicle for retaining coherence in a composition and at the same time maintaining movement. Free imitation lends itself to the exposition type of structure whereby voices can merge at a cadence and then start anew.

FAMILIAR STYLE

The polyphonic music we have been describing scans the text very freely, or not at all, in a poetic sense. One word, even a syllable, may extend over an entire melodic phrase. With regard to the text this often becomes a melismatic style. At the other extreme is a style which we discover in many types of Renaissance music, a style in which the text is declaimed by a group of voices, all singing in a set rhythmic pattern according to the scansion of the text. This is a chordal style, which can be described texturally as isometric (see page 60). It has been given the name *familiar style*. Familiar style is similar to present-day church hymn music. Here the text occupies an important place in the attention of the listener from note to note. The length and structure of the text determine partly how the music will be put together. Familiar style appears throughout the sixteenth century in short sacred and secular works as well as in parts of more extended works. Its simplicity and directness commended it to the Calvinists, and it was the only kind of singing allowed in their churches.

REPETITION AND CONTRAST

As a rule, Renaissance music tends to be *through-composed*, that is, each phrase or each section is freshly composed or worked over. Literal repetitions are relatively infrequent, yet the principle of repetition does operate to bind the music together thematically. Imitation itself is a kind of varied repetition. Moreover, in Josquin's motet, and in much Renaissance music, we hear responsory or echo effects in which one phrase is restated at a different pitch by different voices. This suggests a tiny, balanced, two-part structure embedded within the larger flow of the entire piece.

We do hear repetitions of phrases in the manner of refrains in many secular compositions of the Renaissance. Here an especially striking turn or poignant phrase reappears to emphasize the expressive quality and to bind the form together a bit more clearly. For example, in Marenzio's madrigal *S'io parto,* the phrase *dolorosa partita* (this sad departure), is heard twice at different points in the piece with virtually the identical musical setting, *Masterpieces,* no. 27.

In a style as consistent and smoothly flowing as that of Renaissance music, contrast makes itself felt in a rather subdued and subtle manner. We have nothing of the bold contrasts we associate with symphonic music of a later age. Still, in Josquin's motet, the play of delicate contrasts throws light and shadow and gives distinct profile to the various phrases of the work. Consider the shift from one range to another, the change of motive from a relatively slow subject to one that is quicker, the concentration on major-triad sounds, as at the very beginning, compared with the strong minor flavor elsewhere and at the end. We have already mentioned the shift in meter as a basic structural contrast. Later Renaissance music often veers toward bolder contrast effects, particularly those dealing with harmonic shifts, as in the Marenzio madrigal cited above.

Starting with his subject or his model, the Renaissance composer worked out his composition by imitation or elaboration, or very possibly both. He led the voices smoothly through the consonant harmonic combinations and the suspensions which made up typical Renaissance chord forms. The inner shape and the length of the form were controlled by the various cadences within the piece and by the length of the text or the cantus firmus. These were all quite flexible and were handled differently in each piece. Nevertheless, some well-defined plan is discernible in each piece, representing special applications of the general principles we have been discussing. For purposes of illustration, let us see how a contrapuntal work, the motet *Tristis est anima mea, Masterpieces,* no. 23, has been shaped.

1. Listening to the whole piece, we are aware of the continuing contrapuntal activity organized imitatively. Yet, by contrast, the two sections in chordal style, the *Nunc videbitis* (Now you will see) and the *Ego vadam immolari* (I go to be sacrificed), stand out as being particularly expressive accents.
2. Harmonically, most of the piece appears to remain in the tonal center first established. But we have a striking episode of harmonic contrast when the text gives the words *circumdabit me* (surround me). The motive used at this point is a pictorial representation of the act of surrounding, since it is circular in shape.
3. There are five points of imitation contrasted to the two sections in chordal style. These begin with the following texts:
   a. *Tristis,* a slow and melodically quiet subject
   b. *Sustinete* (Tarry), a somewhat quicker subject with entries coming very quickly
   c. *Et vigilate mecum* (And watch with me), a quick, melodically active subject, treated more broadly and intensively than the first two subjects

   Up to this point there is a steady increase in the pace and intensity of movement.

   d. *Nunc videbitis,* the first section in chordal style, representing a dramatically contrasted slowdown after the accumulated momentum of the previous music

e. *Quae circumdabit,* an intensive treatment of the circular motive, representing the most striking harmonic digression within the piece
f. *Vos fugam* (You will take flight), another tightly woven imitative section, again pictorial in its representation of flight (the term *fugue* in music is derived from the Latin word for flight), the voices here continually chasing each other
g. *Ego vadam,* in a slightly ornamental chordal style

4. In order to create a convincing sense of final arrival, the composer has established a strong harmonic drive. You can hear the bass sustaining the dominant tone of the mode, while the action intensifies by means of the running figures that imitate each other closely in the upper voices. The bass here is a center of gravitation that prevents the flight of the melodic voices from breaking away entirely. This drive to the cadence at the end of a piece is a characteristic feature of Roman and Flemish music of the Renaissance. In this piece, it establishes a large-scale contrast between the continuous and flowing movement within the structure and the sense of arrival at the end.

EXAMPLE 4·6 Diagram of drive to cadence in Lassus: *Tristis*

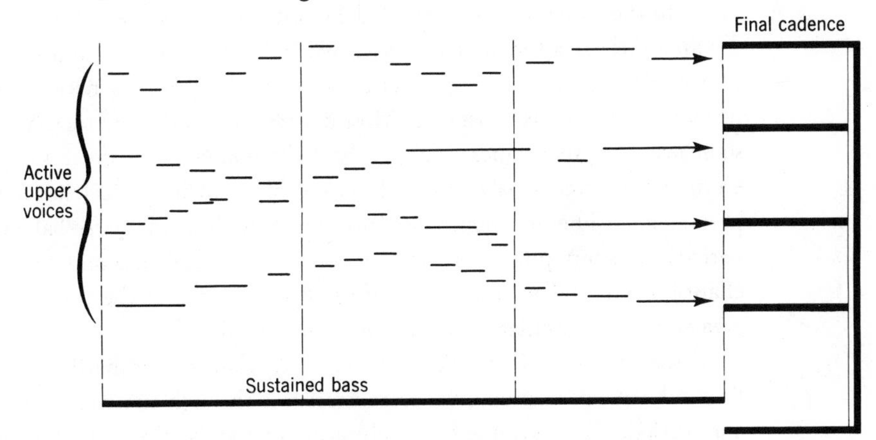

5. Most of the inner cadences which ended points of imitation were covered by new movement, as in the following manner:

(new entry)
tristis est anima mea
tristis est anima mea
(arrival)

or: (new entry)
vos fugam capietis
circumdabit me
(arrival)

From our discussion above, it should now be quite apparent that in listening to a polyphonic piece, it is well to become acquainted with the text beforehand. The composer frequently makes musical references to the meaning of the text, either by creating a general expressive quality befitting the words or by specific instances of pictorialism or expressive nuance. Without knowing the text, the listener will be confused by the mixture of several voices singing different words at the same time.

SYMMETRY IN RENAISSANCE MUSIC: THE DANCE

In the Renaissance music we have examined, there seemed to be relatively little regularity of phrasing. Balanced statement-counterstatement relationships were rare. The polyphonic texture gave rise to a continuous flow which did not admit evenly spaced articulations. In another area of Renaissance music, symmetry is present because it is essential to the spirit and form of the expression. This area is dance music.

During the Renaissance there was an ever-growing interest in dancing and in dance music. Dancing was one of the essential items in the training of a gentleman or lady. Art and literature provide ample testimony to the range and variety of dances during the sixteenth century. Thoinot Arbeau's *Orchésographie,* a work devoted entirely to a discussion of dances and dancing, lists many dances of various nations performed during the Renaissance. Most dances were for polite society, but some were popular tunes, such as the *Gassenhawer,* the street song of Germany, that curiously foreshadows the blues in its typical harmonic progressions. The prevalence of dance music, with its regularly balanced periods, its short phases of movement, its steady accents, and its penchant for what we would call *tunefulness* is evidence of the continually greater role that secular music was beginning to play.

As we have seen in medieval dances, dance music ordinarily crystallizes into two-part structures, from measures through motives, phrases, and periods. The symmetry of physical motion is bilateral, step and counterstep, thrust and counterthrust. In Renaissance dance music, this two-part relationship of phrases and periods was carried out to the extent that separate dances were often paired. A fast dance would follow a slow dance; often in such pairs of dances, the second would be a variation upon the first, as in Lute Dances, no. 22 of *Masterpieces.*

There was a great variety of dances in the sixteenth century. Below are listed some of the more popular types and their special characteristics:

Pavane: a slow dance in duple time, perfomed with ceremonious solemnity after the manner of the peacock, *pavo,* from which it derived its name

Galliard: a rather quick dance in triple time, the after-dance of the pavane
Allemande: a dance of moderate pace in duple time, rather reserved in its motions; its name is the French word for "German."
Courante: a dance of moderately quick pace in triple time, deriving its name from the French *courant,* "running"; the after-dance of the allemande
Passamezzo: a pavane of somewhat quicker pace
Saltarello: the after-dance of the passamezzo, in triple time, quick pace
Branle: a name given to a number of different dances in the sixteenth century, all characterized by being danced in groups, rather than by pairs of dancers
Morisca: an exotic dance, danced in pantomime with grotesque Moorish make-up and costumes; the ancestor of the Morris dance

Dance compositions were popular during this period; they circulated among musicians and frequently were used as subjects for sets of variations. From this time onward, the dance was an important medium of musical composition, and it soon became a formidable influence upon other kinds of music.

Songs were closely allied to dances. When poetry whose lines were equal in length was set to music, the result was a symmetrical structure. In fact some compositions were both danced and sung. The Lute Ayre, *My Thoughts Are Winged with Hope, Treasury,* no. 34, by John Dowland, is composed of six equal phrases, each containing twelve beats. The cadences of the successive phrases can easily be heard, giving a clear sense of open and closed punctuation. Rhythmically, this piece resembles the courante. It also has the pairing of phrases and cadences we heard earlier in the estampie.

The form of Renaissance music may be summarized as follows:

1. Addition and elaboration
   a. Preexisting material (cantus firmus) from sacred and secular sources
   b. Motto subjects
   c. Parody, using all or part of a previously composed work
   d. Transcription and ornamentation of a previously composed work
   e. Variation
   f. Elaborations on a tone
2. Imitation, strict and free
3. Control of the extent of a composition by the text
4. Repetition and contrast of sections
5. Distribution and strength of cadences and tonal centers
6. Balance of phrases and periods in dance music

National Styles in Renaissance Music

During the first half of the Renaissance the countries in the northwestern part of Europe—the Low Countries, Burgundy, and France—took the leadership in musical composition. Flemish composers were the acknowledged masters of their art in all Europe. After the defeat of Charles of Burgundy by the French in 1477 and the incorporation of Burgundy into the French kingdom, Flemish composers began to migrate to other centers of Europe, and particularly to Italy. Wherever they went, they introduced their own craft of composition, adapting it to the local conditions which they discovered. For example, in Venice they developed the polychoral style, taking advantage of the wonderful resonances in St. Mark's Cathedral, which is built on the plan of a Greek cross with four arms. Vocal and instrumental groups were placed in the arms of the cross and answered each other back and forth.

In addition to the travels of Renaissance musicians, which carried musical information by word of mouth, the invention of a practical system of music printing about 1500 increased the dissemination of musical techniques. A give-and-take among composers was facilitated; refinements and innovations were transmitted quickly. Music printing is the counterpart of letter printing, invented by Gutenberg.

ITALIAN MADRIGAL

From about 1500, throughout the century, Italy was the battlefield for the powerful rulers of Europe, those of France, Spain, and Germany, who took advantage of the internal struggles between the Italian states to form alliances and to claim sovereignty. Such struggles established lines of communication to various important points in Italy (Rome, Florence, Naples, etc.), and musicians went along with the armies. It became the fashion to employ Flemish musicians in the chapels and courts of Italy, and so Italy, the theater of war, became also the center for the musical art of the sixteenth century, as it was for literature and painting.

In Italy, Flemish masters found a popular, attractive, yet undeveloped form in the *frottola.* The frottola was composed in familiar style to poetry that had popular appeal yet little elegance or distinction, as for example in Marchetto Cara's frottola *O mia cieca* (Oh, My Fate), *Treasury,* no. 20. By applying their learned techniques and their polished expressive manner to the clear, dancelike forms of popular music of the Italians, Flemish composers evolved the *madrigal,* which is perhaps the most representative and comprehensive embodiment of Renaissance music, both technically and aesthetically. The Italian madrigal is the secular counterpart of the motet, imitative in style and rather similar in harmonic procedure. It became increasingly dedicated to the expression of intense and even violent personal feelings. Musically, this involved more pictorialism, a greater amount of dissonance, striking chromatic shifts, and bolder contrasts between sections and phrases. The Italian madrigal represents one of the forces that eventually destroyed the evenly flowing consistency of Renaissance music and ushered in the Baroque era.

Marenzio's madrigal *S'io parto* represents the Italian secular vocal style at its full flower. It has many special moments of striking emotional expressiveness, yet retains the sense of polyphonic movement that characterizes Renaissance music (see page 117). It is written in the Dorian mode, proper for a sad subject.

ENGLISH MADRIGAL

This was a secular form strongly influenced by the Italian madrigal. It was cultivated during the height of the Elizabethan and Jacobean periods, from about 1590 on. Stylistically it is much like its Italian counterpart, but it shows distinctive qualities of its own, particularly in its touches of fanciful humor and its delightful play upon the rhythms of the English language, in which frequent shifts between various kinds of duple and triple meter create a buoyant yet subtle imbalance in the quality of movement.

The most important collection of English madrigals is *The Triumphs of Oriana*. Many composers contributed to this collection. One of the most brilliant works of the entire set is Weelkes's *As Vesta Was from Latmos Hill Descending*. This piece has a most ingratiating manner; it is full of clever and subtle pictorialism, as noted below:

As Vesta was from Latmos Hill: declaratory opening, full ensemble
Running down amain: descending figures succeeding each other in quick imitations
Two by two: two voices; *three by three:* three voices; *all alone:* solo
Mingling with: intertwining imitative figures
Long live fair Oriana: much-repeated fanfare figures using tonic and dominant harmonies; strong sense of cadential arrival

FRENCH CHANSON

The chanson was the principal French secular form of the Renaissance. It generally dealt with pastoral or amorous subjects, although some highly entertaining descriptive chansons were written in which vivid pictorialism abounded. The chanson was generally imitative in procedure, but the main interest lay in lively dancelike rhythms, rather than in well-rounded melodic phrases. Indeed, this form and its instrumental counterpart, the canzona francese, can be identified by the rhythmic pattern 𝅗𝅥 ♩ ♩ (long short short) which is found at the beginning of most chansons. In some chansons the harmony for long sections alternates between the familiar tonic, dominant, and subdominant chords, a procedure quite different from the subtle shifts of harmony found in the motet. This gives the chanson a modern sound at times.

Thomas Crequillon's chanson *Pour un plaisir* (For a Pleasure), *Masterpieces,* no. 20, is typical of its genre. A very entertaining variety of chanson is the program chanson, which describes special scenes or actions with vivid pictorial effects. Clément Jannequin's *La Guerre* (The War), which tells the story of the battle of Marignan with sounds that describe fanfares, drums, encounters, and the like, is one of the most famous pieces of the entire chanson literature.

French vocal music has traditionally been concerned with a proper and clear declamation of the text, particularly in reference to the length of syllables. Hence, the chanson frequently employs familiar style. One group of poets and composers went so far as to set up strict conditions for measuring music according to the text. They created *vers mesuré,* in which the rhythmic freedom of any voice, or of the entire ensemble, was subordinate to poetic scansion.

GERMAN CHORALE

Martin Luther and other early leaders in the Protestant Reformation encouraged their congregations to take part in the musical portion of the church service. Luther helped to compile collections of *chorales* (hymn tunes with German texts) that could be sung by the worshipers. Lutheran composers quickly took these tunes as the basis for works that resembled the imitative motet with cantus firmus. Later in the sixteenth century, in line with the more direct, down-to-earth religious outlook of the Reformation, composers wrote simpler versions of the chorales, using familiar style. As a rule, then, the chorale tended to be shorter, simpler, and far less pictorial than the motet. The French counterpart of the chorale was the *psalm,* and in England the Anglican church developed a form of sacred song called the *anthem.*

In *Aus tiefer Not, 2000 Years of Music,* no. 10, we can hear an example of the early German chorale. Although it has some contrapuntal action, the interest centers on the chorale melody in the top voice. Note how rarely a major chord is heard. The dark, minor sounds of this piece suggest very strongly the sense of the text "Out of the deepest need, I call to Thee." Listen also to Johann Walther's chorale *Komm, Gott Schöpfer* (Come, God the Creator), *Treasury*, no. 24.

If we were to list the various media, forms, and styles of Renaissance music, sacred and secular, vocal and instrumental, Italian, French, Spanish, German, English, we should see that in spite of the general uniformity of style that governed music of this era, there was a rich variety of local color and expression. Indeed, sometimes the differences are much more noticeable than the underlying unity of style, as we heard when we contrasted the Lassus motet with a set of keyboard variations.

Music historians have borrowed the term *Renaissance* from the history of art, literature, and ideas because music paralleled these other aspects of culture both in time and in certain characteristic features. *Humanism* is the term that Renaissance historians apply to the spirit of this age. Specifically it refers to a new interest in the ancient classic culture of Greece and Rome and the application of classic ideas in literature of the sixteenth century. In a broader sense, and this interests us much more, humanism refers to the new attitudes of the Renaissance, which, as Michelet, the French historian put it, led to the "discovery of the world, the discovery of man." Evidences of this spirit of inquiry are found in Leonardo da Vinci's scientific interest, particularly his studies of anatomy, in Copernicus's new theories of astronomy, in the development of the science of perspective by Renaissance painters, and in the penetrating and comprehensive search into human motivations and emotions which Shakespeare's plays embody. Musically, we find analogies to perspective in the creation of a true bass function in harmony. The awakening of the scientific spirit of inquiry might be compared to the development of a balanced, clear, and logical relationship between tones and voices which consonant, triadic harmony and imitation brought about. Strong personal feelings in drama and poetry are matched boldly by the emphasis on expressive devices and moods, both in the madrigal and the motet.

Historically, the Renaissance saw the first comprehensive effort to break away from the twin authorities of Church and Empire. Political and religious movements had repercussions in the field of fine arts. Much of the music we have examined in this chapter is secular in nature. Both the motivation and the means were present for the Renaissance man to express himself in a personal, warm, and often impassioned

FIGURE 3. Michelangelo: Engraving of the gate called Flaminia but now called del Popolo. Note the symmetry of the design and the combination of classical elements (arch and column) with Christian motifs (keys and papal tiara). (Courtesy of the Stanford University Libraries.)

style. He no longer was concerned entirely with reframing and renewing hieratic, absolute values; rather his attention turned to his own feelings and the way in which he observed the real world around him, the world of senses and solidity.

In the area of religion, the great, conclusive event was the Reformation, the establishment of new churches, locally controlled, speaking the language of their own country. Not long after, in the middle of the sixteenth century, the Catholic Church took steps to counteract this centrifugal tendency that was manifested on all sides, and in the Counter Reformation, made efforts to reorganize itself and reestablish its supreme authority. The sacred music of Lassus and Palestrina which we have heard was composed in the spirit of the Counter Reformation. Although in many respects it embodies the ideals of Renaissance art in its evenness, balance, smooth flow, and harmonious relationship between all parts, it avoids completely that sense of worldly delight and bold emotional projection which was the guiding spirit in the aesthetics of Renaissance art. To this extent, Roman polyphony is anti-Renaissance; it points to certain mystic qualities found in the art of the seventeenth century.

A great deal of Renaissance music was written to be performed on grand occasions, solemn or festive. There was also music written for performance by musical amateurs in the home, at court, or among friends. Music was one of the graces that had a place in the education of the ideal man of the Renaissance. Dancing, poetry, classics, and music were part of his accomplishments. The satisfactions he received from performing madrigals, dance pieces, or other compositions for en semble can be re-created by the modern amateur if he has any training in vocal or instrumental performance. Indeed, he will receive a truer picture of Renaissance music and a deeper personal musical satisfaction if he can perform this music rather than listen to it in concert, a purpose for which it may never have been intended.

The points we have covered in dealing with Renaissance music may be summarized as follows:

1. ***Qualities of sound*** (texture, harmony): consonance, triads, careful use of dissonance; occasional striking chromaticism; development of a true bass; formulation of strong cadences; some codification of chord progression; fuller sound due to greater number of voices; subtle effects of contrast
2. ***Qualities of movement:*** steady, evenly flowing, moderate pace; short, symmetrical phases of movement in dances; long, nonsymmetrical phases of movement with much overlap in polyphonic pieces; some variation within the basic pace due to note values and rhythmic patterns employed

3. ***Form-building factors:*** addition and elaboration upon preexisting material; paraphrase of entire pieces; free ornamentation, imitation, dance forms, repetition, and contrast of material occasionally
4. ***Style and expression:*** growth of secular music and distinctions between national styles; development of an important instrumental music; concern with musical representation of feelings; faithful yet subtle delineation of the text in music; control of expressive values by well-defined musical procedures, such as consonance-dissonance relationships; sense of steady rhythmic flow

Genres and Compositions Discussed in This Chapter

Vocal music, sacred

Mass: *Dufay:* Gloria; *Dufay:* Kyrie from Mass *Se la face ay pâle* (If My Face Is Pale), *Masterpieces,* no. 15; *Palestrina: Agnus Dei* I from Mass *Veni sponsa Christi* (Come, Bride of Christ), *Masterpieces,* no. 24; *Deprès: Missa Hercules*
Motet: *Lassus: Tristis est anima mea* (Sad Is My Soul), *Masterpieces,* no 23; *Deprès: Ave Maria, Masterpieces,* no. 19
Chorale: *Walther: Aus tiefer Not* (Out of the Deepest Need), *2000 Years,* no. 10; *Walther: Komm, Gott Schöpfer* (Come, God the Creator), *Treasury,* no. 24

Vocal music, secular

Chanson: *Crequillon: Pour un plaisir* (For a Pleasure), *Masterpieces,* no. 20
Frottola: *Cara: O mia cieca* (Oh, My Fate), *Treasury,* no. 20
Madrigal, English: *Bennet: Thyrsis, Masterpieces,* no. 28; *Weelkes: As Vesta Was from Latmos Hill Descending*
Madrigal, Italian: *Marenzio: S'io parto* (If I Leave), *Masterpieces,* no. 27

Instrumental music

Canzona francese: *Gabrieli, A.: Pour un plaisir* (For a Pleasure), *Masterpieces,* no. 21
Dances: *Lute dances, Masterpieces,* no. 22 (see also summary in text, page 132)
Toccata (intonation, prelude, fantasia, ricercar): *Merulo:* Toccata, *Treasury,* no. 29
Variations: *Farnaby: Loth to Depart, Masterpieces,* no. 29

Throughout this chapter the unity of Renaissance musical style was the basis from which we proceeded to examine the various facets of that style. Within this unity there was much apparent diversity of procedure. For historians, the end of the Renaissance is marked by a split, a destruction of the basic unity of style; this came partly from the intensification of diverse elements and partly from a new view of musical expression and how it was to be achieved. In the following chapter, we shall observe some of the results of that separation.

Suggestions for Critical Listening

1. ***Sound***
   - *a.* Range: high, low, middle, fluctuating
   - *b.* Amount: number of voices; constant, varied
   - *c.* Timbre: blended, contrasted; voices, instruments (number of each)
2. ***Movement; meter and rhythm***
   - *a.* Pace: slow, quick, moderate
   - *b.* Regularity: maintained, broken
   - *c.* Articulation: continuous, interrupted flow
   - *d.* Groupings: by two, by three, shifting; clear, unclear
   - *e.* Intensity: vigorous, gentle
3. ***Arrival***
   - *a.* Clear, unclear; emphatic, light; final, nonfinal; frequent, widely spaced points of arrival
   - *b.* Approach: strong, light
4. ***Melody***
   - *a.* Type of contour; position of apex, if present
   - *b.* Motives: clearly defined, not clearly defined; repeated, varied, contrasted; degree of "tunefulness"
5. ***Texture***
   - *a.* Interaction of voices: imitation, nonimitative polyphony, familiar style, melody and accompaniment, give-and-take
   - *b.* Relation of performance media to text: blend or separation of various parts
6. ***Harmony***
   - *a.* Emphasis on particular values: major, minor chords; dissonance; chromaticism
   - *b.* Types of cadence: authentic, half, plagal, deceptive, Phrygian
7. ***Structure; statement and counterstatement***
   - *a.* Phrases: long, short; equal, unequal in length; well marked, overlapping
   - *b.* Principal sections: number of sections; repetition, contrast
   - *c.* Use of compositional techniques: imitation, ornamentation, cantus firmus
8. ***Relation of music and text***
   - *a.* Familiar style, melismatic, combination of styles
   - *b.* Expressive quality: general mood of text, pictorialism, special points of expressive emphasis or color
9. ***Type of piece*** (see Genres and Compositions, page 140)

Suggested Listening Projects

1. **Canzona *Tsaat een meeskin, L'Anthologie Sonore,* Vol. 1**

   Listen for: Regular pulse; imitation; use of syncopation; systematic give-and-take among instruments; indications of sectional structure; contrast in change of meter; lack of harmonic contrast. Imagine the enjoyment of playing such a piece. With present-day instruments, this could be easily performed by guitar, flute, and two strings.

2. **Frottola *Dal letto me levava* (I Rose from My Bed), *2000 Years of Music,* no. 7**

   Listen for: Emphasis on compact chordal texture; lively counter rhythms and give-and-take effects; strong cadences; short phrases; lack of melodic elegance; straightforward, gay manner of piece.

3. **Motet *Miserere Mei* (Woe Is Me) (Lassus), *2000 Years of Music,* no. 12**

   Listen for: Emphasis on dark colors; fluctuation between imitative counterpoint and declamatory passages; low center of sound; suavity of movement; arching melodic lines; careful approach and departure from the melodic apices of the piece; strong sense of tonal center; powerful cadences. Relate these to the tragic sense of the text.

4. **Polychoral motet *Laudate Dominum* (Praise God) (Hassler), *Treasury,* no. 28**

   Listen for: Well-delineated structure outlined by contrasts between imitation and familiar style, by alternation of high (women's voices) and low (men's voices) levels of sound, and by effect of arrival when both groups sing together at the end; broad cadences (plagal cadence at end of piece); bright quality of sound; broad melodic lines within a rather narrow range; some repetition of chord progressions; varied restatement of figure first assigned to men's voices; change of meter and pace near end of piece.

chapter five

Baroque Music

The era of baroque music extended from 1600 to 1750. As applied to music, the term "baroque," like "Renaissance," is borrowed from art history. In architecture, baroque style is characterized by certain distortions and transformations of Renaissance style and was originally a term of opprobrium, derived from the word *barroco,* meaning misshaped pearl.

Unlike the Renaissance, the Baroque period in music does not represent a uniformity and refinement of practice throughout its 150 years. Rather, the music falls into three fairly well-defined phases, designated as *early, middle,* and *late baroque.* The dates given below are only approximate.

Early Baroque (ca. 1600-1620)

GENERAL CHARACTERISTICS

Striking changes in musical style appeared to take place around the year 1600. If you listen to such compositions as Giovanni Gabrieli's motet for two choirs with organ and instruments, *In ecclesiis* (In the Congregation), or Giulio Caccini's madrigal for solo voice and lute, *Dovrò dunque morire* (Must I Die, Then) or Claudio Monteverdi's

FIGURE 4. J. Callot: *The Exodus of Israel*. A seventeenth century engraving. Note the intensity of effect created by the grotesque border and the displacement of the groups in the scene itself, requiring the viewer to imagine himself looking from the extreme left to appreciate the symmetry. (Courtesy of Dr. Leon Kolb, San Francisco.)

madrigal for five voices, *Ohimè, se tanto amate* (Alas! If You Love So Much), you will find that they project an entirely different quality of sound and movement than is heard in pieces which are typical of the late Renaissance. In Gabrieli's music we hear (1) brilliant contrasts in qualities of sound; (2) sudden changes in pace and quality of movement; (3) short phases of movement; (4) striking dissonances and frequent cadences.

In the Caccini piece we hear (1) a solo voice separated from an instrumental accompaniment, instead of a number of equally important participants; (2) a stop-and-start quality of movement suggesting outbursts of feeling; (3) frequent cadences; (4) a declamatory manner, intensely personal in feeling.

In the Monteverdi piece we hear (1) again a stop-and-start quality of movement; (2) striking dissonances; (3) contrasts in texture; (4) abrupt changes of manner.

These pieces represent the drastic changes of style that seemed to overtake music about 1600, particularly in Italy. Striking, dramatic, intense, violent, and bizarre effects were sought, instead of the continuous flow and the carefully woven counterpoint of Roman sacred polyphony which, in each piece, embodied but a single, thoroughly controlled expressive idea. The conflict between the two styles was reflected in the writings of musicians at this time. Some, upholding the old style, or *prima prattica,* as it was called, spoke for the polish, skill, and balance of the music itself. They believed music to be more important than the text. Others, championing the modern style, called the *seconda prattica,* felt that music should serve the words, that any device or effect that would intensify the dramatic value should be used, regardless of its consistency or lack of consistency with traditional usage. Music history shows no lack of such controversies between the old and the new. They have flared up as far back as the time of the Ars antiqua, and they rage today between the proponents of conservative and progressive music.

Some of the later music of the Renaissance anticipated the striking changes in musical style that were to take place at the beginning of the Baroque period:

1. Chromaticism was introduced, along with increasingly bold shifts of tonal center, especially in the madrigal.
2. Instrumental music grew, leading to brilliant techniques of improvisation and to the exploitation of contrasting sonorities of instruments and voices.
3. There was a tendency, in compositions scored for four or more voices, to divide the group, sharpening the effect of contrast and delineating phrase structure clearly.

FIGURE 5. Abraham Bosse: *Music Party*. A seventeenth century engraving. (Courtesy of the Metropolitan Museum of Art.)

4. Instruments were substituted for voices, which often resulted in featuring a solo voice that was accompanied.

CONTRAST AND CONCERTATO

The watchword of early baroque music is *contrast.* Contrast intensifies the dramatic values in a composition by throwing individual moments or statements into high relief. In the examples cited above we heard contrasts of sonority, of mood, of movement—often projected within very short phases of movement. Structurally, the effect of such contrast is to destroy the continuous flow; the long line of Renaissance music now has become a series of short, often powerful thrusts. A sectionalized form is thus created, which enables the composer to emphasize a single and striking musical idea. In such a layout, repetition can be used to bind the piece into a unified whole. This is apparent in Gabrieli's *In ecclesiis.* We hear many repetitions, some of which are immediate restatements of a preceding phrase and others of which recall entire sections heard previously. An outline of this work follows:

EXAMPLE 5·1 Outline of Gabrieli: *In ecclesiis*

A. *In ecclesiis* (In the Congregation), soprano; declamatory style	10 measures
B. Alleluia, chorus II alternating with soprano I	9 measures
C. *In omni loco* (In every place), tenor I; declamatory style	23 measures
B. Alleluia, chorus II alternating with soprano I	8 measures
D. Sinfonia: instruments in canzona style	16 measures
E. *In Deo* (In God), alto I, tenor I; short points of imitation	45 measures
B. Alleluia, choruses I and II alternating	9 measures
F. *Deus meus* (My God), soprano I, tenor I; short points of imitation	43 measures
B. Alleluia, choruses I and II	10 measures
G. *Deus adjutor* (God our advocate) choruses I and II (note chromaticism and dissonance)	25 measures
B. Alleluia, choruses I and II (note broadened cadence)	17 measures

The sectional structure, which has a very different effect upon the continuity than the flowing Renaissance style, gives rise to strong inner symmetries (compare sections C and G, E and F) and permits the Alleluia to act as a refrain which binds the form tightly.

One of the chief appeals of *In ecclesiis* is the range and variety of its sonorities. Such contrasts of sonority, created by dividing the total ensemble into smaller groups or single parts and setting them against each other boldly, represent the practice called *concertato*. This means "striving together." The concertato technique is the forerunner of the *concerto* of later baroque music. From this time on, its influence pervades virtually all types of music even to the present day. When a modern symphony sets full orchestra against a few instruments in alternation or makes use of contrasts in color, it is employing a procedure descended from early seventeenth-century concertato style.

HARMONIC SONORITIES; CADENCES; DISSONANCE

The play of sonorities in Gabrieli's piece is embodied in a texture which gives maximum brilliance and power to individual chord sounds. There is relatively little counterpoint, and imitation tends to be reduced to a mere give-and-take. Solid, full *chords* are frequently used for the impact of their particular quality of sound. These chords are the familiar chord types of Renaissance music, but they do not take shape simply as the result of evenly flowing melodic lines accommodating to each other harmonically by combinations of consonant intervals. Rather Gabrieli seems to have used them for their special distinctive sounds; he has considered them as entities, important and valuable in their own right. Example 5·2 illustrates the difference between a chordal section from the Gabrieli piece and the typical Renaissance method of obtaining chords by contrapuntal action.

EXAMPLE 5·2

a. Gabrieli. Solid, separate chords; strong, immediate impact

b. Renaissance. Combination of melodic lines to obtain chords

In the massive chordal texture of a piece such as Gabrieli's, cadences play a very important part in directing and controlling musical movement. The first forty-two measures contain at least twelve strong cadential progressions; the phases of movement are short and the punctuation is emphatic. Movement here is embodied in *harmony,* not in *line,* as in the typical Renaissance texture. As yet, however, the cadences do not focus clearly upon a central tone or key.

In this new style, each chord has considerable harmonic weight. Against such a center of harmonic gravity, it is possible to introduce melodic dissonances effectively for the sake of expressive accents and nuances. For example, at the very beginning of the recitative from Monteverdi's *Orfeo, Masterpieces,* no. 31, where the voice sings *Tu se' morta, mia vita* (You are dead, my life), the feeling of anguish is expressed by sharp dissonances in the voice against the sustained chord of the instruments.

The treatment of dissonance is one of the essential distinctions between Renaissance musical expression and that of the early Baroque. In Renaissance music, the dissonance is carefully reached and left; in early baroque music, the dissonance is often highlighted, with less concern for how it is approached and left. This distinction was the crux of the great controversy between the *prima prattica,* as represented by the style of Palestrina, and the *seconda prattica,* championed by Monteverdi (see page 145).

POLARITY OF TREBLE AND BASS; FIGURED BASS; TRIO-SONATA TEXTURE

In the recitative of Monteverdi that we have been examining, the solo voice is separated by range and color of sound from its chordal support. This creates a contrast instead of a blend in the texture. In this opposition appears one of the principal harmonic aspects of baroque music, i.e., the *polarity of the chordal element,* represented principally by the bass voice, against the uppermost or melodic voice. In Monteverdi's recitative, only the solo voice and the bass were actually composed. It was the responsibility of the keyboard performer (usually an organist or a harpsichordist) to supply the inner notes, to fill out the chord; in this he was generally guided by numbers which indicated what intervals should be played above the bass tone, as in Example 5·3. This system of harmonizing was called *figured bass,* and, as we can easily hear, the principal musical interest lies in the outer parts. We have a reduction of essential parts from four or five to only two; whatever other tones appear do so in order to make the harmony clear and to give a fuller sound.

The pitting of treble voices against the bass leads to a texture characteristic of a great deal of baroque music. It is generally called *trio-sonata*

EXAMPLE 5·3 Figured bass. Bach: Wachet auf (Sleepers, Awake), cantata

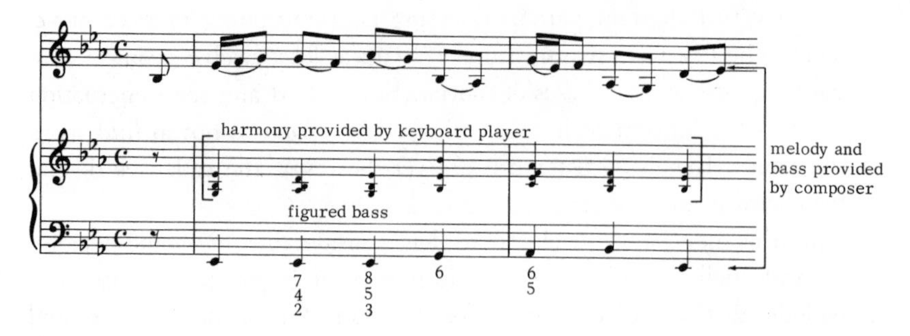

texture, since it is most clearly embodied in a form of composition called the *trio sonata.* In this texture, two competing solo instruments are heard in the treble range; these are supported by a continuous bass part, played by the left hand on a keyboard instrument and by a bass instrument, such as cello or viola da gamba. The right hand on the keyboard fills in the harmonies. Occasionally we hear a lute assuming the role of the keyboard *continuo.*

In the trio sonata, some of the most typical aspects of baroque texture appear in concentrated form. These are (1) polarity between the treble and bass, (2) concertato action in the solo instruments, and (3) chordal texture growing from the figured bass. Example 5·4, taken from a late baroque piece, illustrates trio-sonata layout.

EXAMPLE 5·4 Handel: Trio sonata in G minor, first movement

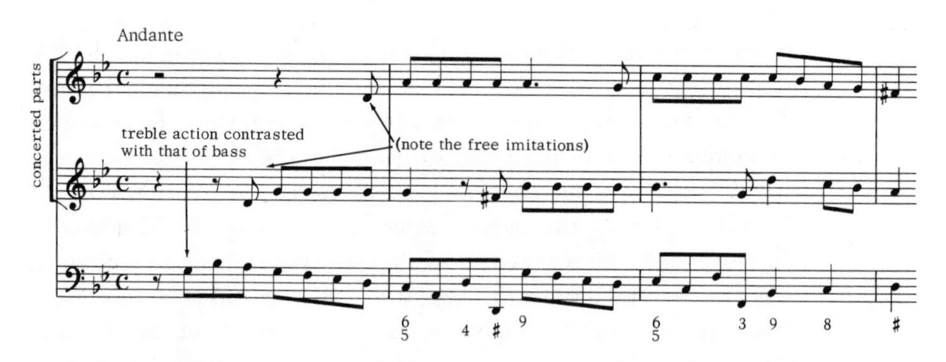

MONODY AND RECITATIVE

The separation of the melody from its harmonic web is most strikingly exemplified in the entirely new technique of composition described variously as *monody, recitative,* or *stile rappresentativo.* This manner, which we heard in the Caccini piece and the Monteverdi recitative, sets the voice free from the remainder of the texture and assigns to it a declamatory melodic line which reflects faithfully the flow of the poetry and its expressive nuances. In the pure recitative, there is no steady, well-defined beat or pulse nor any organization of the melodic line by salient motives. The expressive aim of monody, when it was created by a group of Florentines at the very end of the sixteenth century, was, as Caccini himself put it, "to imitate the conceit of the words." Music was the servant and not the master of the poetry. These Florentine musicians and noblemen, designating themselves the *Camerata,* claimed to rescue music from the artifices of the contrapuntalists and turn it once again to the service of Platonic ideals, to revive the ancient Greek drama in which music was supposed to have played an important yet subsidiary role.

The poets of the Camerata took old Greek tales, such as that of Orpheus and Eurydice, and gave them new dramatic form. These plays were then recited to music in the stile rappresentativo, each voice being accompanied by one or more instruments, which furnished the harmony. This was the beginning of *opera.* Jacopo Peri's *Euridice,* composed in 1600, exemplifies this new idea of the relationship of music and language. It was composed almost entirely in recitative. Although certain moments in this work are projected with dramatic force and intensity, the unrelieved declamation does not create and hold interest throughout the composition. Opera as a purely declaimed revival of Greek drama lasted but a few years. Musical impulses began very soon to assert themselves. Older procedures from polyphonic music were taken up again, and new techniques of composition were evolved, so that opera quickly acquired an independent inner strength based on the interplay of musical and dramatic values.

Monteverdi's *Orfeo,* composed in 1607, represents this new concept of operatic composition. It tells the same story as Peri's *Euridice,* but its internal structure is quite different. Instrumental sections, recitatives, and choruses, representing many different styles of composition, alternate in a lively and always interesting manner. The difference between Peri's and Monteverdi's works shows how opera grew quickly from a narrow, arbitrarily conceived process to one in which many different values and effects were gathered together into a unified yet diverse work. Peri's *Euridice* was conceived in the spirit of the Camerata; *Orfeo* already embodied those elements of dramatic contrast, of spectacle, of brilliant effect, that constitute, to this day, the principal appeal of opera.

The developments in early seventeenth-century music may be summarized briefly as follows:

1. Sectionalism in structure, evolved from the polychoral method of performance

2. The concertato style, combining voices and instruments
3. Further crystallization of harmonic procedures, involving greater concentration on cadential progressions and realized in the figured bass
4. The establishment of polarity in texture, standardized in trio-sonata layout
5. The invention of recitative, with its most significant embodiment in opera
6. Expressively, a style based on bold contrasts, intense outbursts of feeling, shifting qualities of movement, striking dissonances

The immediate appeal of this music must have been strong and compelling; much of it still is for today's listener. The first effects of these new processes were to destroy the continuity that characterized Renaissance music. But special qualities of sound, bold contrasts, and intense emotional outbursts were not enough to build musical movement and sustain it over any considerable period of time. For these purposes, certain procedures would have to be codified and strengthened, as was done in the second stage of baroque music, the middle Baroque.

Middle Baroque (ca. 1620-1680)

In order to see what direction the synthesis and codification of technique, form, and expression took during the middle Baroque period, we shall examine three works from the *Masterpieces* collection: no. 32, Giacomo Carissimi's Scene from *Judicium Salomonis* (The Judgment of Solomon); no. 33, Heinrich Schütz's Sacred Cantata, *O Herr, hilf* (O Lord, Help); and no. 36, Jean Baptiste Lully's Overture to *Armide*.

RECITATIVE

Although the Carissimi piece is written entirely in the recitative style, it does not speak to us in the strongly felt, intensely affective accents of Caccini and Monteverdi. It is quite straightforward—indeed, matter of fact—with the exception of the music of the First Mother, whose poignant distress is expressed by the minor mode, dissonances, chromaticism, and a halting manner of movement. Generally, the accompaniment is extremely simple; many of the chords are sustained for one and a half or two measures. The harmony is not venturesome; rather, it seems to be concerned with making cadences quite frequently. Structurally, we make out seven short but relatively self-contained sections. The last section, being a resolution of the problem and embodying Solomon's judgment in the case of the disputed infant, is somewhat longer than the preceding ones. Note that each of the mothers, in her second statement, echoes the latter part of her first statement. A clever bit of musical analogy takes places in the treatment of the word *dividatur,* that is, "divide." The second mother sings short notes (divisions of the longer note), reflecting her assent to the division, while the first mother sings long notes, protesting the "division" of the child.

The principal distinctions between this music and its early baroque counterparts lie in (1) the simplification of the recitative technique, in both voice and accompaniment; (2) the clearer feeling for tonal center; and (3) the reduction in the amount of striking dissonances previously used for affective purposes. The multisectional structure, on the other hand, suggests a retention of an early baroque formal layout.

The Carissimi excerpt shows what happened to the recitative in the mid-seventeenth century. It no longer assumes the burden of intense musical expression; it moves on a level, at a rather even pace; it is prose-like, declarative. As a type, this treatment of recitative turned out to be very useful for more than two centuries. In opera of the seventeenth, eighteenth, and nineteenth centuries, it served to compress a great deal of narrative or expository material into a relatively short period of time. In this kind of recitative, one does not linger; one hurries ahead. Only the few moments of the First Mother's music were strongly evocative; this kind of recitative represents a more songlike manner, also encountered in later dramatic music.

CONCERTATO PROCEDURE

Like recitative, the concertato style underwent changes during the middle of the seventeenth century. Schütz's Sacred Cantata illustrates what happened. This is a particularly apt example since Schütz was the pupil of Giovanni Gabrieli, the early Venetian master of the concertato technique of composition. First, we immediately notice that striking contrasts of sonority no longer occupy the composer's attention. In line with this, each section carries out one idea for a considerable length of time. The quality of movement is purposeful and vigorous; momentum is maintained by the interplay of motives being worked over very thoroughly. The concertato procedure is embodied in this motivic interplay; the give-and-take between voices and instruments is complex and close-grained. Gabrieli's stop-and-start effects are no longer present.

In this music long-range contrasts help to shape the form. There are three sections, varying in their qualities of movement. The first has a driving quality, in quick, energetic duple meter; the second section is smoother in movement, because of its triple meter; the third section picks up once more the driving quality of the first, but intensifies this vigorous manner by piling up closely spaced imitations and colliding dissonances within each phrase. In this third section, we feel a strong sense of cadential drive augmented by the accumulating dissonances. Thus the final part of this piece serves to round it off by aiming at emphatic points of arrival. Although the concertato procedure dominates this composition, the long-range harmonic drives, the steady vigorous pace, the systematic working over of motives (often in sequences), the elimination of striking contrast—all represent a drastic change from the early concertato manner of Gabrieli. With such compact and unified treatment, a strong sense of accumulation develops. Schütz's music foreshadows Bach's in this respect. The scoring is typically that of the trio sonata.

Lully's overture exploits the brilliance of instruments. The three sections of the piece carry out, at considerable length, (1) the movement of a stately ceremonial march, (2) a buoyant, swinging dance, and (3) a return to the broad manner of the opening march. Within each section, movement continues, well-marked and vigorous. Again we feel that a drive toward a cadential point of arrival focuses the harmonic movement in each section or phrase. Within each section we hear little contrast; on the other hand, the contrast between sections is marked.

Although these three compositions differ from each other in manner and purpose, they do illustrate some of the underlying processes in the development of musical structure during the middle Baroque period.

Middle baroque style may be summarized as follows:

1. In comparison with the very short phases of movement typical of the concertato manner in early baroque music, we have *longer sections* and a sense of unity within these sections; particularly in the Schütz and Lully pieces. Contrast takes place *between* sections.
2. In all three works an even stronger feeling for *cadence* seems to pervade the music. The harmony is directed to strong points of arrival. Naturally, this is associated with a well-defined sectional structure. The sections are fairly long. Strong caesuras and cadential points of arrival are necessary when phrases and sections are to be well defined. The cadential relationships in harmony begin to saturate the music.
3. Unity of manner within fairly long sections is associated with a consistent and skillful treatment of the *melodic material,* the figurations, the ornamentation, and the texture. In a given section the composer took one idea and worked it over systematically and intensively, imitating it, spinning it out, repeating it in many ways.

We might liken the structural tendencies of middle baroque music to a process of crystallization, in which small crystals are gathered slowly into larger and larger clusters. The diffusion, the centrifugal tendencies of the early seventeenth century are turned inward. Controls and codification occupy the composer's attention. This attitude is demonstrated by the fact that one idea, one quality of expression is carried out over a rather long phase of movement; the momentary nuances, the sudden contrasts of early baroque music have disappeared.

Before we proceed to the final stage of baroque music, one point must be made in order to set the record straight. Not all seventeenth-century music participated in this cycle of breakup and re-formation. You will recall that musical tastes at the beginning of the seventeenth century were divided between the new manner and the old, that is, the polyphonic style. Many pieces for sacred performance were written in the manner of Palestrina and the Roman school during the seventeenth century. Indeed, this style has survived, mostly in counterpoint classes, down to this very day. Therefore we cannot look for evidence in *all* baroque music of the developments we have described. Still, a close observer might discover that even the most conservative choral music of the seventeenth century had absorbed some of the modern ways and that dance music began to employ the stronger harmonic language developed in early and middle baroque music.

Late Baroque (ca. 1680-1750)

If we listen to any music by one of the late baroque masters, a chorus by Johann Sebastian Bach, an aria by Handel, or a concerto movement by Antonio Vivaldi, we are struck by the greater sense of breadth and purpose which this music has over comparable works by earlier composers. This music seems to reach farther and to achieve its goals with more telling force than any music heretofore composed. We cannot help being impressed by the structural grandeur of late baroque music, fully realized in large works, but also reflected in the smaller compositions of this era.

It was no accident that, from the middle of the seventeenth century through the early years of the eighteenth century, musical forms steadily grew in breadth, coherence, and balance. The very techniques of musical composition changed so that inner strength and outer clarity were increasingly apparent. Among these techniques, none was more important than the strengthening of the *sense of key* which took place in late seventeenth-century harmony and which provided the basis of the harmonic language of Bach, Handel, their contemporaries, and their successors.

SENSE OF KEY

We have already seen, in Chapter 2, how a cadence gives us a sense of key, or harmonic *position*. By the systematic use of cadences, a composer can create a phrase or period that gives a clear and strong impression of a key. Moreover, when he puts a heavier cadence at the end of such a phrase, the impression of the key is immeasurably strengthened. During the seventeenth century, composers were developing ways in which such impressions of key could be projected in their music. At the same time they found that a *clear harmonic orientation* went hand in hand with *intensive motivic play and development*. Each cadential formula served to hold the music together, while at the same time the melodic and rhythmic energy of the motive propelled the music forward. It was a controlled and balanced flight, an interpenetration of harmonic, rhythmic, and melodic forces that enabled music to expand its phrases and periods to great lengths. Within this plan, contrast was sacrificed, but later in the eighteenth century, as we shall see, contrast was to find a place in this structural scheme. An excellent example of a broad period

EXAMPLE 5·5 Bach: *Brandenburg* Concerto No. 3, first movement

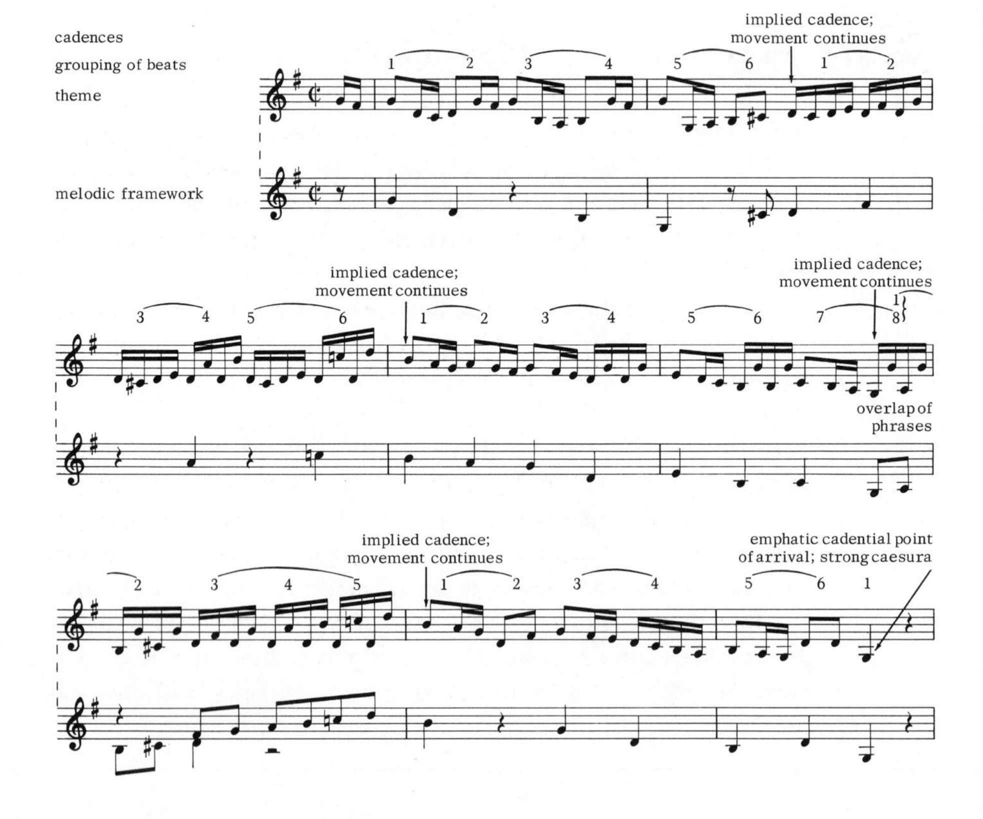

that develops motives intensively and drives with tremendous force to its cadence is the very beginning of Bach's *Brandenburg* Concerto No. 3 in G major. Example 5·5, on the preceding page, illustrates this kind of period, which is a basic structural plan for most baroque music. In this example, we hear a firm announcement of the key of G major, solidly on the tonic. The first phrase ends with a strong half cadence to D, the dominant degree. Then there follow three implied cadences to G, and the period ends with an emphatic cadential point of arrival, confirming the sense of the key of G, not only for the present, but as a central harmonic position for the entire movement.

Associated with this harmonic action is characteristic rhythmic and melodic behavior. The vigorous beats are generally grouped by two; larger units vary in length, so that we have a conflict in rhythm which builds up tension and assigns the role of resolving this tension to the cadence at the end of the period. This is comparable to periodic structure in the rhetoric of language, wherein the idea is not complete until the sentence arrives at its period (see pages 42 and 120). Melodically, we can sense a framework (sketched below the actual music) which creates a shape for the period, moving downward and upward in broad arches. Upon this framework, vigorous and characteristic short figures or motives engage in an intensive exercise to provide the final elements of life and color to the music.

Such a period might be compared to the span of a bridge, anchored firmly by its cadential piers and possessed of great internal strength by virtue of its tightly knit construction and its solid materials. The clearness and the emphasis with which the impression of key is given in late baroque music enabled the baroque composer to build a movement in blocks of key *areas*. Each area represented a sharply defined harmonic *position*, established at a specific distance and direction away from the home key. In some cases the music would pause momentarily at a given position or area; at other times it would settle for a while in a new position. Example 5·6 shows the plan for the harmonic areas of the first movement of Handel's Concerto in C major, *Masterpieces*, no. 43.

Briefly, then, the late baroque formula for the building of structural units involves (1) active, cadentially oriented harmony which projects a strong sense of key; clear, often emphatic arrival; (2) steady, vigorous beats that crystallize into well-marked larger units, eventually forming periods; (3) intensive play of motives, often sequential, forming large melodic contours; (4) structural units linked through key relationships to form a broad harmonic plan.

We receive additional corroboration of this view of late baroque structure from the musical theorists of the early eighteenth century. These

EXAMPLE 5·6 Handel: Concerto in C major

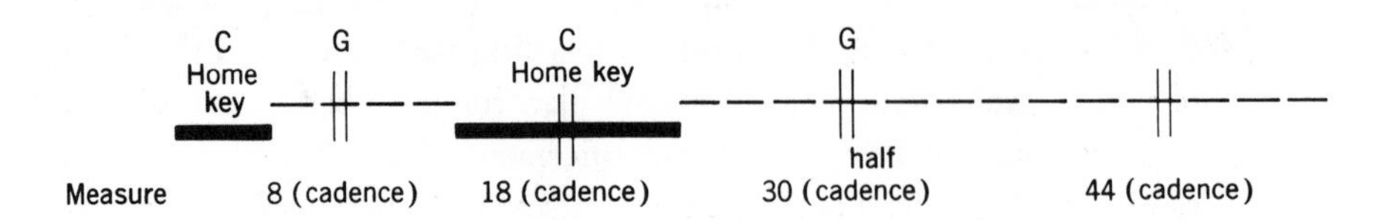

to E minor
Cadential section
Home key C
50 (cadence)
72 (cadence)
(E minor)
100
(final cadence)

formulas are their recommendations for the working out of a musical composition, and we have no reason to suppose that Bach and Handel themselves did not proceed along these lines.

DOCTRINE OF THE AFFECTIONS

Because of this technique of structure, late baroque music is able to carry out one basic idea or expressive value within a given composition or over an extended section within a composition. This reflects the general aesthetic attitude of composers and musical theorists during the Baroque era, an attitude which was codified in the theory called the *doctrine of the affections.* According to this theory of expression, certain types of musical figure were considered proper for the delineation of specific expressive values, especially when a text was involved. Rising figures suggested elation; falling figures suggested sorrow; chromaticism was proper for grief or other poignant, touching feelings. Both in vocal and instrumental music, the composer settled upon a suitable figure and then proceeded to write an entire piece based upon the rhythm, the style, and the affective quality of that figure. After he had established his initial expressive premises, after he had indicated the musical subject of his piece, the composer's main concern was to write as excellent a piece of music as he could. The doctrine of the affections involved a formal symbolism; it belonged to an art in the grand manner, an art with more than a touch of absolutism about it.

The extent to which the emotions were represented in musical thought of the late baroque is illustrated by the affections or attitudes mentioned by Johann Mattheson, the leading spokesman of this era, in 1739: joy, love, hope, sadness, pride, stubbornness, anger, rage, jealousy, fear, calmness, gaiety, majesty, heroism, and many combinations of feeling, such as courage and yearning.

Mattheson and his contemporaries in musical theory and practice represent a carryover of the sixteenth and seventeenth-century notion of the affections which were supposed to characterize various temperaments—the choleric, the sanguine, the phlegmatic, and the melancholic.

Nowhere is the relationship between technique, style, and expression more vivid or dramatic than in the *Crucifixus* (He Was Crucified) of Bach's B-minor Mass and the *Et Resurrexit* (And Was Resurrected) which follows. The contrast between these two numbers represents deepest sorrow followed by greatest joy. The sound of the *Crucifixus* is dark; everything seems to gravitate downward to the lowest notes of the bass. The bass line itself descends, as do the melodic figures of the choral parts. Two aspects are especially to be noticed:

1. At no time does the pace lose its slow, triple beat, nor its grouping into four-measure phrases. The descending bass figure is a *chaconne* pattern, taken from a dance of slow and stately manner. Here the steadiness and clearness of a dance rhythm supports, controls, and directs the tragic expressive flow of the music. Fresh momentum develops each time the bass drops to its cadence note and rises again to begin anew the downward path. Against the bass cadence, the voices and the supporting harmonies create an overlap of harmonic and melodic movement; thus the four-measure articulations are hidden though present, and the renewal and intensification of the tragic affection by fresh entries take place in a free rhythmic scheme at variance with the basic chaconne pattern.

EXAMPLE 5·7 Bach: B-minor Mass, *Crucifixus*

voices
overlapping entries against four measure chaconne pattern
no cadence here
instruments
basic chaconne pattern
chaconne pattern begins again

2. The shifting, chromatic harmonies, saturated with many poignant dissonances project a sense of harmonic instability throughout the piece. The general harmonic quality of the piece is *minor;* all the progressions

work in the area of minor keys. At the very end of the *Crucifixus* the chromaticism reaches its point of greatest intensity; each chord brings a new harmonic inflection; the cup of sorrow is full to the brim. Then, the resolution of all of this is not to the minor, but to a sublime, transfigured *major* chord; the sorrow is completed by a touch of lyric softness. Surprising and unexpected as this ending may seem, it carries out the surprising and unexpected harmonic procedure of the entire piece. We cannot help being moved by the wonderfully affective contrast of minor and major at this point.

In utmost contrast to the darkness of the *Crucifixus* there follows the jubilation of the *Et Resurrexit*. The brilliant sound of trumpets, fanfare figures directed upward, long exultant melismas, a vigorous, quick, light quality of movement, the entirely fresh effect of a new and major key —all these combine to describe the most joyous moment in Christendom, the Resurrection of Jesus Christ. Just as the dissonances pushed downward and the melodic lines sank in the *Crucifixus,* so does everything rise in the *Et Resurrexit.* The piece is treated in concertato style for chorus and orchestra; the exuberant give-and-take between elements of various types is proper to the feeling of renewed hope, energy, and joy that is given in the text. Only at the most important structural cadences does the steady driving movement come to a full point of arrival. Otherwise, throughout the *Et Resurrexit,* the driving pulse and the intensive development of two or three characteristic motives create an unbroken, continually growing sense of movement.

You may have noticed that Bach did not make any concession to the voices as far as brilliance or difficulty of material was concerned. The chorus is expected to handle the rapid virtuoso passages that interlace the entire fabric of the work. The broad and intensively searching techniques of composition are thus matched in scope by the demands made upon the performers.

The classification of musical figures, rhythms, harmonies, and genres in the doctrine of the affections is but one facet of a larger structure of thought in the Baroque period. Music tried to imitate philosophy and religion in codifying and rationalizing the material at hand. Musical rationalism appears not only in the doctrine of the affections but as well in the publication of the first musical dictionaries [Brossard, *Dictionnaire de musique* (Dictionary of Music), 1703; Walther, *Musikalisches Lexikon* (Musical Lexicon), 1728] and in the enormous increase from the early eighteenth century onward in the number of treatises dealing with musical composition. At no time in the history of music do we find a more comprehensive effort to put everything in its proper place than in the eighteenth century; logic and feeling find a common meeting place both *externally,* in the systems that were built, and *internally,* in the clear order and progression of the music. The result was a simpler sense of order in music and a greater accessibility of music for many more people.

ASPECTS OF FORM

In examining structural aspects of late baroque music, we shall examine the topic from two points of view: (1) the procedures used in the building of form and (2) the works which incorporate these procedures and which represent typical layouts for musical composition.

Imitation; Fugue

In the *Resurrexit* and *Crucifixus,* Bach used two very important procedures of composition, procedures that virtually dominate baroque music. These are (1) *imitation,* as in the *Resurrexit,* and (2) *variation,* as in the *Crucifixus.* We have already discussed imitation and variation in Chapters 2 and 4. In baroque music, techniques of imitation were most intensively explored in the type of composition called *fugue.*

Fugue, strictly speaking, is a process in which a given theme or subject is presented and worked over in contrapuntal imitation by two or more voices or parts. This process lent its name to such contrapuntal compositions. Fugues in late baroque music shared in the general stylistic evolution we have described above; thus they are different in layout and procedure from imitative pieces of the Renaissance period. Briefly, the evolution took place as follows:

1. Points of imitation, of which there were many in chansons and motets, were reduced in number and their length increased.
2. In the seventeenth century the canzona and the ricercar often used but one subject; each section might use a variant of the original subject or it might introduce a new counterpoint.
3. An increasingly stronger sense of harmonic drive within each section and the development of intensive techniques for working over short motives enabled composers further to increase the length of sections and at the same time to maintain and augment the sense of movement which gave unity and coherence to the structure.
4. Eventually, sectionalism virtually disappeared and the fugue structure was created largely by harmonic relationships and emphatic cadences; the principal harmonic relationship was exemplified by emphasis on tonic and dominant, as embodied in the entries of the subject. Typically, the first entry represented the tonic, the second entry the dominant (see Example 5·8).

Although their evolution was worked out along similar lines, the canzona and ricercar managed to retain their separate identities as far as style was concerned. The canzona became a quick fugue and very often used dance patterns in its subjects. The ricercar became a slow, serious fugue, retaining the even pace and something of the vocal style of the motet. The first two fugues in Johann Sebastian Bach's *Well-Tempered Clavier* illustrate the two different types. The first fugue is beholden to the ricercar, not only in style, but also in the very thorough way in which it explores the possibilities of its subjects; it uses *stretto,* in which one voice enters with the subject before the preceding voice has completed its entry (see Example 5·8).

The effect of stretto is cumulative; it increases the intensity of musical movement. As a result of the stretto procedure, the subject is called to our attention in an impressive and insistent manner, so that the entire piece projects an impression of substance and importance. Stretto covers the points of arrival for the individual voices; in this piece we can hear only two cadences, each very powerful. The first appears about midway in the piece, while the second takes the form of a broad area of arrival, extending through the final four measures. Throughout the twenty-seven measures of the fugue, we hear the subject more than twenty times.

EXAMPLE 5·8 Stretto from Bach: *Well-Tempered Clavier,* Book I, Fugue in C major. The four entries illustrate how fugal imitation establishes an opposition of tonic and dominant

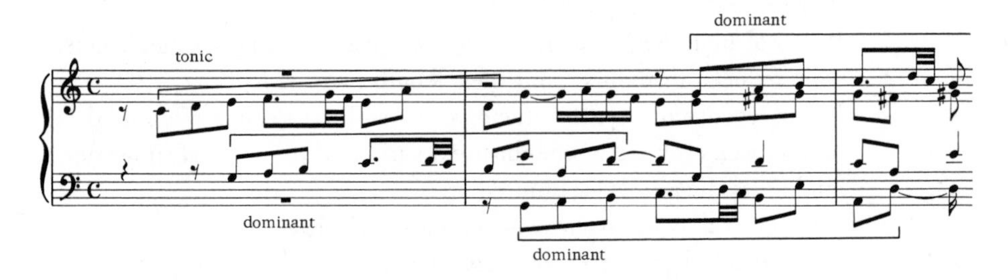

In contrast, perhaps so intended by Bach, the second fugue has a much lighter expressive quality. In style it borrows the rhythm of the *bourrée,* a very popular eighteenth-century dance, written in quick duple time, with a short upbeat. In its thirty-one measures, the subject appears only eight times. It has a thin texture; its quality of movement is light and buoyant, and its concern with its subject far less searching and serious than the first fugue's. Note the very clear sense of punctuation that divides the structure into two-measure groups which tend to form a symmetrical relationship with each other. In spite of its skillfully worked-out counterpoint, this fugue thus retains the spirit of the dance which was its source. Accordingly, a proper performance of the piece should be in the style of a dance. Example 5·9 is a diagram which shows the subject, the episodic material, the harmonic plan, and the phrase structure of this fugue.

EXAMPLE 5·9 Diagram of Bach: *Well-Tempered Clavier,* Book I, Fugue in C minor

Note the disturbance of regular phrase rhythm beginning at measure 17; this intensifies rhythmic action, building up to powerful cadences and a broad effect of arrival. Such interruptions of rhythmic order to prepare for an area of arrival are important aspects of Bach's idea of extended musical structure.

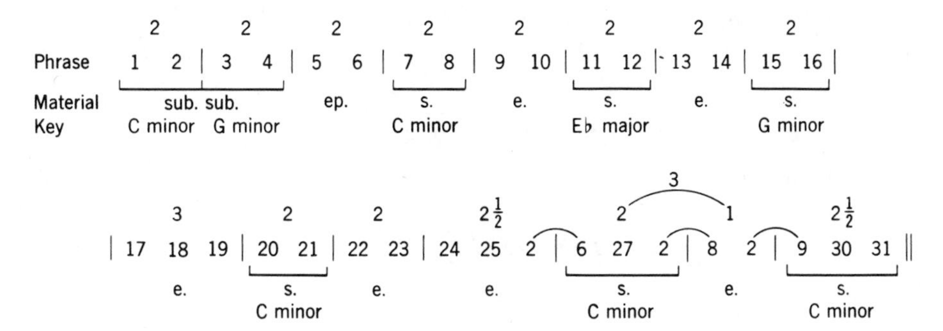

Canon; Alterations of a Subject

Contrapuntal, imitative composition has always presented a challenge to the composer in the treatment of subjects and themes. As early as the fourteenth century (see page 104) composers have displayed their ingenuity in setting a subject against itself in various ways. This procedure is called *canon,* meaning "law, rule." It signifies a relationship between two or more voices that remains constant throughout a piece or a sectioin of considerable length. Canon is distinguished from free imitation (see page 128). In the simplest form of canon the second voice follows the first exactly with respect to the intervals of the melody and the rhythmic values.

EXAMPLE 5·10 Pattern of canon

As a rule, fugal composition has relatively little to do with canon. Bach occasionally designated sections of larger works as being canonic. Canons are found in his *Goldberg* Variations, *The Art of the Fugue,* and the *Musical Offering.*

A musical theme or subject can retain its identity for the hearer, even though it may be altered in some ways. This frequently happens in fugue composition. The theme may be turned upside down (*inversion*); it may be played backward (*retrograde*); it may be compressed in time value (*diminution*); and its time values may be stretched out (*augmentation*). These permutations represent considerable ingenuity; and we as listeners can take pleasure in it. We are intrigued to hear the subject of the G-major Fugue in Bach's *Well-Tempered Clavier,* Book I, turned upside down, i.e., *inverted.* Bach achieves an effect of climax in the final section of the great organ fugue in E♭ major, the *St. Anne's* Fugue, when he brings back the opening subject, the chorale melody, in long

EXAMPLE 5·11 Alteration of a subject

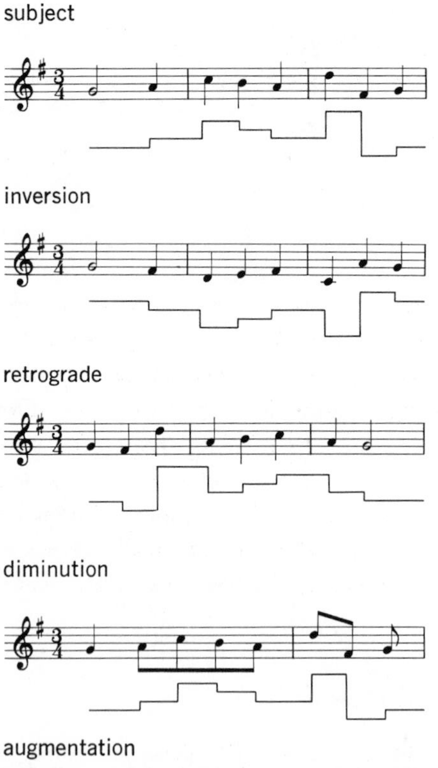

notes in the bass, i.e., *augmented*. Example 5·11 illustrates graphically ways in which a subject can be altered.

In the examples from Bach's keyboard music, we saw that fugal imitation can be adapted to various aspects of musical structure and style. Below are listed additional fugal movements together with some special characteristics which distinguish them:

Bach: Mass in B minor, Kyrie I: long, chromatic subject
Handel: *Messiah*, Blessing and Honor: long, diatonic subject
Corelli: Sonata, Op. 3, no. 7, first allegro: short fugue
Bach: Organ Fugue in A minor: fugue of great length with a very long subject in the style of a gigue
Bach: Sonata No. 2 in A minor for violin alone: very extended fugue on a short subject in the style of a bourrée

Elements of fugal procedure can be found in almost every kind of music during the Baroque era, although frequently an entire piece will not be handled fugally; rather, some sections may begin with fugal imitations. We hear such imitations in the *Et Resurrexit* from the B-minor Mass.

EXAMPLE 5·12 Bach: *Et Resurrexit* from the B-minor Mass

Soprano I
Soprano II
continuation
Alto
continuation
Tenor
continuation
Bass
continuation in concerto style
concerto-like tutti

For the composer of the late Baroque period, fugal imitation was a means by which he could concentrate attention upon his subject, structurally and expressively; he could set the subject to work effectively against itself by (1) carrying it to different harmonic positions and by (2) altering some of its melodic or rhythmic features. Virtually any kind of musical material could be adapted to fugal imitation provided that the range allowed several voices to proceed simultaneously and that the melodic material was distinctive enough to stamp itself upon the attention of the listener.

Fugal composition may be summarized as follows:

1. Fugue is a procedure by which one or more subjects can be exposed or presented in contrapuntal imitation.
2. Fugal structure is built through the presentation of the subject in various keys or harmonic positions.
3. Fugal composition can be adapted to many different styles and varieties of expression.
4. The length of a fugue is not fixed, nor is its internal plan, provided that the basic premises of the baroque style are observed.
5. Fugal procedure may be incorporated with many types of composition that are not primarily fugal in plan.
6. Fugal imitation is a means by which musical movement may be maintained steadily and intensified.

Variation

Another very important type of musical procedure in baroque music was the *variation*. This was an extension of the process of addition and elaboration that was so widespread in Renaissance music. Many variations were written for keyboard performers. This was to be expected, since only the keyboard performer had both the freedom of action and the command of the full range of sound which were desirable in the various settings of the model and its ornamentation. String instruments also partook in performances of variations because of their natural agility. Themes for variations were taken from plain-chant melodies, chorale tunes, popular songs and dances, or simple melodic patterns given to the bass voice.

Bach turned again and again to the variation procedure as a means of building a composition. His *Crucifixus* from the B-minor Mass, which we have already discussed, illustrates variation upon a bass theme, a type of procedure designated as *ground bass* or *ostinato bass*. This composition, a continuously moving, searching, tightly woven work, exemplifies Bach's attitude toward variation procedure. He seeks out the possibilities of the subject and composes an entirely new work, using the theme as a scaffolding. We are not dealing here with decorative ornamentation. Several other examples will show further how Bach made use of the variation idea. In the Passacaglia and Fugue in C minor, the subject is a genuine tune:

EXAMPLE 5·13 Bach: Passacaglia and Fugue in C minor

The procedure in this piece consists of ornamentation surrounding the tune. The principal distinctions of its variation procedure are (1) the striking rhythmic and melodic qualities of the added parts; (2) the sense of well-developed counterpoint in each variation as opposed to a rather decorative manner which was standard for pieces of this kind; (3) the bold and dramatic contrasts that are introduced to set off different sections; and (4) the culmination of the variation concept in a broad fugue which employs a version of the tune as a subject.

In his Canonic Variations on *Vom Himmel hoch* (From Heaven on High), Bach used a familiar chorale tune, the first line of which is quoted in Example 5·14.

EXAMPLE 5·14 Bach: Canonic Variations on *Vom Himmel hoch*

The various phrases of this tune are treated as subjects for canonic imitation. Here the principal distinction is the superlative control of contrapuntal technique, which gives evidence of Bach's unparalleled insight into the nature of musical relationships.

Another famous set of variations by Bach is the *Goldberg* Variations. Here the subject is the harmonic progression which supports a rather florid melodic voice. In the thirty variations that this set comprises, Bach has explored many types of musical composition and style characteristic of baroque music. We find dances such as gigues and courantes; we find one variation cast as a French overture (see page 182); there are nine canons, each set according to its own plan. Each variation, moreover, has its own thematic material; only the rhythmic and harmonic skeleton provides the link between these pieces.

The ornamental type of variation which was a favorite vehicle for keyboard performance since the days of the Renaissance is represented by Handel's tuneful and sonorous piece, the so-called *Harmonious Blacksmith*. It is not difficult to hear the tune or, at least, to imagine it amid the figurations of each variation. The effects of sonority created in this piece, ringing and vibrant as they emerge from the harpsichord, constitute perhaps the principal appeal of the work.

Another important basis of variation composition was the *chorale,* which will be discussed later in this chapter when we cover the topic of church music.

The process of ornamentation is employed elsewhere in late baroque music. Compositions entitled *fantasia, toccata, prelude,* and *introduction* are frequently based upon highly elaborated figurations that expand a harmonic progression or melodic line created by the composer. In these we have no formal set of variations upon a tune or bass; rather, there is an improvisatory manner, a sense of exploration without frequent and regular returns to the beginning of a subject. Such a composition is the toccata of Bach's Toccata and Fugue in D minor. Example 5·15 illustrates two different methods by which a musical framework may be elaborated. The prelude (Example 5·15*a*) shows a repeated pattern by which a chord progression is elaborated; the toccata (Example 5·15*b*) shows a somewhat less regular pattern which ornaments a descending scale line.

EXAMPLE 5·15

a. Bach: *Well-Tempered Clavier,* Book I, Prelude in C major

b. Bach: Toccata in C major

Neither of these pieces is a variation type of composition, yet they employ characteristic means of variation and elaboration, as indeed much music of the Baroque era did (see Example 5·5, and compare it with Example 5·15*b*).

In works of slow tempo, the composer sometimes wrote only the main notes of the melody. The performer was allowed to show his creative ingenuity in elaborating these melodies. Many manuals from the eighteenth century provide instruction in this practice. The theme of Bach's *Goldberg* Variations should be thus performed.

If we should compare typical late baroque variation procedure with that of the early baroque or Renaissance styles, we should discover one significant difference in the treatment of melodic material. In late baroque variations the figures are more sharply etched; they tend to be repeated and to be worked over intensively much more than in the earlier variations; and they gather to form much broader arches of rise and fall, with a far greater sense of harmonic drive than their predecessors. Thus, the variation participates in the general codification and crystallization of structure which is typical of the late baroque style.

Variation procedure in late baroque music may be summarized as follows:

1. Formal variations draw upon three types of subject:
   a. Preexisting melody
   b. Bass figure (ostinato or ground bass)
   c. Harmonic progression
2. Variation procedure is used from time to time in preludes, fantasias, and toccatas.
3. Melodies in baroque music are often built by elaborating a melodic framework.
4. Melodic ornamentation and variation are either:
   a. Written out by the composer
   b. Added by the perfomer
5. Variations in late baroque music tend to be constructed much more systematically upon a given figure than variations of earlier styles.

Dance Forms

Dance forms, as we have already seen, represent established general patterns within which action is strictly controlled by the prescribed length of phrase and by the proper cadences. Reviewing briefly the elements of dance structure that evolved in medieval and Renaissance music, we have (1) symmetry of structure, most often expressed in pairs of phrases or periods, (2) an open cadence answered by a closed cadence, and (3) characteristic tempos and rhythmic patterns.

These elements were also present in late baroque dance music but were subjected to the codification of procedures we have discussed above. Symmetry, a fundamental element in the dance, is universally represented in late baroque dance music by the two-reprise or binary form. This form consists of two sections which complement each other in the following manner:

1. They are built from the same or similar melodic material.
2. The first section ends with a nonfinal or open cadence; this may possibly be a cadence to the dominant key or a half-cadence in the home key. In minor keys, the first part may end in the relative major. The second section ends with an authentic cadence in the home key.
3. In the simplest forms the second section is the same length as the first; in larger forms it is usually made longer, especially toward the cadence. The term *reprise* comes from the custom of repeating each section: AABB. Often the repeated section undergoes some variation. François Couperin's gigue *La Galante, Masterpieces,* no. 4, incorporates these structural elements.

To a composer like Bach, this sharply defined, easily managed plan was more than a convenient framework in which to enclose characteristic dance melodies. The two-reprise form is capable of great internal expansion; as this takes place, there develops a stronger drive toward the cadence which ends the reprise. A strong sense of accumulated energy, rising above the level of gallant pleasantry, pervades the quality of movement in such a work, intended not for dancing, but as a serious exercise in musical composition. The final movement of Bach's Sonata No. 3 in C major for violin alone demonstrates how far a dance type, the *polonaise,* and the two-reprise dance form can go beyond the category of mere entertainment, while retaining the essential features of the original pattern. The first reprise is forty measures in length; the second, sixty. Within these boundaries, the violin engages in an intensive, unrelenting elaboration of a purposeful harmonic progression. As we examine such expansions of the two-reprise form in eighteenth-century music, we can understand their coming to life only because of the precise codification of the small-scale form, as represented in Couperin's piece. Further consideration of the two-reprise form will be given in Chapter 6, for in classic music the form enjoys even greater importance than it does in baroque music.

Dances were also codified by being put together to form the *suite,* a set of dances. The suite evolved from the pairing of dances in Renaissance music. Eventually, in the second half of the seventeenth century, the sequence of dances was standardized according to the following order:

Allemande. A dance of moderate pace, duple meter, and rather heavy quality of movement

Courante. A moderately quick dance in triple time, frequently employing momentary shifts of accent, creating a rather blurred imbalanced rhythmic feeling

Sarabande. A rather slow dance in triple meter, generally with an accent of length upon the second beat of the measure

Gigue. A quick dance, often handled imitatively, in various kinds of triple meter

The four movements of the suite show its international flavor, since the allemande is German, the courante French or Italian, the sarabande Spanish, and the gigue English. After the standardization of the suite, the practice of adding optional dances to the basic four grew up. For example, in Bach's French Suite No. 6 in E major, the movements are Allemande, Sarabande, Gavotte, Polonaise, Bourrée, Menuet, and Gigue. The Suite in E minor by Froberger, *Masterpieces,* no. 35, illustrates the mid-seventeenth-century suite at about the time of standardization.

The two-reprise plan could serve music in styles other than the dance. The chorale characteristically has two parts, although it lacks the melodic and harmonic symmetry of the dance to bind the two sections. On the other hand, the first prelude of Bach's *Well-Tempered Clavier* fulfills the conditions for a two-reprise form as given above although the manner is that of a harmonic improvisation. Part I ends at measure 11 and part II at measure 19, followed by a magnificently broad cadential extension to measure 36.

Domenico Scarlatti used the two-reprise form in his sonatas (*essercizi*) for harpsichord. While many of these pieces are in the style of a dance, they involve bold contrasts of material, strikingly inventive passages, frequent repetitions, often in echo manner, and a capriciousness that breaks the continuity of expression and rhetoric which characterizes most baroque music. His Sonata in C minor, *Masterpieces,* no. 42, is typical of his style and structure. The rhythm is that of an allemande. Note that measures 2, 3, and 4 have the same melodic material and that 6 repeats 5, 8 repeats 7, and 11 and 12 repeat measure 10 with some small changes. Reprise II is a partial review of reprise I, with the return to the home key balancing the departure at the beginning. The entire plan is neat, perfectly symmetrical, and well punctuated, so that change in manner is easily accomplished and indeed emphasizes the tidy form.

Dances included in a suite, sonata, concerto, or overture were often arranged so that two dances of the same kind were paired—for example, Minuet I, Minuet II, Minuet I (without repetition of each reprise). Later, in the classic period, this arrangement was employed in the minuets of larger works.

Dance music contributed significantly to the baroque doctrine of the affections. Characteristic dance styles and orderly, clear arrangements of phrases made it possible for baroque composers to take up one idea or figure and to expand it at length throughout an aria or a movement of an instrumental work. Without these stylistic and structural elements taken from the dance, baroque expression could not have achieved its characteristic monumentality. The *Crucifixus* from Bach's B-minor Mass illustrates this point.

Baroque dance forms may be summarized as follows:

1. Dances are cast in the two-reprise form, with an open cadence at the end of part I, a closed cadence at the end of part II.
2. Dances range in length from short pieces (8 + 8–12 measures) to broadly extended works of more than 100 measures.
3. There were many types of dances, often reflecting national styles.
4. The order of dances became standardized in the suite, whose four basic types were the allemande, courante, sarabande, and gigue. (See Glossary for specific descriptions of baroque dances.)
5. Dance forms were used in music representing styles other than dances and lent their symmetry to the orderly presentation of affections.

The Concerto

Finally, among late baroque structural principles, we shall investigate the *concerto,* which is a special codification of the concertato form of the early and middle baroque styles.

The principal structural element in the concerto is the competition, the give-and-take, between the various participants in the performance. This is typically embodied in an alternation between a large group, the *tutti* or *ripieno,* and one or more solo instruments:

Tutti—solo—tutti—solo—tutti—solo—etc.——tutti

In the final codification, the number of alternations between tutti and solo tended not to exceed four or five, although in some cases, tutti and solo often alternate very quickly and overlap, heightening the sense of competition.

When the solo element involved several instruments, the concerto was designated a *concerto grosso,* as distinguished from the concerto with a single soloist. In the concerto grosso, the solo group was called the *concertino;* the full orchestra, the *ripieno.*

The sense of competition in the concerto lends itself to the play of brilliant, rapidly moving patterns of figuration. Give-and-take and the characteristic figuration are both clearly represented in the first movement of Bach's *Brandenburg* Concerto No. 2 in F major. As you listen to this piece, you will have no difficulty hearing the contrasts of the full orchestra with the brilliant solo instruments: the violin, the bell-like high trumpet of Bach's time, the oboe, and the flute. The opening theme of this piece, announced boldly by the tutti, is a typical concerto theme, somewhat square, vigorous in effect, angular in shape, anchored upon the principal tones of the major or minor triad. This theme is illustrated in Example 5·16.

EXAMPLE 5·16 Bach: *Brandenburg* Concerto No. 2 in F major, first movement

EXAMPLE 5·17 Handel: Concerto Grosso in D major

EXAMPLE 5·18 Handel: Concerto Grosso in F major

EXAMPLE 5·19 Bach: Concerto for Violin in E major

The opening passage for the orchestra, with its distinctive theme, is called the *ritornello,* since it returns throughout the movement and at the end to establish the structural pillars of the form.

Themes such as this (Examples 5·16 to 5·19) have a great deal of propulsive power. As you can hear in the first movement of the *Brandenburg,* No. 2, they break out easily into florid passages, generally taken by the solo instruments. These florid passages consist of chains of rapid, mechanically regular notes put together in stereotyped patterns. They are supported by a vigorous, regular motoric beat in the bass instruments and the supporting parts.

The concerto, along with much other baroque music, absorbed its characteristic manner of figuration from English keyboard music of the seventeenth century. English musicians and actors had traveled through Europe, often by necessity to escape the authoritarianism of the Commonwealth. Wherever they went, their keyboard style was taken up by local composers and also transferred to other instruments. These figures, originally employed as a means of variation, became the staple ingredient in the late baroque instrumental concerto. Example 5·20, from the *Brandenburg* Concerto No. 2, shows the solo performers working through a set of such figurations. Notice here the sense of progression created by the systematic rise and fall of the various parts, in sequential patterns so often found in baroque music (see Example 5·15).

EXAMPLE 5·20 Bach: *Brandenburg* Concerto No. 2, first movement

Over the entire movement that we have taken as an example, the form builds an alternation of tutti and solo. Typically, in the concerto, the tutti opens and closes the movement with its bold thematic statement in the home key. Within the movement, the treatment of tutti and solo will vary according to the style and the type of instruments used. Our present example, with its brilliant solo participants, emphasizes the contrast between these and the tutti. The solo episodes stand out. In the *Brandenburg* Concerto No. 6, Bach has a thoroughly homogeneous group of instruments, *viola da braccio* (arm viol), *viola da gamba* (knee viol), cello, and bass. He therefore concentrates upon an intense and compact interweaving of melodic material and does not attempt to project a brilliant soloistic quality, although we can detect the tutti-solo alternation if we listen closely. Harmonically, the concerto follows the plan of other late baroque music. A key is set at the beginning. The music seems to describe an orbit around the home key, now taking one direction, then another, sometimes passing through but never straying very far, as we can see in Example 5·21.

EXAMPLE 5·21 Diagram of key scheme. Bach: *Brandenburg* Concerto No. 2, first movement

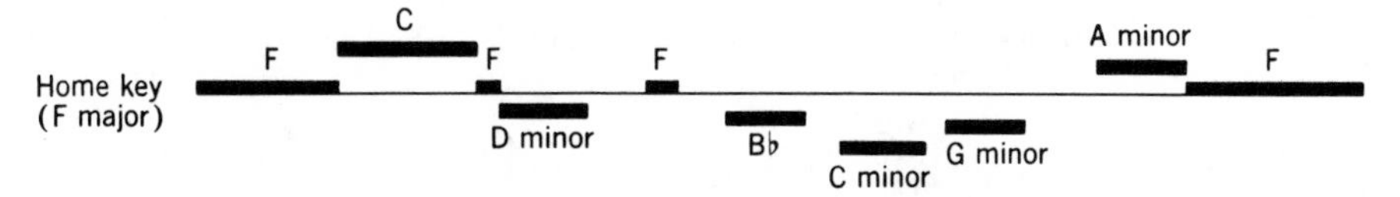

The heavy black lines represent areas of harmonic stability; the thin black line represents the home key as a level of reference throughout the movement; areas where there is no heavy black line represent shifting, relatively unstable harmonic action.

The concerto is usually a three-movement piece. The first movement displays most typically the concertato and virtuoso aspects; the second movement is frequently patterned after the slow arias of opera; the last movement may take up again the manner of the first movement, or it may assume the style of a dance, such as a gigue or minuet. In the Baroque period, the concerto, more than any other type of composition, provided musicians the opportunity to exercise themselves boldly and exuberantly, with no end in view except the sheer pleasure of making music together.

We can hear concerto elements in many compositions in the late baroque style. For example, the *Et Resurrexit* from the B-minor Mass of Bach is actually a concerto for chorus, soloists, and orchestra. Solo music can imitate concerto procedure, as in Scarlatti's Sonata in C minor, *Masterpieces,* no. 42, which contains four tutti enclosing three solo episodes. Concerto and dance are combined here in a composition whose title gives no indication of these stylistic characteristics (see page 171). Concerto procedure, as represented by tutti-solo layout and by bold figuration, is also carried over into classic music; the first movement of Mozart's *Prague* Symphony contains many brilliant effects drawn from the style of the concerto.

Concerto procedure may be summarized as follows:

1. The baroque concerto is characterized by sharply contrasting amounts of sound. The contrasts result from alternation between an orchestra and one or more solo instruments.
2. A brilliant patterned figuration is perhaps the most characteristic melodic ingredient of the concerto.

3. The harmonic plan of the concerto involves moving to and from keys that surround the principal key.
4. Concerto procedure is used in various forms and media of late baroque music.

In the next major section of this chapter, we shall examine some aspects of musical performance; in this connection other forms of baroque music will be examined, but, as we shall see, they draw upon the elements of procedure and structural plan described above.

Performance of Baroque Music

One of the most important and illuminating tasks of musical historians recently has been to ascertain how early music was actually performed. In establishing valid methods of re-creating older music, these scholars have shown us the beauties and the charm, the freshness of sound, the buoyancy of movement, the piquancy of arabesque that emerges from Renaissance and baroque music. One result has been the recorded *Masterpieces* set, which has been used as a reference here. The delight which this music can give would be lost to us if it were performed with the heavier, broader tones of today's instruments or in a manner of playing reminiscent of Tchaikovsky and Wagner.

The sound of baroque music, particularly music for groups of instruments, is quite different from the sound of chamber or orchestral music of the late eighteenth and nineteenth centuries. This is due partly to the different qualities of instrumental tone and partly to a different disposition of instrumental sound. As far as the constitution of an instrumental ensemble was concerned, there was no strict standardization. An orchestra might consist of ten or of thirty, forty, or even more performers. Whatever instrumentation was used in any particular piece, however, the instrumental layout exemplified the three characteristics described above on page 150. When a number of concertato instruments were employed, they would share the responsibilities of the upper parts. Without exception, a keyboard instrument would be on hand to fill in the harmonies from the written-out bass part. We thus have a kind of layered texture, which preserved its essential uniformity of manner, regardless of how many or how few instruments were playing at any time.

With respect to the amount and strength of sound, the dynamic levels, increase and decrease, we have not, as a rule, heard either very loud or very soft passages. Still, in the concerto, for example, the contrast between solo and tutti inevitably creates a contrast in dynamics, a sharp rise or fall between relatively loud and relatively soft. This sudden change is typical of much baroque music, particularly that laid out along the lines of the concerto. This type of dynamic style is called *terrace dynamics*. When the same material is first played loud and then soft, we have the typical baroque effect known as the *echo*. Although crescendo and decrescendo probably occurred in performance, they were not a primary resource of expression, as, for example, in Wagner's or Tchaikovsky's music.

Historians are still seeking answers to the question of how baroque music was performed. We may never find a complete answer because we cannot turn time back and duplicate the conditions of performance. Yet even the approximate solutions have opened a new world of sound and expression to the listener of today.

We have a good deal of information about *where* and *when* music of the seventeenth and early eighteenth centuries was performed. Generally speaking, there were three kinds of occasions that called for music. Representing the oldest tradition was *worship music* and its concomitant, solemn public ceremony. *Domestic music* was performed for the entertainment of a court or household. It also included pieces used for teaching purposes. *Theater music* was embodied, of course, in opera and ballet. The three types of music were classified by baroque theorists as *church, chamber,* and *theater styles.* Ordinarily, the church style leaned toward a contrapuntal exposition of musical materials; the chamber style employed dance idioms or dealt with brilliant studies for solo performers; the purest embodiment of theater style was recitative. The three styles intermingled, however; they traded and borrowed from each other to such an extent that by the beginning of the eighteenth century, these classifications referred to occasions, but not necessarily to techniques or styles of composition.

Theater, church, and chamber music was performed all over Europe during the seventeenth and eighteenth centuries. Still, because of political and economic conditions, the leading musical countries of Europe—Italy, France, Germany, and England—took different directions in the cultivation of various media and idioms of performance. We shall look at these directions now, taking into account the type of occasion and, where pertinent, the type of environment.

THEATER MUSIC

In music for the theater we find the most intensive and the broadest application of the doctrine of the affections. The language of poetry and drama is specific in its expressive intent. Musical composition for the theater shaped itself to the emotional qualities of the text, so much so that an extensive vocabulary of conventional figures and styles was built throughout the seventeenth and eighteenth centuries in connection with composition for the stage. These figures were also carried over into purely instrumental music, so that many such compositions are imitations of dramatic music. Because the dramatic elements in unstaged works—cantatas, oratorios, the Passion—derive largely from opera, it may be said that baroque dramatic music is virtually synonymous with opera. Of the several schools of opera, the Italian is much the most significant; the French cultivated their own type, while the English, thanks to the genius of Henry Purcell, had a brief moment of glory in their own sphere of opera during the latter part of the seventeenth century.

Italian Opera

Earlier in this chapter, we learned something of the beginnings of opera, about monody and recitative. The first operas were intended for performance at court. Reports tell us that these early operas were lavish, grandiose entertainments, providing full scope to ballet, massed ensembles, scenery, and novel stage effects, in addition to the primary purpose, which was dramatic representation. The Roman opera of the early seventeenth century was among the most elaborate that has ever been staged. The Church was not slow to take advantage of this new and highly appealing spectacle. In pursuing the objectives of the Counter-Reformation, it sponsored operas on sacred subjects, as well as oratorios.

This double blessing, from temporal and spiritual authorities, gave tremendous momentum to operatic composition so that, quite early in the century, thousands of operas had already been written and many opera houses sprang up in Italy.

When musical values began to reassert themselves in the early opera, one of the most important forms of vocal music started to take shape. This was the *aria*. In contrast to the freely composed recitative, the aria had some consistent, regular, and fairly extended plan. It leaned toward song or dance rhythms; its melodic material was more continuous and rounded in quality; it made use of repetitions and neatly balanced contrasts. Its quality of movement was more flowing than that of the recitative, and its points of arrival clearly indicated the ends of long phrases or periods. It worked over one idea at considerable length, thus paralleling the structural evolution we have described in instrumental music.

FIGURE 6. Andrea Pozzo: Baroque stage design, from *Fernsehkunst* (The Art of Perspective), 1700. Note how the domed ceiling with its painting creates the illusion of unlimited space (continuous expansion). (Courtesy of the Stanford University Libraries.)

The specific forms in which arias were cast were quite varied, but toward the middle of the seventeenth century one type began to dominate. This was the *da capo aria.* (*Da capo* means "return to the head, or beginning.") It comprised (1) a first section, in rather brilliant style, followed by (2) a middle section that was shorter, provided a contrast in key to the principal section, and, at the option of the composer (depending on how he interpreted the text) might be similar or contrasted in style to the principal section, and (3) a return to the first section. The da capo form was especially suited to the musical styles of the later seventeenth and the eighteenth centuries in which consistent and thorough exploration of a single musical value or effect had become the principal procedure, and contrast occurred between movements or extended sections.

The excerpt from Handel's *Rinaldo, Masterpieces,* no. 44, shows a number of different musical procedures associated with opera. We first have a recitative similar to that which we heard in the Carissimi piece; next a canzonalike instrumental interlude, indicating furious action on the stage. The da capo aria that follows is a slow, tragic piece; it takes advantage of the halting, somewhat imbalanced rhythm of the sarabande; and a hint of fugal exposition is heard at the beginning to suggest a serious, even grave, expressive quality. The middle section, changing to a mood of defiance, takes up again the brisk canzona style. The entire scene is rounded off by a return to the principal expressive value, the sense of tragic loss, as projected in the first section of the aria. At the beginning and end, the orchestra provides the equivalent of the first and last tutti in a concerto; it frames the aria, establishing the style and the breadth of the piece. Throughout the aria it is constantly active as a partner in the musical discourse and at no time becomes mere accompaniment.

In Italian opera of the late seventeenth and eighteenth centuries, some arias assumed the proportions and manner of a vocal concerto, with brilliant ornamental passages, difficult figures, and a generally flamboyant style. Indeed, dramatic values in Italian opera receded in favor of the brilliant, highly polished, and stereotyped music. Operas featured virtuosi; the elaborate arias were frequently extended by interposed passage-work of enormous difficulty, negotiable by only a very few singers. The composer had to write this music to order; he was not free to experiment with new musicodramatic ideas. In reaction to this rigid view, which allowed but one affection to be expressed, and that quite formally, some composers in the middle of the century, notably Christoph Willibald von Gluck, composed operas that achieved a different balance between musical and dramatic values.

In the time of early Italian opera, it was the custom to perform a canzona, called a *sinfonia,* before the main presentation began. The sections of the sinfonia became standardized into the typical three-movement form of the seventeenth century. Because the sinfonia was intended to collect the attention of the audience for the performance to follow, it began in a brilliant, brisk manner, often with fanfares, running figures, unisons for full orchestra designed for emphasis, and frequent bold strokes for punctuation. The second movement borrowed the style of the aria, in a rather slow tempo; the third, again quick, was dancelike —most often a gigue or minuet.

The sinfonia rarely lingered over any idea for long, nor did it develop a thread of meaning. It simply made more brilliant use of the effects of sectional contrast of the early canzona. Indeed, many critics during the eighteenth century considered this genre a most superficial kind of music. The sinfonia was first programmed independently at public concerts in the middle of the eighteenth century, and it was the ancestor of the great symphonies of a later age.

Unlike other kinds of baroque music, the Italian opera sinfonia did not survive to be performed by musicians of the twentieth century. Very few recordings are available, and the operas themselves are not performed. A typical example is found in *Treasury,* no. 44, the sinfonia to *La Caduta de Decem Viri* (The Fall of the Decemvirate) by Alessandro Scarlatti. Its three movements take up in turn the style of the concerto, a slow dancelike style, and a quick gigue. In Scarlatti's piece we can hear a skillful use of counterpoint, much more so than in the usual sinfonia of that era. Several generations later, Mozart's early symphonies still echoed the structure and spirit of the Italian opera sinfonia.

French Opera

In France political conditions led to a very different kind of musical situation from that found in Italy. Politically the Italian peninsula was broken up into many kingdoms, principalities, and minor states, most of which were under the control of some foreign power. There was great dispersal, no strong center. France, under Richelieu and later Louis XIV, became a highly centralized state, independent of the Papacy, the embodiment of monarchical absolutism, and the strongest kingdom of Europe. Controls were set upon many aspects of French life; order was established by court edict, and style was dictated. Supporting and glorifying this centralized absolutism, magnificent displays in all the arts were offered during court entertainments.

Mirroring the absolutism of the king, French music had its own dictator, its own absolute monarch during the late seventeenth century. This was Jean Baptiste Lully, who was granted supreme powers over French music by express order of the king. With power, funds, and resources at his command, Lully created the finest orchestra in Europe, the "twenty-four violins." Indeed, the formation of the modern orchestra is largely traceable to the great interest and activity in orchestral music stimulated and directed at first by the example of Lully and expanded during the first half of the eighteenth century.

French opera developed distinctive characteristics in response to the grandeur of Louis XIV's court. Instead of a series of brilliant solo numbers which gave musical heroes opportunities to show off, French opera was a brilliant spectacle. Ballet was of primary importance in the scheme; there was more instrumental music than in Italian opera, because of the superlative orchestral establishment; arias were shorter, often dancelike in style; the dramatic situation was given a greater place in the total scheme, and instead of the matter-of-fact recitative found in Italian opera, a special kind of recitative, declaimed in fluctuating time values and fitted to the peculiarities of the French language, was developed. One further distinction is that Italian opera was performed all over Europe and often had to pay its own way; French opera centered at the court of Louis XIV and was heavily subsidized.

Lully displayed his superlative orchestra at its greatest brilliance in the overtures which opened the festivities of a grand entertainment, accompanying the king as he was making his way into the theater. These pieces acquired the name *French overture*. They begin characteristically with a stately marchlike pace and are distinguished by the snappy dotted rhythms which enabled the orchestra of Lully, with its matchless precision, to display its famed virtuosity. The slow ceremonial pace of the opening section of the French overture also gave the orchestra a chance to show off its richness and fullness of tone. (No. 36 from *Masterpieces*, the Overture to Lully's opera *Armide*, illustrates these qualities of the genre.) Following the slow opening section, a quick canzonalike piece provides a contrast, with lively rhythms and imitative layout; after this stately, important beginning, the French overture might conclude with a set of dances.

Throughout the eighteenth and nineteenth centuries, the pattern of a slow, solemn introduction followed by a quick, brilliant movement represents, in sonatas and symphonies, the heritage of the French overture. Mozart's *Prague* Symphony, Beethoven's Symphony No. 2, and Haydn's *London* Symphony all begin with stately, serious introductions that recall the manner of the French overture.

FIGURE 7. Engraving of a scene from Molière's comedy *Le Malade Imaginaire,* in the garden of Versailles in 1676. Note the grand symmetries, both on stage and in the total scene itself, reflecting the notion of classical order that was characteristic of the time of Louis XIV. The music was very likely composed by Lully. (From the Gracely Collection, Stanford University Libraries.)

English Theater Music

England's musical position during the Baroque period suffered through the years of the Commonwealth. A ban was placed on the English court entertainments, the masques which were produced on a remarkably lavish scale during Tudor and Stuart times. A considerable amount of domestic music was performed throughout the century, but the luxuriance and vigor of musical activity that are needed to define a distinctive style were lacking in England. Upon the Restoration, French and Italian music were imported, intermingling with English dances and songs in the revived masques and in opera.

English music of the late seventeenth century is party to a strange and curious paradox in the history of opera. Despite the lack of a concentrated home-fed musical style, the one opera dating from the late 1600s that appears in today's repertory, is an English work, Purcell's *Dido and Aeneas.* We rarely hear any French or Italian dramatic music from the middle or late Baroque period, although we would certainly be impressed by this music if it were available. But *Dido and Aeneas* has such a poignant and moving dramatic appeal, its music is so wonderfully fresh and colorful, it offers so few problems of staging, and it has such a wealth and variety of styles and attitudes that it has commended itself to modern concert or dramatic performance with equal ease. It has been staged effectively by both amateur and professional groups. Since it represents, structurally, the middle baroque style, its individual numbers are relatively short; they make their dramatic point and move on to the next without the intrusion of the personality or prowess of the singer. (The work was composed for a girls' school.) *Dido's Lament,* at the end of the opera, is one of the most touchingly sorrowful expressions in the entire history of opera. Like the *Crucifixus* of Bach's B-minor Mass, it reveals its basic affective quality in the descending chromatic line of an ostinato bass, above which the perishing Dido sings a melodic line burdened by dissonances and particularly expressive intervals. Example 5·22 shows both the bass line and Dido's song. Compare this with the example from the *Crucifixus.*

Within the short space of little over an hour, Purcell takes us through a grand sweep of events, from Dido's awakening love, through the plotting of the sorceress to force Aeneas's departure, to the final tragic death of Dido. Note the brilliance of the triumph music, the imaginative tone painting of the sorceress's music, the infectious buoyancy of the sailors' dance.

Aside from this more or less isolated masterpiece, the English developed no momentum in the composition of opera. But a foreign product, Italian opera, was being imported in vast quantities; by the beginning

EXAMPLE 5·22 Purcell: *Dido and Aeneas,* Dido's Lament

(The dissonances are indicated by the sign +.)

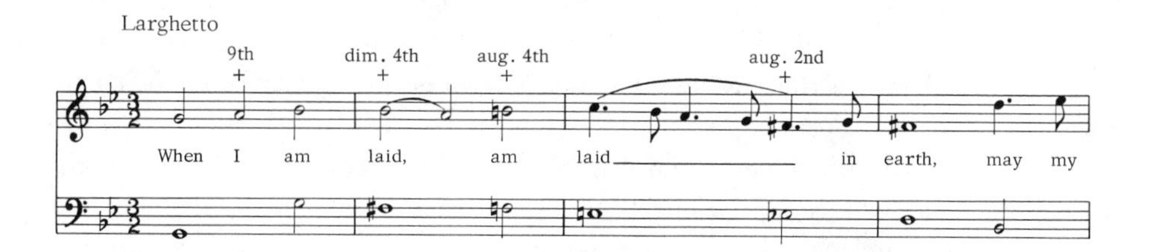

of the eighteenth century and until its very end, Italian opera was à la mode in London.

Most of the music we have been describing was composed and performed for the benefit of the aristocracy, for kings, princes, nobles, and the great personages of the church. The opera which was performed at court or in opera houses dealt with serious subjects and was called *opera seria.* In France the opera was designated as *tragédie lyrique.* Gods, ancient heroes, mythological personages—these were the characters in opera seria. The plots dealt with noble events and emotions, qualities which were supposed to reflect the nature of the patrons of opera. Generally, the conflict between love and duty was the central dramatic theme.

The long, concertolike aria, which expressed but one affection, was the ideal structural vehicle for such opera; it could provide the desired brilliance. Furthermore, in its coordination of text and music, it was a powerful means for the expression of one affect on a monumental scale, an objective highly valued in opera seria. Indeed, it would appear that the operatic aria was the one form that most fully realized the doctrine of the affections.

Comic Opera

Popular music, music intended for the middle and lower classes, had existed for centuries before the Baroque era. We have few documents relating to this music before the seventeenth century, but we know that much of it was performed in connection with improvised stage presentations, the most celebrated of which was the *commedia dell'arte.* In this form the traditional characters of broad farce, Harlequin, Punchinello, Columbine, Pantalon, etc., were first encountered. The nobility liked to watch episodes of comedy as relief between the acts of their serious operas. As this custom grew, a new form of opera took shape, the comic opera or *opera buffa.*

Aristocratic opera tells us something about the façade of seventeenth- and eighteenth-century history—the magnificent courts, the absolute monarchs, the ideas of grandeur and power. Comic opera deals with the down-to-earth play of situation and often with the overturning of tradition or authority. Comedy thrives on punctured pomposity and outraged dignity. The classic theme of opera buffa shows the servant winning over the master. Giovanni Battista Pergolesi's *La serva padrona* (The Maid as Mistress) is the most famous early eighteenth-century opera buffa. It created a sensation when it was performed in Paris in 1752. As its title clearly indicates, it represents a triumph for the servant. Indeed, as far back as we can penetrate into the history of folklore, the king for a day theme echoes and reechoes. In Mozart's great comic operas, Figaro masters Almaviva, the count; the buffa characters of *Don Giovanni,* Leporello, Zerlina, and Masetto, come out best in the end. In a more serious vein, the middle-class philosophy of Sarastro, whereby a man can succeed on his merits alone, overcomes the absolutism of the Queen of the Night in the opera *The Magic Flute.* Note here that Zerlina, Figaro, Leporello, and others in these works are transformations of the old *commedia dell'arte* types.

Musically, opera buffa also represents a contrast to opera seria. Instead of grandiose arias that developed one affective quality at great length and displayed the arts of the virtuoso singer, we find short, tuneful songs, with emphasis upon a sparkling, witty text. One of the most amusing techniques was *parlando,* a quick patter in an even, steady tempo. Parlando became virtually a trade-mark of comic opera, surviving many changes of style. (A Gilbert and Sullivan piece would certainly lose much of its appeal without its patter songs.) Comic opera relied upon quick-witted acting and singing, and particularly upon the ability of the performer to etch sharply parodied characterizations or to splash about with broad farce. Needless to say, it focused attention upon incident and plot much more than opera seria did. As a result of the interplay of incidents and characters, opera buffa developed the ensemble number, in which a number of characters sing together in a lively give-and-take, often using figures and motives that are sharply contrasted to each other. We might take this to be a lighthearted concertato procedure. Later composers transplanted the ensemble technique to serious moments in opera. In Chapter 6, we shall see how this was done during the first scene of *Don Giovanni,* by Mozart.

Two examples from Pergolesi's operas can serve to illustrate the typical styles of opera buffa. The first, a duet from *La serva padrona* (The Maid as Mistress), *Lo conosco,* has Serpina, the servant girl, trying to persuade Uberto, her master, to agree to do what he will eventually do, that is, take her as his wife. She is teasing and seductive; he is stubborn but intrigued. The music shows some typical late baroque features: steady movement, play of short figures, a firm continuo. But the grand spirit of the baroque is somehow gone; the mood is lighthearted and humorous. Motion is regularly arrested by strong cadences; figures are repeated again and again; the texture is thin, and there is little sense of development or exploration. The motion is often represented by parlando, which narrows and straightens the melodic curve. There is a mixing of figures, rather than a unity of affect. Although Serpina and Uberto do sing the same melodies frequently, they have their own special moments: Serpina with a soft, flattering figure; Uberto with a grumbling, low-pitched expression of his stubbornness. Here the musical authority of the late baroque style is being undermined as well as the social authority of the master who will yield his power to the servant girl.

The second example is pure farce. It is the aria *Le virtuosi* (The Virtuosi) from *Il Maestro di musica* (The Music Master). Here Pergolesi begins in the pompous style of the French overture and, as the piece goes on, pokes fun at many of the typical figures which virtuoso singers prided themselves on being able to perform well. Long sustained tones, great leaps, trills, and cadenzas—all these are slipped into the basic march style, completely destroying the unity of affection and employing comic contrast as a principle of construction.

Opera in the late Baroque period may be summarized as follows:

1. The two most important centers for opera were Italy and France.
2. Italian baroque opera comprised two types: *seria* and *buffa.*
   a. Opera seria dealt with one affection in each number; this was carried out at considerable length, with the key scheme and the unity of figure typical of late baroque style.
   b. Opera buffa involved short numbers, ensembles, a lighter style that incorporated the humorous values of contrast, and the buoyancy of the gayer dances.
3. Italian opera—composed and performed throughout most of Europe—consisted mainly of long arias, preceded by recitatives.
4. The instrumental introduction of the Italian opera, the *sinfonia,* was composed much like the concerto, in three movements, fast-slow-fast;

the first movement reflected concerto procedure; the second movement was a short aria (without words); the last movement was generally a dance—a minuet or a gigue.

5. French opera included ballet, short arias, full orchestration, and a recitative style that fluctuated in meter. The introduction, played by the orchestra, was called *overture;* it featured the precise performance of dotted rhythms (possibly imitating the military tattoo) followed by a quick movement using fugal procedure; it usually ended with a set of dances.

CHURCH MUSIC

We have become acquainted with some examples of baroque church music, having discussed Gabrieli's *In ecclesiis* and works by Schütz and Carissimi. Church music in this era was composed in one of two general styles: (1) *stile antico,* consciously modeled on the masses and motets of Renaissance music, or (2) *stile moderno,* using the concertato technique, the recitative, and other procedures evolved during the Baroque era.

Church music in Baroque times reflected social and political conditions in the various countries of Europe. Nowhere was this more clearly demonstrated than in Germany. Germany's musical history during the seventeenth century reads quite differently from that of Italy or France. Germany was the battlefield for the last and most bitter phase of the conflict between Catholicism and Protestantism, the Thirty Years' War, 1618–1648. The country was devastated and its resources were exhausted. Grand entertainments at the courts of the warring princes were out of the question, despite the attractiveness of French and Italian ways. Opera, therefore, did not find the conditions which caused it to flourish in Italy and France.

On the other hand, the ideological strength that Protestantism was able to gather in this religious struggle gave great encouragement and impetus to church music. Of all the countries in Europe, Germany was the one in which a fresh, vigorous, and extensive art of sacred music was cultivated.

Chorale

German church music is centered upon the chorale (see page 136). During the seventeenth century the melodies used in Lutheran worship became subjects for many other kinds of elaboration, generally by organists. The congregation sang the chorale proper, which was preceded by an organ *chorale prelude* by way of introduction. The forms of the chorale prelude are those of other types of baroque music. The melody might be broken up into its phrases, and each subject treated as a point of imitation, as in a ricercar; it might be given in long notes, while a considerable amount of contrapuntal activity took place in the other parts. [The first number in the cantata *Wachet auf* (Sleepers, Awake) represents this kind of chorale prelude.] In other cases, the chorale might be treated as a set of variations, a fugue, or an ornamented aria (see page 180).

The original melody was felt to be the musical counterpart of the sacred text upon which a sermon would be based; the elaboration, the exegesis, corresponded to the preacher's development of the subject of the sermon. Unlike the motet, which used the plain chant as an invisible skeleton within the contrapuntal web, the chorale and the chorale prelude give bold prominence to the chorale tune. This reflects the Lutheran attitude of worship; the message must be direct, simple, clear, and understood by all.

Many of you have heard the organist in a church perform a chorale prelude on such traditional tunes as *Ein' feste Burg* (A Mighty Fortress Is Our God), *Vom Himmel hoch* (From Heaven on High), and *Christ lag in Todesbanden* (Christ Lay in the Bonds of Death). As the theme moves forward, supported and strengthened by its elaborations and imitations, the idea of faith is conveyed to the worshiper with overpowering conviction.

Church music in North Germany developed, through its intensive and widespread activity, an important school of organists. In the early Baroque era, German organists studied in Italy and elsewhere, borrowing techniques of composition from the Italian canzona and ricercar. Through Johann Froberger, Johann Pachelbel, Jan Reinken, and Dietrich Buxtehude, predecessors of Bach, North German polyphony matured and techniques of fugue composition were evolved that found their ultimate realization in the great preludes, toccatas, fantasias, and fugues of Bach. Bach represented the culmination and indeed the end of an era in Germany dominated by organ playing and composition for the organ.

Cantata

The *cantata,* meaning a "sung piece," took several different forms in the Baroque era. The most important type is the church cantata, which evolved in North Germany as Lutheranism became more and more firmly established. Each Sunday and feast day of the year called for a cantata, based on a liturgical text, to be sung in German and performed by the musical establishment of the church for which it was composed.

Hence, the cantata is a type, rather than a specific form, of composition.

Cantatas consist of a number of movements embodying various styles and forms. Some movements may be grand concertato pieces, using orchestra and chorus; others may be solo songs, preceded perhaps by recitatives; if the cantata uses a chorale, one or more movements might be settings of the chorale melody. To illustrate the range of procedures in a typical cantata, and to show how the cantata draws from the general reservoir of baroque style, we shall describe briefly the respective movements in one of Bach's best-known works of this type, Cantata No. 80, *Ein' feste Burg* (A Mighty Fortress Is Our God). This work is scored for four-part chorus and soloists, supported by an orchestra of two oboes, three trumpets, timpani, strings, and organ. The size of the orchestra and the presence of trumpets and timpani indicate that this is a brilliant, festive work; it was composed to commemorate the Reformation.

1. The first movement is a monumental ricercar, using the various phrases of the chorale as subject for imitation. The orchestra chimes in from time to time with phrases from the chorale in augmentation, set canonically between oboes and trumpets above and bass with continuo below. The long notes in the bass, especially at cadences, represent graphically the firmness of God as a fortress. At the very outset the joyous and vigorous affection is announced by the special instruments, trumpets and timpani. Hardly another work in the entire literature of music gives so intense and searching a treatment of its subject as this movement does for the chorale tune that is its basis.
2. The second movement is a brilliant duet for soprano and bass in the manner of an operatic aria or instrumental concerto. It will be easy to hear the opening orchestral passage returning from time to time and at the end as a typical aria or concerto ritornello. The soprano sings melodic material from the chorale. The texture exemplifies polarity of soprano and bass.
3. The third movement is a recitative and arioso (a style incorporating the recitative elements of declamation and well-defined melodic contour from aria) for bass.
4. The fourth movement is an aria for bass in slow tempo, using the rhythm of the siciliano. It, too, borrows from the opera, with florid passage work for the soloist, and from the concerto, with the orchestral ritornello heard punctuating the movement by means of entries in B minor, F♯ minor, and D major and finally returning to the home key, B minor, to conclude the aria.
5. The fifth movement is an ornamented chorale. The chorus sings the simple chorale tune while the orchestra engages in elaborate figurations,

some of which have the shape of the chorale figures. The style is that of a slow gigue.

6. The sixth movement is a recitative for tenor.
7. The seventh movement is a duet for alto and tenor, again in the operatic style; being in rather slow triple time, it might be thought of as borrowing the rhythm of a minuet. Note the chromatic inflections at the end of the movement, at the word "death."
8. The final movement is a setting of the pure chorale melody in four parts, each part being reinforced by the orchestra.

The melody *Ein' feste Burg* which provides the cantus firmus for this cantata is one of the early Reformation tunes, probably composed by Luther himself.

Bach's cantata exemplifies the best-known type within this genre; that is, a church cantata. The term cantata is also applied to secular compositions for voices which are the equivalent of instrumental sonatas. Early in the seventeenth century the cantata replaced the madrigal as a vocal form; from the beginning it too was organized in the sectional form, of which *Ein' feste Burg* is an example. Many composers, including Bach and Handel, composed secular cantatas, often modeled upon the recitative and aria styles of opera.

Oratorio

In Italy a distinctive form of church music arose through the transplantation of opera techniques into chapel music. This was the *oratorio.* Since medieval times, religious stories had often been presented in dramatic fashion, with characters and scenery. The medieval church dramas are among the ancestors of modern drama, and insofar as they employed music, might be considered to be indirect forerunners of the oratorio, a dramatic presentation of a religious or thoughtful subject or story. The oratorio became established in the seventeenth century. It resembled opera in its component parts, using recitatives and arias; it relied, however, more than opera upon the chorus. Occasionally recitative might be assigned to a narrator, whose contribution would serve to provide a frame for the dramatic action. In its musical aspects, the oratorio might be considered an extended cantata, but both oratorio and cantata, as we have observed, borrowed much from opera.

Handel's *Messiah,* familiar to all, and one of the most celebrated works ever composed, not only exemplifies the oratorio but is a treasure house of musical riches and a compendium of baroque techniques of composition. As a rule, we find Handel's music less dense than that of Bach; Handel's counterpoint is more likely to give way to massive effects of sonority and brilliant passage-work; the intertwining of contrapuntal lines is more loosely carried out. Handel more than makes up for this by a wonderful sense for the dramatic nuance, by the elegance of his melodic lines, and by the brilliance and power of his sonorities. All these are illustrated in the *Messiah,* and, lest we overlook his contrapuntal skill, one of the most impressive movements of all is the fugue *And with His Stripes.*

The Passion

A special type of oratorio, particularly representative of baroque ideas of expression, was the *passion.* This told the story of the sacrifice of Christ in quasi-dramatic form. For his great *Passion According to St. Matthew,* Bach composed shorter individual numbers than those of the Mass in B minor. Thus, he was able to change the expressive value more quickly, to develop dramatic contrast more vividly, and to carry the story forward more powerfully than had he written long, broadly developed pieces. The latter course was proper for his Mass, which establishes monumental and timeless attitudes of faith. But for the Passion an intense personal message was intended. The arioso *Ach Golgotha, Masterpieces,* no. 49, illustrates this value. Its broken melodic line, framed around angular intervals above a pulsating accompaniment, is an expression of profound sorrow. We receive much the same musical impression from the final chorus, with its characteristic descending figure that embodies the typical baroque melodic motive of the sigh.

The catalog of baroque church music includes many other forms and types. Mass, motet, anthem, service, magnificat, and instrumental works incorporated into the celebration of worship—these all represent various conditions of performance, belief, and expressive intention.

Sacred music in the late baroque may be summarized as follows:

1. Germany was probably the most important country in the field of church music during the Baroque period.
2. The cantata was the most important form of church music in Germany.
3. The cantata took many forms and incorporated techniques of composition from other types of music.
4. The chorale was the cornerstone of German church music. It was incorporated into cantatas, sung as an independent composition, and used as a basis for a wide range of compositions, principally for organ.
5. The oratorio applied operatic techniques in telling a story drawn from sacred literature; orchestra, soloists, and chorus were used.
6. The Passion was a favorite topic in baroque oratorios.

CHAMBER MUSIC

Like theater and church music, chamber music in the Baroque period derived its name from the place of performance. This might well be at home, in a salon, or at court, and by stretching the point a little, could include open-air music in a garden or perhaps on the street. Wherever one or more persons made music for entertainment or instruction, the music they played could properly be called chamber music.

Suites, concertos, secular cantatas, songs and arias, and even preludes and fugues—some of which we have examined—all may be included in the category of chamber music. The range of performance media extended from a single instrument such as violin or flute to full orchestra. The range of difficulty covered such simple pieces as those found in Bach's *Notebook of Anna Magdalena Bach,* which are very easy studies, to the brilliant virtuoso concertos of Vivaldi and Handel.

Sonata

Originally one title for instrumental chamber music was *canzona da sonar,* a canzona to be sounded instead of sung. This was shortened to *sonata.* Early sonatas, calling for various types of instrumental performance, either in chamber or church, followed the pattern of other music of the early Baroque period. They were composed principally in short, contrasted sections involving a number of different styles or manners. These sections became longer in line with the general trend of middle baroque music and were more or less standardized into an alternation of slow and fast movements. In many sonatas dance movements were included.

Sonatas were used in two different connections: (1) in the church, where they were called *sonate da chiesa;* (2) for domestic use, where they were called *sonate da camera.* Sonate da chiesa were supposed to use a more serious style than the sonate da camera; yet, dancelike movements, which predominate in the sonata da camera, are found in both types. Arcangelo Corelli's Sonata da Chiesa in E minor, Op. 3, no. 7, *Masterpieces,* no. 39, illustrates the ecclesiastical type. You will observe the severe style of the slow movements, the purposeful polyphony of the first quick movement, and the dancelike manner of the final quick movement. Notice, particularly in the slow movements, how skillfully Corelli uses tightly bound dissonance-resolution patterns to create a strong harmonic forward drive, aimed at broad cadences.

In the sonata, written as it is for one instrument or two supported by basso continuo, the treble-bass polarity is most clearly discerned; the

Corelli work, a so-called trio sonata, has the characteristic texture associated with that form (see page 150).

French Chamber Music

In our discussion of baroque dance forms we have already had occasion to describe the suite (see page 170). Suites were a favorite genre of chamber-music composition in France. The French cultivated dance music passionately, but the kind of music we find in French seventeenth- and eighteenth-century dance suites is quite different from that com-

FIGURE 8. François Boucher: *Dispatch of the Messenger*. A French rococo painting illustrating a wealth of ornamental detail. (Courtesy of the Metropolitan Museum of Art.)

posed in England, Germany, or Italy. Indeed, a very distinctive kind of chamber-music style evolved in France. French musicians preferred the lute particularly as a domestic instrument.

The lute, a plucked string instrument, could neither play in a genuine polyphonic manner nor sustain a tone, once it had been plucked. In this respect it is similar to the present-day guitar, of which it is a direct ancestor. The role of the guitar, when we hear it now, is to provide a rhythmic-harmonic support to a singer or some instrument that can take a melody conveniently. Likewise, in the seventeenth century, the lute was used for accompaniment, very often as the continuo. However, by ingenious modifications, French lute composers used that instrument in solo performance. They interspersed runs of rapid notes and arpeggios between the principal tones of the melody to create a more continuous effect of movement; they alternated melodic motives between several strings, giving the impression of polyphony; and they created ornamental clusters of rapid tones around the principal tones to give the illusion of a sustained sound. All in all, French lute music had an airy, insubstantial, highly ornate, delicate, and precious manner, entirely in contrast to the monumental style of the French orchestra and suggestive of French court society as it was at that time. The courtier was frivolous and of little weight, and so was his music. In the latter part of the seventeenth century, French musicians turned to the harpsichord as the principal solo instrument, but they transferred the style of the lute to the keyboard.

Lute music gave rise to a typical French manner of performance, well-known in the eighteenth century and called the *stile brisé,* the broken style. Couperin's piece for clavecin, *La Galante,* illustrates the ornamental French style (see *Masterpieces,* no. 40). Bach turned to the French manner again and again, providing many of his slow movements with a rich embroidery of ornaments.

Chamber music in the late Baroque period can be summarized as follows:

1. Chamber music was composed either for entertainment or for instruction.
2. It included a great many types of composition—concertos, suites, preludes, fantasias, fugues, cantatas, songs, and chamber sonatas.
3. The sonata, when it is distinguishable from the suite, consists of an alternation of slow and fast movements, drawing upon typical idioms of the late baroque style.
4. The French developed a special style of chamber music, based upon the "broken" style of lute playing, which involved a rich texture of ornamentation.

Combinations of Procedure in Late Baroque Music

In this chapter we have discussed late baroque music from the point of view of its categories. Classification in all areas of thought and experience was a most important preoccupation in the seventeenth and eighteenth centuries; music joined this trend. The classification of things and processes represented the *static,* absolute aspect of the times. But classes were not established for themselves alone. They constituted areas in which the play of elements could take place. Combinations, expansions, contractions, modifications—all manner of manipulation was possible, using materials that were clearly defined and universally understood. Musical fission and fusion occurred constantly to enrich the substance of musical communication and to expand the range of available usage. This was the *dynamic* aspect of late baroque music, one that created a virtually inexhaustible reservoir of procedures for composers of that era. To the listener who could recognize these "artificial" combinations, the music offered striking and meaningful facets of content.

1. Dance rhythms were used to provide characteristic patterns in instrumental music (e.g., the second fugue (page 163) as well as the third—a gavotte—from Bach's *Well-Tempered Clavier*) and in vocal music (e.g., the aria from Handel's *Rinaldo,* page 180).
2. Dance form was embodied in single movements [e.g., the first movement of Scarlatti's sonata (page 171).
3. Concerto layout was transferred from the orchestral realm (e.g., in the Scarlatti sonata and also in the subject of Bach's great fugue in A minor, where the first two measures represent a tutti and the next four measures a solo).
4. Aria style was transferred to instrumental music, as in the second movement of Bach's *Brandenburg* Concerto No. 2.
5. Concerto figuration was assigned to the voice (e.g., the middle part of the aria from Handel's *Rinaldo*).

The *Crucifixus* and *Et Resurrexit* of Bach's Mass in B minor demonstrate a number of these stylistic transferences; we have the dance form (chaconne) treated in motet (imitative) style by the voices, the concertato scoring for voices and instruments, the fugal entries in the *Et Resurrexit,* which itself has the rhythm of a minuet, and the da capo structure of the *Et Resurrexit,* borrowed from the aria. The summit of the trend, thus, appears to be the music of Bach, where the combination of styles, density of texture, tightness of harmonic and rhythmic action, and breadth of structure work together to create a kind of "ideal" style for baroque music, which, in fact, rises far above the typical music of this period.

Precise, reasoned, yet imaginative treatment of material in music parallels the scientific and mathematical developments of the seventeenth century. We have only to think of Newton, Leibniz, Descartes, Kepler, Harvey, and Pascal, among many, to realize how thoroughly the scientific attitude permeated the spirit of these times and guided the thoughts of men.

Scientific methods exerted a strong influence upon musical speculation in the eighteenth century. The most important result was the work of Jean Philippe Rameau, who published treatises in which he tried to show how harmony is derived from natural acoustical phenomena. Unlike other theorists, who were content to classify chords according to their usefulness, Rameau wanted to demonstrate that music had as firm a basis in nature as physics, astronomy, or mathematics. He was only partly successful; yet his theories have had a profound effect upon musical thinking to this very day.

The four principal areas of musical activity in the seventeenth and early eighteenth centuries, Germany, Italy, France, and England, each contributed something distinctive to the synthesis of style in late baroque music. Of these, Italy's activity, while not so productive of great monuments as Germany's, was more pervasive and persuasive than any. The Italians worked out brilliant styles of instrumental performance just as they did for solo vocal music in opera. They were also responsible for the final evolution of the modern violin. Such names as Stradivari, Amati, and Guarneri are legendary in the history of violin making, and the Italian violins have not been equaled to this day in beauty of tone. Wherever Italian musicians traveled they carried their style of playing and the musical forms which they had evolved. The very language of opera and chamber music was Italian, as the titles and terms bear witness.

Such widespread popularity grew from the pleasing nature of Italian music itself. Ingratiating melody, sensuous appeal of sound, brilliant and facile passage-work, regular rhythms, a feeling for easily perceived order, a sweetness and logic of harmony—all these were qualities which combined to gain for Italian music a popular success all over Europe and to establish the Italian style as a kind of norm for eighteenth-century music.

When the continuous flow and expansion began to break up, when the long line became a series of short fragments, when cadences and caesuras occurred frequently and regularly, showing shortening of breath, then the baroque itself no longer lived. There was a foreshadowing of this in the Italian opera sinfonia. In opera buffa, in salon pieces for keyboard written in the middle of the eighteenth century, and in short and simple songs and dances that appealed to middle-class listeners, the process of breakup spread. Eventually, this disintegration opened the way to the re-formation of musical structure which took place during the Viennese classic era of the late eighteenth century.

Summary

1. *Sound:* In ensemble music, well-defined levels maintained; in solo music, fairly wide range covering several levels; transparency of sound; retention of one color value; contrast achieved by concertato procedures and by tutti-solo alternations
2. *Movement; meter and rhythm:* Steady, purposeful, energetic, regular, except in fantasias and recitatives; one quality for a movement or principal section; characteristic rhythmic patterns of dances often used; well-defined duple and triple meters; organization of statement and counterstatement in groups of two; in dance music, clear symmetry of phrases; occasional mixtures of meter between duple and triple, as in the courante
3. *Arrival:* Clear, often emphatic, strongly directed, rather frequent, but often overridden
4. *Melody:* Sharply defined motives, treated systematically to form broad melodic arches; motives often arranged sequentially; much use of variation; irregular, declamatory style in recitative
5. *Texture:* Basic trio-sonata layout; strong sense of polyphonic action, due to active part writing; much use of imitation
6. *Harmony:* Strong sense of key; circular or "solar" arrangement of degrees within a key, supported by cadences and sequential action; very strong cadential action at the end of major sections; exploratory harmony in recitatives with considerable chromaticism; some chromaticism to enrich the key feeling
7. *Structure:* Fugue, concerto, two-reprise forms, da capo forms, French overture, variation; form expressed through departure from and return to home key; tendency to alternate slow and fast movements; combinations of forms, idioms, types
8. *Expression:* Doctrine of the affections, establishing a style or manner for each piece, which was then carried out at length; strong characterization of expressive qualities; some pictorialism
9. *Performance:* In theater, church, and chamber

Genres and Compositions Discussed in This Chapter

Theater music

French overture: *Lully:* Overture to *Armide, Masterpieces,* no. 36

Italian opera sinfonia: *Scarlatti, Alessandro:* La Caduta de Decem Viri (The Fall of the Decemvirate), *Treasury,* no. 44

Opera buffa: *Pergolesi: Lo conosco* from *La Serva Padrona* (The Maid as Mistress); *Le virtuosi* (The Virtuosi) from *Il Maestro di Musica* (The Music Master)

Opera, early baroque: *Monteverdi: Tu se' morta* (You Are Dead) from *Orfeo, Masterpieces,* no. 31

Opera seria: *Handel: Cara sposa* (Dear Spouse) from *Rinaldo, Masterpieces,* no. 44

Opera, English: *Purcell: When I Am Laid to Rest* from *Dido and Aeneas*

Church music

Cantata: *Bach: Wachet auf* (Sleepers, Awake); (*Ein' feste Burg*) A Mighty Fortress Is Our God; *Schütz: O Herr, hilf* (O Lord, Help), *Masterpieces,* no. 33

Concertato motet: *Gabrieli: In ecclesiis* (In the Congregation)

Chorale prelude: *Bach:* (*Wachet auf*) (Sleepers, Awake)

Fugue: *Bach:* Kyrie I from Mass in B minor; *Handel: Blessing and Honor* from *The Messiah*

Mass: *Bach:* Mass in B minor

Passion: *Bach: Ach Golgotha* from *St. Matthew Passion, Masterpieces,* no. 49

Variation: *Bach:* Canonic Variations on *Vom Himmel Hoch* (From Heaven on High); *Crucifixus* from Mass in B minor

Chamber music

Concerto: *Bach: Brandenburg* Concertos, no. 2 in F major, no. 3 in G major, no. 6 in B♭ major; *Handel:* Concerto in C major for oboe, strings, and continuo, *Masterpieces,* no. 43

Dance: *Bach:* Sonata No. 3 for violin alone (polonaise); *Couperin: La Galante* (gigue), *Masterpieces,* no. 40; (See also suite and sonata)

Fugue: *Bach:* Organ Fugue in A minor; Sonata No. 2 for violin alone, second movement; *Well-Tempered Clavier,* Fugues, Nos. 1, 2, 3; *Corelli:* Sonata da Chiesa in E minor, Op. 3, no. 7, first allegro

Madrigal: *Caccini: Dovro dunque morire* (Must I Die), *Masterpieces,* no. 30; *Monteverdi: Ohime, se tanto amate* (Alas! If You Love So Much)

Monody: (See *Caccini* under madrigal)

Prelude: *Bach: Well-Tempered Clavier,* Prelude No. 1

Sonata: *Corelli:* Sonata da Chiesa in E minor, Op. 3, no. 7, *Masterpieces,* no. 39; *Bach:* Sonata No. 2 in A minor and No. 3 in C major for violin alone; *Handel:* Sonata in G minor; *Scarlatti, Domenico:* Sonata in C minor, *Masterpieces,* no. 42

Suite: *Bach:* French Suite No. 6 in E major; *Froberger:* Suite in E minor, *Masterpieces,* no. 35

Toccata: *Bach: Toccata* from Toccata, Adagio, and Fugue in C major

Variation: *Bach: Goldberg* Variations; Passacaglia and Fugue in C minor; (See also church music)

Suggestions for Critical Listening

Many of the criteria given in Chapter 4, page 141, are applicable in evaluating baroque music. In addition, the following points may be noted:

1. ***Sound:*** Use of tutti-solo layout (concerto procedure)
2. ***Movement; meter and rhythm:*** Typical rhythmic patterns derived from dance music
3. ***Melody:*** Amount of ornamentation; regular or free
4. ***Texture:*** Handling of treble-continuo relationship
5. ***Harmony:*** Many or few shifts of key; clarity of key feeling
6. ***Structure:*** Key scheme; two-reprise form; da capo form; number and character of movements within a large piece
7. ***Expression:*** Type of affective value suggested

Suggested Listening Projects

1. **Monteverdi, Claudio: *Lamento d'Arianna, 2000 Years,* no. 18**

   Listen for: Stile rappresentativo; poignant, often chromatic supporting harmonies; strong cadential effects; particularly expressive intervals in solo voice line; varied settings of the refrain *Lasciatemi morire* (Let Me Die).

2. **Vivaldi, Antonio: Concerto in G minor, Op. 3, no. 2**

   Listen for: Very clear distinctions between tutti and solo; mechanical stereotyped figures, especially in solo passages; continuous motoric drive; cadential drive, particularly toward end of a section. Compare the transparent part writing of this piece with the densely woven counterpoint of the first movements of Bach's *Brandenburg* Concertos, Nos. 3 and 6.

3. **Handel: *The Messiah,* For unto Us a Child Is Born**

   Listen for: Concertolike style and layout; contrast between the three principal motives: *For unto us, And the government, Wonderful!*; incidental imitations not thoroughly carried out; virtuoso demands upon chorus; transparent textures; four important points of arrival; stretto and broadening effects at end.

chapter six

Classic Music

Today's listener needs no introduction to classic music. Haydn, Mozart, and Beethoven are familiar concert names. Mozart is a best-seller in recordings of serious music. For almost two centuries classic music has had a tremendous appeal to listeners, performers, composers, and scholars.

Let us begin by listening to a work that is familiar to most concert-goers: the first movement of Mozart's Symphony No. 41 in C major, the *Jupiter*. In many respects this music is different from any that we have thus far heard in our survey of music's growth. There is a greater brilliance and fullness of sound; there is a tremendous variety of texture and color; we hear many sharp contrasts of style and dynamics. The marchlike pace builds up into long phases of movement projected on a grand scale; the points of arrival are emphatic and act as long-range harmonic goals, indeed, as areas of arrival following intense action. The shift from one expressive value to another is striking, often surprising. Marches and flourishes, a song, a dance, vigorous contrapuntal wrestlings, and grand climaxes—all find their place within the framework of this piece, a piece that impresses us also by its imposing length. Throughout we sense undercurrents of dramatic force, ready to explode at any time. With all this variety and richness of content, we are constantly aware that the form, long as it is, remains entirely under control, that it seems to pursue its ends with clarity, breadth, and force.

From our listening, we know that classic music contains many works that are comparable to the *Jupiter* Symphony in scope and in richness of content. How did this come about? What are the conditions and procedures that underlie the classic style and its forms? To answer these questions, we must first set the stage.

Stylistic Materials of Classic Music

In the first movement of the *Jupiter* Symphony, we heard many musical styles. Some of these had a popular flavor. There were march patterns, a number of charming songlike moments, and a captivating little dance that Mozart let us hear a number of times. These are all symptoms of what was taking place culturally and socially during that era.

During the eighteenth century a new audience began to exert a strong influence upon musical style and taste. The middle class, growing in prosperity and strength, became an important patron and consumer of music. The preferences of the middle class ran to simple dances and songs, to short and easy pieces of obvious and strong popular appeal. This represented a drastic shift in musical taste from that of the aristocratic connoisseurs of the Baroque period. Dances themselves reflected the change in style. For example, earlier in the eighteenth century, at the court of Louis XV, dances were intended for a small group of experts. There were many subtle variations of movement in the dances themselves and a corresponding free ornamentation of the music with which they were accompanied. This was an art meant for the delight of sophisticated noblemen. On the other hand, the popular dances of the later eighteenth century were mass dances, characterized by a vigorous, simple, and down-to-earth quality; and the music for these dances corresponded in style.

The history of the minuet, the most popular dance of both eras, illustrates the change strikingly. In the earlier period the minuet was an elegant and elaborate dance of rather moderate and restrained quality of movement. By the time of Haydn and Mozart it became a sturdy and forthright dance with a briskly swinging quality of movement. Contrast J. K. F. Fischer's Menuet with the Menuetto from Haydn's *London* Symphony. In the former the very pace seems uncertain, because of the elaborate ornamentations; we hear no strong sense of accent. The Haydn Menuetto, on the other hand, has a direct, earthy manner, arising from its vigorously accented beat and its unadorned melody.

EXAMPLE 6·1 Change in style of minuet

a. J. K. F. Fischer: Menuet (1696)

b. Haydn: Menuetto from *London* Symphony (1795)

The ever-growing influence of popular idioms, which we have been tracing during our survey of the medieval, Renaissance, and Baroque periods, reaches its point of saturation in Viennese classic music. In the later eighteenth century, dances, songs, and marches were so strong in their appeal and influence that they became common denominators for musical style. The principal materials for many sonatas, symphonies, and concertos were drawn directly from these idioms.

Listen to the opening of Haydn's Sonata in C major. It is in the manner of a march.

EXAMPLE 6·2 Haydn: Sonata in C major

The Allegro of the first movement of Mozart's Symphony No. 39 in E♭ major, K. 543, begins as a *Ländler,* a German dance resembling the waltz.

EXAMPLE 6·3 Mozart: Symphony No. 39 in E♭ major, K. 543

The final movement of Beethoven's Concerto in G major for Piano and Orchestra, Op. 58, is in the style of a contredanse.

EXAMPLE 6·4 Beethoven: Concerto in G major for Piano and Orchestra, Op. 58

Another strong popularizing influence in music was comic opera. In its various forms, as *opera buffa, opéra comique, Singspiel,* and *ballad opera,* this type of stage entertainment was enthusiastically patronized everywhere in Europe during the eighteenth century. As in other times, comic opera of this era made use of popular song and dance idioms. In fact, it often acted as a kind of central clearinghouse. Well-known tunes might be inserted into the music of a comic opera; and, on the other hand, a fetching new song from a comic opera often became a current favorite. In those times it was perfectly in order to "adapt" great music to popular usage. In a letter to Baron Gottfried von Jacquin in 1787, Mozart said, "all these people (in Prague) flew about in sheer delight to the music of my 'Figaro' arranged for quadrilles and waltzes." To be sure, the line between popular and serious music was a bit more difficult to draw in the eighteenth century than it is at present.

Mingled with popular idioms we find, in classic music, many serious styles and idioms drawn from the reservoir of eighteenth-century musical practice. Taking a bird's-eye view of these will help us to appreciate the stylistic content of classic music. Thus, we can better understand one of the basic principles of classic musical aesthetics, namely, *the contrast and the reconciliation of divergent and often opposing musical qualities.*

As you listen to classic music, you will notice certain characteristic features of sound, movement, and arrival:

1. The sound tends to be transparent, even thin, and is set at a rather high level, as a rule. The bass does not have the heaviness of the baroque continuo.
2. Movement is much more regular, more symmetrical than in baroque music. The effect is often that of a clockwork (which eighteenth-century society dearly loved in many forms). The bass does not move as heavily and purposefully as in baroque music. It serves very often to punctuate the music at points where the symmetry has to be reinforced,

i.e., on the strong parts of measures or phrases. Otherwise, it rests, to allow the upper voices freer play of figure and motive.

3. Arrival can be anticipated more easily and is sensed more clearly than in music of preceding eras. Furthermore, the effects of arrival seem to be arranged in a sort of rank, to reinforce the impression of symmetry.
4. Further, you may notice that the texture changes every few moments, sometimes with great contrast; associated with such changes is a diversity of rhythmic patterns in the figures and motives.

The division below has been made according to (1) *types*, which represent fully formed pieces or sections thereof, and (2) *styles*, which represent a manner of composition. In practice, the two categories often overlap; for example, a march is a style as well as a type.

TYPES

Dance Music

The later eighteenth century had its distinctive dance music—minuets, gavottes, polonaises, gigues, écossaises, contredanses, etc. As in the dances of earlier times, each type had a characteristic rhythm, tempo, and manner. The *Little Music Book* that Leopold Mozart gave to his son Wolfgang on his seventh birthday contains many examples of dances current at that time. It provides evidence of the importance that dance music had as an ingredient in the musical education of Wolfgang. Examples 6·1, 6·3, and 6·4 illustrate some later eighteenth-century dance types.

Marches and Fanfares

Marching music and fanfare signals were heard everywhere in eighteenth-century Europe. Every court, large or small, had its military music. Entertainments opened with festive little marches. In opera and concert the march style was also a great favorite, so much so that the first movements of many symphonies and concertos are based upon it. Fanfare signals, often used as the basis for march tunes, ring the changes on the tones of the major triad, as in military bugle calls. Examples 6·2 and 6·5 illustrate march rhythms.

EXAMPLE 6·5 Mozart: *Little Music Book*

Songs

These were lyric pieces of flowing melodic quality, often intended for amateur performance. Many songs were dances to which words had been added. Example 6·6 is a passepied, a dance in moderately quick triple time. It also is from Mozart's *Little Music Book*. [See also *La ci darem la mano* (Give Me Your Hand) from his opera *Don Giovanni*.]

EXAMPLE 6·6 Grafe: From Mozart: *Little Music Book*

The French Overture (see Chapter 5)

The opening of Mozart's Symphony in E♭ major, K. 543, illustrates the French overture manner in classic music.

EXAMPLE 6·7 Mozart: Symphony in E♭ major, K. 543

Recitative

Two kinds of recitative were standard in the eighteenth century. The first was called *secco,* meaning "dry." It was a close approximation to ordinary speech, accompanied and punctuated with occasional chords played by a keyboard instrument. Secco recitative told a great deal about the plot or the situation in a very short space of time. Frequently it lent itself to the sharp thrusts of comedy. The example following, from the first scene of Mozart's *Don Giovanni,* comes immediately after Don Giovanni has killed Anna's father. The matter-of-fact, flippant manner is a shocking contrast to the tragic death scene that has just run its course. Nowhere in his music has Mozart projected the contrast of serious and comic elements so boldly as at this point.

EXAMPLE 6·8 Mozart: *Don Giovanni*

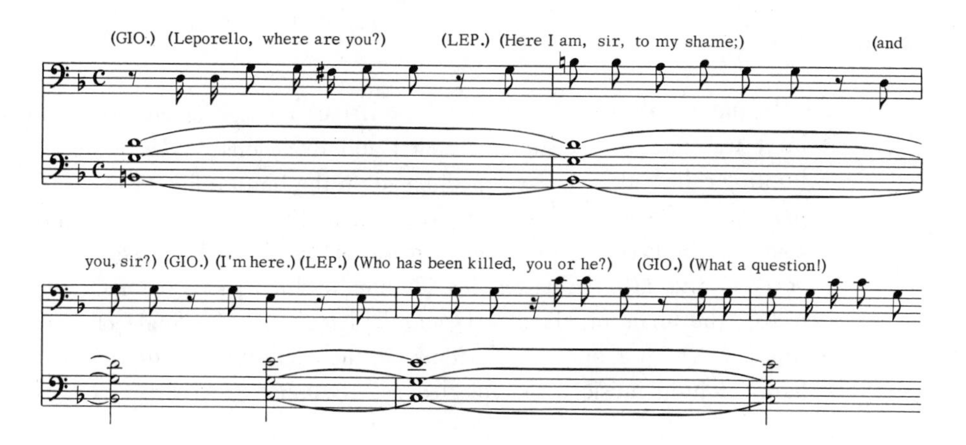

The other type of recitative was called *accompagnato,* meaning "accompanied." In its strongly emotional quality, accompanied recitative recalls the stile rappresentativo of the early opera and the arioso from Bach's *St. Matthew Passion,* page 192. Here we have fragments of expressive melody, pathetic touches, outbursts of strong feeling. Anna's recitative, after she has discovered the body of her father, is set in this manner. Here is an excerpt from this passage:

EXAMPLE 6·9 Mozart: *Don Giovanni*

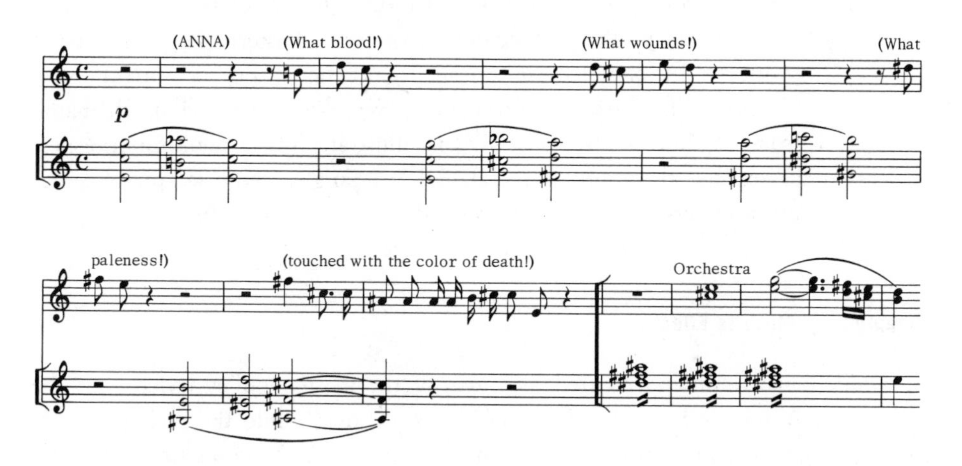

Note the striking shifts of key and the sequential organization of the vocal and instrumental figures, both of which contribute to the expressive intensity of the above excerpt.

STYLES

Hunt Style

In the courtly world that had existed since the age of chivalry, the hunt was one of the supreme sports and diversions. A literature of hunting calls had been developed, based on the fanfare figures of hunting horns. Classic composers made much of these figures. Again and again the hunt echoes in the great masterpieces of the Viennese classic era. Mozart's *Hunt* Quartet, his Quintet in E♭ major (see Example 6·10), the finale of Haydn's *Drumroll* Symphony, the finale of Beethoven's Violin Concerto—all combine the characteristic figures and flavor of hunt music with typical dance rhythms.

EXAMPLE 6·10 Mozart: Quintet in E♭ major, K. 614, opening of first movement

Turkish Music

Eighteenth-century interest in the Orient, stimulated by travels to the East and by the presence of envoys from Eastern potentates at the courts of Europe, led, in music, to occasional use of Orientalisms. Mozart's *Alla Turca,* his Overture to *Seraglio,* and the Turkish march from Beethoven's *Ruins of Athens* illustrate this curious exotic aspect of eighteenth-century musical style. Triangle, cymbals, piccolo, and drum effects were used or imitated.

Bagpipe and Musette Effects

In imitating contredanses, one of the most popular devices was the bagpipe effect. One tone is held as a drone, while the melody travels its way in a rather simple manner. The trio in Mozart's Quintet in E♭ major is a lovely little drone-bass piece. Haydn, in the finale of the *London* Symphony, also made use of a bagpipe effect. *Musette* is the name sometimes given to such pieces, the musette being the French bagpipe.

The Singing-allegro Style

The lyricism which eighteenth-century music had acquired from Italian opera was incorporated into instrumental music in a characteristic manner called the *singing-allegro*. In this manner, a songlike melody with rather long notes and a rounded contour was accompanied in quick, even notes; a rapid, dancelike pace was typical of this style. The singing-allegro was particularly favored in piano music; and many of Mozart's piano sonatas begin in this fashion (see Example 6·22).

The Soloistic Style

This was a style in which the soloistic capacities of the performer were displayed. It consisted of brilliant passages in bold style, in both instrumental and vocal music. Soloistic music was generally laid out according to the concerto-grosso plan, that is, alternation of passages for full ensemble with passages for solo. Example 6·21 shows an unusually brilliant use of soloistic style, beginning at the ninth measure.

The Storm and Stress Style

Both the Storm and Stress style and the Sensibility style—which will be described next—represented eighteenth-century metamorphoses of aesthetic values cultivated in the Baroque period. They were concerned with the delineation of certain well-defined, expressive, and emotional qualities. Both involved relationships between music and literature. The tie between opera and drama was relevant to the Storm and Stress style; song and poetry found a common expressive area in the Sensibility style.

Although both these styles, the Storm and Stress and the Sensibility, showed the influence of the doctrine of the affections, still their expressive values had become much less stereotyped and well defined. The composer and performer were supposed to show that they were moved intensely at every moment in the composition. The composer now introduced many striking changes and contrasts, instead of carrying out the procedure of the late baroque style, which was to work out a piece in a consistent manner with a few similar figures that signaled the affective value. The result was that music tended to give an impression of subjective feeling, not of objective attitude, and it introduced kaleidoscopic shifts of mood instead of retaining a single and specific emotional quality. The Storm and Stress and Sensibility in their subjective and personal aesthetic view are early manifestations of romanticism in music and literature. There is a closer connection between them and the romantic age to follow than there is with any other aspect of classic style.

It was in the keyboard sonatas of Karl Philipp Emanuel Bach, as early as the 1740s and 1750s, that the Sensibility style was intensively explored. The Storm and Stress in music was represented in the works of Haydn during the 1770s. The examples we quote below illustrate the application of these styles in works that were composed later, when the classic style had achieved its full stature.

Storm and Stress had a stronger impact on classic composers than the Sensibility style had. Storm and Stress qualities were more challenging and, when merged with the sustained structural strength of classic music, could create a tremendously dramatic impact. The specific features of this style, illustrated in Example 6·11, are rhythmic agitation, chromaticism, dissonance, minor mode, compact texture, and the expressive qualities which the name itself so well describes.

EXAMPLE 6·11 Mozart: Fantasia in C minor, K. 475.

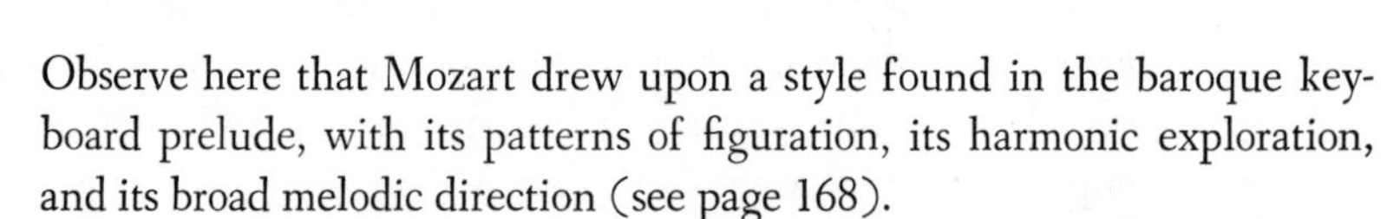

Observe here that Mozart drew upon a style found in the baroque keyboard prelude, with its patterns of figuration, its harmonic exploration, and its broad melodic direction (see page 168).

Most of the first movement of Beethoven's Symphony No. 5 is in the Storm and Stress style.

The Sensibility Style

The Sensibility style and its German equivalent, the *Empfindsamkeit,* were intimate and capricious in manner, with rapid changes in mood and feeling. Phrases were irregular; there were many stops and starts without strong rhythmic propulsion. Example 6·12 is typical of this style.

EXAMPLE 6·12 Mozart: Fantasia in D minor, K. 397

Example 6·12 begins with a plaintive little melody. Suddenly at the fifth measure a strong, impulsive exclamation is interjected. There is a suspenseful pause, and the music continues with an uncertain, broken, chromatic descending figure, suggesting perhaps sighs or the spasmodic breathing that attends weeping. Again a pause of suspense, then an emphatic figure hammers away at one tone while the accompaniment descends, the dissonances accumulate, and the music finally reaches a highly ornamented cadence. Such sudden changes of mood and expression called for an intimate type of performance. Sensibility and *Empfindsamkeit* were typically keyboard and song styles, by which the performer could make as intimate a contact with the listener as possible.

Galant and Learned Styles

Most of the musical types and styles listed above represent what was called the *galant style* in the eighteenth century. It was so designated because its gay, pleasing, entertaining qualities were preferred in the salons of the aristocracy, the galant world, to the serious discourses of contrapuntal composition. Technically, this style was also referred to as the *free style;* apart from its often "playful" aspect, it involved a bolder, less careful treatment of dissonance (see *prima* and *seconda prattica,* page 145) in which emphatic dissonances did not have to be prepared in the manner of a suspension; there was much contrast in musical materials; the phraseology was looser, with frequent and emphatic punctuation. All this gave rise to a much less deliberate sense of consequence than is found in music of the older style.

The galant style was considered to be opposed to the *learned* or *strict style,* whose principal condition was the binding of the dissonance to its prepaartion, followed by careful resolution (see page 120). Thus the learned style was also called the *bound style,* or *stile legato.* Consistent with the laws of dissonance treatment, the learned style maintained a steady and continuous flow in which unity of effect was present and in which punctuation was less palpable than in the free style. The learned style was, of course, applied in the contrapuntal and fugal compositions of the eighteenth century, and it found a place in the catalog of resources and devices that classic composers used. Haydn, Mozart, and Beethoven grew up with counterpoint; their training included intensive study of cantus firmus elaboration, canon, fugue, and figured bass. This is evident in their music, especially when they made deliberate use of devices from the learned style, as in Example 6·13. Note in this example that Mozart has alternated sections of galant and learned procedure.

In Example 6·13 the strong punctuation and the clear sense of phrase balance limit the extent to which contrapuntal action is carried. This limitation is typical of the classic use of imitation; it is rarely far-reaching and is governed by the symmetry of galant phrase structure. The entire piece is in the galant style. Indeed, most music of the classic era is galant in intention. Still, as we said before, the influence of the learned style with respect to counterpoint and imitation is strong in the works of classic composers; where the learned style is incorporated, it adds a powerful element of musical action.

In the eighteenth century many theorists and critics debated the pros and cons of the learned and galant styles. Jean Jacques Rousseau, reflecting his back-to-nature philosophy, preferred the galant; Johann Quantz, a highly trained German musician, had much admiration for the subtleties of the learned style. We can easily see a parallel between the rise of the galant style in music and the rise of individualism in eighteenth-century thought; the decline of the learned style suggests the decline of absolutism.

Other examples of the use of the learned style in classic music are:

Beethoven: Symphony No. 3, *Eroica,* second movement and finale (see pages 252, 254)

Haydn: Symphony No. 103, *Drumroll,* finale (see page 230)

Mozart: Sonata in D major, K. 576, first movement

EXAMPLE 6·13 Mozart: Quartet in C major, K. 465, finale

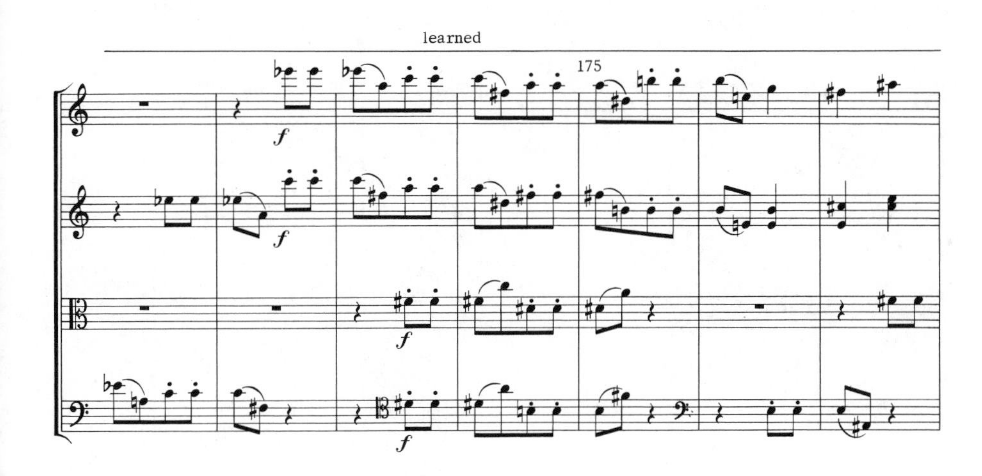

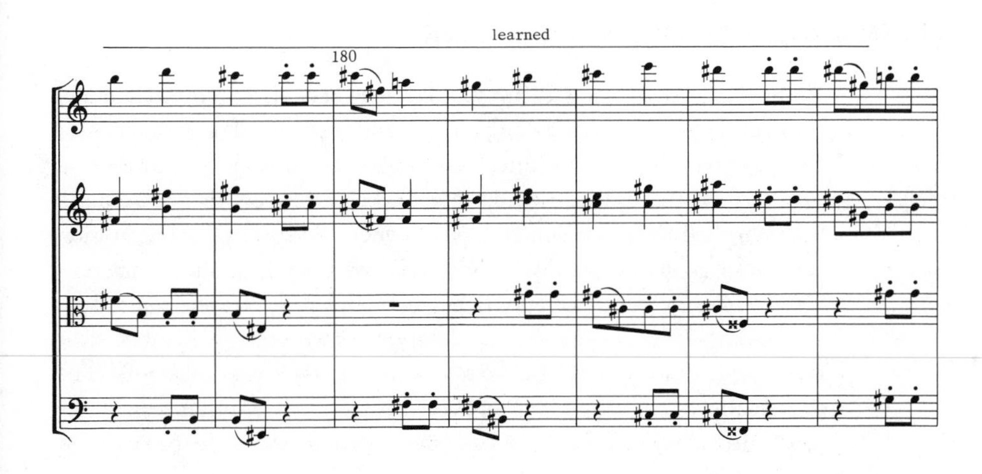

(EXAMPLE 6·13 *continued*)

USE OF STYLES AND TYPES IN CLASSIC MUSIC

All the highly mannered idioms that we have been describing were easily recognized by the listener of the eighteenth century. For him, and for the composer, they constituted materials for musical conversation—a conversation that was carried on among the performers themselves, and between composer, performer, and listener. Borrowing an expression that belongs to rhetoric, we might very well say that these materials were musical *topics*. A composition might deal with but one topic, or it might range over a wide variety of topics. Often enough, we find that the topic is quite specific; the composer is making a particular reference or actually telling a story. Probably the most noted instances of this procedure are Haydn's oratorios *The Creation* and *The Seasons*, in which each number is vividly descriptive of its text. In music that was not especially geared to telling a story, a connoisseur might, to his surprise and delight, discover a reference which added a piquant new value to his pleasure in listening. Although we have no proof of the following interpretation in Haydn's words, we would not violate the spirit of eighteenth-century music if we read the following allusions into these sections of his Symphony No. 103 in E♭ major (*Drumroll*):

1. The entire piece has a military flavor, owing to the fanfares of brass and winds heard in each movement.
2. The military mood is set at the very beginning by a roll on the timpani, which was, for the eighteenth century, a regimental instrument.
3. Following the roll on the timpani, the lower instruments play a melody in unison, composed in the manner of a plainsong, punctuated as if with "amens" at each cadence; this melody is repeated by the violins, with a counterpoint added, in the manner of organum (a prayer before the battle?).
4. The actual battle might be visualized in the second movement. Everyone in Europe knew of the battle of Vienna in 1683, when the Turks were repulsed at the gates of the city and the Ottoman advance into Europe was finally halted. One theme serves both parties, Turks and Viennese. The minor version, with its augmented second, is Oriental in flavor, while the major version, with its hint of fanfare, speaks for the imperial Austrian forces. These versions alternate, in the course of which the Turkish champion, represented by the oboe, and the Austrian hero, the *Konzertmeister* violin, have opportunities to declare themselves. A melee follows—the battle itself—signaled by drum tattoos. At the end, the Viennese prevail, since it is their music which we hear last.
5. The finale is a symphony of victory, a *chasse* (hunt) with fanfares ringing throughout the movement.

In view of the popularity of battle music in the eighteenth century (and long before), and considering Haydn's delight in the picturesque, we are quite in the spirit of the times to take up these fancies, for they may enrich our appreciation of the symphony, which on musical grounds is one of the great masterpieces of the age.

This is by no means a recommendation that the listener try to find a story in every piece he hears. But when the composer seems to incorporate such allusions in the fabric of his music, we should miss something were we not to recognize them. In very much the same way, we can watch a Shakespeare play and receive a strong emotional impact from the attitudes and events that are represented. But in Shakespeare there is such a rich by-play of reference that only by understanding it can we fully savor what Shakespeare is telling us. The music of the classic style is particularly given over to the play of topic, both general and specific. Much of this topical material represents the influence of opera; a great deal of instrumental music is an imitation of opera, with its characteristic expressive values and its lively play of situation in a give-and-take manner.

The better the listener of the eighteenth century knew the musical language of the time, the keener would be his judgment with respect to the skill and imagination of the composer. He could recognize the winning, the elegant melodic phrase, the moving harmonic gesture, the well-placed effective contrast, and he could distinguish these from music that was commonplace, dilute, and awkward. To us today, these values also can come alive if we develop some acquaintance with classic ideas and techniques.

If you listen once again to the first movement of the *Jupiter* Symphony, noting carefully how and when Mozart uses material in various styles, you will see that he is not content to use this material in a matter-of-fact way. Rather, he makes something of each gesture, repeating it, developing it, returning to it at strategic moments. There is balance, control, and drive, a grand scheme in which each measure and motive has its place, giving evidence, like so many other works written at this time, that classic composers were vitally concerned with building form of monumental proportions. They had the raw materials, the techniques, the impulse of expression, and the imagination to accomplish this. Our next step is to get some idea of the ways in which classic forms are built.

The stylistic materials of classic music may be summarized as follows:

1. Types
   a. Dances: minuets, gavottes, contredanses, waltzes, polonaises, etc.
   b. Marches and fanfares: military and hunting
   c. Songs: often based on dance tunes
   d. French overture: stately manner, dotted rhythms
   e. Recitative
      a. Secco: in speaking manner
      b. Accompagnato: in arioso manner
2. Styles
   a. Hunt
   b. Turkish: triangle, cymbals, piccolo, drum
   c. Bagpipe and musette effect: drone basses
   d. Singing-allegro: quick, songlike melodic style
   e. Soloistic: virtuoso, "concertante"
   f. Storm and Stress: agitation, powerful effects
   g. Sensibility: sentimental, intimate, ornamental
   h. Learned: contrapuntal texture (contrast to galant)

3. Combination and coordination of styles and types in classic music
   a. Possibility of using many different styles in a single piece
   b. Referential and topical material

Form in Classic Music

We would probably all agree that the principal impression we receive from classic form, large or small, is the idea of balance. By the time a classic piece has run its course, all problems have been solved and a satisfying sense of equilibrium has been established. This, of course, is more readily felt in short pieces, in which our aural perspective, our overview of the entire work, becomes clear upon the first hearing and in which the symmetry and balance between the various sections can be immediately and directly felt.

For this reason, then, we turn once more to dance forms, where symmetry governs musical events in a most apparent fashion. We shall find, later, that there is a strong family resemblance between dance forms and the larger structures of classic music.

As we have seen in previous chapters, symmetry in music grows by statement paired with counterstatement. Motive answers motive; phrase answers phrase; cadence answers cadence. Nowhere is this more obvious than in eighteenth-century dance music. When one phrase ends with a half cadence and is answered by another phrase ending with a full cadence, we have a symmetrical period. When such a period is answered by another of comparable length, we have a symmetrical two-reprise form. With few exceptions the popular music of the eighteenth century is made up of periods and phrases arranged symmetrically.

To build small pieces, eighteenth-century composers connected two or more periods, arranging matters so that a final sense of arrival came only at the end of the piece. Let us have a look at some of these.

SMALL FORMS: TWO-REPRISE; THREE-PART

The most prevalent structural plan for small pieces in eighteenth-century music embodies *two* relatively equal periods, or two groups of periods; this, as we know, is called *two-reprise form.*[1] We have become familiar

[1] The more familiar designations for this form are *two-part* or *binary*. Two-reprise is used here because technically it describes the sections more accurately; as a rule they each were repeated or *reprised*. In cases where the repeat is not indicated, the harmonic structural layout that made it possible to repeat each section is still present.

with the genealogy of two-reprise form in the dances of medieval, Renaissance, and baroque music, the estampies, the pavanes, the allemandes, etc. Classic composers found the small two-reprise form quite sufficient to contain some of their most delightful and winning music, as the examples below bear witness.

As you listen to the following pieces in two-reprise form, try to determine how completely balance is maintained, or where it has been disturbed. Also, listen for the strong cadence points within the piece and at the end.

EXAMPLE 6·14 Mozart: Menuetto from *Eine kleine Nachtmusik*

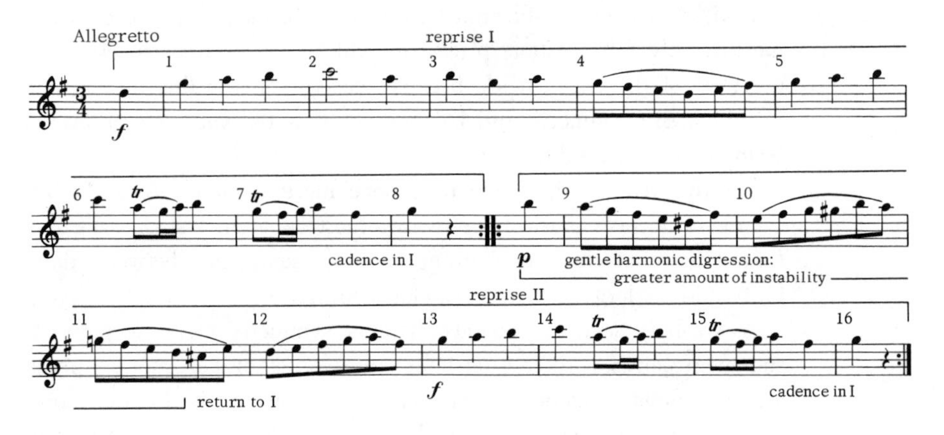

We sense perfect balance in this piece. The two reprises are exactly equal in length. The cadences are equal in strength. The cadence at the end of Reprise I is, to a certain extent, final-sounding because it ends solidly in the home key. Yet we do not accept it as the end of the form because the music has not been in progress sufficiently long to call for a full stop. However, when the very same cadence appears at the end of Reprise II, we can accept its finality because it completes a symmetrical pattern involving two periods. Here is an example of the simplest kind of counterstatement: an answer by repetition. To be sure, the slight harmonic digression at the beginning of the second period makes a great difference, enough to give the cadence of Reprise II a greater feeling of weight and arrival. As you listen for the harmonic flow of classic music, you will become aware that the broader and bolder a harmonic digression is, the stronger will be the cadence which subsequently brings matters back into balance.

Example 6·15 is different from the Mozart example. First, we cannot find perfect symmetry between Reprises I and II, because Reprise II is longer again by one-half. How did this come about? Reprise I pro-

EXAMPLE 6·15 Haydn: Rondo from Sonata for Clavier in D major

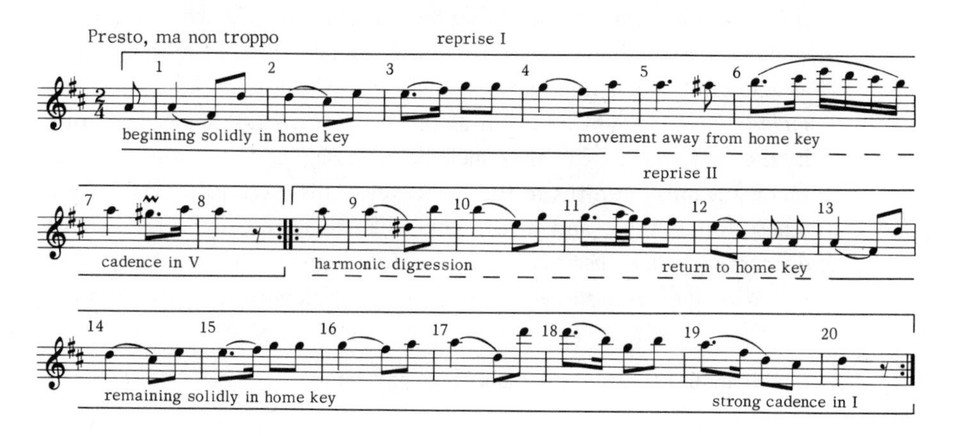

vides a clue. If you listen carefully, you will hear that the cadence in Reprise I goes afield; it does not end in the home key. This is a modulation that is secured by a strong cadence in the new key, the dominant (see page 69). Since the harmony has digressed, has gone off base, it must make its way back home. Having set up such a problem, the composer was, in a sense, obligated to explore before he turned back to his home key. In making such explorations, the mathematically perfect balance of two equal parts was destroyed. No matter; he finished the period solidly in the home key and we have a satisfying sense of completion. The cadential question of Reprise I is balanced by the cadential answer of Reprise II. Here is a diagram of this two-part form (in this diagram, and subsequently, "X" stands for harmonic digression or instability):

EXAMPLE 6·16

	REPRISE I		REPRISE II	
If the piece is in the major key	I	V I	X X	I
If the piece is in the minor key	I	III	X	I
	Presentation of tonic key	Contrast key: strong cadence	Harmonic digressions	Return to tonic: final cadence

You may have noticed that the melody presented at the beginning returned again toward the end. To be exact, it returned when the music came back to the home key. Indeed, the reappearance of the theme acted as a kind of signal for the reestablishment of the tonic key. Thus, the *melodic layout* might be taken as *three-part:* (1) the theme, beginning in the home key; (2) other melodic material; and (3) return of the theme, as music returns to the home key. This gives us an ABA form. These forms, then, and many others like them, are hybrids; *their cadences and their periods crystallize into two-reprise structures; their melodies shape into three-part forms,* as the following diagram shows:

EXAMPLE 6·17 Thematic plan: Three-part form

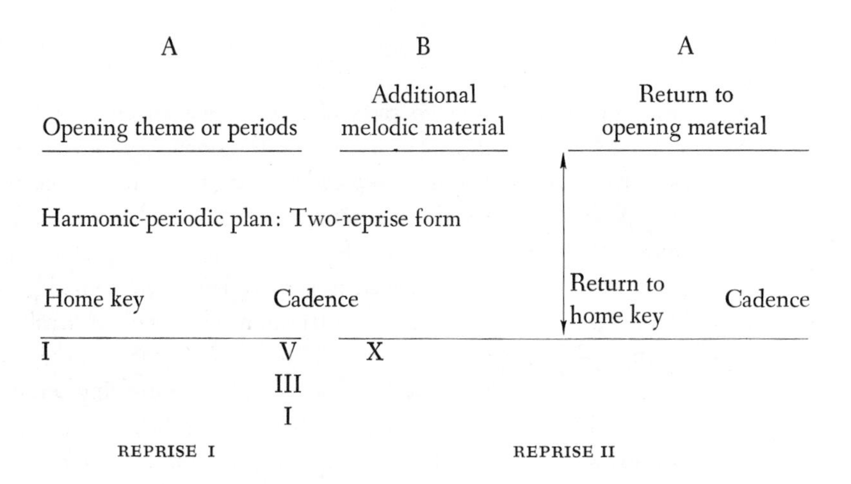

To illustrate the widespread and virtually unlimited possibilities offered by the two-reprise form, let us look at still another example, the duet *La ci darem la mano* (Give Me Your Hand) from Mozart's opera, *Don Giovanni.* Mozart, with his superb insight into the relation of music and dramatic action, has ingeniously used a formal dance as the musical setting for Don Giovanni's attempt to lure Zerlina away to his castle. A symmetrical period form is apt here, since there is a regular give-and-take between the two singers in alternate phrases. Don Giovanni has a rather forceful melodic line; Zerlina sings the same material, but with graceful ornamentation suggests a yielding quality. This ornamentation provides the springboard for a somewhat extended form with broader and more elaborate cadential effects, especially in Part II. In its elegance and grace this melody is one of the choicest examples of Viennese classic music.

Small two-reprise forms are rarely offered as complete compositions. They are combined with each other to make up larger pieces. This procedure stems from earlier music, in which dances were often played in pairs or groups. For example, in minuets there was a first dance, rather vigorous in style, followed by another minuet, possibly more lyric in style. This second minuet was played by a smaller group of instruments, often a trio; thus the second minuet acquired the name *trio*. After the trio, the first minuet was repeated. This plan was taken over in classic music with or without modifications. Listen to the trio of the Menuetto from Mozart's *Eine kleine Nachtmusik*. In this middle piece, we hear a more flowing manner, a lighter texture, and a change of position since we visit another key. Mozart here has contrasted a sturdy minuet that seems to *walk* along with an elegant trio that floats and touches ground but occasionally and lightly.

In the performance of two-reprise compositions it is customary to play each reprise twice and, upon the return, to play each reprise but once; therefore:

MINUET	TRIO	MINUET
A A B B	C C D D	A B

In larger forms repetitions are generally indicated by the composer, although at present many performers do not observe these instructions. For the performer, and especially for the listener, there are good reasons for making such repeats:

1. Since such movements are essentially dance forms, the patterns and the balance of the dance conception are better realized and given scope by twofold statements.
2. Upon the repetition of a reprise, particularly in slow movements, it is legitimate for a performer to vary or elaborate the melodic material somewhat; this adds an element of immediate interest for the listener.
3. Since this music is a discourse, restatement increases familiarity for the listener, fixes the order of musical events, and adds to the scope of the listening experience.
4. The possibility of taking one of two directions at the end of a reprise (forward or return) throws a fresh light upon the structure of the piece.

As you may surmise, it was not difficult to turn out a routine piece in two-reprise form. Literally, hundreds of thousands of such pieces appeared during the later eighteenth century. This was the bread-and-butter music upon which Haydn and Mozart and all the other composers of the time were nourished and raised. Dilettantes and amateurs also

FIGURE 9. Frontispiece of musical dice game published in Paris around 1790. The publisher's catalogue ascribes the authorship to Abbé Maximilian Stadler, friend of Haydn and Mozart. Other such games were supposed to have been composed by Haydn and Mozart themselves. (From a private collection.)

tried their hands at writing little dances and minuets. They were taught to compose these pieces along with their lessons at the keyboard. Among the teaching manuals we find such titles as *The Ever-ready Minuet and Polonaise Composer* by Johann Philipp Kirnberger and the *Philharmonic Game* attributed to Haydn. These books provided simple melodic fragments; by throwing dice, the rankest amateur could put together a minuet from certain of these fragments. Serious instruction in musical composition in the eighteenth century also made use of the two-reprise form as a framework within which the virtually limitless combinations, permutations, and arrangement of musical materials could be explored.

BROADER PHASES OF MOVEMENT

Popular idioms and their neatly balanced little forms were common property in eighteenth-century music. The Viennese masters' distinction in small genres lay in the elegance of their melody, the fine detail work of their texture, and the subtlety of their harmony. But they truly showed their genius in going beyond this small scope to marshal many forces and to build musical structures of grand proportion. It is not often that the lay listener has the opportunity to follow closely and clearly the constructive processes of a great style. In much music the materials themselves are difficult to shape or even to understand. But in classic music, the sense of balance in period structure and the disruption of that balance are so well projected and address themselves with such telling force to the listener that we can proceed quite far toward an understanding of the ways in which classic structure takes shape.

In the examples to follow, the full import of the broadening of structure will be felt only if you listen to what precedes and follows; in fact, listening to a fairly substantial portion of each movement would be the best way to grasp the relationship between the intensity of action on the one hand and breadth of structure on the other, and to realize in what way the example is a consistent part of a larger design.

The first example is taken from the Violin Concerto of Beethoven:

EXAMPLE 6·18 Beethoven: Violin Concerto in D major, Op. 61, first movement

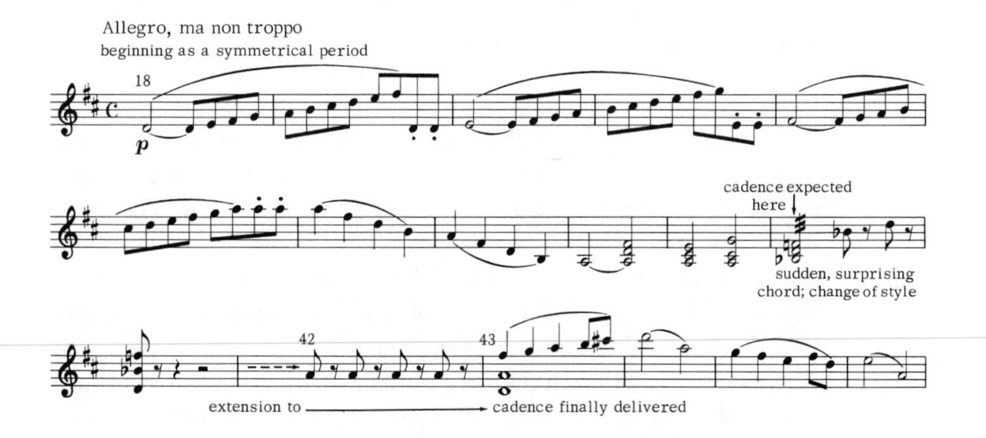

Just at the moment of the cadence, the music suddenly crashes forward with a completely unanticipated surge. A deceptive cadence, a new motive, a change of rhythmic intensity—all these give a new momentum to the music, causing the period to become enormously extended. The cadence we wanted, and which we still hope for, arrives—but twenty-eight measures later. Meanwhile, what a wealth of musical interest has been added to the original material of the period! The critical moment for this period was the *deceptive cadence* at measure 28.

EXAMPLE 6·19 Beethoven: Quartet in C minor, Op. 18, no. 4, opening of first movement

In Example 6·19 the driving quality of the period sets up a momentum which overrides the normal cadential point at measure 8. At this point a light cadence articulates but does not halt movement. The music reaches forward, rising dramatically to a climax just before the broad cadence which resolves the tension. At the cadence, the idea of arrival is pounded home by violent strokes of tonic and dominant. The extension of this period is certainly its most engrossing moment. (Note that Beethoven has used much the same material to achieve his cadence here as he did to thwart it earlier. Compare measures 6–8 with measures

10–12. This rhetorical restatement for emphasis and affirmation is a very powerful means for building up the drive to a periodic cadence.) The structural plan of this extended period, and, indeed, of many such periods in classic music might be drawn as follows:

EXAMPLE 6·20

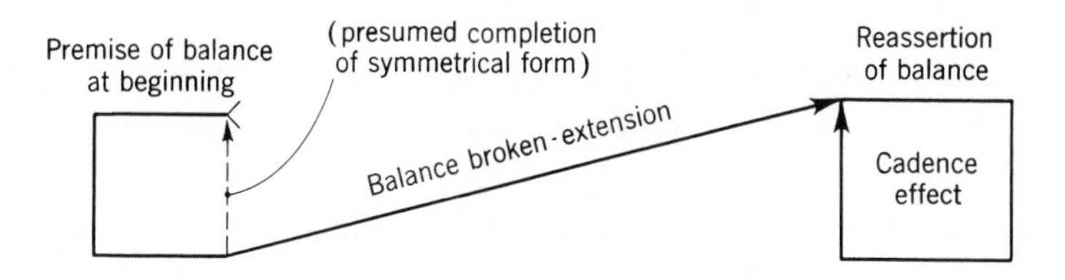

Despite the absence of perfect symmetry, a psychological sense of balance is very effectively projected by this kind of structure. It both challenges and satisfies our feeling for movement and arrival. Example 6·21 illustrates another interruption of symmetry and the subsequent reassertion of balance.

EXAMPLE 6·21 Mozart: Quintet in E♭ major, K. 614, first movement

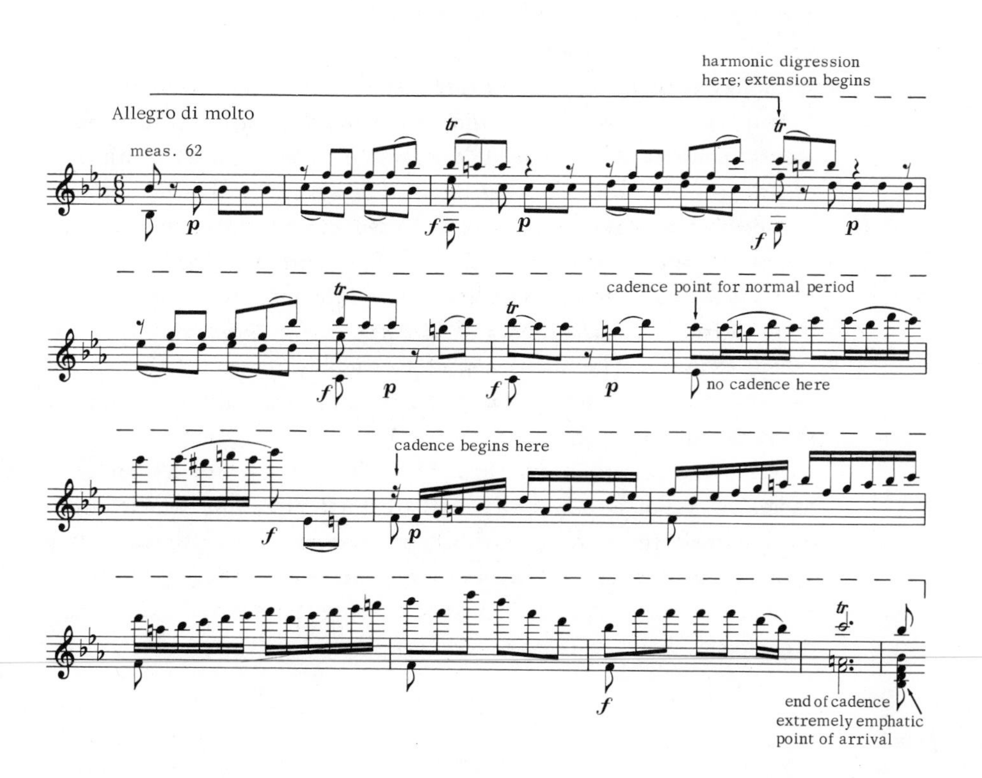

At measure 66, the harmony moves afield: this not only initiates an extension, but actually prepares for a greatly extended cadence. At first we hear a comfortable give-and-take (measures 62–65); but when the digression interferes, there is a tightening of movement which explodes into a soaring, brilliant, climactic flight that settles to a point of arrival only at the cadence. The extension has exactly doubled the length of the period.

Example 6·22, taken from Mozart's Quartet in C major, is still another instance of a broadening of the phase of movement. At measure 31 in Example 6·22 (on the following page), the instruments become very active in working against each other; this is in contrast to the simpler and lighter texture of the first phrase. The singing, lyric melody of the first phrase descends to a lower register and becomes more impassioned and eloquent; tension is increased by the tug and pull of the voices accompanying the melody. Even after the activity of the other parts slacks off and they are in a position to make a cadence (see measure 40), the momentum that was developed throughout the period is so strong that the melodic action does not subside; when the postponed cadence does take place (measure 43), the melodic action carries right on into the beginning of the next period. Here we have heard an active interplay among the component parts. This interplay had an intensifying effect and caused momentum to carry beyond the point of arrival for the period. Classic composers were always alert to give accompanying or subsidiary parts some rhythmic and melodic life of their own.

Still another way of generating more intense and sustained movement is *contrast*. The classic style makes bold contrast a basic principle of structure. Much of the dramatic quality we hear in Haydn, Mozart, and Beethoven arises from skillfully placed, often sudden, contrast. We might compare the expansive effect of such contrast to the energy that is released when two forces collide or two substances work against each other in friction. The opening of Mozart's *Jupiter* Symphony is an excellent example. The alternation of two highly contrasted, juxtaposed motives sets off a momentum that eventually runs down only some thirty measures later.

Not every period in Haydn's, Mozart's, and Beethoven's music is expanded, yet it is principally this structural procedure which distinguishes their forms from the ordinary layouts of eighteenth-century popular music. These techniques for expansion are among the principal resources classic composers had for conveying the sense of exhilarating excitement, dramatic climax, and logical resolution that characterizes all classic music.

EXAMPLE 6·22 Mozart: Quartet in C major, K, 465, first movement

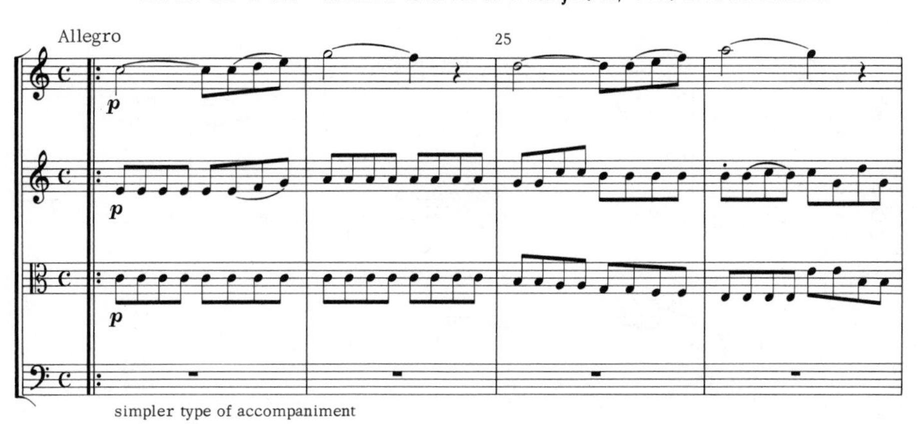

30

f

more elaborate part-writing begins here

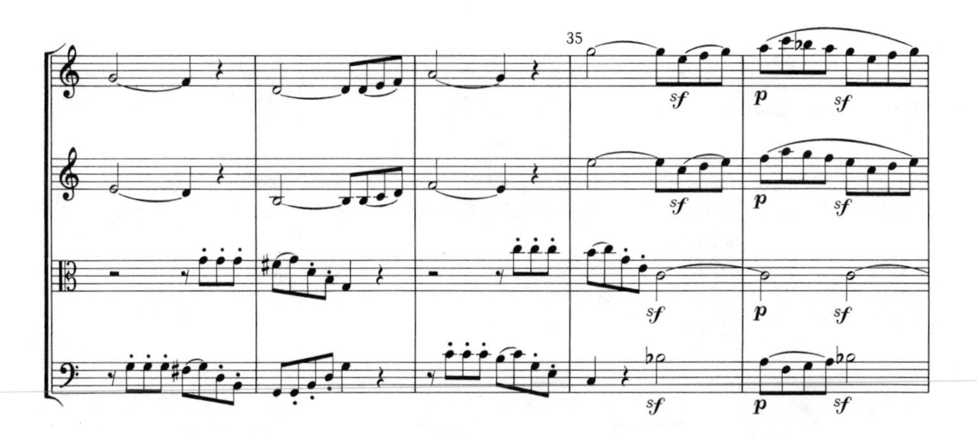

(EXAMPLE 6·22 *continued*)

TREATMENT OF MOTIVES

In the extended periods discussed above, observe what happens to the melodic material while the extensions grow. The melodic phrases are broken up into their constitutent motives, and the motives are worked against each other in a tightened interplay. They contribute their own push to the increasing momentum of the period.

Such play with motives represents one of the greatest skills of classic composers. As you listen to the first movement of the *Jupiter* Symphony, you will find that much of the interest is created by the resourceful methods Mozart employed to work over the dozen or so salient motives in the work. One great tour de force of classic composition is the finale of Haydn's *Drumroll* Symphony. The melodic material of this entire movement consists of but *two* motives. Observe the amazing variety of treatment which Haydn has given to one of these motives.

EXAMPLE 6·23 Haydn: Symphony No. 103 in E♭ major (*Drumroll*), finale

a. Motive, answered by a variant four measures later

b. Four and one-half statements of motive, two measures apart, answered by a swiftly descending contrasting figure; tighter construction than in *a*

c. Motive answered by totally contrasting figure

d. Shortened statements of motive piled on quickly; very tight construction

e. Motive used against itself in learned manner

In listening to the entire movement, notice how Haydn uses this motive again and again to propel the music forward. He rarely lingers; the motive constantly gives the music fresh momentum.

CLASSIC HARMONY

All that we have described so far in classic music, its styles, its phrase structure and periods, its melodic and motivic material—all the salient and rather easily noticed aspects—would not add up to the classic style itself were it not for the highly characteristic classic treatment of harmony. The classic sense of harmony, particularly the classic sense for key, is a framework for all classic procedures of composition. Observe, in the simplest period, the neat opposition of half and authentic cadences that projects the key so clearly. Observe, in the grand extended periods of large works, how their cadences drive toward the goal which is the confirmation of key.

No other style in the history of music makes as clear and emphatic a point of setting forth the key as classic music. The entire cycle of a classic form, large or small, involves presenting a key, departing from it, and returning to end the piece with conviction in the home key, as in the plan I–V, X–I. Thus a sense of key in classic music is very much like the sense of spatial or geographic orientation in the physical world. Home, the tonic key, is the point of departure and arrival. Regardless of the excursions one takes, far or near, long or short, the return to home is made, and there, in the home key, one remains. The difference between classic music and its predecessors in this respect is the dramatic emphasis and the extensive preparations which classic music gives to the various points and areas in this cycle of departure, exploration, and return.

Nothing can demonstrate the importance of a triumphant affirmation of key better than the very end of Beethoven's Symphony No. 5. For many measures we hear nothing but fanfares and flourishes on the tonic chord, C major. Again and again Beethoven drives the impression home, so that, by sheer weight and mass, he will create the harmonic area of arrival he feels is necessary to anchor the entire symphony in the home key. It is not enough simply to reach the tonic chord; the impression must be deep, lasting, and final. While the emphasis is rarely so great, similar gestures are heard at the end of many classic movements.

Intimately associated with this sense of key is the periodization we have observed. Periodization provides the light and strong cadences, those points of arrival which are necessary to give clarity and dramatic emphasis to the projection of a key.

With this basic idea of classic structure in mind—the interaction of key with period structure, framing a rich and varied melodic content —we can now proceed to describe the larger forms in which classic music is most fully realized.

Classic form-building factors may be summarized as follows:

1. Normal period: two phrases; half cadence; full cadence
2. Two-reprise form
   a. Two normal periods: I–I, X–I; or I–V, X–I; or I–III, X–I
   b. Second period extended
   c. Restatement of opening theme in second period, giving ABA melodic plan
   d. Combinations of two-reprise forms as in minuet

3. Broader phases of movement: normal period extended by:
   a. Deceptive cadence
   b. Reinforced cadence
   c. Harmonic digression
   d. Melodic action at cadence
4. Manipulation of motives
   a. Rearrangement that creates altered period
   b. Development that intensifies movement
5. Harmony
   a. Universality of I–V, X–I plan
   b. Classic emphasis on key, especially at points and areas of arrival

LARGE FORMS

Classic symphonies, concertos, quartets, sonatas, and other comparable works are extensive, ambitious compositions that require perhaps as much as thirty minutes to perform. They are made up of three or four movements, each of which stems from a slow or fast type of movement found in a baroque concerto, sinfonia, sonata, or suite. The extensiveness of classic form is a reflection, in part, of the circumstances in which the music was performed. For example, the symphony and concerto were presented to a large public audience, sitting in a large public concert hall, listening to an orchestra that was larger than those customary in the private courts of the earlier eighteenth century. Moreover, the audience was listening to the music itself, not associating it directly with dance, dramatic action, ceremony, or worship. Nor was the music taken as casual entertainment; it was intended to absorb the listener entirely.

The individual pieces in the three- or four-movement cycle drew upon the standard idioms of the time. Following is a brief description of the typical styles of the movements:

1. The opening movement was serious, broad, brilliant and searching; it brought all the skills and imagination of the composer into play. Often its basic pace was that of a march; sometimes it assumed the manner of the eighteenth-century concerto grosso, or a dance, or the singing-allegro. The first movement of the *Jupiter* represents the first movement of the eighteenth-century symphony in the grandest manner.
2. The slow movement appealed to lyric sentiments. Here composers sought for broadly singing, well-rounded, winning melodies. The style was generally that of a song or aria, but occasionally it was a slow dance or march, as in the slow movement of the *Drumroll.* These movements gained breadth by their slow pace and expansive lyricism, rather than by extensive and searching development.

3. In four-movement cycles, one of the middle movements was generally a dance, a minuet or scherzo. Mozart and Haydn preferred the minuet, but Beethoven quickened the pace to establish the scherzo as the dance movement. We observe, in spite of the dance style and form, much play with motives and part writing, many surprises, contrasts, and unexpected turns of phrase in most of the minuets and scherzos of classic music.
4. As a rule, the last movement was a quick dance, often in hunt style. At other times it matched the first movement in brilliance and scope, particularly in the *Jupiter* Symphony. The last movement often achieved a pitch of excitement toward the very end unequaled by anything previously heard in the entire work. This, of course, was intended as a fitting climax and windup to the whole composition, as at the end of Beethoven's Symphony No. 5.

In compositions intended primarily for purposes of entertainment, such as serenades, divertimenti, and cassations, there was likely to be a greater number of movements. These would be additional minuets, dances, or slow movements. The order of movements given above represents the usual plan; nevertheless, the arrangement is by no means fixed and many pieces show a different order. In all cases, slow movements were placed to provide a strategic contrast in style and pace with neighboring quick movements. Moreover, a work might begin with a slow movement, but it would rarely end with one.

SONATA FORM

A movement from such works as Beethoven's Third, Fifth, or Seventh Symphonies or Mozart's *Jupiter* Symphony is a complex structure; its musical path traverses many kinds of terrain, and the distance covered is great. There is a tremendous difference between the simple, small, and crystal-clear structure of the two-part dance forms of the eighteenth century and the imposing masterpieces that represent the culmination of classic musical art. Yet despite the vast gulf which separates the dance from the symphony, structurally there is a family resemblance between the two. We can use this resemblance to help us get a clear picture of longer classic form. To use an analogy: in architecture the motive of the rectangle may be taken as a basic principle of structure. We recognize the function and position of the rectangle when we see it, whether it be realized in a skyscraper or a small house. Similarly, there are certain points of reference which classic structure uses very consistently, both in large and small forms. No matter what the scope of the form may be, these points of structural reference react upon each other in much the same way.

Returning to our two-reprise form, especially that represented by Example 6·15, we can picture it as a bridge, in a harmonic sense. Terra firma is represented on both sides, or at the beginning and end, by the solid sense of the home key. There are two spans to this bridge, anchored in the middle by a strong cadence in the dominant key. Example 6·24 shows this scheme graphically:

EXAMPLE 6·24

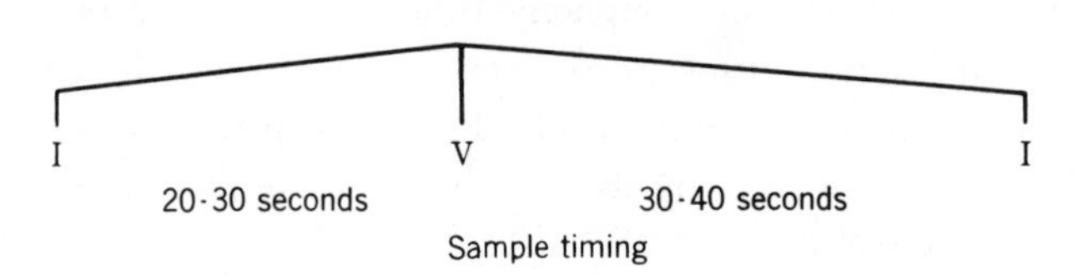

In point of time, this is a small structure, taking less than a minute to traverse its harmonic ground. Now, imagine the same structural plan extended to cover an enormous area. The pillars would have to be anchored much more strongly; the spans would have to be strengthened and perhaps supported by subsidiary pillars. Perhaps also the bridge itself would have to be reached and left by approaches. Yet the basic plan can very well be left unchanged, regardless of size, as illustrated in Example 6·25.

EXAMPLE 6·25

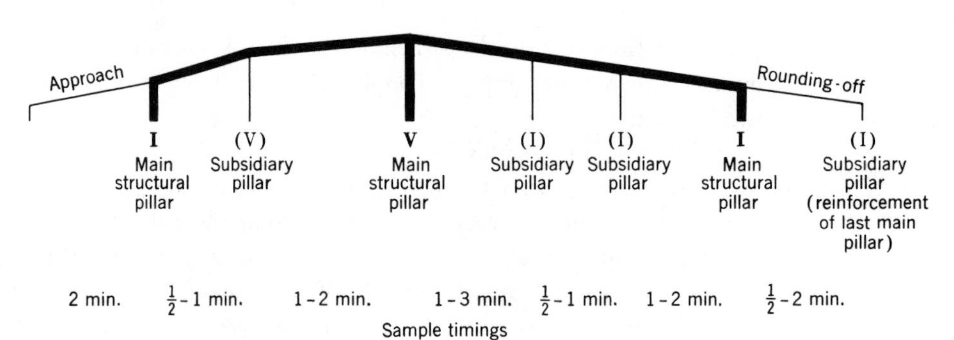

Example 6·25 shows the harmonic plan of sonata form; it is not easy for the listener to hear the harmonic progress of the form, particularly during the first time or two that he listens for it. He is attracted principally by the more apparent qualities: the themes, the contrasts, the textures, the dramatic gestures. Still, underneath these surface manifestations, he may sense, without realizing it, the broad and purposeful onward flow of the music toward its grand points of harmonic arrival.

At critical moments these harmonic objectives assert themselves in unmistakable terms; these correspond to the pillars of our bridge. Such points can be recognized by the emphatic cadential gestures which anchor the form at spaced intervals.

In the final movement of Mozart's *Prague* Symphony, there should be little trouble in locating two extremely important points of arrival, one shortly before the movement has run half its length, and the other at the very end of the movement. Try comparing the two cadences by putting the phonograph needle down on the record just before each passage. The two cadences use the same melodic material, yet you should hear easily that the first is in the dominant key and the second in the tonic. This represents the I–V, V–I plan described in Chapter 2.

It should also be apparent that strong cadences and the harmonic stability they embody can be anticipated for a long time; during the course of this expectation the composer can introduce many striking, interesting, ingratiating, or impressive musical details. Relying on the *unity* and strength which his harmonic objectives provide, he can achieve an amazingly rich local *variety* of expressive content. The two processes work hand in hand. *Broad scope invites richness of content; richness of content gives fresh momentum and energy toward the mounting of a broad phase of movement.*

Thematic Material in Sonata Form

In a sonata form, one or more salient themes will be heard. For both the listener and the composer themes are landmarks; they help us to get our bearings within the form; they act as areas of arrival and departure. As we studied the small two-reprise form earlier in this chapter, we noticed how the theme, stated at the beginning of the piece and in the home key, returned later to signal the reestablishment of the tonic, or home key. Sonata form uses thematic material in the same way.

At the beginning of the form, when the home key is presented, we hear what is generally the most important theme of the entire movement. This is the theme that the composer associates with the tonic key. Therefore, at the moment of recapitulation, when the home key returns, it is almost invariably signaled by the opening theme. When the music moves to the contrasting key of the exposition, it, too, will be announced in many cases by a distinctive thematic statement. We shall hear this again in the recapitulation, *but in the tonic key*. A very clear example of the association of themes with keys is the first movement of Mozart's Quintet in E♭ major. There are two salient themes, one in hunt style, and the other in a singing-allegro manner. The first announces the tonic key; the second introduces the dominant.

Composers differ in the treatment of thematic material in their music. Haydn is well known for using a variant of the opening theme to begin the second *key area.* Mozart and Beethoven tended to use several distinctive themes in each key area. Mozart's use of many themes came from the Italian influence in his music, characterized by the appeal of ingratiating melodic materials. Mozart was also fond of striking contrasts in texture; there was no better way to highlight such contrasts than to introduce them with new themes. Often when Beethoven introduced new themes other than at the beginning of key areas, it was to establish additional areas of departure and arrival for his more extended forms. A thematic statement is like a station that acts as a point of rest in a long journey. We shall see how this comes about when we discuss the first movement of his *Eroica* Symphony.

You may have heard somewhere about the *first* and *second themes* of sonata form. Most descriptions of this form characterize the first theme as bold or *masculine* and the second theme as lyric or *feminine.* This thematic contrast is supposed to establish the fundamental structure of sonata form. However, in classic music such thematic contrast is not always clear to the listener. There are sharp local contrasts; some forms have more than two salient themes; Haydn will frequently use the same theme for both key areas. The principal themes become sharply differentiated in style as a basic rule only in sonata forms of the romantic period; thematic contrast is not the *basis* of classic sonata form.

In order to come to terms with the conventional idea of sonata form described in most textbooks, the following plan is given:

HARMONIC PLAN		CONVENTIONAL DESIGNATION OF SECTIONS	
Reprise I	*Home key area*	A. *Exposition*	Main theme
	Contrasting key area		Subsidiary theme
Reprise II	Harmonic explorations	B. *Development*	Themes worked over
	Home key area	A. *Recapitulation*	Themes restated

You will notice that the same discrepancy between harmonic plan and thematic order that we discovered in the small two-reprise form is present in the sonata form. If we turn our attention to the themes, we make out a three-part form. If we recognize the organizing power of the harmony, the two-reprise form appears to be basic. The two-reprise versus three-part controversy concerning sonata form is still alive today. Here we shall recognize its two-reprise origin and harmonic layout, and at the same time acknowledge that it was becoming a hybrid form as its thematic relationships became stereotyped.

When we listen to a sonata form movement, our concern with themes should be to appreciate the skill and imagination with which the composer has introduced and used them. Are there many or few? How are they introduced, restated, and worked over? Frequently the number of themes has much to do with the character of a piece. One salient theme developed extensively gives the impression of compact structure and driving momentum; many themes in a movement convey a broad and luxuriant quality to the listener. The presentation of an appealing theme is essential to the balance of the form and a grateful contrast to the tensions of development and cadential drive. We rest awhile and enjoy the melody before resuming the business of moving ahead. In the themes of sonata form we have the manifestation of the popular eighteenth-century manner which established so strong a contact with the listener.

With the foregoing in mind, we shall look at a movement in sonata form, the first movement of the Mozart *Jupiter* Symphony, with which we introduced classic music in this chapter.

Exposition

Two large key areas are contrasted. We have already described the extended period which comprises the *first key area* of this piece (see Example 2·23). This key area is marked off by a grand pause in the full orchestra. When the opening theme starts again, gently, and with a delicate contrapuntal texture, Mozart has begun his journey to the second key. He takes his time about arriving, making a few excursions along the way. Another full stop after a great deal of flourish prepares for the *second key area,* introduced by a graceful theme that begins in singing-allegro style, but capriciously changes its motion after two measures to become a dance.

EXAMPLE 6·26 Beginning of second key area

Mozart does not linger long; suddenly the Storm and Stress breaks in, driving the music forward. This excitement grows, maintains a high level for a while, then rather quickly trails off. After another complete stop, a sprightly little dance tune in the manner of a gavotte makes its appearance. It provides a restful contrast to the foregoing struggle, settling the preceding vigorous action into an area of arrival. When a stabilizing theme of this sort appears at the end of a reprise or large section, it is called a *closing theme;* the sonata form characteristically signals the end of the second key area by such a theme. Following this closing theme in the first movement of Mozart's *Jupiter,* a few flourishes, using motives heard previously, clinch the effect of arrival. A closing theme and repeated cadential flourishes give us a very strong impression of the dominant key—a most emphatic and broad commitment. The basic contrast of key has been confirmed. At this point in sonata form, if the exposition is not repeated, the music continues into the development. If the exposition is repeated (the reasons for repetition have been given above, page 221), the composer directs the dominant harmony back to the tonic whence it came and the movement returns to the opening measures.

Development

In the development we hear movement *away* from the second key, harmonic exploration, and an approach to the home key. When the sonata form reaches the final cadence in the second key, it has come to a critical point. From this moment on, the ultimate harmonic objective will be to find a way back to the home key and to complete the form by means of an extended section in the home key. This will prove that, after all, the tonic key is the most important element in the harmonic scheme. The first stage in this return is to undermine the feeling of assertion which the second key gave at the end of the exposition. There are countless ways of doing this; each sonata form seems to take another road. This is one of the points where the resourcefulness and imagination of the composer are challenged. As a rule, the section called the *development* goes far afield harmonically, creating a great deal of instability; toward the end the harmony settles so that a cadence to the home key is first promised, then accomplished at the recapitulation.

In the later classic era, composers found the development to be a great challenge. They worked their thematic materials over intensively, guided the harmony through bold tangents, and introduced sharp contrasts, often in a most unexpected way. The development was becoming the most exciting part of the form.

Mozart, in our example, throws the listener off balance immediately. Starting on the tone which ended the exposition, he engages in a bit of harmonic prestidigitation, which lands us, in four tones, in a faraway key. Blithely, then, the little dance tune takes up again as if all were calm and placid. This cheerful latecomer is destined for great things, however. Hardly has it come to a cadence when it breaks apart and begins to struggle with itself in a tight contrapuntal duel that goes on for many measures. When matters are finally settled, we find ourselves arriving at the opening theme. But still we are not home. *It is not the right key!* After a momentary rest, we resume our harmonic wanderings, while the opening motive is being whipped around mercilessly. Finally, there comes a sense of leveling off. We are being made ready to hear the advent of the home key, and with a grand gesture, it arrives.

Recapitulation

The home key is reestablished. Officially, the recapitulation stays firmly in the home key and reviews the thematic material given in the exposition, and in the original order. The thematic material first heard in the second key area now appears in the home key. The hegemony of the tonic key is secured by this harmonic adjustment. We might think of the sonata form in this connection as being one immense musical rhyme in which the melodic material of the recapitulation rhymes with that of the exposition, but has a different meaning by ending in the tonic instead of the dominant key.

MEANING	SOUND	
Key Area I tonic	A	thematic material
Key Area II dominant (III in minor)	**B**	thematic material ⟍
X		rhyme
Key Area I tonic	A	thematic material
Adjusted Key Area II tonic	**B**	thematic material ⟋

As a matter of fact, such musical rhymes frequently occur in small two-reprise forms where the cadence to reprise I is repeated at the end of reprise II.

As you come to know a particular movement in sonata form, look for local changes in the way the material of the recapitulation is handled as compared with the exposition. To the alert eighteenth-century listener, such changes represented freshness, cleverness, and imagination. One such change is the shift into minor after the first period of the recapitulation in the first movement of the *Jupiter*.

Coda

The coda is a cadential section or area of arrival for the entire movement. In many sonata forms the cadences which end the exposition and which are restated as a rhyme at the end of the recapitulation are not sufficiently broad and emphatic to bring the movement to a proper conclusion. A stronger sense of finality is needed. In order to accomplish this effect, the composer supplies a section whose primary purpose is cadential; the authentic cadence of the home key is stated and restated in a variety of ways. Sometimes the final section, called *coda* (meaning "tailpiece"), is short, as in the first movement of the *Jupiter* Symphony, where Mozart has added just four measures of fanfare to end the movement with a flourish. At other times, the coda undertakes other business before it makes its cadences. In such cases, where we may hear harmonic digressions, some thematic development perhaps, and often another reference to the opening theme, the added material creates a strong drive to the actual cadential section, a sort of "whiplash" effect that gives powerful rhetorical emphasis to the cadence. In the finale of the *Jupiter* Symphony Mozart engages the music in a broad contrapuntal development before winding up the movement with brilliant cadential formulas. The extent to which the coda may be built is discussed below in connection with the first movement of Beethoven's Symphony No. 3 (see page 250).

As we have presented it here, the sonata form has something of the character of a formal argument. It may be helpful to visualize it in the following manner:

The first premise is the home key, represented by thematic material which we shall call A.

The second premise is the contrasting key, represented by thematic material which we shall call B.

The home key makes its point with A; the point is refuted by the contrasting key with B. This refutation takes longer to accomplish than the initial argument; it also makes its final point with great emphasis. (We are now at the end of the exposition.)

The premise of contrasting-key B material is undermined by the digressions and explorations of the development.

Home-key A material returns (recapitulation) to reestablish the first premise, *but* in order to settle the argument and reconcile the two contrasting premises, the home key later incorporates the B material, showing that there can be unity, after all, between A and B. To make its point more powerfully, the home key asserts itself with great emphasis (coda).

Each movement in sonata form represents an individual way of using the general harmonic framework and the common stylistic materials. For example, in Haydn's *Drumroll* Symphony, the exposition is quite short; it is concerned mostly with motives heard in the opening theme.

There is no break in the lively pace until very near the end of the exposition; at this point, we hear, as a refreshing contrast, a bouncing waltz tune that serves to stabilize the second key and to provide an area of arrival for the exposition. On the other hand, the development is extensive and searching. It works through all the material heard in the exposition. There is also a coda in this movement, prepared for by a sudden harmonic digression, an interruption in pace, and a reference to the motive heard in the slow introduction.

In the first movement of Mozart's Quintet in E♭ major, there is constant alternation between two contrasting elements, the hunt music and a brilliant soloistic style. With dramatic surprise the development introduces a completely new theme, in a new mood, the Storm and Stress. Listening carefully, you will hear that neither the exposition nor the recapitulation ends with a full sense of arrival. At the very last moment, in each section, an element of harmonic instability is introduced. In the exposition, this leads directly into the development. In the recapitulation, it makes way for a brilliant, expansive coda full of excitement, with the instruments moving at striking tangents to each other.

As sonata form evolved in the classic era, it was adapted to many types of expression. Quick movements and slow movements, brilliant, gay and reflective lyric qualities—the sonata form was a proper vehicle for them all. Its application in opera, in the concerto, in the rondo, and in the operatic overture will be observed as we deal with these aspects of classic music. Also, we shall see how the sonata form achieves its greatest scope when we consider the structure of Beethoven's Symphony No. 3.

The sonata form was a kind of synthesis, a summing up of all the different techniques, idioms, and styles of the eighteenth century. It used harmonic logic, period structure, and thematic clarity from the song and dance styles; it took richness and variety of manner from the Storm and Stress, the soloistic, and the Sensibility styles. It developed its exciting and lively handling of voices from the learned style; it acquired both a singing manner and the idea of dramatic contrast from the Italian opera. Most important, music written in the sonata form was intended primarily to be listened to, not to accompany singing or dancing. It was concert music, and therefore could make a strong challenge to the listener, to say nothing of the composer himself. Its principal distinction was its breadth of dimension, which came about from the interplay of strong propulsive forces and compensating emphatic points of arrival. The most imposing sonata forms were those found in music intended for literate and appreciative audiences, audiences which learned to enjoy the combination of galant and learned styles. Such listeners frequented the concert halls of Paris, London, Vienna, and Prague in the late eighteenth and early nineteenth centuries. Mozart's piano concertos, Haydn's London symphonies, and Beethoven's orchestral and chamber music represent the zenith in the evolution of sonata form.

One final comment is in order before we proceed to the other forms of the classic style. The term *sonata form* was assigned to the plan we have been studying by nineteenth-century writers. It does not describe what takes place, as do the terms fugue, variation, concerto, rondo, and two-reprise for their respective forms. A more appropriate term for the sonata form would be *key area form,* since this does suggest the basic organization; however, usage has established the term sonata form, and for this reason we have employed it here.

Classic sonata form may be summarized as follows:

1. Extended use of I–V, X–I plan (I–III, X–I in minor)
2. Major sections of form designated as key areas
3. Exposition: key areas I and II, each with its own distinctive thematic material but no fixed number of themes; end of key area II point of strongest harmonic contrast
4. Development: X; nature and order of thematic material optional but usually taken from exposition; harmonic preparation for return to home key
5. Recapitulation: resolution of harmonic contrast of exposition by incorporating all thematic material in home key, usually in order of original presentation
6. Coda: cadential area for entire movement; some digressions possible before final arrival
7. Sonata form used principally for first movement; occasionally for slow movements, sometimes without X section; rarely for dance movements; often for finales; also in opera and in opera overtures

RONDO FORMS

From the grandeur of the sonata form, we shall return for a while to less challenging music of the eighteenth century as we become acquainted with rondo forms. The finale of Haydn's D-major Sonata, of which we have already heard the opening two-part section, has as its most prominent structural feature a main section that returns a number of times. This periodic return identifies the piece as a *rondo.*

The principal idea of the rondo was to entertain, to please the listener without particularly exciting him or taxing his intellectual powers. Therefore the rondo presented a group of attractive song or dance tunes. One of these tunes, generally the first, was the most important and was interspersed between the others. The rondo comes *around* to its refrain, or main tune, again and again; thus it acquired its name. The intervening tunes are called *episodes*. Rondos differ in form according to the distribution of refrains and episodes. Here are some examples:

A B *A* C *A*	Haydn: Sonata in D major, finale Mozart: Sonata in C major, K. 545, finale Mozart: Piano Concerto in C minor, K. 491, slow movement
A B *A* C *A* B *A*	Mozart: Sonata in D major, K. 311, finale Haydn: Quartet in D major, Op. 64, no. 5, finale
A B *A* C B *A*	Mozart: Sonata in C major, K. 309, finale Haydn: Symphony in B♭ major, no. 102, finale (A B A C [A shortened] B A)
A B *A* C *A* D *A* B *A*	Mozart: Sonata in B♭ major, K. 281, finale
A B C *A* D C *A* B	Mozart: Quintet in G minor, K. 516, finale

In earlier eighteenth-century music, rondo forms were used for dances and songs. They had, therefore, the following characteristics: (1) normal period structure; (2) strong melodic appeal throughout; (3) steady, even movement; (4) a minimum of harmonic instability and exploration within a given section. The finale of Haydn's Sonata in D major still exemplifies this type of rondo.

In the simpler rondo forms, where each section is a complete but small two-reprise form, larger structural issues do not enter the picture. We are concerned here with local excursions, each of which starts out from home. The form can grow simply by adding on excursions, as the diagram shows:

EXAMPLE 6·27 Diagram of rondo forms

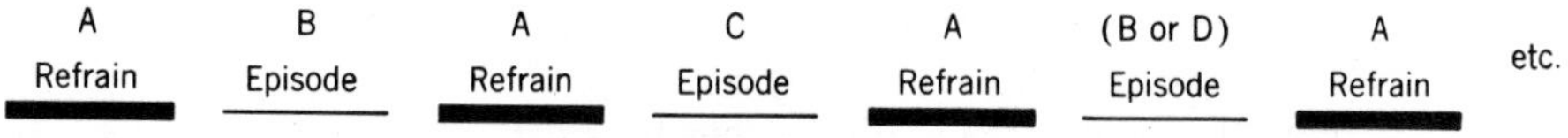

A	B	A	C	A	(B or D)	A	
Refrain	Episode	Refrain	Episode	Refrain	Episode	Refrain	etc.

Conceivably the piece could end after any refrain except the first; on the other hand, new episodes and additional refrains could be added very easily.

An example of the treatment of the rondo form by a Viennese master, is the second movement of Mozart's Quintet in E♭, K. 614. We hear first a graceful, beautifully poised theme, set out in normal periods as two small reprises. Mozart does not let us forget this tune. As a matter of fact, it is the only melody in the entire movement; but changes in key, structure, and mood provide the contrast necessary for the episodes of a rondo.

The most remarkable feature of the movement is the way in which Mozart handled the texture. By this time in his life (1791), he was the transcendent master of part writing, of elaboration, of the precious detail. In every moment of this piece some new delight of ornamentation, give-and-take, filigree work, or texture appears. It is a masterpiece of decorative art, built upon a simple gavotte rhythm.

Later eighteenth-century rondos, those which served as final movements of sonatas, symphonies, or concertos, show the same kind of internal expansion that we have seen in the sonata form. Moreover, they approach the style and manner of the sonata, exhibiting the following characteristics: (1) extended periods, except when themes are being presented; (2) much development of motivic material; (3) broad phases of movement, frequently with contrasts of strong dramatic impact; (4) extended harmonic digressions and broad cadential drives.

Probably the most remarkable example of the later rondo is the finale of Haydn's Symphony No. 103. The entire motivic material of this movement is presented in the first eight measures. Two motives, a hunting fanfare and a lilting dance tune, are set against each other contrapuntally. How typically classic this is: to set galant themes against each other in the learned manner!

EXAMPLE 6·28 Haydn: Symphony No. 103 in E♭ major, finale

Hardly a note in the entire movement is not related to these two figures (see Example 6·23).

The form of this movement is delineated by key relationships in the following manner:

SECTION	A	B	A	C	A	B	Coda
KEY	I	V	I	X	I	I	I
MEASURE	1	91	158	182	264	300	351

It is apparent that this movement approaches the sonata form very closely. Movement and interest are maintained by an incredibly imaginative treatment of harmonies, part writing, contrast, and motive relationships. Not only in the opening subject but throughout the form, this piece represents a complete interpenetration of the dance style with the learned and serious techniques of later classic music. Visualize the situation when this rondo was first performed. The listener was familiar with rondo forms and with the usual procedures of late eighteenth-century music. From the very beginning, every figure, every turn involved a surprise. Yet not one bit of logic was sacrificed; the thread of the musical discourse remained clear. The effect must have been electrifying. No wonder Haydn was cheered when his music was performed in London, for all of it had the same lively, attractive, fanciful, and at the same time profoundly logical quality.

VARIATION FORM

As we look back upon classic music from the mid-twentieth century, the most impressive works of the period seem to be those written in sonata form or in the larger rondo forms. For the composer and performer of the eighteenth century the variation form, while generally not as imposing as the sonata or rondo, was most useful. It served as a vehicle for the kind of elaboration which delighted the listener and which showed the ingenuity and fantasy of the composer. Often the theme that was varied was familiar to the listener (Mozart's Variations on *Ah, vous dirai-je Maman,** for example); the appeal of such a work would partly be in hearing a well-known tune in a new guise.

The variation form was a legacy from an earlier age, as was the dance and the rondo. It consists of a set of small pieces based upon a theme heard at the beginning. Typically, this theme is in two-reprise form and has the character of a song or dance; its melodic outline is easy to follow; its harmonic progressions are clearly laid out and relatively uncomplicated. Each variation retains the general rhythmic and harmonic layout of the theme and, as a rule, follows the melodic contour of the theme. In a given variation there may be changes in style, figuration, texture, or harmony, but always some similarity to the original theme is retained. If the theme is in a major key, a variation in minor in the middle of the series or toward the end provides a contrast for the piece.

While there is no given order for the types of variation, nor a prescribed number, we often find that the composer has organized the

* French children's song, the tune of which is familiar to us as *Twinkle Twinkle, Little Star.*

individual pieces so that there is a sense of grouping and progression. Perhaps one variation will elaborate the theme in eighth notes; the succeeding variation may use sixteenth notes to give a sense of quickening action as well as a connection between the two sections. Following, there may be an abrupt but grateful contrast through the use of longer notes. One variation may actually elaborate on a preceding section, rather than on the theme itself. This, indeed, is one of the principal appeals of the variation—we do not quite know what to expect in the forthcoming treatment of the theme.

Variation form was occasionally used for opening movements, as in Beethoven's Sonata in A♭ major, Op. 26, and Mozart's Sonata in A major, K. 331. Haydn's Symphony No. 103 in E♭ major has a slow movement in variation form, as has Beethoven's Quartet in A major, Op. 18, no. 5. The finale of Mozart's Sonata in D major, K. 284, is also in variation form. (See page 254, where the finale of Beethoven's Symphony No. 3 is discussed at some length as a special example of variation form.)

Variation procedure is often applied to pieces in other forms so that when a distinctive theme returns, it is altered in its texture or melodic details. The diverting effect of a new dress adds interest at such points. Variation then becomes a resource for heightening the interest of a counterstatement, which would ordinarily be a simple repetition. Example 6·29 from the slow movement of Mozart's Quartet in C major, K. 465, illustrates such elaboration. The first excerpt is from the exposition; the second from the recapitulation.

EXAMPLE 6·29 Mozart: Quartet in C major, K. 465

The dotted lines indicate the original notes of the rather simple melody and their place in the decorated version of the recapitulation.

Beethoven employed the technique of variation extensively, developing ever more searching and imaginative ways of treating his original theme. One of his last and greatest works, a monument in the history of the variation—is his 33 *Variations on a Waltz of Diabelli,* Op. 120. Diabelli's tune has all the common features of a popular two-part dance form: symmetrical construction, a simple tune built on the notes of tonic and dominant chords, a stock harmonic digression to the dominant and then back. There is also a sequence in the tune. Beethoven enriches each of these formulas in incredibly imaginative and subtle ways, intensifying every gesture, creating in each variation a new composition, and yet retaining the skeletal structure of the model.

THREE-PART FORMS

Since the melodic material of slow movements is lyric rather than energetic, the forms of such movements sometimes involve no more than several broadly singing, well-rounded melodies. In the simplest versions there is a principal melody, a contrasting melody in a different key, and a return to the first melody. A three-part form is created, as in the slow movement of Haydn's Trio in G major. The outline of the movement is given below:

A (E major)	B (A major)	Transition	A (E major)
1–16	17–36	37–44	45–69

In more highly organized three-part forms, some of the harmonic and periodic techniques of sonata form are used. In the slow movement of Beethoven's Piano Sonata in E♭ major, Op. 7, extensions, harmonic explorations, and broad cadences give the movement a very impressive air.

The designation *three-part form* is also applied to dance movements in which two dances are performed in succession and then the first is repeated. The most familiar example of this form is the minuet-and-trio. Beethoven cast the second movement of his Symphony No. 3 in this form, as march-trio-march; a description of this movement is included in the analysis of the complete symphony (page 252).

THE INTRODUCTION

The first movement of a symphony, sonata, or quartet sometimes has an introduction in slow tempo. Such an introduction is derived from the opening section of the French overture (see page 182). In the introduction of Mozart's Symphony in E♭ major, K. 543, the typical dotted rhythm of the French overture is used (see Example 6·7). In other introductions, the slow tempo was retained, but a more singing style, as in Italian opera, was substituted, as in the introduction of Haydn's Symphony in B♭ major, No. 102. (See also Haydn's Symphony No.

103, whose introduction suggests a church sonata.) In all cases, much of the introduction was dedicated to a cadential preparation for the beginning of the main part of the movement. The introduction of Mozart's *Prague* Symphony is by far the most impressive section of its kind in all eighteenth-century music. Here is a brief description:

The piece opens with the three *coups d'archet* (bow strokes) so frequently found in eighteenth-century music. The quality of movement is broad, impressive. Striking contrasts pile up in a very short time; *texturally* by tutti-solo contrasts; *rhythmically,* by changing patterns; *stylistically,* by fragments of *Empfindsamkeit* and the singing style; *harmonically,* by exploration. Three times we move toward a cadence; three times the resolution is held off by deceptive cadences. The third time there is a cadence to the minor (not the major, as expected). Such a change is far-reaching, for key regions remote from the home key are now being explored. The exploration becomes systematic, the phrase structure balanced. The whims, the surprises of the first part are answered here by a purposeful drive that gradually focuses on the dominant of the home key. The resolution to the tonic major, the home key, comes only when the quick part begins. This introduction takes thirty-six measures of very slow four-four time and lasts about four minutes. The quick part of the first movement is a worthy counterstatement to the introduction, which it matches with its brilliance, its verve, and its great skill in handling a rich variety of materials.

THE FANTASIA

Classic forms are based upon clear-cut period structure. The fantasia is a different kind of piece (see page 210). It appeals to the sense of improvisation; the element of surprise is cultivated; the music seems to wander freely without balance of phrase or well-defined cadences. The figures in a fantasia are brilliant; the harmony is boldly exploratory. Now and then, a period or two of more balanced quality appear by way of contrast. The Sensibility, the Storm and Stress, and the soloistic styles are favored in this kind of piece. Since it changes pace and manner quickly, the fantasia is best suited to keyboard perfomance. The impulsive moods of the fantasia foreshadow similar pieces for the keyboard written by Schubert, Chopin, and Schumann in the romantic era. Mozart's Fantasia in C minor, K. 475, is probably the most celebrated example of this kind of composition. It is organized as follows:

Exploratory section, many deceptive cadences: 1–25
Stable section, singing theme: 26–41
Exploratory section, brilliant virtuoso style: 42–90

Stable section, new singing theme: 91–129
Exploratory section, brilliant virtuoso style: 130–155
Stable section, area of arrival using material of Part 1, and in C minor: 156–172

Each section, except Part 6, uses new material. Harmonically and thematically Mozart rounded the form of this piece by Part 6.

Beethoven subtitled each of his two piano sonatas, Op. 27, *quasi una fantasia* (in the manner of a fantasia). In the first of these, the movements are played without pause; the structure is rather episodic, less tight than is customary in a sonata. The second, the famous "Moonlight" Sonata, carries out, in its well-known first movement, a figuration characteristic of keyboard fantasias, above which the sustained melody gently moves. We might even go so far as to consider the final movement of his Symphony No. 9 a fantasia for chorus, soloists, and orchestra, in view of its highly episodic structure.

PLAN OF AN ENTIRE WORK: SYMPHONY NO. 3 IN E♭ MAJOR, OP. 55 (*EROICA*), BY BEETHOVEN

In order to show how various types of form are combined in a composition of great length, we shall analyze the Symphony No. 3 by Beethoven. This work has been chosen for several reasons: (1) It represents classic principles of structure in instrumental music in their broadest scope; (2) it embodies some unique features of structure, which grow out of the expressive aspects of the work; (3) for all its great length, it achieves a coherence that rises above the general consistencies of the classic style.

First movement: Allegro con brio (691 measures)

Exposition (1–148)	Relatively short first key area (KA); very long second key area
KA I (1–37)	One theme, waltzlike, quick introduction of harmonic instability, imbalance of phrases; different instrumental colors in presentation of theme (measures 3, 15, 37); note drive created by rhythmic imbalance (23–37; see p. 38); shift to second key (45–56), new theme
KA II (57–148)	Many motives, frequent harmonic digressions, long periods, much rhythmic imbalance; trailing off after cadence (148–152)

Development (152–398)	Two large cycles of action
Part I (166–233)	A. Stable section (166–178), theme from measure 45 B. Unstable (178–220), several motives combined A. Stable (220–236), theme from measure 46
Part II (233–397)	C. Unstable (236–284), fugato building up to a tremendous cadential drive D. Relatively stable (284–337), a new theme in a distant key, opening theme in several keys, new theme restated E. Unstable (338–397), return to home key, extended cadential drive, suspense by understatement just before return
Recapitulation (398–556)	Recomposition of first key area, virtually literal restatement of material from original second key area: exact rhyme
Coda (557–691)	A. Another development section (557–631), using opening theme and new theme from development (D); broad drive to cadence (595–631) B. Opening theme (631–662) presented for *first* time in phrases that alternate tonic and dominant in absolute symmetry, four times C. Cadential section (663–691), quoting theme from second key area

Of all the single movements in Beethoven's music, this is perhaps the most impressive from a structural point of view, and certainly one of the most significant in its impact on the future history of music. In sheer length it is virtually double any sonata form previously composed (a fact that impressed later composers). But this, of course, means very little unless we understand some of the circumstances surrounding this great length.

How is this gigantic form justified? The answer to such a question remains essentially a mystery; nevertheless we may point out some clues. In Chapter 2 we have looked at some of the special qualities of this piece. Principal among these is the immensely vital and vigorous quality of movement, especially intense when syncopations pile up at strategic moments. Beethoven's choice of three-four meter for this composition is decisive for its style and structure. In triple meter, the beats that represent movement occupy more time in the measure than the beat that represents arrival, i.e., two-thirds as against one-third. (In two-four time, movement and arrival have equal shares.) Furthermore, triple meter invites a shift of stress or accent in several ways; apart from the usual **1** 2, 3, we can have 1 **2** 3, 1 2 **3**, or **1** 2 **3**. In two-measure groups the patterns of shifted stress can become more complex, particularly when several voices are assigned different patterns. Beethoven exploits these possibilities to the fullest. (See also the groupings in Example 2·9.) Musical movement is thus intensified, and a drive is created which carries many of the long periods in this piece to very emphatic points of arrival. One way to appreciate this rhythmic action is to count steadily by threes throughout the movement.

In every measure of this work there is furious activity, an electric quality of action. We might draw an analogy with physics; the microscopic collision of musical particles sets free a tremendous outburst of energy which must necessarily give rise to an extended form. As compensation for this intense quality of movement, important points and areas of arrival are reached with great dramatic emphasis. Moreover, in this movement much of the expansion takes place at points that the eighteenth-century sonata form was content to pass over rather quickly —in the development section and at the cadential area of the entire movement that completes the recapitulation. Both the development and the coda of this movement are extremely long. In order to support and give point to this length, Beethoven establishes new piers to his structural bridge, new areas of arrival within the form. The diagram below illustrates what happens:

EXAMPLE 6·30 Diagram of Beethoven: Symphony No. 3, first movement

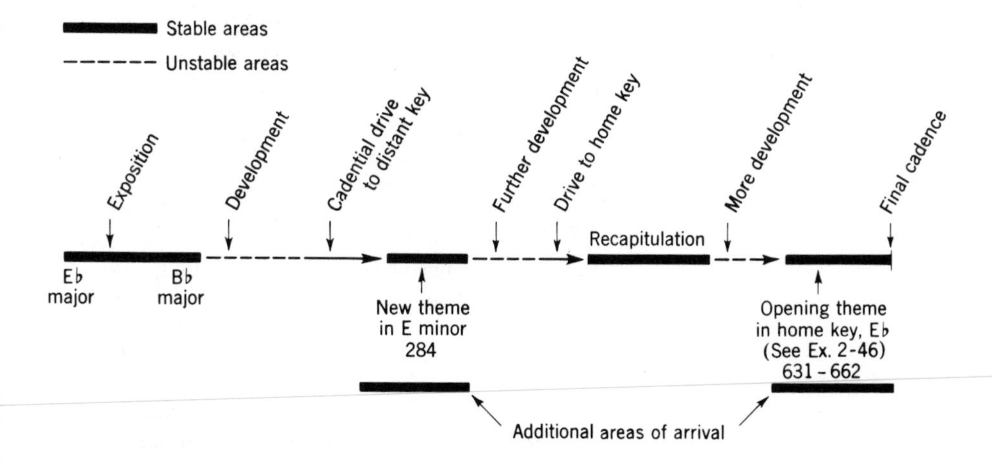

In the development section, a new theme is presented in E minor, a key far removed from the home key, E♭ major. This section represents a kind of apex, the point of farthest exploration, or of greatest distance from home. From here onward, the harmonic objective is the return to the home key, a return which takes considerable time to accomplish. It is this development section, of such length and dramatic power, that has been responsible for the concept that the development is the crucial area of sonata form, that it is a psychological climax.

A counterweight to the section just described, and an additional strong point of arrival in the form, appears at the final return to the home key in the coda of this movement. At this point the opening theme, for the *first* time in the movement, appears in a normal balanced arrangement, its phrases alternating in simple fashion between tonic and dominant harmonies. The theme is allowed to become a straightforward melody. This is the area of arrival for the entire movement. Here we find the classic viewpoint made clear: The form must be rounded off; it must finish properly; all instability must be set to rights; full compensation must be made. It is remarkable that in a movement of such grandiose conception and realization, the music returns to its origins, to the straightforward, sturdy values of a popular art.

In listening to this movement, you will help clarify its action and structure for yourself by noting the following points: (1) When and how are rhythmic imbalance and harmonic instability introduced after the symmetrical beginning of a phrase or period? (2) When are important points of arrival, generally authentic cadences, reached?

Second movement: Marcia funebre: Adagio assai (247 measures)

A. (1–68)	A very slow funeral march in two-reprise form (each part repeated with some changes) followed by a concluding cadential section; minor mode
B. (69–101)	A contrasting trio, also in two-reprise form (with neither part repeated), in a lyric style, interrupted by fanfares that provide a rhyme for the two sections
A.′ (105–113)	Fragmentary return to the march, as if a da capo were to be used to round off the form
C. (114–173)	An X or development-like section, beginning with imitative polyphony on a new theme
A.″ (174–209)	Return of the march
Coda (209–247)	Cadential section for the movement, first digressing harmonically and using a new theme, then returning to a fragmentary restatement of the march

After the first movement, with its compression of time, movement, and action and the resultant explosion into flights of enormous breadth and vigor, the second movement provides a contrast on a comparably grand scale. Here we have the slowing down of time; events are stretched out; there are instants where everything seems suspended. The result is again great breadth of structure, achieved by expansion rather than by compression. In the extremely deliberate motion of the funeral march, activated and yet held in check by the dotted rhythms which signify the tattoo of muffled drums, the filling-out of a two-reprise form takes considerable time. But Beethoven adds another dimension to this form by breaking off the march upon its return; he leaps to another plane of action. The notes gradually become quick; the spaces in time are filled in until we have virtually a hurricane of action. Then, suddenly, like the eye of the hurricane, there is an interval of almost dead quiet (measures 154–158) and the storm breaks in with renewed violence, gradually to subside during the restatement of the march. The cycle of action is not yet completed when the march has been repeated; therefore, Beethoven denies the listener the cadence that might have ended the piece at this point and leads, by means of a deceptive cadence, into the final phase. The process of expansion continues until the last measures, where the march theme is broken into fragments, punctuated by intervals of total suspension of action. The tragic implications of this kind of play with musical movement can certainly be felt strongly.

Third movement: Scherzo: Allegro vivace (442 measures)

Scherzo (1–166)	Reprise I (1–28) Reprise II (29–166)
Trio (167–255)	Reprise I (167–197) Reprise II (198–255)
Scherzo da capo and coda (256–442)	

Again, in this movement, Beethoven takes a view of musical action that seems to go beyond the typical classic contrasts of slow and fast. Here we have a headlong momentum, as it were, a virtually pure expression of musical energy; there are fleeting hints of a theme in the scherzo, but these occupy but a small part of the total plan. One of the basic premises of this movement is the four-measure phrase; if you should count by fours throughout, you would find that at some points there is a rhythmic conflict, but at others, particularly in the latter part of the scherzo, the groups of four are clearly marked, rectifying the imbalance, and you can sense the great accumulation of movement which is piled up thereby.

The very beginning poses a rhythmic problem. The first reprise, which is hardly a complete section but rather like the topic of an argument, may be sensed rhythmically as 6, 5, and 3. This rhythmic ambiguity appears whenever we hear the theme itself. Also, Beethoven merely touches upon the home key, then moves off quickly, making a cadence in the dominant at the end of the reprise. Both this harmonic and rhythmic instability is resolved in a grand manner by the very extended cadential section of the second reprise; this may suggest why there is such a discrepancy between the dimensions of the two reprises. The trio, with its tune and greater harmonic stability, has a more obvious balance of reprise length.

Beethoven writes out the entire da capo, instead of instructing the performers to play the scherzo once more. He does this because he makes one startling alteration in the fanfare figure toward the end of the scherzo; he interrupts the quick triple motion which creates the momentum and writes the fanfare in duple time. This has the effect both of holding back momentarily and of adding an extra thrust to the final measures upon the resumption of triple time. It demonstrates how Beethoven can give broad structural importance to a single gesture, and how judiciously he plans such moves.

Fourth movement: Allegro molto (473 measures)

Opening flourish (1–11) (see Example 2·2)

Home key
1. Decorative variations on the bass (12–75)
2. The melody with ornamental garlands (76–107)
   Transition (107–116)

Other keys
3. A fugal passage on the bass subject (117–174)
4. A dance, using the melody (175–198)
   Transition (198–210)
5. A march, using the bass (211–256)
6. A songlike variation, using the melody (257–277)

Home key
7. A fugal passage, on the bass, with the melody chiming in (277–348)
8. A slow aria, using the melody (349–380)
9. A grand chorale, using the melody (381–396)

Coda (397–473); note return of opening flourish (431–434)

In this movement, we might say that Beethoven has returned to the "real" world of musical time and movement, to familiar ground. The piece is a set of variations built upon a contredanse tune and its bass, which Beethoven had used before as melodic material in several compositions. He does not construct this movement through the purposeful manipulation of musical time; rather, he returns to the eighteenth century to characterize the sections of his movement according to familiar types, as the outline above shows. The subject itself is in a two-reprise form; the following example gives the tune and its bass:

EXAMPLE 6·31 Beethoven: Symphony No. 3, finale

After the chorale, Beethoven abandons the variation procedure. He is making a coda; thus, we hear some free harmonic exploration preparing the final exultant cadential section. The movement concludes with fanfares and rushing passages, incorporating the exciting figure that began the movement with a challenge.

As you can see, Beethoven is not content merely to put together a set of interesting elaborations upon his subject. Instead, he gives the form a broad overall structure by using (1) large key areas: tonic—shifting keys—tonic; (2) an integrated phrase structure, in which cadences are often not clear-cut. Thus two neighboring variations can be linked without a break. As with so much of Beethoven's music, the impression is one of broad gestures, violent drives, and grand ideas; the whole piece is "written large."

Apart from its monumental structure, the *Eroica* is noted for a rather spectacular circumstance concerning its subtitle. Originally composed in honor of Napoleon Bonaparte as a republican hero, the symphony was later given the title *Sinfonia Eroica* when Beethoven learned that Napoleon had had himself proclaimed Emperor of the French; any mention of Bonaparte was removed from the title page.

Structural types in classic music may be summarized as follows:

1. *Sonata form*
2. *Rondo form:* Organized around a refrain which alternates with epi-

sodes; constructed with (*a*) well-marked, symmetrical sections or (*b*) elements of extension and exploration taken from sonata-form procedure

3. *Variation form:* (*a*) Formal variations, optional in number; (*b*) combination of variation procedure with other forms
4. *Three-part form:* Sectional, as in rondo, generally lyric in style; also ABA as in minuet
5. *Fantasia:* Episodic, without regular refrain, much more exploration and improvisation than in other classic forms

In the preceding survey of classic forms, we have seen that they represented ways of using harmony and the period forms of late eighteenth-century music. There were two general methods of building forms: (1) in *sectional arrangement,* as in dances, small two- and three-part forms, and simpler rondos; (2) in *integrated arrangement,* as in the sonata form.

In sectional arrangement, normal period structure predominated; the forms grew by addition and repetition of sections. There was a straightforward rhythmic and melodic appeal in such movements. Integrated arrangement involved internal expansion and a more closely knit connection between succeeding periods. The forms grew from within. The principal appeal of such movements was the challenging excitement that broad concepts could stimulate. As the classic style evolved, integrated forms grew more and more impressive while sectional forms acquired some of the continuity and expansion of integrated arrangement.

Analysis of a movement according to the methods worked out here would proceed along the following lines:

1. Establishment of perspective by determining the harmonic plan and the nature of the period structure
2. Noting of highlights, important landmarks, by examining thematic distribution
3. Observation of significant detail work, such as specific harmonic progressions, interplay of parts and motives, handling of texture
4. Consideration of the general expressive qualities of the piece, especially in relation to the style or styles used

Particularly interesting will be the relationship of statement and counterstatement. When a progression, a theme, or a texture is repeated later on in a movement, it very often is changed in some way. Fresh interest is thus given to the counterstatement; and to the perceptive listener, this new light thrown on a familiar musical quality is one of the great pleasures of the classic style.

Media of Performance in Classic Music

The styles, forms, and techniques we have described were all used in the principal media of performance in classic music. Although one style may have been evolved in a particular medium, it would be borrowed for use in a different setting. Transferring styles and idioms from one type of medium to another was characteristic of late baroque music, and this trend was maintained in classic music. Thus, a section in an orchestral piece might be in the aria manner of Italian opera, or a piece for keyboard alone might emulate the tutti-solo arrangement of the concerto. Nevertheless the medium of performance did have some effect upon the music that was written. The amount of sonority available, the types and varieties of color values, the size of the place in which the music was to be performed, the kind of audience and the sort of attention it would give—all these influenced the composer's decisions with regard to form and style.

THE ORCHESTRA

Orchestras differed in size and personnel in the eighteenth century. Small opera houses and court orchestras generally had few string instruments, a pair or two of woodwind instruments, such as oboes and flutes, two horns, perhaps timpani, and a keyboard player who directed the orchestra while filling in the harmony at his instrument. Mozart's early symphonies use this orchestration. The large orchestras, which furnished the instrumentation for music of the late eighteenth century and became models for nineteenth- and twentieth-century orchestras, functioned in large cosmopolitan centers and in celebrated courts, such as Mannheim and Berlin. They had many strings and pairs of flutes, oboes, bassoons, horns, trumpets, timpani, and often clarinets. Although the keyboard leader was still present, he was no longer needed to complete the harmony and keep the music going. This was because of the much fuller sound of these larger orchestras, their greater competence, and the ability of the brass and lower strings to provide a strong support to the harmony.

The principal advantages of the orchestral style were brilliance and full mass of sound as well as variety of color. There was a tremendous range of dynamics; striking contrasts between loud and soft effects were exploited; crescendo and decrescendo passages added to the excitement of an orchestral performance. The classic orchestral style, evolved principally in Mannheim and Paris, made use of these "new" orchestral values, and yet retained the tutti-solo procedure of the baroque concerto grosso.

From about 1730, orchestral concerts became important areas of activity. Many of the items in the programs of these early orchestral concerts were sinfonias borrowed from Italian opera. Opera sinfonias are the ancestors of the classic symphony. Indeed, many of Mozart's early symphonies are typical examples of this kind of composition.

It was in the late eighteenth century that the modern procedures of orchestration were developed. In order to see how these were employed in a typical orchestral composition, let us return once more to the first movement of Beethoven's Symphony No. 3. It is scored for the following instruments:

2 flutes	2 timpani
2 oboes	14–16 first violins
2 clarinets	12–14 second violins
2 bassoons	10–12 violas
3 horns	8–10 cellos
2 trumpets	8 string basses

Playing all together, as they frequently do, these instruments can create a very large amount of sound. Most often, however, they are set against each other with respect to both tone color and action. Generally, there is one principal melody, carried most of the time by the first violins, although flute, clarinets, or oboes often partake in the melodic leadership, particularly in lyric moments. Now and then, a horn or bassoon is given a solo passage appropriate to its style of performance. Against the principal melodic line, much subordinate action takes place. We hear typical accompaniment figures, generally taken by the middle string instruments, second violin and viola, and sometimes the cello.

In Beethoven's orchestra, the underlying support is assigned principally to the lowermost strings, the cello and the bass. If we listen closely to what these low strings do, we can see that Beethoven has managed to give them an amazing variety of figures and functions. They support the harmony; they provide rhythmic spark to a passage; they punctuate; and now and then they take on the principal melodic role. Aside from their occasional fanfare themes, the brass give body to orchestral sound; also, because of their bold attack, they can accent a chord or a point of arrival. The timpani also serve a purpose of accent; their other role is to reinforce the bass.

The crescendo, of which we have already taken note, plays a vital role in the structure of the *Eroica* Symphony, as it does in many other classic works. An extended period receives its final shape by reaching its point of arrival at the peak of a rising dynamic curve, at the moment of the greatest impact of sound. In the first movement of the *Eroica,* the second period of the first key area and all the periods of the second key area provide striking examples of rising dynamic curves.

Beethoven took not only form but also orchestral procedures from late eighteenth-century music, and he expanded them notably. His orchestration set the pattern for nineteenth-century scoring. In this respect, Berlioz, Wagner, Brahms, Liszt, and many other romantic composers were influenced directly by Beethoven, taking their cue from his boldness of effect, his fullness of sound, his variety of texture, and his brilliance of manner.

Orchestral performance in the classic period included symphonies, overtures, serenades (see chamber music), ballet music, and the concerto, which we shall consider next.

THE CONCERTO

The classic concerto, along with the symphony, represented the most impressive type of instrumental music in the late eighteenth century. Carrying on the tradition of baroque music, the solo or concertino element might be drawn from the orchestra itself. Concertos were written for clarinet, flute, horn, bassoon, cello, and harp. But as classic music expanded its techniques and intensified its expressive qualities, the more brilliant, the more impressive instruments—the violin and particularly the piano—became the leading solo instruments in the classic concerto.

The late piano concertos of Mozart, those he wrote for performance by himself in Vienna, give a panorama of concerto composition that has had implications for concerto procedure over a period of almost two hundred years. In these works we find the lively give-and-take that characterizes the baroque concerto grosso and also the dramatic opposition of forces that distinguishes classic musical expression. Further, in Mozart's piano concertos we meet the brilliant virtuoso soloist, the immediate ancestor of the romantic hero-musician of the nineteenth century, as well as the descendant of generations of composer-performers.

Structurally the concerto is laid out like other works of big scope. Generally there are three movements. The first is a quick piece in sonata form, modified to include an orchestral tutti in the tonic key at the opening before the key area plan begins to unfold. The orchestral tutti replaces the repeat of the exposition in other sonata form movements, although the tutti and the repeated exposition do *not* come from the same source. Classic music, in the first movement of the concerto, combined the baroque concerto-grosso layout with the sonata-form key scheme: it thereby created a synthesis, much as it did in other areas of style and structure. The middle movement is a slow piece. The finale is again quick and usually has a frankly dancelike quality.

Of all Mozart's piano concertos, perhaps the most unusual is the Concerto in C minor, K. 491. From the very first tones, we can perceive immediately that this work will not move in any standard eighteenth-century groove. Instead of a flourish, a fanfare, a *coup d'archet,* or even perhaps a singing melody—gestures which might be expected to begin a concerto—we hear a disembodied, winding, chromatic, and harmonically ambiguous line, a motive that suggests doubt and emotional unrest.

EXAMPLE 6·32 Mozart: Piano Concerto in C minor, K. 491, first movement

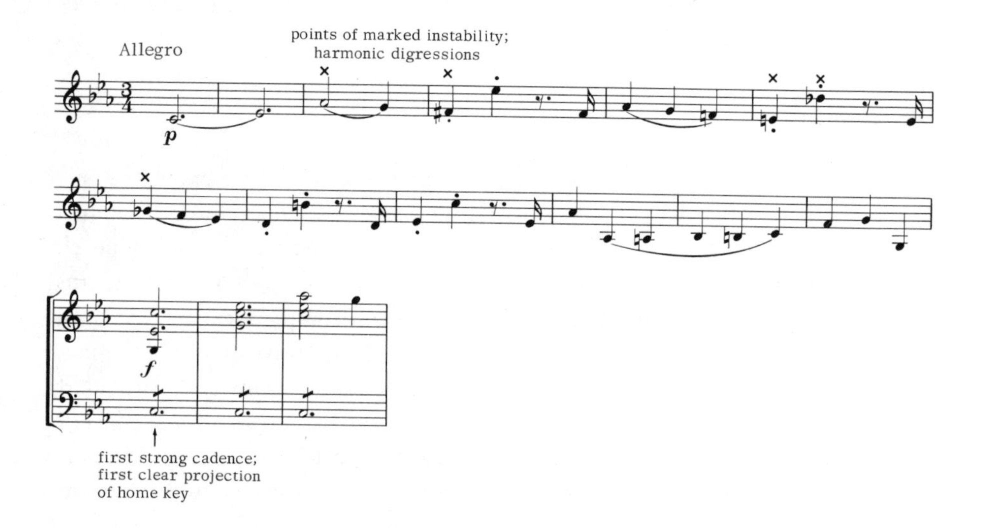

Such imbalance at the very beginning certainly betokens a series of crises that will force the movement to be worked out in an extensive manner, structurally, expressively, and texturally. We are not disappointed in this expectation. Throughout the first movement we find a tremendous wealth of melodic material, a breadth of periodic structure, and a fantastic variety of textures. Here is no solo display discreetly supported by accompaniment figures in the orchestra. Listen to the bold manner in which Mozart uses the woodwinds, setting their airy, fluid tones against the percussive, crisp quality of the solo piano. Listen for the various roles the piano plays in this piece, solo, ornamental, contrapuntal, and even accompaniment. Only the piano, among all solo instruments, can match the orchestra in range, fullness of sound, power, and complexity of action. Like Beethoven in his *Eroica* Symphony,

Mozart has searched deeply and ranged widely in this concerto, which is, in a sense, his own *Eroica*.

As a rule, the solo concerto in classic times treated popular idioms in a brilliant fashion. Thus, the piano concertos of Mozart in G major, K. 453, and C major, K. 467, begin in the march style, as do Beethoven's first, second, third, and fifth piano concertos and his violin concerto. Mozart's Concertos in A major for piano, K. 488, and in B♭, K. 595, take up the singing-allegro manner.

CHAMBER MUSIC

In the middle of the eighteenth century and before, instrumental ensemble music could often be played either with one or more performers to a part. Trios or quartets, for example, might be presented by single players for each part or by a small string orchestra with a leader at the keyboard, as in the first quartets of Haydn and the orchestra trios of the Mannheim School, about 1750–1760. As the new orchestral style evolved, a split took place between orchestral and chamber music. Composers either wrote with orchestral sonorities in mind or wrote with the knowledge that a few expert players would perform the piece. Often these experts were the principal instrumentalists in the large orchestras.

In chamber music there is a great flexibility of part writing. The relationships of texture and sonority are more intimate, less dramatic than those of the orchestra. Contrasts are not as sharp as in other media of performance. Hence, in chamber music, we are likely to find more extended lines, a considerable amount of fine-drawn ornamentation, and a great deal of interweaving among the parts. Since the performers were skillful, there was a great deal of soloistic writing, which might, at times, compensate for the lack of massive sound.

Many varieties of chamber music were written, according to the number of performers and the purpose of the performance. Two general types are to be noted:

1. Serious, thoughtful works intended for small concert performance. The broad forms and all the stylistic resources of classic music were used. Mozart's, Haydn's, and Beethoven's string quartets represent this type.
2. Pleasantly entertaining pieces intended for amusement at a party or festive occasion. The movements were in the style of dances, songs, and marches; each work contained four, five, six, or more of these popular pieces. Very little serious material was introduced. Wind instruments were often used, particularly when the performance was to take place out of doors; the sound of wind instruments carries better in the open

air than the sound of strings. *Serenade, divertimento,* and *cassation* were names given to such pieces.

Beethoven's Quartet in F major, Op. 59, no. 1, Mozart's Quartet in C major, K. 465 (see Examples 6·13 and 6·22), represent the serious style; Mozart's *Eine kleine Nachtmusik* is a very famous serenade, whereas Mozart's Quintet in E♭ major, K. 614, has elements of both styles. Chamber music style is illustrated in Examples 2·34, 6·13, 6·19, 6·21, 6·22, 6·29.

It was Joseph Haydn who was most responsible for the kind of part writing and motive play that characterizes the fully evolved classic chamber music style. In his quartets he combined amazing skill, freshness of manner, and wittiness of rhetoric that continue to delight listeners to this very day, as in the finale of his Quartet in F major, Op. 77, no. 2, his last listed work in this medium. The movement is in the style of a polonaise, a point which bears strongly upon the way in which Haydn manipulated the rhythm. The accent in the polonaise comes upon the second beat in a triple meter, going against the normal metrical accent. Haydn adds to the rhythmic question so raised by using a motive that could easily be heard as being in four-four time. Example 6·33 gives this motive, including the pauses at the beginning which further add to the uncertainty:

EXAMPLE 6·33 Haydn: Quartet in F, Op. 77, no. 2, finale

It is only at measure 13 that we settle comfortably into a triple meter. The movement is in sonata form; the second key area comes at measure 30, but it involves absolutely no thematic contrast. In fact, this movement is a prime example of Haydn's use of a single motive to provide most of the thematic material for an entire movement (see page 229). What is lacking in melodic contrast (except for local incidents) is more than made up for by a fantastic play of part writing, imitation, give-and-take, soloistic flights—all in all, an electrifying display of learned techniques cast in the galant vein, full of humor and irrepressible vitality that never flags in its momentum.

An area of chamber music that is rarely represented in present-day concert programs but which was very important in the musical life of the eighteenth century was lighter chamber music—solos, duets, and trios for strings or winds, or both. In this music, we find, aside from original compositions, pieces that used popular songs and adaptations of concertos, symphonies, and operas, and in which the tune and the bass alone often sufficed for purposes of performance. For today's musical amateurs, these works offer a rich source, almost untapped, of musical entertainment and recreation.

SOLO KEYBOARD MUSIC

Keyboard music has the advantage of the flexibility that comes when one performer has control of the musical performance. The principal keyboard instruments in the later eighteenth century were the harpsichord and the early piano, neither of which had the massive quality of sound that the modern piano can command. Classic keyboard music was often composed in but two lines, one for the right hand and one for the left; the result was a very transparent texture, in which frequently only two notes were heard simultaneously. Idiomatically, classic keyboard music falls into two categories:

1. Music with characteristic keyboard figuration, clearly written with the piano in mind (in the late eighteenth century the piano was the preferred keyboard instrument, rather than the harpsichord). The figuration might be brilliant, to try the prowess of a virtuoso performer, or it might be scaled to the modest skill of an amateur or dilettante.
2. Music which imitated various familiar styles of the classic era. The piano was the favorite house instrument; it was the readiest source of music for an evening's entertainment. Music intended for such diversions often had a picturesque quality, as if to bring the outside world into the home. Military, operatic, ecclesiastical, Turkish, characteristic dance music—all were imitated in solo keyboard music. We have only to glance through the piano sonatas of Mozart to see how he tells the performer and listener about the great world outside the chamber. There is virtually a narrative quality to the play of topics. One example is to be found in his Sonata in D major, K. 284. The first movement is a faithful copy of an Italian opera sinfonia, with its brilliant tutti, its rushing figures, and its general air of busyness.

In keyboard music a characteristic type of figuration, called the *Alberti bass,* was taken over by classic composers from the earlier school of Italian keyboard composers. This figuration consisted of a regular alternation, in a narrow range, between tones of a chord in the left hand, while the right hand played a singing melody. Classic music for solo keyboard also received much from the German *Empfindsamkeit* through the influence of Karl Philipp Emanuel Bach. Anyone who has had some training in piano has probably become acquainted with samplings of classic solo keyboard music. The sonatas of Haydn, Mozart, and Beethoven are standard items in the teaching repertory.

Aside from its role as a solo instrument, the piano took part in chamber music. It performed sonatas with another instrument, and it joined two or more instruments in trios, quartets, etc. In some cases, as in the Mozart piano quartets and trios, the effect is that of a concerto for piano, adapted to the smaller group, with some sharing of the solo role. At other times, the piano might act as the tutti element to the solo of the violin or flute; still again, the right hand of the piano might have a play of dialogue with another treble instrument. See Examples 2·28, 2·32, 2·46, and 6·11 for samples of classic keyboard style.

In the last years of the eighteenth century, piano virtuosity developed greatly. This topic properly belongs to the Romantic period and will be discussed in Chapter 7.

FIGURE 10. Manuscript of recitative from Act 4, scene 7 of Mozart's *Marriage of Figaro*. The excerpt is in Mozart's own handwriting. (Courtesy of the Memorial Library of Music, Stanford University Libraries.)

mia Cerimonia ... ei godeva leggendo: e nel vederlo io rideva di me senza saperlo.
o Susaña, Su=
=saña, quante pene mi costi!
Con quell'ingenua faccia...
Con quegli occhi innocenti...
chi creduto l'a=
=vria!
ah che il fidarsi à doña à doña
è ognor follia.
attaca subito l'aria di

OPERA

Opera offered the classic composer the maximum in dramatic contrast of sonority values. The human voice, with the strong and immediate emotional quality of its impact, could be contrasted with the various sonorities of the orchestra. Because of the plot and the text, gesture and emotion have a much more specific meaning in opera than in instrumental music. Musical figures can underscore and highlight these dramatic values. The baroque doctrine of the affections was concerned principally with the use of appropriate musical figures when a text was being set. Classic opera continued this tradition but, because of the flexibility of classic techniques of composition, was able to add sharp contrast to strong affective quality. In Mozart's last operas, each character is portrayed in a musical style fitting to his nature and his dramatic function. Furthermore, within the general style for each character, subtle musical nuances reflect shades and variations of meaning.

We have already mentioned the rise of opera buffa in relation to the change in social structure during the eighteenth century. Opera, like instrumental music, achieved a synthesis in the works of Mozart. Comic opera (buffa) and opera seria were merged. For example, consider the order of events in the first part of his *Don Giovanni:*

1. The overture begins with a slow introduction, echoing the powerful, very deliberate manner of the French overture. Its content, however, represents the style of the *ombra,* i.e., ghostly music, which was a familiar device in operatic composition of the seventeenth and eighteenth centuries (Purcell's music for the Sorceress in *Dido and Aeneas,* Gluck's music for Orestes' vision in *Iphigenia in Tauris*). This Storm and Stress style, associated with the Commandant, forecasts the tragic fate of Don Giovanni.
2. The body of the overture provides a total contrast to the introduction. It is a brilliant example of the galant style, in which fanfare, singing-allegro, concerto, and the learned styles intermingle. Since it is in sonata form, with well-marked key areas, we might expect it to wind up with great flourishes to settle the final arrival in the home key. To our surprise, there is a sudden shift of key at the very end, a chord of suspense which pulls us into the drama and prepares for Leporello's entrance.
3. Leporello's song is typical buffa music, perky, simple, tuneful, set in a light texture. He is grumbling and wishing that he might change places with his master. Mozart introduces some deft topical nuances here. Leporello's pacing back and forth as sentry is easy to picture in the simple march figure which we hear at first. When he sings of his master, we hear a hunting fanfare, suggesting the pleasures of the cavalier

gentleman. This song does not come to a full close but moves into a transition that picks up the pace and leads into the scene of the struggle, duel, and death.

4. The scene of conflict that follows is an ensemble piece, an example of vocal chamber music in which the music for each character reflects faithfully the role being played. Anna and Giovanni are struggling; their music is tense; it tends to rise in pitch. Leporello retains his buffa manner. Suddenly, the action focuses more sharply; the key changes abruptly, and the pace slows to a more deliberate and ominous tempo. The Commandant enters. The quality of his voice, a basso, and the slow, dignified nature of his music give a more weighty and tragic aspect to the action. As the duel between Giovanni and the Commandant begins, the music is quite literally pictorial; the parries and thrusts are portrayed by rapid scale passages, and at the death blow all movement stops, while the orchestra sustains a sharply dissonant chord. As the Commandant dies, the harmonies are minor and chromatic and the melodic lines all descend. Yet, at this point, when Leporello sings, he retains his buffa manner! This part has no cadence; it dissolves into a recitative secco whose humor has a shocking effect so closely following the death (see Example 6·8).
5. After the death, the action is cast in recitative secco and accompagnato (see Example 6·9). When Anna and Ottavio learn what has happened, they resolve vengeance. This is the final number of the scene, a duet which uses the dramatic elements of key contrast inherent in the sonata form, as outlined below:

HARMONIC FORM		DRAMATIC FORM
Part I	First key area, minor key	Anna sings; rejects Ottavio in her despair.
	Second key area, related major key	Ottavio offers consolation; contrast to opening mood.
Part II	Shifting harmonies	Both swear revenge; emphasis and accent of accompanied recitative.
	Return to home key	Firm resolution for revenge; Anna's key and the mood of her opening music overcome the contrast of Ottavio's mood and key of consolation.

Special gestures within this form highlight the dramatic situation and help to clarify the underlying structure. The exposition has ended with a somewhat more relaxed quality of movement than we heard at the beginning. Suddenly the music stops short, underlining the change of mood and dramatic meaning. The incisive strokes of the recitative section tell us that a grim purpose has been formed. The restatement of the recitative drives home the sense of purpose, and the duet moves steadily to its end from that point on with an accumulation of momentum, shaping a broad area of arrival for the entire form. The regular, unbroken movement of the final section is proper to the sense of high resolve that finally unites the lovers after their despair. There is hardly a more perfect example of the dramatic possibilities of sonata form than this duet, yet, strangely enough, in spite of its melodic elegance and richness, there is not one theme by which the listener can find his way through the form. Mozart does not develop or recapitulate the thematic material of the exposition!

Viewing the entire first scene, we can see that it has an internal structure which binds the various sections together in a tight and continuous plan of musicodramatic action. The overture and the final duet, pillars to the form, are in the same key (D), and each uses the sonata form. Indeed, the cadence in D, averted in the overture, is reinforced at the end of the scene as an answer to an important harmonic question. Leporello's music suggests the dance movement of a symphony; the struggle is like the opening key area of a sonata form; the death and recitative have the expressive value of a slow movement. In the following diagram we can see the drop and rise of expressive intensity throughout this scene:

Overture	Leporello	Struggle	Death; Revenge
Tragic			Tragic
Galant		Furious action	
	Buffa		

In order to sample more fully the musical content of *Don Giovanni,* considered by many the greatest opera ever written, we shall touch briefly upon some other numbers:

1. When Elvira, who has recently been betrayed by Don Giovanni, appears, in a rage, to find and punish him, she is brought on stage with a rather flamboyant march. She is highborn, but there is a faintly ridiculous touch to her character. She sings a melody which leaps about, and at the end, when she says *gli vo cavare il core* (I'll carve his heart out), she sings a brilliant coloratura melodic arch on the syllable *-vare,* which suggests the twisting and turning of the knife.
2. In one of the most famous songs in all opera, the *Catalogue* aria, Leporello explains to Elvira the quantity and quality of Don Giovanni's

loves. In the first part, he enumerates his master's conquests (in Italy, 640; in Germany, 231—countesses, peasants, baronesses, etc.). Here Leporello sings a good deal of parlando, except when he reports 1,003 in Spain; at this point he slows down momentarily and repeats the number, as if in disbelief. Part I is in quick duple time, proper to the ticking off of numbers. Part II, in which the qualities of Giovanni's women are mentioned, is a slow minuet in triple time, a more "rounded" style of performance. We cannot point to all the delicious nuances with which each type is described, but note, as you listen, the manner in which the blondes, the brunettes, the fat, the thin, the majestic, the petite, the old, and the young are each deftly characterized in a few notes.

3. In the champagne aria, *Finch'han del vino,* Mozart composed a brilliant piece to suggest the intoxication of a carousal; he drives the music through breathlessly, without a pause, so that Don Giovanni himself is virtually reeling at the end from a lack of respite in singing.
4. Much of this opera is conceived in the buffa manner, but some numbers recall the seria style. The most formalized character of all, Don Ottavio, sings the most formal music. Typical of his music is the aria *Il mio tesoro* (My Treasure). An elegant melody, a broad form, with roulades added upon repetitions and at cadential points—these demonstrate that Mozart was master of the seria as well as the buffa style; the juxtaposition of this aria with the other elements in the opera, however, give it a dimension of characterization that would be lacking in a pure seria work.

Classic opera owed much to Gluck, who took the stance of a reformer of dramatic music; he espoused a more "natural" representation of lyric and dramatic values, believing that the story of an opera should be told in a moving, flexible way. He stood against the formalism and artificial techniques of baroque opera seria, with its static plots and its extreme codification of musical procedures. The overture and opening scene of his opera *Alceste* represent this view. The overture is a mood piece, not a sinfonia or brilliant French overture. It sets the tragic mood (note the similarity to the opening measures of the overture to *Don Giovanni*), and it moves without break into the highly charged dissonances with which the Greek chorus prays to the gods for the life of their king, Admetus. We are pulled into the drama immediately, without any formal posturing. Gluck's influence on Mozart in matters of musical dramaturgy was considerable, as scholars have noted in many specific instances.

As we studied *Don Giovanni,* it must have been clear that simply to listen to it as a piece of music would be to know only part of it.

FIGURE 11. M. Gauci: Scene from the opera buffa *Il Fanatico per la Musica* (The Musical Fanatic) composed by Simon Mayr and performed in London in 1805 and 1806. The music that the singer is playing on his imaginary flute is notated below the picture, and the text reads, "What a beautiful passage! What pleasure it gives me." (Courtesy of the Gracely Collection, Stanford University Libraries.)

Beyond the wonderful melodies and exciting passages in the music, there is the visual picture, then the general sense of the words, and finally the subtle nuances in which specific words (in Italian) are shaped and highlighted by the music. We hear, in short, all that gives it its expressive power as staged drama. As we go from one degree of comprehension to the next, we lose none of the preceding values; rather, the fuller knowledge of music, staging, and text is incorporated into our listening pleasure. This topical content is also present in instrumental music, which often imitated opera in its style; as we suggested previously, to recognize these topical references is to gain an added delight in listening. Classic music is certainly not to be taken as purely abstract.

CHORAL MUSIC

Nearly all choral music in the late eighteenth century was intended for church performance or for other purposes of devotion. There was a strong influence of conservative traditional practice in choral music, most of which consisted of Masses or individual numbers from the liturgy. Traditionally certain portions were handled in a fugal style; other sections, not bound by tradition, showed operatic and galant qualities. In the sections not dedicated to the learned style, the forms were those of other music: sonata, three-part, rondo, etc. Like orchestral music, the texture of choral music (almost always accompanied by instruments) varied from transparency and thinness to the mighty effect of massed voices and instruments. These contrasts were often juxtaposed.

All serious composers in the eighteenth century had a thorough training in church music. Much of the early output of Mozart and Haydn was in the form of music for sacred services. It was principally from this source that they acquired the discipline and strength in part writing and harmony that enabled them to transform the somewhat frivolous popular music of the time into important and enduring masterpieces.

Choral music in the classic era was generally intended for purposes of worship and was therefore supposedly restricted in its range of expression. Actually, a wide range of style, structure, and expression was used in this medium by classic composers, as we can see in the following compositions:

Mozart: *Regina Coeli* (Queen of Heaven), K. 108. This motet, written for performance in Salzburg, shows a complete absorption of Italian opera and instrumental style. It is galant throughout; the plan is that of an Italian opera sinfonia or early concert symphony —a fast, brilliant movement, a second movement in the style of a moderately paced minuet, an adagio, and a brilliant contredanse finale. It is distinguished from its model, the sinfonia, by the presence of voices, by the use of a continuo (prescribed for church music), and by a more active and deftly wrought play of figure and motive, which does not, however, disturb the galant symmetry of the phrase structure.

Haydn: Mass in D minor (*Lord Nelson*): *Dona nobis pacem* (Give Us Peace). Curiously, this piece does not reflect the sentiment of its text, "give us peace." Rather, it is a brilliant concertato piece, brisk, punctuated by trumpet and drum signals; it is very much in the vein of the festive choral music of Bach and Handel. Haydn employs the learned style in fugal expositions, but does not allow himself to be carried away by the counterpoint. The discourse of the fugue is interrupted by declamations; the cadential structure is clear and decisive in its punctuation; and the entire movement embodies the key area structure of the sonata form.

Beethoven: *Missa solemnis,* Op. 123: *Donas nobis pacem.* In contrast to the examples from Mozart and Haydn, which stand firmly in the classic world, Beethoven's music in this case has the impact, the feel, of the grandiose choral style of the nineteenth century. It has a very broad range of sound, with respect to both volume and timbre (disembodied winds, solo timpani); a vast palette of rich combinations gives us expressive values that move from the terror of the last judgment to the final peace which the last downward-bending phrase evokes. There is also a tremendous contrast of material—recitative, march, fanfare, and a principal theme of pastoral quality. The entire piece has a strong declamatory character, so much so that when the orchestra is playing alone, one can imagine that some poetic image related to the text is impelling the music. Formally, we have episodes, as in a fantasia, but the principal material, in the pastoral vein, shows elements of sonata form, especially in the similarity of cadential sections which end the exposition and recapitulation.

Finally, in classic choral music we should mention Haydn's oratorios *The Creation* and *The Seasons,* both of which are celebrated for their frank pictorialism.

Classic music may be summarized in terms of its media as follows:

1. Orchestral music: symphony, overture, concerto, ballet, serenade
2. Chamber music: for two, three, four, or more instruments; for entertainment or serious concert performance
3. Keyboard music: principally piano, some harpsichord; in all forms

4. Opera: buffa, seria, intermingling of the two styles
5. Choral music: principally for church; motets, masses, oratorios
6. Transcriptions and transfers of music from one medium to another, generally to make orchestral or operatic music available for chamber music performance
7. Sound and texture ranging between two extremes:
   a. "Skeleton" layout using but two lines, treble and bass, as in keyboard music, duets, and few-voiced chamber music; musical action is emphasized.
   b. Richness and fullness of texture in which the chords are filled out considerably from bottom to top; sound is emphasized as an expressive value to create a broad and massive effect as in orchestral music, some chamber music, and choral works.

General Survey and Summary

In our study of classic music, we considered the fully matured style of Haydn, Mozart, and Beethoven. Our principal concern was to determine how this music, at once so appealing and so challenging, had reached its culmination. To do this, we examined styles, types, forms, and idioms—always in reference to their use in the great masterworks of the period. We discussed the mid-century, with its crosscurrents of learned and galant and its early formation of what would later be classic procedures. It would be a serious distortion to assume that classic music consisted only of the three titans and a few lesser figures preceding and surrounding them. In fact, one of the wonders of the eighteenth century is the sheer volume of music produced by thousands of composers all over the Western world. Still more amazing is that this music runs so true to type. We could not begin to make a count of how many pieces, large and small, were written in the two-reprise form, how many minuets, contredanses, rondos, even sonatas and symphonies. Everyone who had status above that of peasant, be he nobleman or businessman, had the opportunity to dabble in the fashionable art of music. We see a sharp increase in the publication of music; instruction books, often intended to simplify performance and composition, appeared by the hundreds. At worst, the music was neatly put together; at best, the felicitous combination, the imaginative turn, produced works of elegance and genius. One would need a biographical dictionary to cover the roster of composers in such centers as Paris, London, Vienna, Berlin, Mannheim, Prague, Dresden, Naples, Milan, Rome, St. Petersburg, and Leipzig. The mid-century change in taste, and the shifts in style and structure associated with it, has not yet been fully documented in music-historical studies.

We should further realize that the evolution of the classic style was not accomplished piecemeal, with each composer handing in some special bit of progress or inventing some special formal device. If we survey the works of Haydn and Mozart, we can see that they themselves grew enormously and that the history of the general style is written in their own works, from typical galant works, rather small in scale, to the distinctive monuments of their maturity.

Let us touch upon some distinctive samples of the work that other composers of the classic era produced:

K. P. E. Bach: Fantasia in E♭ from the Fourth Collection of Sonatas and Free Fantasias, 1783. This was intended as a show piece, technically, and as a vehicle for free, rather extravagant expression. The work is so free and improvisatory in style that Bach did not provide bar lines for most of it. We are offered a full share of the Sensibility style: many changes of figure, restless harmony, stop and start rhetoric. There is restatement of material in the latter part of the piece, but nowhere do we find the orderly statement-counterstatement arrangement that we heard in Mozart's Fantasia in C minor.

J. C. Bach: Overture to *Lucio Silla*. This is also programmed as Sinfonia in B♭. An Italian-style sinfonia, but with much more highly developed melodic content and colorful orchestration than is usual in this form.

The contrasts are very neatly managed, and the twofold statement of almost every phrase provides the listener with ample opportunity to enjoy each melodic fragment; at the same time, it establishes typical classic balance. The second movement, a slow aria in rondo form, is given over entirely to luminous, exquisitely beautiful melody, while the finale, a gigue in rondo form, has one of the catchiest tunes in the entire classic literature.

Boccherini: Quintet in D major, Op. 37, no. 2, first movement. This is scored for two violins, viola, and two cellos. The first cello shares the concertante or solo role with the first violin; the second cello provides the true bass. Here we have a typical Italian style, influenced strongly by the concerto in the vigorous passages and by the operatic aria in the singing episodes. This is a virtuoso piece, with much idiomatic string writing; also, the richness of texture with the added cello gives a characteristic flavor that differs from the lighter sound of the string quartet. The punctuation is very clear, even more so because of the solo-tutti texture. We can make out a sonata form, but note that the opening flourish does not return at the recapitulation; it serves to provide a final area of arrival at the end, a neat accommodation to the style and scoring of the piece.

Johann Stamitz: Sinfonia in D a 8 (*Melodia Germanica*). This is a typical "Mannheim" symphony, of the kind that strongly influenced Haydn and Mozart. Note especially the concertolike contrasts, the use of crescendo (an effect to show off the orchestra), short sections, characteristic pairing of winds to achieve a very "sweet" effect, very little harmonic exploration, many salient melodic figures, action of a brisk but not intense quality.

Cherubini: Overture to *Medea,* 1797. A work of great intensity, powerful sonorities, reflecting the agitated expression of postrevolutionary French opera. Cherubini had strong influence on Beethoven, whose overture to *Egmont* shows many affinities to this work. There is intense development of two motives, both heard in the first key area, which provide the melodic material for the entire piece. Note the dramatic contrast of loud and soft, the suspenseful pauses, and the reiterated F minor at the end.

Before we conclude this survey of classic music, a final comment on Beethoven is necessary to fill out the picture of his role.

Historically he stood with Haydn and Mozart as one of the three great masters of the classic style. In most of his works we find the basic premises of balance-imbalance adjustment worked out in proportions that conform to classic usage. Yet the expressive content of his music represents such an intensification over that of Haydn and Mozart that a greater momentum was developed, a more violent surge forward created. Because of this drive and intensity Beethoven had a strong kinship with the age that followed, the romantic period of the nineteenth century. Romantic composers were strongly influenced by Beethoven in many respects. For example, the thematic concept of romantic sonata form is already realized in the first movement of Beethoven's Sonata for Piano in E minor, Op. 57, the *Appassionata.* There are three distinctly different episodes that constitute the exposition, each with its salient theme and each in a different key. This is quite different from the integrated exposition of the typical classic sonata with its drive from the tonic to the structural cadence in the contrasting key. In addition to its form, the first movement of the *Appassionata* Sonata contains a number of striking effects, each of which shows a romantic flavor:

1. Extreme contrasts in range
2. Extreme contrasts in dynamics
3. Constant use of Storm and Stress values
4. Brilliant virtuoso pasages
5. Sudden, unexpected changes in pace

Other qualities of Beethoven's music that attracted and influenced romantic composers were:

1. Striking sonority effects, as in the *Pastoral* Symphony, the *Leonore* Overtures, Nos. 2 and 3, and the *Missa solemnis*
2. Recitative passages for instruments, as in the first movement of the Sonata in D minor for Piano, Op. 31, no. 2, and in the last string quartets

3. Passages of great harmonic instability, as at the beginning of the String Quartet in C, Op. 59, no. 3
4. The idea of the hero, so dramatically presented in the *Eroica* Symphony

Beethoven inherited Mozart's sense for the dramatic and contrasting relationship; he also learned a tightness of development and motivic interplay from Haydn. He lacked Mozart's spontaneous lyricism; therefore, he did little in the field of opera. He lacked Haydn's spontaneous sense for the play of phrase and effect; therefore, he had to wrestle mightily with stubborn materials. Rarely does a Beethoven phrase or period wind its way comfortably to its end. His imbalances were the grim crises of the romantic age to come, not the inflections and nuances of the eighteenth century. Still, the explosion had not yet come; the centrifugal forces contained in Beethoven's music are controlled by a sense of musical balance, of *gravitation to a long-range point of arrival.*

Regular dance and song patterns and a well-defined sense of key provided classic composers with a sturdy framework upon which to build extended phases of movement and large-scale forms. Richness and variety of expression were drawn from idioms that were available in eighteenth-century musical life. Change in the type of audience and fewer restrictions upon musical idiom provided a powerful stimulus in the late eighteenth century for more imposing compositions. At this time the sonata form became the most important structural plan. Its importance lay in its long-range harmonic scheme that could organize and focus the activity and momentum of a large number of periods. As the inner content of a movement grew more intensely expressive, the form broadened.

There is a strong temptation to draw a parallel between rationalistic thought in the eighteenth century and classicism in music. Actually this is only partly valid as an analogy. Rationalism might be compared to mid-eighteenth-century music, in which a balanced, clear, uncomplicated, and down-to-earth quality was predominant.

Toward the end of the eighteenth century, unsettling forces were at work. The middle-class revolutions in America and France had taken place. Early romanticism had made its first appearance in the *Sturm und Drang* period of German literature and in the writings of Rousseau. German idealism, with affinities to the romantic movement, was being developed by Fichte, Kant, and Hegel. We have seen the analogy to this unsettling influence at work within the harmonic and rhythmic structure of the classic period form. Yet, in no way did this unseat the fundamental premise of classic music, which was the final and complete victory of stability after an engrossing musical experience that involved strong elements of instability. Classic music, through its synthesizing power, was able to assimilate the incipient romanticism of the Sensibility and the Storm and Stress qualities, and to assign these qualities their proper function in the stream of musical movement. Thus, it turned what might have been a hostile force into an ally.

The musical objective of the classic composer was to entertain, stimulate, and challenge the listener, and at times to touch his emotions more profoundly. Neither he nor the listener was supposed to lose himself in the tide of the music, as in a later era. Classic music was neither a purely rationalistic art which disallowed all terms save those that were easily reconciled nor a mystic art reaching for goals that were unattainable. Somehow, it managed to stand poised between two opposing forces and receive maximum benefit from both.

Thus, classic music faces both ways. This ambivalence is also seen in many details of classic composition. Very often a chord or melodic figure was approached in one meaning, as an item in one pattern, but was given a different meaning as the point of departure in another pattern. The very fact that any musical idea can be both statement and counterstatement gave rise to this equivocality. Classic composers delighted in making a play with ambiguous relationships; like Shakespeare with his puns, they liked to assign more than one value to a musical term. Nevertheless, this uncertainty was only an internal detail of action; it was a contribution to the sense of movement within a form. Never did it become so powerful as to weaken the strength of the form itself. The last phase of the classic relationship between form and content was reached in Beethoven. Afterward, the individual moments of intensity or color in the music began to assume more importance for the composer and the listener than the balanced perfection of the form. This was the way to romanticism.

Summary

1. Qualities of sound: much contrast in level, strength, and color; use of crescendo and diminuendo; sharp accents; exploration of higher registers; lighter bass; overall transparency and brilliance; range between two-voiced treble-bass and very full sound.
2. Qualities of movement: in a given movement, maintenance of one pace, as a rule; strongly influenced by typical song and dance patterns; characteristic use of syncopation for purposes of intensifying movement; vigorous, accentuated pace, even in slow movements.
3. Arrival: extremely important; frequent clear strong points of arrival; entire sections geared structurally to broad effects of arrival.
4. Movement and arrival: clarity of phrase and period structure; symmetrical structure, often broken to extend periods.

5. Melody: essentially built on characteristic motives in a statement-counterstatement relationship; frequency of real "tunes;" clarity of phrase and period structure. Many melodies express harmony built largely on the notes of a chord.
6. Rhythm: steady, vigorous, characteristic patterns; often subject to irregularities which are later resolved; dance rhythms dominate; diverse rhythmic patterns; strongly differentiated motives.
7. Harmony: strong, clear sense of key; complete saturation by cadential action; characteristic opposition of I and V; periods of broad exploration and instability; cadential drive a basic structural force.
8. Texture basically homophonic, i.e., melody and accompaniment; some polyphony, much give-and-take; polarity of treble and bass; two to four parts, occasionally more; many changes in texture throughout a composition.
9. Performance outdoors and in theater, home, concert hall, and church.
10. Wide range of expressive and stylistic material.

Genres and Compositions Discussed in This Chapter

Styles and types

Bagpipe and musette: *Mozart:* Quintet in E♭ major, K. 614; *Haydn:* Symphony No. 104 in D major (*London*)

Contredanse: *Beethoven:* Concerto for Piano and Orchestra in G major, Op. 58, no. 4; Symphony No. 3 in E♭ major, Op. 55 (*Eroica*); *Mozart: Motet, Regina coeli* (Queen of Heaven)

Hunt: *Beethoven:* Concerto for Violin and Orchestra in D major, Op. 61; *Haydn:* Symphony No. 103 in E♭ major (*Drumroll*); *Mozart:* Quartet in B♭ major, K. 458 (*Hunt*); Quintet in E♭ major, K. 614

French overture: *Mozart:* Symphony No. 38 in D major, K. 504 (*Prague*); Symphony No. 39 in E♭ major, K. 543; Overture to *Don Giovanni*

Ländler: *Mozart:* Symphony No. 39 in E♭ major

Learned style: *Beethoven:* Symphony No. 3 in E♭ major (*Eroica*); *Haydn:* Symphony No. 103 in E♭ major (*Drumroll*); *Mozart:* Quartet in C major, K. 465; Sonata in D major, K. 576; *Haydn: Lord Nelson* Mass

March: *Beethoven:* Symphony No. 3 in E♭ major; *Haydn:* Sonata in C major; *Mozart:* Concerto in C major, K. 467; March from *Little Music Book*

Minuet: *Fischer,* J. K. F.: Minuet; *Haydn:* Symphony No. 104 in D major (*London*)

Oriental and Turkish: *Beethoven:* Turkish March from *Ruins of Athens; Haydn:* Symphony No. 103 in E♭ major; *Mozart:* Sonata in A major, K. 331; Overture to *Il Seraglio*

Recitative accompagnato: *Mozart: Don Giovanni*

Recitative secco: *Mozart: Don Giovanni*

Sensibility: *Bach,* K. P. E.: Fantasia in E♭ major; *Mozart:* Fantasia in D minor, K. 397
Singing-allegro: *Mozart:* Sonata in C major, K. 545
Song: *Gräfe:* Aria from *Little Music Book* (Mozart)
Soloistic: *Mozart:* Quintet in E♭ major, K. 614
Storm and Stress: *Beethoven:* Symphony No. 5 in C minor, Op. 67; *Mozart:* Overture to *Don Giovanni;* Fantasia in C minor, K. 475

Forms

Fantasia: *Bach,* K. P. E.: Fantasia in E♭ major; *Beethoven:* Sonatas in E♭ major and C♯ minor, Op. 27, nos. 1 and 2; *Mozart:* Fantasia in C minor, K. 475; Fantasia in D minor, K. 397
Introduction: *Haydn:* Symphony No. 103 in E♭ major; Symphony No. 102 in B♭ major; *Mozart:* Symphony No. 38 in D major, K. 504; Symphony No. 39 in E♭ major
Rondo: *Haydn:* Symphony No. 103 in E♭ major; *Mozart:* Quintet in E♭ major, K. 614
Scherzo: *Beethoven:* Symphony No. 3 in E♭ major
Sonata form: *Mozart:* Symphony No. 41 in C, K. 551 (*Jupiter*); *Beethoven:* Symphony No. 3 in E♭ major
Three-part form: *Haydn:* Trio in G major
Two-reprise form: *Haydn:* Sonata in D major; *Mozart: La ci Darem* from *Don Giovanni;* Serenade *Eine kleine Nachtmusik*
Variation: *Beethoven:* Symphony No. 3 in E♭ major; *Diabelli* Variations, Op. 120

Media of performance

CHAMBER MUSIC

Quartet (string): *Beethoven:* Quartet in C minor, Op. 18, no. 4; Quartet in C major, Op. 59, no. 3; *Haydn:* Quartet in F major, Op. 77, no. 2; *Mozart:* Quartet in C major, K. 465
Quintet (string): *Boccherini:* Quintet in D major, Op. 37, no. 2; *Mozart:* Quintet in E♭ major, K. 614
Trio (violin, cello, piano): *Haydn:* Trio in G major

CHORAL MUSIC

Mass: *Beethoven: Missa solemnis,* Op. 123; *Haydn: Lord Nelson* Mass
Motet: *Mozart: Regina coeli,* K. 108
Oratorio: *Haydn: The Creation; The Seasons*

KEYBOARD MUSIC

Beethoven: Sonatas in E♭ major and C♯ minor, Op. 27, nos. 1 and 2; Sonata in D minor, Op. 31, no. 2; Sonata in F minor, Op. 57
Haydn: Sonata in C major; Sonata in D major
Bach, K. P. E.: Fantasia in E♭ major
Mozart: Fantasia in C minor, K. 475; Fantasia in D minor, K. 397; Sonata in C major, K. 545; Sonata in D major, K. 576

OPERA

Gluck: Alceste; Mozart: Don Giovanni

ORCHESTRAL MUSIC

Concerto: *Beethoven:* Concerto in G major for Piano and Orchestra, Op. 58; Concerto in D major for Violin and Orchestra, Op. 61; *Mozart:* Concerto in C minor for Piano and Orchestra, K. 491

Overture: *Bach,* J. C.: *Lucio Silla; Beethoven: Egmont; Leonore,* Nos. 2 and 3, Op. 729; *Mozart: Don Giovanni*

Symphony: *Bach,* J. C.: Sinfonia in B♭ (*Lucio Silla*); *Beethoven:* Symphony No. 3 in E♭ major; Symphony No. 5 in C minor, Op. 67; Symphony No. 6 in F major, Op. 68 (*Pastoral*); Symphony No. 9 in D minor, Op. 125; *Haydn:* Symphony No. 104 in D major; Symphony No. 103 in E♭ major; *Mozart:* Symphony No. 38 in D major, K. 504; Symphony No. 39 in E♭ major, K. 543; Symphony No. 41 in C major, K. 551; *Stamitz: Sinfonia* in D a 8 (*Melodia Germanica* No. 1)

Suggestions for Critical Listening

1. *Sound*
   - *a.* Range: high, low, middle, broad or narrow, fluctuating
   - *b.* Amount: number of parts; constant or varied
   - *c.* Strength: degree of strength; constant or varied
   - *d.* Timbre: types of instruments or voices used, to what effect
2. *Movement; meter and rhythm*
   - *a.* Pace: degree of speed; regular, irregular
   - *b.* Articulation: degree of separation of tones and figures
   - *c.* Intensity: vigorous, gentle
   - *d.* Meter: duple, triple; shifts of accent
   - *e.* Degree of symmetry among motives and phrases
   - *f.* Typical patterns (march, dances)
3. *Arrival*
   - *a.* Cadences: frequent, widely spaced; heavy, light; types
   - *b.* Approach to cadence: gentle, strong (sense of drive)
4. *Melody*
   - *a.* Motives or complete tunes
   - *b.* Degree of repetition, variation, contrast
   - *c.* Number of distinctive melodic ideas
5. *Texture*
   - *a.* Types used: melody-accompaniment, imitation, chordal, give-and-take, nonimitative polyphony
   - *b.* Changes: many, few
6. *Harmony*
   - *a.* Diatonic, chromatic
   - *b.* Many, few, no shifts of key
   - *c.* Use of dissonance
7. *Structure:* Statement and counterstatement
   - *a.* Phrases and periods: symmetrical, nonsymmetrical, long, short, clearly punctuated, run together, extensions

b. Key scheme: key-area form, remains in one key mainly, visits many keys, key areas well defined, not well defined
c. Principal sections: how many, how related: repetition, variation, contrast
d. Use of special techniques: imitation, dance, variation, development, improvisation

8. *Expression*
   a. Styles or types used: (see No. 11 of summary)
   b. Topical or pictorial elements
9. *Forms and media* (see page 278)

Suggested Listening Projects

1. **Haydn, Joseph, Quartet in D major, Op. 76, no. 5, finale**

Listen for: Intensive working over of two contrasting motives stated in the first twelve measures; shaping of form entirely by key areas; interweaving of parts; striking harmonic surprises; absence of many strong cadential points of arrival; imbalance of phrase relationships; two strategically placed pauses, one in the middle, one near the end, just before the cadences in the dominant and tonic, respectively; the new melodic material used to make these cadences; the general contredanse quality of the entire piece.

2. **Bach, K. P. E., Sonata in B minor, last movement**

Listen for: The general sentimental quality, *Empfindsamkeit;* the elegant ornamentation; expressive intervals; the exactly regular phrases and periods, four and eight measures in length; a complete sense of balance in phrase structure; chromaticism; thin texture; rondo form; small-scale concept; gentle quality of movement.

3. **Mozart, *Magic Flute*, Aria of the Queen of the Night, *Die Hölle Rache* (Hellish Rage)**

Listen for: Storm and Stress character of entire aria; contrast of key areas; emphasis on pointed figures and motives rather than upon fully formed themes; active give-and-take between voice and orchestra in concerto manner; the breaking into coloratura at the moments of greatest passion; dramatic effect of recitativelike passage at the cadential section of the entire aria, as if the Queen's rage had crystallized into a decisive plan; compare with the revenge duet at the end of Scene I of *Don Giovanni* (same key, similar idea, same harmonic plan, similar use of recitative).

4. **Beethoven, Symphony No. 7, Scherzo**

Listen for: General headlong pace of Scherzo; setting of short opening motive as statement, long-spun-out melody as counterstatement; striking, unexpected shifts of tonal center; use of orchestration to contribute to off-balance effects of movement; striking contrast of Trio to Scherzo in every respect: sonority, movement, melodic style, texture, phrase structure.

chapter seven

Romantic Music

Romantic music is familiar territory for today's listener. And for many, its terrain is the most attractive and picturesque in the entire field of music. It has much to offer that is immediately appealing and moving—the lyricism of Schubert, Frédéric Chopin, and Mendelssohn, the verve and warmth of Tchaikovsky and Anton Dvorak, the imposing grandeur and introspective profundity of Brahms, the intensity of Robert Schumann, the fantasy of Berlioz and Liszt, the overpowering eloquence of Wagner, the dramatic passion of Giuseppe Verdi—this and much more the nineteenth century has given to music.

It is difficult to define romanticism in music, as in other fields of expression. It has so many facets, each brilliant and each facing in its own direction, that we can often mistake one aspect for the entire structure. Individualism—the characteristic personal language—takes precedence over a common or universal style of expression. Each composer adopts his own distinctive posture and finds special resources which are peculiarly suited to his own genius. In classic music, the sense of structural authority stands above the individual nuance; in romantic music the nuance often asserts itself at the expense of structural balance and clarity. Thus, romanticism in music breaks away from a central authority; it exhibits a centrifugal motion, emphasizing the facets, rather than the form.

Romanticism appears in its fullest flower in such works as the Prelude to Wagner's opera *Tristan und Isolde,* Chopin's Preludes for piano,

Schumann's *Carnaval,* Berlioz's *Symphonie fantastique,* Schubert's song, *The Erlking* and Liszt's Sonata for Piano in B minor. Each of these works has some qualities that mark it especially as being romantic. And of all these compositions, perhaps the most typical of romanticism, and at the same time a unique work in many respects, is the Prelude to Wagner's *Tristan.* For us, it can be a central area of reference from which we can start down the devious paths of musical romanticism.

Wagner, the wonder-worker of harmony, draws us into the mood of the entire opera with the very first chord. What a world of intense feeling, of longing, of frustration and unhappiness it seems to suggest! Restless, unstable, dissonant, and tense, it has a rich, almost luxuriant quality of sound, produced both by the intervals and by the manner in which the chord has been set for instruments.

EXAMPLE 7·1 Wagner: Prelude to *Tristan und Isolde*

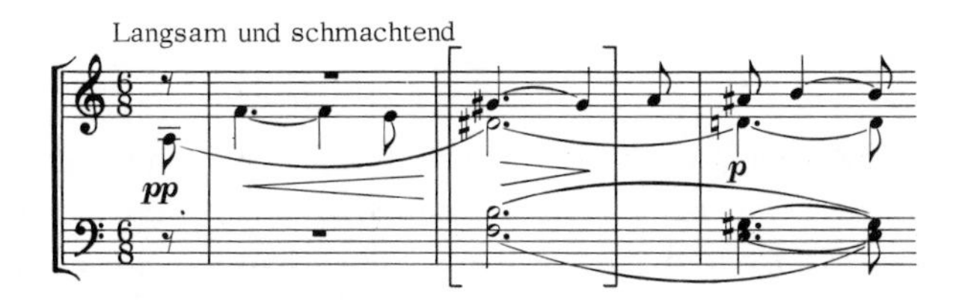

This chord has become famous in music; it has been labeled the *Tristan chord* and is felt to symbolize the world of romantic harmony. Indeed, an entire book has been written upon it and its implications for the history of harmonic expression.*

As the music moves forward, the first impression is maintained and augmented. Every chord, every sound, has a richness of color as well as some element of dissonance or instability. At no time do we reach a point of final arrival, an authentic cadence, or for that matter an entirely stable chord. We listen for a clear definition of tonal center; yet the music only hints at keys and refuses to establish or confirm them. *Harmonically,* everything seems to be in a state of flux. This constant movement is the harmonic basis of what Wagner himself called *endless melody.*

Melody, rhythm, and texture add their share to this general impression. At first the flow of sound proceeds without a defined beat or pulse; only later, when activity becomes more animated, does the underlying meter of the piece make itself felt. *Texturally,* the music is dense; the component voices all move slowly, shifting constantly and subtly. Above

* Ernst Kurth, *Die Romantische Harmonik und ihre Krise in Wagner's Tristan,* Berlin, 1920.

and through this dense mass of sound, the melodic line floats and spins out. *Expressively,* the music seems to be reaching, groping, striving; yet it never reaches a final goal. We are not certain where we are going, nor exactly why, but the striving itself is portentous, and each moment in the music stirs us deeply.

As we proceed through this chapter, various aspects of the style and structure of the Prelude to *Tristan* will be touched upon. Of these, the most significant element is harmony. To a very great extent, romantic composers found their touchstone for musical expression within a rich and colorful harmonic vocabulary. Each handled the harmony differently, but all addressed themselves to color and intensity when they wished to embody the spirit of their age.

Romantic Harmony

HARMONIC TENSION

Most of the chords in the Prelude to *Tristan* have one feature in common: they are chords that have been traditionally used to *create the tension* necessary to make a cadence. They have a strong leading-tone action. Such unstable harmonies convey a sense of movement in addition to projecting an effect of richness in color. The example below illustrates some of these wonderfully evocative combinations:

EXAMPLE 7·2 Typical chords in the Wagner vocabulary

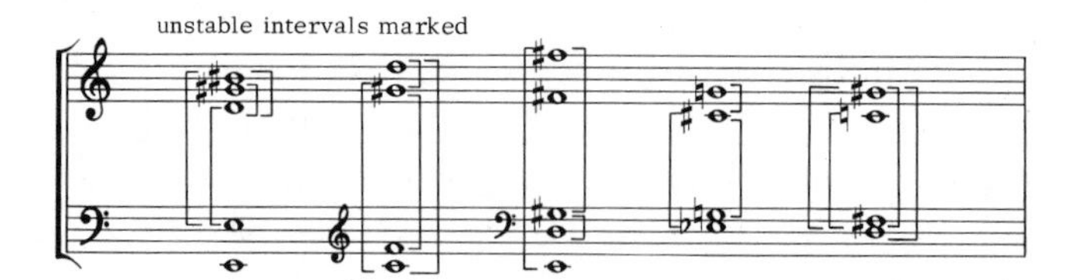

How did Wagner arrive at such a harmonic vocabulary? To answer this we must retrospect a bit. In the evolution of music from the early Middle Ages on, there was a gradual increase in the strength and frequency of leading-tone action in harmony. In plain chant, Ars antiqua, and Ars nova, cadential action took place only at the ends of phrases, simply to round off a phase of movement conveniently. In Renaissance music, there was greater concentration on cadential arrival; the action of leading tones became more prominent. Also chord progressions began to group themselves around tonal centers. In baroque and classic music, this process became increasingly important. Dominant harmonies and leading tones occupied a more and more prominent place within the phases of harmonic movement, creating more and more frequent cadences.

Here and there in classic music, leading-tone harmonies became so densely concentrated as to bypass completely their chords of resolution, that is, tonic harmonies. Often in the keyboard fantasy, and in developments and introductions, we may have no clear sense of a specific tonal center, as a result of saturation by chords of tension. Still, at no time did a period fail to arrive at a satisfying tonic eventually; also, it generally took off from a clearly defined harmonic position. In *Tristan,* this is no longer true; the leading-tone factor reaches its point of greatest concentration. Tonic harmony is more conspicuous by absence and implication than by its palpable presence. (Actually, the note A can be taken as a tonal center, but only by analyzing harmonic movement *around* it, not *to* it.) Wagner's use of this leading-tone harmony is highly controlled and systematic, a mastery that is evident in all aspects of his style. After Wagner, the process continues; elements which create tension are isolated and used independently. The other tones, those which create a body and a rich sonority for the chord, are eliminated. This takes place in the music of Gustav Mahler and Arnold Schönberg, as well as in the music of many other twentieth-century composers. Wagner, therefore, represents a critical stage in the history of harmony. In his music the acme of cadential tension is reached by the avoidance of chords of resolution. After Wagner, the tension elements in harmony lose their contact with any specifically indicated resolution and they are used as free agents. (It should be understood that the process described above represents the most significant *new* developments in harmony in the nineteenth century. Tradition still was very strong, and the notions of cadence and key still very much alive, even where they were affected by these trends.)

HARMONIC COLOR

At the beginning of *Tristan,* the characteristic qualities of the individual chords can attract us simply as a play of kaleidoscopic, shifting effects. Each combination of sounds has its own appeal within a generally consistent mood. Again and again in romantic music we encounter moments and perhaps even extended passages in which the composer seems to be probing deeply into the effect that a special chord or sound creates. Here are the first few measures of Schubert's song *Der Doppelgänger* (The Phantom Double). Note the weird, ghostly effect created by the low-placed, slowly moving chords.

EXAMPLE 7·3 Schubert: *Der Doppelgänger* (The Phantom Double)

Molto adagio

(Still is the night. The streets are quiet.)

pp

In such music, the principal appeal—and it is generally very strong—centers upon tone color and its ability to establish and maintain a consistent and evocative mood. In contrast to the growing and collapsing tension of music that relies on *instability,* this other kind of romantic music assigns a relatively *stable* quality to its harmonies, even though there may be dissonance contained in the sounds. The harmonies are not used primarily for their tensions or their driving quality of movement; rather, they are precious for their intrinsic qualities of sound. Of course, an emphasis on instability does not preclude the attractions that arresting sonorities can exert. Perhaps this explains partly why the music of Wagner exerts such fascination. The sense of urgent emotional necessity created by his unbroken chains of tension chords is clothed with a rich luxuriance of immensely attractive sound.

As a virtually pure example of a mood created by a steady flow of one kind of sound, listen to the song *Wohin* (Whither) from Schubert's song cycle *Die Schöne Müllerin* (The Fair Miller Maid). The song describes the flow of a brook and the wistful speculation which this flow suggests to a wanderer in the country. The murmur of the water is depicted by a rapid little figure in the piano, repeated over and over again within very simple and sweet harmonies. The steady flow is embodied in a gentle pulse which gives life to the sound. Over this current the melody floats, giving point to the glow of the harmony and texture. The entire song envelops us in one sustained mood, which, although it fluctuates somewhat, is faithful to the first impression it makes.

Schubert, among all romantic composers, was the most skillful and appealing in his use of harmonic color. He could give entire phrases and periods within a composition a special glow of beauty through striking coloristic shifts of key, as he does in the Quintet in C major, Op. 163, and the introduction of the Overture to *Rosamunde.*

Harmonic color in romantic music is intimately associated with the means used to produce it, that is, the exploration of sonority values in the piano, in the orchestra, and to a lesser extent in chamber music. This topic will be covered later. Our immediate concern will be romantic ideas of musical expression and the implications (touched upon in the preceding discussion) of harmonic tension and color.

Romantic harmony may be summarized as follows:

1. Harmonic tension
   a. Tristan chord as representative of tension effects
   b. Concentration of leading-tone harmonies
   c. Avoidance of clear resolution
2. Harmonic color
   a. Interest in sound of chords for special effect
   b. Maintenance of special color
   c. Exploration of extreme registers

Expressive Values

EMOTIONAL INTENSITY

Tristan's harmony symbolizes a new world of expression in nineteenth-century music. We meet violent emotional outbursts, restlessness of the spirit, intense desires and yearnings, and ideas of foreboding, tragedy, and doom.

If we recall the duel and death in the first scene of *Don Giovanni,* we see a foreshadowing of this type of expression in the strikingly dissonant chord that accompanies the death stroke. Also, the overture of *Don Giovanni* creates an impression of doom by the dark and unstable harmonies at the beginning. At such moments Mozart points to musical romanticism. A similar concentration of unstable, shifting harmonic effects again projects an atmosphere of terror and doom, of damnation, in the wolf-glen scene from Karl Maria von Weber's opera *Der Freischütz.* Violent, impetuous feeling is frequently suggested by the music of Schumann; this quality is supported by restless, shifting harmonies, as at the beginning of his Overture to *Manfred,* after the poem by Lord Byron.

All these qualities of expression seem to involve personal feelings, personal destinies. Art, music, literature, and philosophy during the nineteenth century are passionately concerned with the individual and his fate. They deal with personal reactions, experiences, and emotions. Man quests and probes, seeking the solution of the problem of good and evil. Nineteenth-century music draws heavily upon such literary and philosophic concepts. The power of music to convey strong emotional effects was geared to these grand and profound ideas, some of which are discussed in the following paragraphs.

GOOD VERSUS EVIL

In nineteenth-century thought, the conflict between good and evil took many forms. Certainly the most celebrated version of this theme was the Faust story, which tells of a compact made with the Devil for the sake of worldly power and personal advantage. Faust's redemption comes about through the intercession of Marguerite, a heroine whose pure and holy love for Faust overcomes the power of the Devil. To be sure, Faust is not saved in every version of the story, but in each case, the struggle between the diabolic and the angelic forms the body of the story. Berlioz, Wagner, Liszt, Charles Gounod, and Arrigo Boïto all took the Faust theme as a subject upon which they based musical compositions. Moreover, we do not have to look very hard to find the Faust story in disguise in Weber's opera *Der Freischütz.* Max, the hunter hero, represents Faust; Zamiel is the counterpart of Mephistopheles, the Devil; the magic bullets represent the temptation of power and worldly success; and Agatha is Weber's Marguerite.

Wagner himself was deeply concerned with such problems. In each of his music dramas the central issue seems to be a metaphysical conflict. In *Tristan,* love is pitted against honor and tradition; in *Tannhäuser,* sacred love against profane love; and in *Parsifal,* the holy against the impious. In the *Ring* cycle, a godlike race struggles against the force of giants and dwarfs; love, honor, and power are set against each other.

We can find some of these ideas prefigured long before the romantic era. For example, Don Giovanni pays his price in Hell for his thoroughly evil and selfish life on earth. In Mozart's *Magic Flute,* the line between good and evil is drawn again, this time with a sociologic and political intent. Good is represented by Sarastro; only those who are proved worthy may enter his temple; evil is personified by the Queen of the Night, whose power lies in spells and incantations. Sarastro thus stands for the newly rising *individual,* who was coming into his own during the latter part of the eighteenth century; the Queen is the symbol of centuries-long entrenched hereditary *autocracy.* Insofar as Mozart incorporates symbolism of this kind into his bold, searching, and imaginative treatment of dramatic themes, he anticipates romanticism.

Closely linked to the idea of good is the search for the ideal in romanticism. This might have religious connotations, as in Parsifal's search for the Holy Grail. In the case of Tristan and Isolde, it involves the longing for the bliss that only a perfect realization of love can embody. Siegfried is the ideal of a hero; Wotan seeks the absolute power that only the Ring can confer. At the end of Liszt's *Faust* Symphony, we hear the words, "The eternal woman draws us onward." (See also Liszt's quotation concerning his symphonic poem *Les Préludes,* page 330.) Strauss's Don Juan seeks but never finds the perfect woman. As we might expect, the ideal is rarely attained. Frustration and death are the answers to all the seeking and yearning.

Evil, especially the diabolic, seemed to fascinate many romantic composers. Modest Moussorgsky's *St. John's Night on the Bare Mountain,* Liszt's *Mephisto* waltz and his *Totentanz,* the Witches' Sabbath from Berlioz's *Symphonie fantastique,* the wolf-glen scene from Weber's *Der Freischütz*—all depict the Devil and his cohorts afoot in the dead of night.

In suggesting these concepts and themes, the music explores and develops harmony that is unstable, agitated, restless, making bold use of dissonance for striking effects. As we said before, *Tristan* epitomizes this view. Also, if we take the Prelude as representing restless yearning with its unsettled harmony, then the final section, the Love Death (with which the Prelude is often paired in concert performance), acts as a kind of resolution to the Prelude, since its harmonies have a stronger *major* quality.

NATURE: DESCRIPTIVE MUSIC

The coloristic aspects of romantic harmony and sonority were employed for specific purposes of description. These were frequently associated with images of natural phenomena. Nature, in many forms, attracted composers of the nineteenth century.

The play of water, the rhythm of sea waves, the murmur of the countryside, the rush of wind and rain, the shepherd's and the hunter's horn echoing over the hills—all these and many other fancies provided frameworks for the play of colors, figures, and textures in music.

1. Beethoven's Symphony No. 6, called the *Pastoral,* projects a distinctive quality of sound in each movement. The first movement, with pleasantly monotonous dronelike sounds, sustained or endlessly repeated, describes pleasant feelings upon arrival in the country. The slow ambling of a brook is suggested in the gently swinging motion of the second movement. The fourth movement creates the impression of a sudden storm with sound effects borrowed from eighteenth-century Storm and Stress music.

FIGURE 12. Pierre Rousseau: *Edge of the Woods.* (Courtesy of the Metropolitan Museum of Art.)

2. Wagner himself set the stage for his gigantic work *Der Ring des Nibelungen* (The Ring of the Nibelung) by describing the flow of the river Rhine in the Prelude to *Das Rheingold* (The Rhinegold). This is a most remarkable piece of music, since it contains but one harmony, the chord of E♭ major, upon which all the flowing, rolling figures are based.
3. Mendelssohn's *Hebrides* Overture, descriptive of a trip to the western islands of Scotland, is a landmark in the history of descriptive music. Listen to the strange harmonies within the first few measures. How

EXAMPLE 7·4 Mendelssohn: *Hebrides* Overture

striking is their suggestion of bareness and desolation on a tossing open sea! The whole piece explores such harmonies, balancing them, to be sure, with the traditional cadential progressions of classic harmony.

FIGURE 13. Gustave Doré: Illustration for *The Wandering Jew*. Nineteenth-century romantic motifs of the wild sea, of terror, and of the supernatural characterize this engraving. (Courtesy of the Stanford University Libraries.)

Mendelssohn achieved his effect by using harmonies that belong to the natural minor mode, the mode that lacks a leading tone. In classic music the chords that might be used in the third and fifth measures would probably bring the harmony around to a cadence; Mendelssohn's choice of chord leaves the music "dangling," doubtful, and without cadential drive. Worked into the harmonic structure a short motive is repeated again and again, like little points of color in a painting. The scene, the harmony, the melodic arabesques—these point the way to *musical impressionism,* a style of the late 1800s and early 1900s that devoted itself almost entirely to the description of strange and exotic scenes.

4. Weber begins the overture to his opera *Oberon* with a slow sustained call on the muted horn that seems to come from deep in the elfin woods of Oberon's realm. Fairy flutes and trumpets add to the atmosphere of magic which Weber so effectively creates in the introduction to this piece. Strikingly enough, the body of the overture, the Allegro, is worked out very much as a classic type of piece, in which Weber shows his great debt to Beethoven in matters of orchestration, part writing, and development.

Descriptive music is called *program music.* Much has been written for and against the propriety of composing music with a story or scene in mind. While pictorialism and affective values had for centuries been part of the aesthetics of music, it was in the nineteenth century that the tendency to link music with extramusical ideas became so strong and all-pervading that it was a basic issue among musicians and critics.

Interest in a program for musical composition was inevitable in the intellectual and artistic climate of the nineteenth century, with its grandiose, picturesque, sentimental, and nostalgic feelings and concepts. Moreover, the increased resources of harmonic color and texture lent themselves to special effects of pictorialism and mood. Program music, as a genre, is neither good nor bad. Each composition has to be taken separately and judged according to general standards of effectiveness, imagination, and taste.

Richard Strauss, in his tone poem *Till Eulenspiegel* managed to link an amusing yet pathetic story to a composition that is a masterpiece. The mischievous humor of Till is delightfully suggested by capricious turns in the music, by an effervescent manner, and by a highly imaginative set of musical materials. Although each can stand alone, the story and the music very aptly complement each other. The very same composer, Strauss, fails to convince us of the validity of his intention in another work, the *Sinfonia domestica,* although this piece has many realistic touches of description.

NATIONALISM; LOCAL COLOR

The romantic artist's interest in nature represents an escape from the dull or oppressive realities of everyday existence. Such flights are typical of romanticism. The artist wants to explore different, faraway, and strange worlds; he wants to free himself from the center of gravity which is his own mundane life; he strives to expand the world of his imagination in every direction. All the favorite subjects of romanticism typify this expansion, this centrifugal motion. The nineteenth century, itself an era of great expansion, is truly reflected in its music.

Sometimes the romantic composer's imagination turned to his own national culture and its origins. Folk music, national legends, the quintessence of national spirit were all expressed with great enthusiasm, particularly by composers in the Slavic and the Scandinavian countries, which had been on the periphery of European music during the preceding centuries.

Russia, with Moussorgsky, Aleksandr Borodin, Nicholas Rimsky-Korsakov, and others, developed a new and highly significant musical language, based upon folk rhythms and Oriental qualities of color. These characteristics give a special distinction to such works as Moussorgsky's opera *Boris Godunov,* Borodin's opera *Prince Igor,* and Rimsky-Korsakov's Overture *La Grande Pâque russe* (Russian Easter). In all these works you will hear brilliant flashes of color, odd-sounding melodies based on exotic scales, and a violence of rhythm not encountered in Western music. They represent a deliberate effort to break away from Western European style; they assert the distinction and separateness of a national culture.

Local color is closely associated with nationalism in nineteenth-century music. Actually, the distinction lies in the fact that nationalism represents the use of material from a composer's own country or area of origin, while local color may incorporate material from other regions. Thus, Tchaikovsky used Italian melodies in his *Capriccio Italien,* Bizet and Rimsky-Korsakov turned to the music of Spain in *Carmen* and the *Capriccio Espagnol,* respectively, while Mahler introduced an Oriental quality in his *Lied von der Erde* (Song of the Earth). To be sure, there is a further distinction: in nationalism, the impulse is directed toward history, countryside, and legend, while in local color, special values of exoticism, the faraway, the mysterious seem to draw the composer.

Some examples of nationalism and local color in romantic music follow:

Dvorak: *Slavonic Dances,* Op. 46 and Op. 72. These sixteen dances for orchestra, brilliantly scored, were originally written for piano.

Dvorak's material is original; he used no popular melodies. Among the dance types we hear the polka, the furiant (a quick dance in triple time), the polonaise, and a number of characteristic Slavonic dance types. Emphasis here is on intriguing rhythm, ingratiating melody, bold scoring, colorful harmony—all contained within a symmetrical periodic layout.

Rimsky-Korsakov: Overture *La Grande Pâque russe* (Russian Easter), Op. 57. Russian themes are used here. At the beginning, we hear antiphonal effects that recall the chant of an Orthodox church service; the harmonies are modal, as befits the scene. Later, bell effects in many versions, solos, and orchestral tutti add their share to the color of the piece. The main body of the work, the allegro, is cast in sonata form.

Tchaikovsky: *Capriccio Italien,* Op. 48. Here, the composer used melodies he had heard in Florence; he also borrowed from a published collection. The piece itself is a kind of potpourri, with contrasting sections rather closely juxtaposed. Fanfares, songs, dances—all imbued with a Latin warmth of harmony and orchestration—demonstrate how closely Tchaikovsky's own personal style approached that of his subject.

Brahms: *Hungarian Dances.* These short arrangements of preexisting dance melodies are familiar to most listeners, in arrangements for piano as well as for orchestra. Brahms also used Hungarian models in music of greater scope. The finale of his Piano Quartet in G minor, Op. 25, begins as a dance with a characteristic punctuation in three-bar phrases.

In addition to the examples cited above, we can mention Berlioz's use of the tarantella, an Italian dance, in his overture *Roman Carnival;* Chabrier's use of the Spanish jota, with its typical shifts between duple and triple meter, in his rhapsody *España;* Rimsky-Korsakov's use of the jota and fandango, as well as the improvisatory style of the flamenco in his *Capriccio Espagnol.* In all these works the emphasis is upon striking color, highly delineated style, and picturesqueness—qualities which exploit the resources of the nineteenth-century orchestra to the utmost.

MUSIC AND LANGUAGE

The titles and subjects that we have discussed above show that romantic music has close ties with literature and with ideas borrowed from the world of language. But these connections extended beyond the use of literary associations in musical compositions. Many composers were both writers and critics. Weber, Berlioz, Schumann, Liszt, and Wagner produced interesting and often excellent prose in their writings that dealt with musical criticism and aesthetics. Conversely, E. T. A. Hoffmann, one of the strongest spokesmen for romanticism in his writings, was a composer of some prominence in his time.

The connection between music and literature went even farther. Music became poetic, and poetry strove to become ever more musical. Composers tried to approximate the declamatory accents of poetry and dramatic speech in an effort to make their music more eloquent and persuasive. Liszt, at the beginning of his B-minor Sonata, suggests a profound and impassioned soliloquy; within this piece we hear passages in recitative style, as if a text were being declaimed. Indeed, in Wagner's later music dramas, the entire vocal content is cast in the manner called *Sprechgesang,* "speech-song," in which the inflections and rhythms of the German language are delineated in the music.

EXAMPLE 7·5 *Sprechgesang* (speech-song). Wagner: *Tristan,* Act III

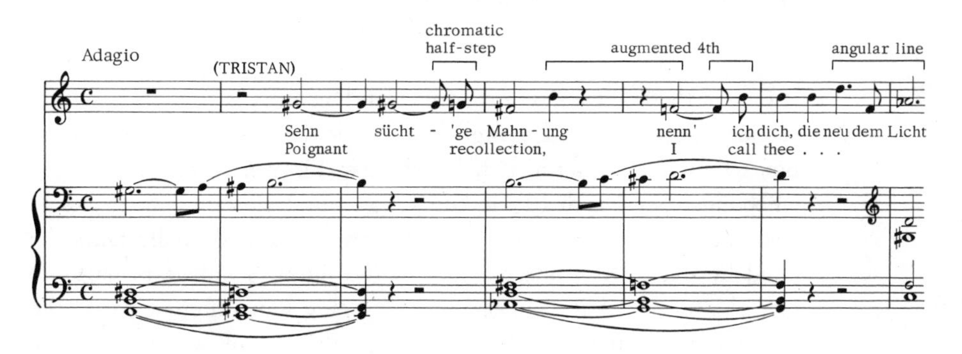

The entire song literature of the nineteenth century, one of the most distinctive contributions of romantic music, depends upon the close union of words and music. The eloquence, charm, and pathos of poetry is closely matched by the music which romantic composers set to lyric poetry.

While music was striving to become ever more poetic and speechlike in its expression, poets, on the other hand, made efforts to create a musical quality in the sounds of their words. The dark mood of the following excerpt from Edgar Allan Poe's *Ulalume* is measurably enhanced by the vowel sounds he has chosen, framed by alliteration among the consonants and by a singsong rhythm.

It was night in the lonesome October
Of my most immemorial year.
It was hard by the dim lake of Auber
In the misty mid-region of Weir.
It was down by the dank tarn of Auber
In the ghoul-haunted woodland of Weir.

POE

In an entirely different mood, John Keats enhances the richness of the scene he is depicting in *The Eve of St. Agnes* by choosing words which have a strongly resonant quality:

While he from forth the closet brought a heap
Of candied apple, quince, and plum, and gourd;
With jellies soother than the creamy curd,
And lucent syrops, tinct with cinnamon;
Manna and dates, in argosy transferr'd
From Fez; and spiced dainties, every one,
From silken Samarcand to cedar'd Lebanon.

KEATS

One of the finest songs of the nineteenth century is Schubert's setting of Goethe's poem *The Erlking.* Goethe tells the story of a father riding home through the storm with his child in his arms. The Erlking, the embodiment of Death (again the supernatural element), first tries to coax the child to come with him, then threatens, and finally takes the child by force. By subtle changes in the music Schubert manages to give the solo voice the appearance of singing four different parts: the narrator, the father, the child, and the Erlking. He mirrors the emotional values of the poetry in subtle, yet telling fashion. Here are samples of each part:

EXAMPLE 7·6 Narrator

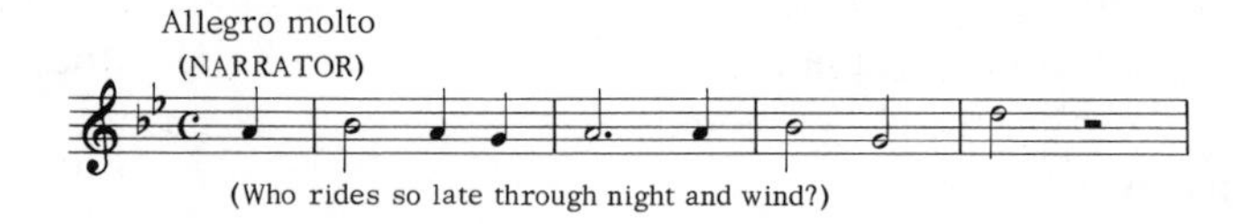

First, the narrator tells of the father hurrying home through the storm and wind. The music begins in a somewhat level, matter-of-fact manner, although the agitation that the storm music in the piano creates tells us that this quiet manner is but a foreboding. As the narrator continues to sing, his melodic line grows active, to signify greater tension.

EXAMPLE 7·7 Father

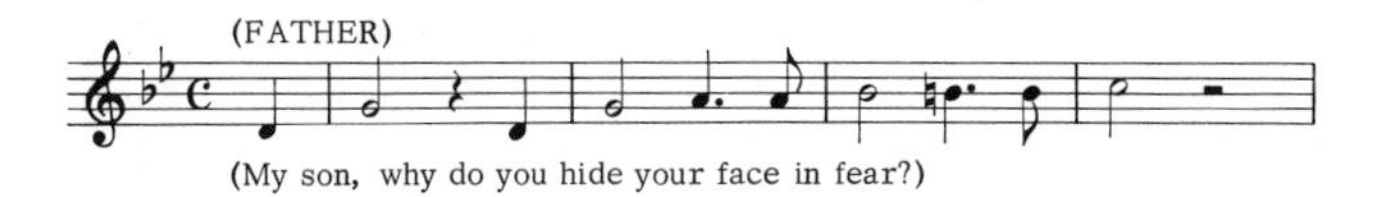

The father's music begins on a low pitch and throughout the piece is generally placed low, with the exception of his last phrase, when the terror of the situation seems to communicate itself to him. The sturdy interval of the perfect fourth, rising from dominant to tonic, characterizes the father's music; traditionally, it has a connotation of authority (as in a trumpet call).

EXAMPLE 7·8 Child

The child, in contrast, is given a high-pitched melodic part, of which the example above is the most characteristic excerpt. Three times we hear this outcry, each time a major second higher, and each time it is a refrain that answers the Erlking's persuasions. Schubert has assigned to the child's music the most unstable harmony in the piece; the pleas of the child are sung over dissonant, unstable harmonies.

EXAMPLE 7·9 Erlking

a.

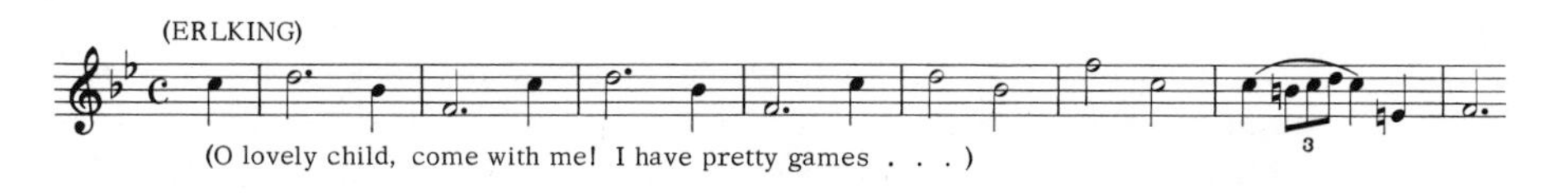

b.

The two melodies above represent the Erlking's music. Notice how sweet and ingratiating they are, like candy offered to a child. This is a master touch in composition, to coat the deadly intent of the Erlking with cloying sweetness. Listen also to the manner in which Schubert lightens the driving accompaniment figure whenever the Erlking sings.

EXAMPLE 7·10 Narrator; recitative

At the very end comes the finest touch of all, as the momentum which carried throughout the piece is broken and the narrator announces in halting recitative that the child is dead. Nothing could portray so well the absolute horror of the tragedy as this bare final statement.

The affinities that music, poetry, drama, and pictorial art have had for each other during the many centuries of Western civilization concerned Wagner deeply. He expressed his idea of merging the arts in his book *The Art Work of the Future.* In his plan Wagner not only brought music and poetry together, but included the graphic arts and pantomime to create his idea of a timeless, universal composition whose subject matter was neither current nor historic, but rather drew upon the legends of German antiquity in order to develop the simple and monumental values associated with man's origins. In Wagner's scheme, music was to play a complementary role, supporting and assisting the dramatic idea. Wagner himself described the relative importance of various arts in this scheme. He said:

> True drama can be thought of only as arising from the drive of all arts to communicate in the most immediate way to a general audience. . . . All of the richly developed possibilities of individual arts will be used in the comprehensive art work; in this form, these possibilities will reach full stature.

Paradoxically, the artistic residue of Wagner's work is almost entirely musical. We are no longer stirred by his grandiose scheme or his racial pageants, but we find that his music is a living experience for us today.

The two harmonic tendencies we have observed in romantic music, harmonic tension and harmonic color, each proceeded farther in its own course; each gave rise to a distinct style of composition in the late nineteenth and early twentieth centuries. The emotional conflicts, the introspection, and the unrest suggested by harmonic tension led to the style called *expressionism.* The shadings, nuances, and textures suggested by color in harmony led to the school called *impressionism*. In Chapter 8 we shall again pick up the threads of these particular lines of musical evolution.

Expressive values in romantic music may be summarized as follows:

1. Emotional intensity
2. Conflict
   a. Good versus evil
   b. Life versus death
   c. Individual versus society
3. Search for the ideal
4. Nature: descriptive music
   a. Natural phenomena: water, wind, sea, countryside
   b. Faraway and long-ago
   c. Fantastic and exotic
5. Nationalism and local color
   a. Stories and scenes from the past
   b. Glorification of national image
   c. Dances, songs
   d. Borrowing of national flavor by foreign composers
6. Music and language
   a. Close ties between music and literature
   b. *Sprechgesang:* imitation of speech in music
   c. Attempts of language to become "musical"
   d. Composers as writers
   e. The merging of language and music in an effort to create a higher art form.

Instruments and Performance

Returning once again to the beginning of *Tristan,* we can very easily see that much of the color effect comes from the way in which the instruments are used. The rich chords would lose much were they to be played by light or thin-bodied instruments. The scoring is for low-pitched wind instruments, massed together; they merge and blend to produce a full, throaty, and vibrant sound. Indeed, throughout the piece our attention is drawn to wind and brass instruments used with great prominence. We hear the orchestral effect at the beginning expanded, varied, and developed as the Prelude unfolds.

Such concentration on the special effects that instrumental sounds can produce is to be found in much nineteenth-century music. Romantic composers give special attention to instruments in two general ways:

They are concerned (1) with instrumental color and sonority; and (2) with virtuoso, soloistic treatment of instruments, both singly and in groups. As we shall see, these two areas often overlap.

THE ORCHESTRA

The development of the art of orchestration involved the efforts of many composers; writing for the concert or symphony orchestra had already grown into an important branch of musical composition in the eighteenth century. Instruments had assumed the state and function which they occupy at the present time, except for some refinements and improvements that developed more fullness of tone, greater accuracy of intonation, and greater ease of handling. By the beginning of the nineteenth century, the orchestra and its instruments were ready to participate in the flights of exploration that romantic composers were about to take. No one exemplifies the imaginative treatment of the orchestra better than Hector Berlioz. His *Symphonie fantastique* represents him best in this vein.

As we listen to his *Symphonie fantastique,* we are struck immediately by the entirely different qualities of sound which distinguish this piece from the Prelude to *Tristan.* In the music of Berlioz there seems to be a brilliance, a sharpness, and a transparency of tone which borders upon thinness. In *Tristan,* the composer seeks a richness and a fullness that borders upon heaviness and opacity. Wagner's tone color suggests a massive emotional upheaval; Berlioz's tone color connotes an intense nervous excitement. Wagner broadens and weights the line of melody by assigning it to a number of instruments which may duplicate each other in several octaves. Berlioz prefers to emphasize the play of melodic fragments against each other, projecting brilliant flashes of color in mid-air. The center of Wagner's tone mass is rather low; he fills in the spaces, from top to bottom, with tones that add body and richness to the sound. In contrast, Berlioz's center of tonal gravity is high, and open spaces may be sensed between the various levels of pitch. Thus, the texture of Berlioz seems well layered; Wagner's is thoroughly mixed.

Continuing with our comparison, we find that Wagner creates, varies, and develops one general quality of sound throughout an extended passage. His orchestration is dedicated to the same expressive purpose as his harmony: to carry out a special mood to its peak of intensity. On the other hand, Berlioz appears to seek out change and contrast, often in the boldest and most unexpected manner. We have unusual juxtapositions of high and low sounds, sometimes together, sometimes in alternation. The tone colors themselves often represent explorations of regions previously untrod.

As we might expect, the expressive purpose of Berlioz is far removed from Wagner's. Berlioz has a darting, lightninglike imagination; like the Viennese classic composers, he projects and reconciles contrasts, although in his case, the boldness of the contrast frequently overrides the resolution. With respect to melodic material, Wagner uses motives that resemble each other in general style; these he works over intensively, and he returns to them constantly for the very fabric of his musical discourse. The component voices in Wagner's music wind in and out in a semi-independent manner, suggesting a constant undercurrent of movement. Berlioz's material shows great variety and sudden contrast. When two or more voices are set against each other, they frequently project a bold conflict in the respective qualities of movement; they proceed at striking tangents to each other. This effect comes about through sharply contrasted rhythmic patterns and the deliberate avoidance of blend between the instruments involved.

Berlioz and Wagner each represent a characteristic attitude of romanticism, and the above comparison only underscores the rich variety to be discovered in the music of this time. Moreover, we shall find much in both composers that is similar. Each was well grounded in the standard orchestral techniques of nineteenth-century music. Each learned much from Beethoven in the way of orchestration. But, in his characteristic vein, each struck out in a different direction. Wagner sought greater fullness and richness of sound to support his grandiose conceptions; Berlioz sought to evoke new impressions by exploring new techniques of scoring, and he highlighted them with a transparent quality of sound.

By way of illustration, listen to these passages from the *Symphonie fantastique:*

1. In the second movement, the hero's dream of a grand ball is told. At the beginning, the misty atmosphere of the dream is depicted by murmuring strings and an ensemble of harps playing brilliant, skyrocketing arpeggios.
2. Distant thunder is suggested by the roll of four timpani at the end of the third movement, *In the Country*. This is certainly one of the most striking passages in all orchestral literature. Tuned to four different tones, these instruments project a strange, muffled, and veiled quality, in which the listener may detect, but cannot fix, a pure pitch. Beethoven, in his *Leonore* Overture No. 3 and in his Symphonies Nos. 8 and 9, had already used the timpani as a solo instrument, but only in its normal function of projecting a bass line. Berlioz goes far beyond this usage, and his low, murmuring chords for timpani, associated with a description of a scene in the country, constitute a bit of pure musical impressionism.

FIGURE 14. Excerpt from Berlioz's *Symphonie fantastique,* March to the Scaffold. Note the massing of instruments in contrasting groups, quick give-and-take, sudden contrast of pianissimo and fortissimo, striking harmonic shifts, brilliance of effect increased by high register of bass instruments. Key to abbreviations of the names of the instruments:

Fl.——Flute(s)
Ob.——Oboe(s)
Cl.——Clarinet(s)
Fg.——Bassoon(s)
Cor.——Horn(s)
C. à p.——Cornet(s)
Tr.——Trumpet(s)
Tbni.——Trombone(s)
Tb.——Tuba(s)
Timp.——Timpani
Ptti.——Cymbal(s)
G.C.——Bass drum
Vl.——Violin(s)
Vla.——Viola(s)
Vc.——Violoncello(s)
Cb.——Double-bass(es)

3. In the country one might hear the shepherd's horn echoing in the distance. Berlioz evokes this picture by using the English horn, an oboe of rather low pitch and full sound. Its rather dark tone quality suits it admirably for playing the *ranz des vaches,* the herder's theme in the third movement. Ordinarily, the English horn did not figure prominently in early nineteenth-century music.
4. The last movement describes a diabolic orgy. At one point, the doom of sinners is foretold by a quotation from plain chant, the *Dies irae* (Day of Wrath). We hear this solemn tune first intoned by tubas and large bells, as it might resound in a cathedral, but immediately each phrase is taken in turn by different groups of instruments, higher, more quickly, and with increasingly grotesque effect, as the devils take over.

In this symphony, as in his other orchestral music, Berlioz often assigns material of striking sound or design to instruments that would ordinarily play a subordinate role in the texture or that were not part of the standard complement in the early-nineteenth-century orchestra. Some of the most vivid moments in this piece feature the harp, timpani, bells, tuba, and English horn. Berlioz seems to have created his rhetoric directly for the orchestra; his feeling for the quality of an instrument was the spark to his melodic, rhythmic, and textural invention. In this respect, he steps beyond his colleagues in the nineteenth century; one must look ahead to the orchestral texture of Strauss and Mahler to discover a similar view. His electric, kaleidoscopic boldness and verve of effect grew out of his keen feeling for the evocative power of the grand romantic orchestra. One interesting concomitant of this superb orchestral mastery was his sense for contrapuntal action whenever a figure made its appearance in the texture. Berlioz's instruments, as they work against each other, project that sense of counterthrust which is the essence of counterpoint.

By and large, during the nineteenth century, orchestral music leans toward the Wagnerian idea of orchestration, with its fullness and power, its richness of color. Brahms, Tchaikovsky, Dvorak, César Franck, Liszt, Bruckner, and the earlier Mahler, often seem to be concerned with the massive, the grand, the heroic sound of the orchestra. As a reaction, toward the end of the nineteenth century, the orchestral qualities we have observed in Berlioz's music began to exert more influence. Transparency, strikingly unusual effects, economy, and lightness appear in the music of Claude Debussy and Ravel, in some of Strauss and Mahler, and in much contemporary music.

As evidence of the tremendous appeal of nineteenth-century orchestral music, one has but to tabulate the orchestral repertoire of present-day symphony orchestras. It leans heavily to the large-scale works composed during the romantic era. Indeed, to many listeners, the entire world of music consists of compositions which embody the romantic orchestral idea of sound. Nowadays, the voicings of many jazz orchestras represent a modified version of Wagner's or Brahms's scoring, rich, compact, and full. Much motion-picture music, not only in its scoring, but in its way of appealing to the feelings and sentiments of the moviegoer, echoes the sound of romantic orchestral music.

We have mentioned other examples of colorful scoring in nineteenth-century orchestral music, as, for example:

Weber: Wolf-glen scene from *Der Freischütz*
Wagner: Prelude to *Das Rheingold* (The Rhinegold)
Mendelssohn: *Hebrides* Overture
Rimsky-Korsakov: Overture *La Grande Pâque russe* (Russian Easter)

In addition, the following are of special interest:

Wagner: Prelude to *Die Walküre* (The Valkyrie). This music suggests the storm through which Siegmund is struggling before he reaches the house of Hunding. We hear three levels of action:

a. There is steady, agitated tremolo in the strings.
b. Below this, the bass instruments reiterate a restless "walking" scale motive, punctuated and accented by rapid scales.
c. Later, fanfare signals enter in the winds and brass.

The entire Prelude is cast as a huge authentic cadence, proceeding from tonic through subdominant and dominant harmonies (note the arrival at the dominant by means of an explosive roll on the timpani); upon the resolution to the tonic the curtain rises and action begins as Siegmund enters. In this excerpt Wagner has made use of classic harmonic techniques to control and focus romantic color and mood. Compare this with Schubert's *Erlking*. The similarities at the beginning are quite striking.

Mahler: Symphony No. 1 in D major, first movement. At the beginning, Mahler has created an extremely tenuous "curtain" of sound by spreading the strings over seven octaves; each section takes the note A at a different level and plays very softly. Against this background, fragmentary signals by winds and brass appear and disappear. Here we have both clarity and elusiveness; the scoring sets the stage for a work of grand proportion.

Brahms: *Variations on a Theme by Haydn,* Op. 56*a*. The variation procedure gives Brahms the opportunity to explore orchestral color in a rather formal manner. Each variation has its own texture and sound. The precise pronunciation of the winds in the theme itself changes, in the first variation, to a flowing string style. Later, scherzando winds, hunting-horn fanfares, a graceful siciliano in strings and winds—each comments upon the original theme. The finale directs attention to the bass, assigning to it a motive treated as a passacaglia, with its own set of variations.

Berlioz: *Romeo and Juliet,* Op. 17, Queen Mab Scherzo. This is a tour de force of orchestral scoring; it would be difficult to characterize it in a few words. The quick, nervous manner of the material is enhanced by many unexpected shifts—irregular give-and-take and offbeat interruptions. We feel here, as so often with Berlioz, that he is scoring his music much as an artist might paint a fresco; a color suggests a figure.

VIRTUOSITY

The search for new, more impressive, richer, and more striking effects in orchestral music is all part of romanticism's urge toward expansion. Scoring was not the only aspect of performance that was affected. New effects made new, and often greater, demands upon the performers. Greater virtuosity was required in all fields of performance. This applied particularly to solo performance. The nineteenth century begins the era of the musical hero, the Paganini, the Liszt, the Rubinstein, the Von Bülow. Both the difficulties of performance and the strangeness of the music itself acted to create a tremendous chasm between the artist and the listener. It was as if the artist were endowed with mysterious magic powers that set him apart from ordinary human beings. It was said of Niccoló Paganini, the great violin virtuoso, that he was in league with the Devil. Not only the performer, but the composer himself was being separated and estranged from his audience, largely because of the elusive or difficult music he wrote in his search for individuality. It was said of Brahms that his violin concerto was not *for,* but *against* the violin. Here is a sample of the sort of figuration the violinist was expected to negotiate:

EXAMPLE 7·11 Brahms: Concerto for Violin, Op. 77, first movement

In Brahms's figuration, the listener feels that the powerful and complex musical rhetoric dictates the difficult figuration; it could not have been said otherwise. Contrary to this expressive posture, the Concerto for Violin No. 1 in D by Paganini, which has even more difficult technical demands, appears to be much more ornamental in the eighteenth-century sense. Paganini, in the truly Italian style, builds elaborate and sparkling patterns over a simple, most agreeable singsong arrangement of symmetrical statements and counterstatements; in these he employs, as a rule, broad blocks of tonic, dominant, and subdominant harmonies to support the flight of the solo violin.

THE PIANO

Aside from the orchestra and violin, the principal medium in which the trend toward brilliance, color, and virtuosity developed was the piano. Like the orchestra, the piano received its present definitive form in the nineteenth century.

Refinements and improvements in the structure and action of the piano were developed that gave it a much wider range of tonal effects and a more brilliant sound than its predecessor of the eighteenth century. The limits of pitch were pushed both higher and lower, and the new registers were effectively employed.

EXAMPLE 7·12 Piano ranges

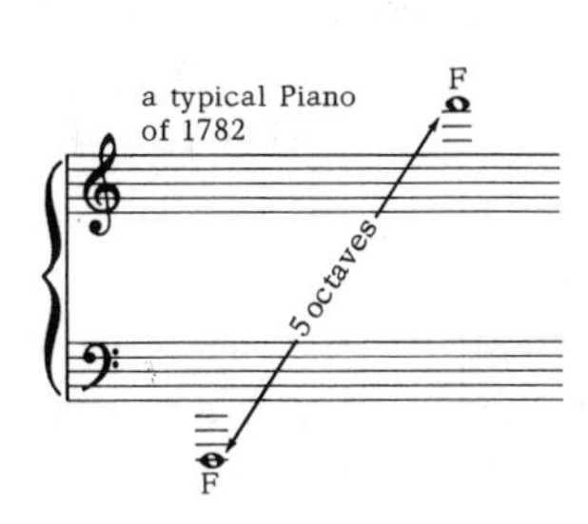

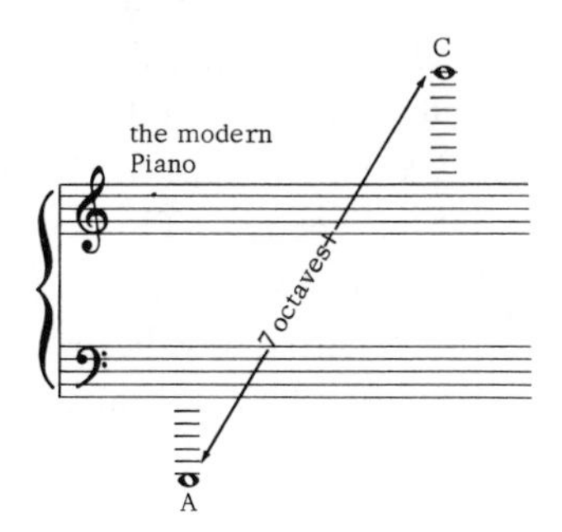

Romantic piano music shows an amazing variety and range of effects. We find the sharpest contrasts between loud and soft, high and low, full and thin, and these seem to have been negotiated by the performer with perfect ease. Of all the refinements, possibly the most important was the perfection of the sustaining pedal, which allowed a tone to reverberate for a time after it had been struck. This one resource opened an entire new world of tone color. (You can easily test this effect for yourself. At the piano, hold down the sustaining pedal, that is, the pedal at the right, and play the chord C–E–G. Release the keys and keep your foot on the pedal. Not only will you hear the reverberations of the tones that were struck, but you will hear, accompanying these tones, *all* the Cs, Es, and Gs above chiming in by *sympathetic resonance.*) Such atmospheric, delicate effects were exploited to the utmost in romantic piano music. Moreover, the sustaining pedal augments the mass of tone, so that grandiose effects are easier to achieve. Finally, much of the singing quality and warm tone which one hears from a fine piano performance comes from wise use of the sustaining pedal.

With its increased resources, the piano stimulated the development of distinctive personal styles. In each of the three works for piano mentioned at the beginning of this chapter, Chopin's Preludes, Schumann's *Carnaval,* and Liszt's Sonata in B minor, we discover a highly characteristic treatment of the keyboard.

Of all nineteenth-century composers, Frédéric Chopin probably explored the capacities of the piano most thoroughly with regard to texture and coloristic effects. The first Prelude gives us a typically Chopinesque miniature. We hear a singing melody floating above a fine network of sound. Although the melody itself is straightforward and symmetrical, the coloration of the tune by use of inflections seems to create a kind of urgency. A complex figuration supports this melody, but the pattern is repeated under each motive and is carried out during the entire piece. Chopin was a master at devising such figurations, such sonorous and airy laceworks of sound (see Example 7·13).

Naturally, these arabesques would require the use of a sustaining pedal to create the desired atmospheric mood and to maintain an adequate body of sound throughout the duration of the chord. Actually we are hearing just a few notes struck at any instant, perhaps no more than one or two. Thus, in Chopin's music, we receive the impression of easy but swift and soaring movement, sometimes gentle, sometimes stormy, but rarely heavy or strained. Chopin's keyboard effects lend themselves best to compositions in which a single mood prevails, or in which episodes of different moods alternate. The first Prelude sings, but has an undercurrent of agitation. The second, an unusual work of Chopin's, moves lugubriously, with a dark and tortured effect; it exploits the heavy, obscure lower sounds of the piano. The third is completely light and effervescent; the sixth, elegiac; the eighth, stormy; the ninth, broadly singing; and the eighteenth, an explosion of violent melodramatic fury. Each of the pieces in this work is a short, highly characteristic

EXAMPLE 7·13

a. Chopin: Prelude in C major

b. Chopin: Prelude in F♯ minor

piece, in which strongly provocative expressive qualities address themselves to the listener. At the same time, they are not so specific in their emotional connotations that the listener is prevented from finding his own particular or general reactions.

Robert Schumann, contemporary of Chopin, and very close to him in stylistic and aesthetic respects, nevertheless developed a different manner of composing for the piano. As we listen to Schumann's *Carnaval,* we hear much that is similar to Chopin in general mood. But the quality of sound in Schumann's music for piano is heavier, more massive than Chopin's. The center of sound seems lower. Therefore, the quality of movement appears to be less light and to involve something of a strain. Typically, Schumann uses more notes at a given time than Chopin. Often the performer has to negotiate massive chords which move rather quickly. While Chopin's harmony seems to change at an even, rather slow rate, whether the piece be slow or fast, Schumann's chords change quickly; the harmony boils up, exploring and restless.

EXAMPLE 7·14 Schumann: Chiarina from *Carnaval*

We hear greater rhythmic imbalance in Schumann than in Chopin. This, together with the restless harmony, gives an impression of instability and constant massive motion (see Example 7·14).

Briefly, Chopin gives the impression of an elegant ease of movement and a transparent quality of sound, while Schumann gives the impression of a rather heavy movement with a denser quality of sound. For that reason Schumann frequently has a more forceful emotional impact upon the listener than Chopin does. There is a personal quality, often impulsive and fantastic, to his music. Chopin's texture and manner point the way to musical impressionism. Liszt, Ravel, and Debussy are his stylistic descendants. Schumann's texture, both in piano and in orchestral music was adopted by his protégé, Johannes Brahms, and his harmony is a direct forerunner of the harmonic style of *Tristan*. Liszt also learned much from Schumann.

The demands made upon the pianist by nineteenth-century composers exceed anything that had been required previously for piano performance. At the summit of virtuosity stands the Sonata in B minor of Franz Liszt. This work embodies all the varied styles and techniques of piano performance that had been evolved up to this time; it also represents the trend of the later nineteenth century to encompass an entire world of expression and feeling in a monumental composition. Everything in this piece seems to have the air of bigness. Most of the music is phenomenally difficult to play. The range of sound covered is tremendous. The volume of sound moves from the loudest possible sonorities to the merest whispers. Most important of all, the expression in this piece covers a huge range. The low-pitched hollow passages at the beginning, with their uncertain harmony, suggest a kind of thoughtful foreboding. Suddenly this mood is broken by an explosive outburst, a wild crash of dissonant harmonies, spearheaded by a boldly arresting theme. Later, a grandiose and sweeping melody enters, to provide a contrast to what has preceded it. Lyricism, impassioned declamation, delicate fantasy, grim purpose set up in fugal manner, and, at the very end, beatific resignation are some of the moods that succeed each other in this piece, much as scenes in a tableau.

In its effort to encompass a gigantic range of expression, this sonata seems to go far beyond the idiomatic style of the piano at many points. Most of the music is what we would call *pianistic*, yet many passages appear to imitate orchestral sounds. We can imagine bassoons and horns sustaining the first low tones while the string basses and celli take the slowly descending figure. Certain lyric passages call for flute or oboe; other massed effects suggest a compact sound of brasses. On the other hand, Liszt is apparently seeking the eloquence that is the special property of vocal music when he composes recitative and declamatory passages in this piece. Everywhere, in almost every respect, there seems to be some kind of push outward, an effort to exceed the limits of usual or ordinary sound, technique, and expression. Thus, like *Tristan,* the Sonata in B minor is truly a representative work of musical romanticism. Further evidence along these lines will turn up when we turn to form in romantic music (see page 328).

Considering the dominating position of the virtuoso in the musical scene of the nineteenth century, it is not surprising that many important concertos were written during this period. Indeed, most of the solo concertos you will hear at symphony programs were written after the year 1800. Beethoven, Mendelssohn, Schumann, Chopin, Liszt, Brahms, Tchaikovsky, and Rachmaninov wrote concertos for solo violin or piano and orchestra, all of which are in the vein of the grand virtuoso style. Today we are still under the spell of the musical wonder-workers; it is the soloist who captures the imagination of the audience and draws the full houses.

CHAMBER MUSIC

Many composers in the nineteenth century continued the tradition of chamber music so firmly established in the eighteenth century. Schubert, Schumann, Brahms, Mendelssohn, Franck, Dvorák—each produced a number of works in this medium; the principal influence seems to have been that of Beethoven, with his serious and searching sonatas, trios, and quartets. Chamber music in the romantic era, however, does not occupy the central position in the musical scene that classic chamber music did. As you may recall, eighteenth-century chamber music was a matrix from which orchestral procedures were drawn and amplified. Much of it was not difficult, and its object was to provide a musical conversation for performer and listener. There was much light interplay among the few voices; sonority was pleasant and sweet, but its texture, in range, color, and grouping was dedicated to a clear distinction between the conversing participants.

In some romantic chamber-music works, the conversation element still comes to the fore; Brahms's violin sonatas represent a serious and intimate dialogue between the violin and the piano. But more often we encounter works in which the music seems to be struggling to reach beyond its established limits of sound and movement. It is as if, in these works, the chamber-music idiom were borrowing from orchestral color and from the virtuoso style. As a result of this trend, romantic chamber music does not really have a field to call its own to the extent that was true of classic chamber music. Consequently, with some notable exceptions, chamber music is not as important a medium in the nineteenth century as it was previously, and its total output is less significant. Below we cite some special instances of characteristic romantic style in chamber music, with particular reference to effects of color and virtuosity:

Schubert: Quintet in C major, Op. 163, first movement. The very first sound in this piece draws us into a strange, sweet mood. Its major harmony, closely spaced, floats in mid-air, sustained, and without any rhythmic action whatever. Here is pure string color, first sweet, then bitter, then even more sweet again as the dissonant chord is followed by a return to the first major chord. When this passage is counterstated a few measures later, in a minor harmony, the low register is used for greater density of sound. The Quintet is scored for two violins, viola, and two cellos. This majority of tenor and bass string instruments provides a much richer palette of colors than is possible in the string quartet. Throughout the piece Schubert exploits this color resource, as in the counterstatement referred to above.

In the second movement of this work, Schubert treats his material in somewhat the same way that Chopin did in fashioning keyboard arabesques. The harmonies move very slowly and regularly; whatever melodic material there is appears in the second violin, with which the viola and first cello are linked in a chordal texture. The first violin and second cello answer each other back and forth with short figures, as if to punctuate and animate the sustained lyric sound of the middle instruments. With but slight variation, this pattern is maintained and repeated in each measure for fourteen measures. One could almost say that this is a piano prelude adapted for strings; the texture is very similar to that of the second movement of Schubert's Sonata in B♭, composed in the same year, 1828.

Mendelssohn: Octet in E♭ major, Op. 20, for four violins, two violas, and two cellos. Throughout this piece, and typically at the beginning, the richness and breadth of sound that eight string instruments provide is an important element in the style and expression. At the beginning, there is a denseness of sound, created by rather active broken chord texture in the seven lower instruments. Over this, the first violin rises in a florid melody which calls for a virtuoso performer. Here is a case in which the opening theme behaves as though it were a song, a broad melody with accompaniment. Color, romantic lyricism, and virtuosity are all incorporated in these first measures; we can easily imagine that we are listening to the string section of an orchestra rather than to a chamber-music ensemble.

Schumann: Quintet in E♭ major, Op. 44, first movement. The opening measures of this piece seem to be reaching for greater power and fullness than would be comfortable for four strings and piano. The brilliant percussive chords come from the orchestral style. If you pay particular attention to the piano part, you will hear many passages of extreme brilliance and difficulty throughout this work.

Brahms: Quintet in F minor, Op. 34, first movement. Brahms's reputation as a "difficult" composer is certainly reinforced by this work, which demonstrates some of the demands the romantic composer made upon his performers in order to negotiate complex material and sustain an eloquent manner. Both the piano and the strings must work to utmost capacity if the powerful sonorities and the intricate and highly charged melodic material are to be projected adequately. In addition, rhythmic complexities abound, especially those which involve rapid and often syncopated interchanges between instruments. In this work, as in many others, Brahms shows his commitment to the classic style through his maintenance of a substantial conversation among the various parts of the texture.

Instruments and performance in romantic music may be summarized as follows:

1. Orchestra
   a. Fuller and more brilliant scoring than in classic style
   b. Special instrumental effects using instruments that are usually less prominent, i.e., timpani, tuba, harp, viola, English horn, percussion
2. Virtuosity
   a. Soloist as hero
   b. Complex figurations and brilliant passage-work
3. Piano
   a. Expansion of register
   b. Exploitation of sonority values through pedaling and figuration
   c. Piano as a "complete" instrument emulating the orchestra
4. Chamber music
   a. Role less prominent than in romantic era
   b. Coloristic effects and trend toward fullness of sound
   c. Some retention of classic "conversation" ideal
   d. Prominent virtuoso element

Heretofore we have been concerned with technique and expression in romantic music. Taking its harmony as a point of departure, we explored some of the expressive implications suggested by that harmony, its color and tension. We dealt with intense emotional expression and with ideas of good and evil, the ideal, the supernatural, the heroic, the far-away and long-ago, simplicity, and the charm of nature; and generally, we considered that this all represented a flight from reality, from the everyday world. Associated with this trend, lending it material assistance, was the expanded world of performance, involving new sounds, greater brilliance, range, and virtuosity.

The rich content of romantic music is somewhat difficult to manage, and you may wonder how such materials can shape themselves into musical forms. Having learned about the expressive values of romanticism, we can now turn our attention to form in romantic music. As always, the proper way to understand musical form is to see how it grows out of the nature of the thing to be expressed.

Form in Romantic Music

First, we must say that there is no consistent principle of structure that governs romantic music. A prelude by Chopin and Liszt's sonata are not manifestations of the same guiding plan, as was the case with the classic minuet and sonata form. The harmonic and rhythmic forces in classic music set up lines of attraction which held both large and small forms in tight control. The *antigravitational* impulse of romantic music destroyed these lines, or at least made them much less powerful. The wide variety of expression and style in the nineteenth century created new problems of coherence and contour with virtually every composition. Rather than discuss established forms, we shall be concerned with certain aspects of structure that reflect romantic trends.

THE DYNAMIC CURVE

Again we return to our source piece, the Prelude to *Tristan und Isolde*. We recall its dissolving harmony, its fluid rhythms, and its dense interweaving of melodic lines. We have difficulty in orienting ourselves, in grasping the structure of the piece. If we listen for landmarks, for clear points of structural arrival, we shall remain confused. But if we enter into the romantic world of expression, to sense the rise and fall of emotional intensity, we can get a fairly good idea of the structure of the Prelude. Each phase of movement begins on a relatively low level of pitch and intensity and builds up to a climax; after each climax, the music drops and new tension begins to develop. Moreover, each successive phase of movement seems to reach a slightly higher point of climax. The entire piece builds up to the final climax, which is the most violent, impassioned, and sustained of all. Correspondingly, the collapse afterward is the most complete; exhausted, the music sinks back to its first gropings. Structurally, we sense a contour, rather than well-defined positions. The form takes shape in successively larger waves of sound, upon a curve of rising intensity. Its outline might be illustrated graphically as follows:

EXAMPLE 7·15 Pattern of dynamic curve

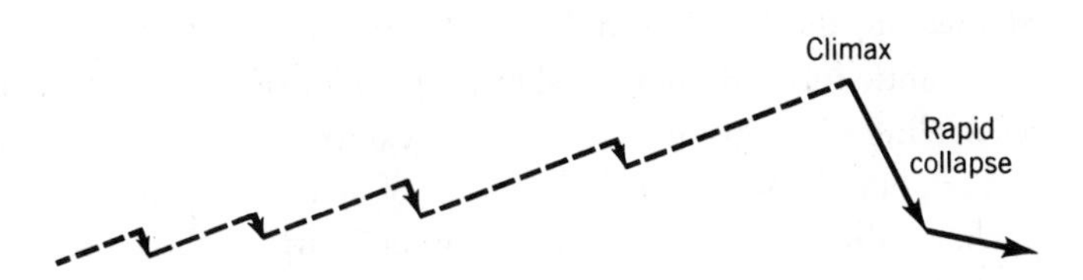

This rise and fall in strength of sound, this *dynamic curve,* is an important resource for building structure in nineteenth-century and early twentieth-century music. (You will recall in *The Erlking* how the emotional value of terror is steadily intensified by the higher pitches of the successive outcries of the child. Schubert has here used a dynamic curve as a form-building factor.) In a small way, Chopin used the dynamic curve in his Prelude in C major. (The word *dynamic* as used in the concept of the dynamic curve should not be confused with the word *dynamics* as applied to the loudness or softness of musical sounds. The term *dynamic curve* expresses a line of action in which intensity increases through various musical means—loudness, pitch, texture, melodic contour, harmony—until it reaches a significant climax.)

In the dynamic curve of the Prelude to *Tristan,* Wagner has epitomized the entire dramatic idea of the opera. Such a plan corresponds very much to the way in which our own emotions grow and ebb. In this music, the composer seeks empathy from the listener; he wants to bring his hearer entirely into the state of feeling set up by the music, so that the listener will lose himself in the music. Such an attitude is very different from the seventeenth- and eighteenth-century idea of projecting affective qualities, wherein the sympathetic response of the listener was evoked without any intention of overwhelming him.

In its plan of mood value, the Prelude assumes rounded form; the piece ends very much in the mood of its beginning, although a literal repetition does not take place. We receive the impression of an ABA form, without the usual balance of sections and the clear definition of the boundaries of each part. Again, the emotional conditions indicated by the music help to define the form. The uncertainty at the beginning is matched by the collapse at the end. The final section, as in all ABA forms, acts as a counterstatement to the first section; therefore, it serves as an area of arrival. But the return does not sound like the triumphant and glorious achievement of a goal, as it would in sonata form; it is rather a sinking back, an exhaustion, a defeat, and a surrender.

WEAKENING OF CADENCES

In its lack of authentic cadence, in the absence of a sense of unequivocal completion, the Prelude to *Tristan* represents another important aspect of romantic form. By now we have some idea of the role that the cadential feeling plays in musical form. Not only does a cadence round off a section, but it acts as a goal, as a point of arrival toward which the music pushes. While much romantic music does arrive with a flourish at the end of a section or movement, a great many compositions of this era fail to arrive emphatically; they trail off, leaving a question unanswered. Liszt's sonata, for all its heroic wrestling and searching, evaporates into thin air at the end. Schubert's song *Die Stadt* (The City) ends with the sound of a dissonant chord; his song *Thränenregen* (Teardrops) is in the major mode but ends in the minor. Chopin's first Prelude trails off; so does his A-major Prelude, that brief, delicate, and wistful fragment of a waltz. The lack of cadence seems to leave something unsaid, so that the mood will continue and the listener will furnish, in his imagination, the resolution of the story. Romantic poetry, too, frequently employs this device. In the two short poems below, much more is hinted at than is actually said. In Wordsworth's poem, the simple lines hint at a deep and lasting sentiment. In Shelley's poem, we are awakened to the lingering fragrance of flowers, the reverberations of tones, the recollection of love, all of which echo far beyond the actual time of experience.

She Dwelt Among the Untrodden Ways

She dwelt among the untrodden ways
Beside the springs of Dove,
A Maid whom there were none to praise
And very few to love:

A violet by a mossy stone
Half hidden from the eye!
—Fair as a star, when only one
Is shining in the sky.

She lived unknown, and few could know
When Lucy ceased to be;
But she is in her grave and, oh,
The difference to me!

WORDSWORTH

To—

Music, when soft voices die,
Vibrates in the memory—
Odours, when sweet violets sicken,
Live within the sense they quicken.

Rose leaves, when the rose is dead,
Are heaped for the beloved's bed;
And so thy thoughts, when thou art gone,
Love itself shall slumber on.

SHELLEY

The two poles of romantic expression, the intimate and the grandiose, are embodied in two different kinds of structure: the short composition, which explores one type of effect, and the extended piece, which is frequently in one unbroken movement but may include many different episodes.

THE SHORT PIECE

Piano

Short piano compositions that deal with one expressive value are typical of nineteenth-century music. These pieces take their momentum from the impulse of the original idea; the brevity of the form needs no contrast or additional force in the way of development or extension. The inner structure of these short compositions tends to accommodate the expression of a single mood or feeling; their lyric value is best projected in a song or dance form. Thus, in Schubert's *Moments musicales,* Chopin's preludes and études, mazurkas, waltzes, and nocturnes, Schumann's many piano works, and Mendelssohn's *Songs without Words* (note the title!), the form comes out typically as a series of well-defined, balanced periods and phrases, recalling the small two- and three-part forms of the eighteenth century. Here we find relatively little extension, although frequently, as we have mentioned above, the final cadences of these pieces are not calculated to bring matters sharply to an end. Indeed, the composers we have mentioned tend to be even more rigid in their phrase structure than Haydn, Mozart, and Beethoven. The classic composers had a flexibility within the period which was balanced by a strong sense of cadence at the end. The romantic composers had an automatic, almost singsonglike evenness in the phrases of their short pieces, but they often surprise us by their indeterminate endings.

These short compositions have a wonderfully spontaneous charm. Composed in series of six, twelve, or more to a set, they can touch upon many different moods in succession. Chopin, Schubert, and Brahms preferred to give them general, nondescriptive titles: impromptu, nocturne, ballade, intermezzo. Mendelssohn and Schumann made a point of assigning characteristic titles to such pieces, as, for example, *Spring Song, Venetian Boat-Song, Papillons* (Butterflies). In one set, his *Kreisleriana,* Schumann went so far as to identify each piece with an imaginary character, either *Florestan,* the impulsive spirit, or *Eusebius,* the introspective spirit.

To illustrate some stylistic and structural aspects of the short piano piece in romantic music, we cite the following examples:

Chopin: Prelude in E minor. The framework of the piece is the period form. There are two phrases, each beginning alike and ending with half cadence and authentic cadence, respectively. The slowly sinking chromatic flow of the bass disturbs the inner balance of each phrase; the repeated two-note motive of the treble is an obvious unifying element against the bass. Together, they create a reflective but troubled mood.

Mendelssohn: *Songs without Words,* Op. 19, no. 2. This piece has the characteristic broad melodic arch and easy, regular flow that is so often found in Mendelssohn. Its grouping into four-measure phrases is unmistakable. These in turn make up a two-reprise form with the familiar contrast of key at the end of reprise I and the clear rhyme to end reprise II. There is some broadening of periodic structure and a coda that has the typical romantic gesture of fading away. The precise structure, with its regular, clear punctuation, accommodates Mendelssohn's gentle, melancholy lyricism. In all his music we find this balance, coupled with a singing style and a facility of movement.

Schumann: *Carnaval,* Op. 9, no. 10. This is a brief waltz, whose opening figure is built on the notes A, E♭, C, and B, which in German are A, S, C, and H. (Asch, the name of a town in Bohemia, served as a motto for most of the pieces in *Carnaval.*) The two-reprise form is used to frame this restless dance, which never makes a strong cadence, although the punctuation is strictly maintained every four measures. Note the rapid changes of harmony and the shift of accent, as well as the extremely light resolutions of the harmony upon beat 2 or 3.

Beyond this small scope, there are piano works of greater length that nevertheless have some of the immediate impact of the short piece. Often, these are built up in sections or episodes, as in the fantasia, and each part has its own character. In such cases, it would seem that the short piece has been incorporated into a larger framework. Chopin's

Ballade in F is a clear example. Its first section is very lyric, a rather slow dance; the second section is highly agitated. These two sections alternate throughout the piece to create an episodic structure of relatively short parts. Other works (Prelude in D♭) are laid out as three-part ABA forms, similar to a minuet and trio.

Song

To study the forms in which songs were written in romantic music, we can best refer to Schubert. One of his songs, *The Erlking,* we have already discussed in some detail. In form this work is not a miniature but rather a fairly extended dramatic scene. It is *through-composed;* that is, for each line of text new melodic material is provided. This is opposed to *strophic* form, in which the same music serves for all stanzas. Through-composed music tends to develop the ideas being expressed, the music sharing significantly in the unfolding of the idea. In strophic settings, the music, charming though it may be, is often only a suitable framework for the general mood of the poem.

The song *Thränenregen* (Teardrops) from *Die Schöne Müllerin* just misses being a fully strophic song, and by just that much becomes an exquisitely touching work of art. The poem speaks of the reflection of the stars and the moon in the brook for the first three stanzas. Schubert has set this as a sentimental melody, with a few melting chromatic nuances; but the mode is *major.* The fourth stanza breaks the spell. Schubert suddenly places his music in the *minor,* makes a turn back to major, but no! at the very end, the minor, the question, the doubt returns and leaves the final impression. Nothing could better suggest this melancholy, this clouding of intimate romantic mood, than the sudden darkening of the harmony.

Another song, a familiar one, *Ungeduld* (Impatience), is entirely strophic. The basic form is short; each stanza is but eighteen measures long. But notice how convincingly Schubert suggests impatience by a quick pace and restless piano music. Each phrase of the voice is short; there are no real points of arrival, only momentary rest before the pace is picked up again. Each phrase reaches higher than the previous one, until finally the dynamic curve achieves its peak with its refrain, "You are my heart!" Only at this end do we reach our cadence! This is truly a miniature, yet the fervor and the expanse of feeling it suggests carry far beyond its actual extent in time.

Robert Schumann's songs, together with his piano pieces, represent his most characteristic and successful work. In both genres, Schumann was able to project intimacy and immediate intensity of feeling, a sharply delineated sketch that would appear to be improvised upon the instant. In his song cycle *Dichterliebe* (Poet's Love) to texts by Heinrich Heine, we meet, again and again, a subtleness of expression coupled with a simplicity of means that speaks feelingly and winningly and is sheer magic in its evocation of mood. The fourth song, *Wenn ich in deine Augen seh'* (When I look into your eyes) is short—only two periods in length with a brief epilogue that trails off. The harmony is simple, mostly cadences and a few modest digressions; the texture is uncomplicated, the melody like that of a popular folksong. Yet Schumann has employed these materials in a very special way. He has alternated motion and rest between the voice and the piano; the result is a chamber-music texture, a close conversation, rather than melody and accompaniment. At times motion overlaps; at times it pauses momentarily. Through this distribution of movement, Schumann has added a new dimension to the music, reflecting the dialogue of the lover and the unspoken response of his beloved.

Many nineteenth-century composers turned to the song as a vehicle for romantic lyricism. Brahms, Hugo Wolf, Richard Strauss, Mahler, and others found a strong personal style in the genre. Mahler wrote a number of song cycles for voice and orchestra, adding an extra element of color to the expression, while still remaining faithful to the intimate manner that probably represents nineteenth-century chamber style even more typically than chamber music itself.

THE EXTENDED PIECE

In building larger forms, nineteenth-century composers used the models that they had received from the classic style. The sonata, the rondo, two-reprise forms, three-part forms—these were all accepted as standard schemes for musical structure and indeed were often more stereotyped than their counterparts of the classic era; many textbooks on musical form were written during the nineteenth century, bearing witness to the complete codification of these structural layouts.

As we shall see, the external features of romantic form are often easier to recognize than those of classic form; yet the changes in style and expression that took place during the nineteenth century affected the internal structure of extended forms, so much so that a different structural principle appears to be at work in many compositions.

Sonata Form

You will recall that classic sonata form, as it appeared in the symphonies, sonatas, etc., was a big structure. Much of the expressive content of a classic sonata form was buoyant, tuneful, even popular in vein. Nevertheless, much was serious, important, and challenging; and this aspect of expression was responsible for the expansion of the form.

Romantic composers, who were concerned greatly with mood, manner, and gesture, addressed themselves directly to the characteristic grand and serious style of the sonata, the symphony, and the concerto. Relatively few nineteenth-century pieces in sonata form are light or cheerful in mood. The romantic symphony, in developing the grandiose manner, tended to be an extremely long work. Some of Mahler's and Bruckner's works take more than an hour to perform. Beethoven's Symphony No. 3 and Symphony No. 9 stood as models for later compositions of extreme length.

The differences between classic and romantic sonata form stand out very clearly in the ways in which the expositions of the two forms are built. Classic sonata form was set up in two large key areas, with a considerable variety of material, much local contrast in style, and a broad drive to the cadence that ended the exposition. The composer was free to introduce a new theme as he saw fit, at any place; or he might be content to work upon one theme. Nevertheless, we observed a tendency to introduce an important new theme at the beginning of the second key area, a theme which might represent a contrast to the opening subject of the movement.

The vividness of expression and the search for distinctive, impressive moods in romantic music led its composers to underscore the characteristic thematic content of sonata form. To them it was important to find an arresting, serious subject, to work this theme over for a time, and then to introduce, as a contrast, a songlike theme which would be the counterstatement to the opening theme. The *personalities of the themes* and their dramatic opposition became the basic structural idea, not, as in the eighteenth century, the *opposition of two keys* and the harmonic-rhythmic pull of grand cadences.

Here are some examples of thematic contrast in nineteenth-century symphonies:

EXAMPLE 7·16 Schumann: Symphony No. 1 in B♭ major

a. First or masculine theme

b. Second or feminine theme

Mahler: Symphony No. 2 in C minor

a. First theme

b. Second theme

Such a sharply marked thematic contrast between a bold, masculine, aggressive theme and a lyric, gentle, feminine theme can also be heard in the first movements of Brahms's Symphony No. 3, Franck's Symphony in D minor, and Tchaikovsky's Symphony No. 6. Each theme, in these examples, has something of the character of an independent piece or episode; thus, there is a kinship with the small lyric pieces we described earlier.

Because of the episodic structure of the romantic symphony, momentum over an entire movement is sacrificed for the sake of highlighting individual moments of striking intensity or appeal. The price paid for this is a looser, less compact form with many stop-and-start effects. Such a structural plan is in line with the basic aesthetics of romanticism. The individual moment, the individual idea, the individual person himself, demands and receives room for expression, even at the expense of the structure of the entire organism. We are handsomely compensated, of course, by the charm or the bold impact of the individual gesture.

Even in the symphonies of Brahms, who of all nineteenth-century composers represents the spirit of classicism most vigorously, we find moments in which the romantic loosening of structure is apparent. One of his finest movements, and one which represents the grand manner of the romantic symphony, is the first movement of his Symphony No. 1. The description of this movement, given below, touches upon certain characteristic features of his style and summarizes the overall structure of the movement.

We know immediately in the first few measures that we are going to hear a big piece. Not only the fullness of sound, but the breadth and sustained manner of the melodic line and the quality of movement indicate spaciousness to the listener. Curiously enough, the first few notes in the upper line are very similar to one of the motives at the beginning of *Tristan*. Also Brahms's harmony has strong chromatic flavor. Yet the contrast is even more striking than the similarity. Listen to the inexorable beat, hammered out by the timpani. There is no question about the rhythmic meaning here. Also, despite the chromaticism in the upper voices, the sense of key is set and maintained through the pedal-points (the repeated and sustained tones in the bass) which hold firmly to the tonic note of the key. This introduction builds to a series of strong cadences and thus prepares very effectively for the main part of the movement. It is an introduction conceived in a classic vein.

The chromatic motive of the introduction is built into the opening theme of the Allegro. In the first key area, note how Brahms has taken the syncopation of the opening motive and used it again and again to lead to a strong cadence. In this respect he follows his master, Beethoven. Here is the motive, and the manner in which it is used later:

EXAMPLE 7·17 Brahms: Symphony No. 1 in C minor, first movement

a. Introduction

b. Allegro of first movement

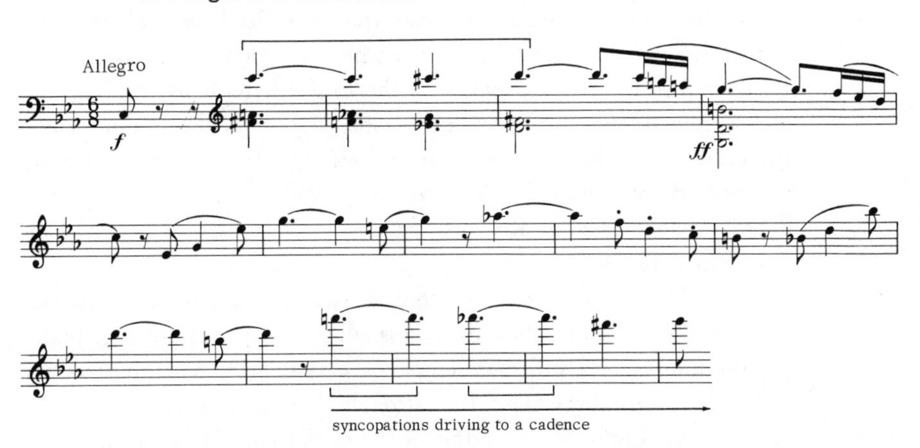

For the second key area, Brahms has actually composed two different pieces. The first (Example 7·18) is the usual lyric section with a theme that is the antithesis of the opening theme in most respects.

EXAMPLE 7·18 Brahms: Symphony No. 1 in C minor, first movement; lyric section

The second section, used as a closing theme, picks up again the manner of the opening Allegro:

EXAMPLE 7·19 Brahms: Symphony No. 1 in C minor, first movement; closing section

Note, in the second phrase of this period, how Brahms creates a striking counterstatement by reversing the positions of the upper and lower themes: a technique of *invertible* counterpoint which adds stress to the stormy manner of the theme. Most of the first movement embodies the vigorous style. The second theme appears only as an episode.

Brahms's development section, spacious yet closely knit, has the driving quality that brings him so close in spirit to Beethoven. This is most dramatically evident in the manner in which he planned the development. Less than half of the 174 measures is devoted to harmonic explorations which move outward and away from any fixed tonal center. The remainder centers upon the dominant harmony of the main key. Like Beethoven in the first movement of the *Eroica* Symphony, Brahms creates a tremendous drive toward the tonic key at the beginning of the recapitulation. The binding, the integrating effect of this gigantic cadential drive is entirely classic in its intention, although many incidental nuances betray the richness of harmonic detail we find in romantic harmony.

Brahms's recapitulation carries out the usual restatement of material heard in the exposition, but his coda is another matter. Instead of building up another and still more emphatic closing section in the manner of Beethoven, Brahms shows how strongly romantic procedures affected his thinking. Listen to the ending of the movement. After all the Storm and Stress, the coda relaxes into a calm, reflective sort of afterthought. The slowing down and the final cadence with its poignant plagal quality create the kind of inconclusive and suspended ending which we find in so many romantic works.

Brahms, in this movement, created a valid compromise between classic and romantic aspects of sonata form; at times he maintained the momentum at critical points and developed strong drives to points of arrival; at other times he allowed the rich and intense immediacy of romantic expression to make itself felt. In order to show the range of treatment that the nineteenth century accorded to sonata form, several additional examples are discussed briefly below:

Tchaikovsky: Symphony No. 6 in B minor (*Pathétique*), Op. 74, first movement. Following a slow introduction, the body of the movement begins in an agitated style, with intensive development of a few short but sharply defined motives. A climax is reached rather quickly, followed by a rapid drop in intensity to reach a moment of complete silence. There ensues, in a slower tempo, the second theme. It is a completely different piece, and it may seem as though we had come to the slow movement of the symphony. The entire second key area is built as a three-part ABA form, A and B each having its own tune. The A tune is one of the most ingratiating melodic inventions in all musical literature. One must pause to take it in, enjoy it, leave it for a gentle contrast, and then welcome it again. The exposition fades away into nothing. The same order of events takes place in the recapitulation, with some variation. Considering the two key areas of the exposition, there are actually two different compositions, linked by a rhetorical pause. Intensity drops, instead of rising as in the classic sonata. Each section is characteristic, inventive, distinctive, indicating that Tchaikovsky is at his best in individual episodes, as one finds in his ballet music. Unity arises from the compatibility of contrasting moods, not from a grand unbroken sweep forward.

Smetana: Overture to *The Bartered Bride*. This is the overture to a comic opera; throughout the nineteenth century we find that music in the lighter vein, such as that of Johann Strauss and Jacques Offenbach, tends to look back to classic models and procedures. Such is the case in this overture, built on the plan and in the spirit of the classic sonata form. It has tremendous verve, stops for nothing, reaches important points of arrival with purposeful drive. The key areas and themes are well marked, the texture has the quick give-and-take of classic scoring, and yet the piece has a distinctly nineteenth-century flavor because of its Slavonic dance rhythms and the colorful harmonies in the second key area, the development, and the coda.

Brahms: Symphony No. 4, Op. 90, first movement. Perhaps of all the movements in Brahms's symphonic music, this comes the closest to representing classic ideas of structure. In fact, it is much like the first movement of Beethoven's *Eroica* in the distribution of its thematic material. The first key area has but one theme, built as a chain of two-note motives; these will come in for intensive development throughout the movement. The second key area has a group of themes which succeed each other rather quickly. The structure is much tighter than in the first symphony; arrival and departure overlap. Contrast between key areas is not emphasized. Carrying out the classic plan, Brahms reaches the climax of the exposition at the area of arrival for the second key. He thus achieves a rise in intensity throughout this section.

THEMATIC ROLE IN ROMANTIC FORM

Individualism, as a creed, is very significant in romantic philosophy, and aesthetics. Musically, the epitome of individualism, its very signal, is the *theme*. Themes, instead of cadences and key areas, are often used as points of arrival and reference in nineteenth-century music. Thus, it is proper to speak of "first and second themes" in romantic sonata form because the thematic contrast is the structural basis of the form. Beyond this role in sonata form, thematic material in romantic music served other structural purposes. These involve (1) use of the *leitmotif* and (2) thematic transformation.

Leitmotif

In order to achieve a measure of unity and, at the same time, shape the contours of his tremendous music dramas, Wagner assigned significant motives to persons, ideas, or situations. These have been given the name *leitmotifs* or, as Wagner himself designated them, *basic themes*.

EXAMPLE 7·20 Leitmotifs

Love-slumber motive from *Tristan* (Wagner)

Sword motive from *Ring* cycle (Wagner)

Valhalla motive from *Ring* cycle (Wagner)

River Rhine motive from *Ring* cycle (Wagner)

In the Prelude to *Tristan,* for all its spinning out, its endless flow, the melodic material consists of a few well-defined and salient motives, which are worked over in many ways to bind the music together. Wagner's harmony wanders, his rhythm is imbalanced, but his melodic material is striking in its ability to hold the music in place.

EXAMPLE 7·21 Beginning of Prelude to *Tristan*

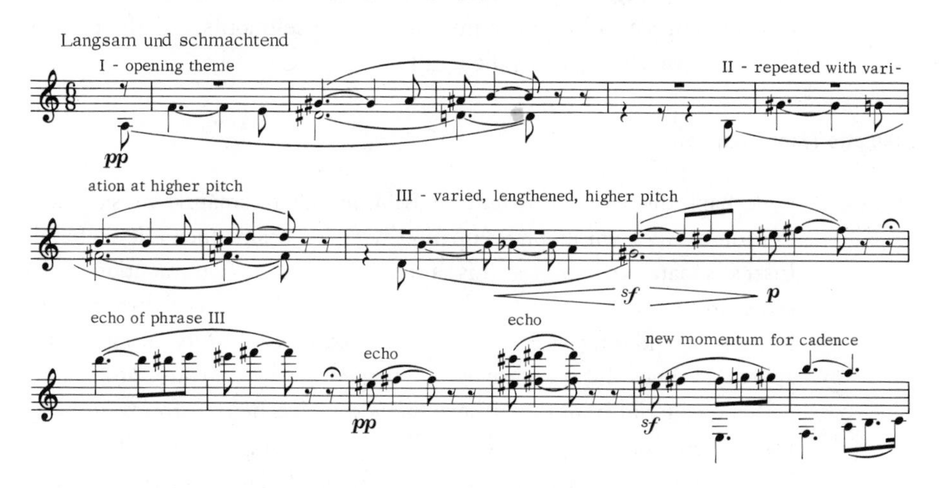

The first phrase announces two important motives. The second phrase takes up the same motives at a higher pitch, the third phrase still higher and noticeably altered. Most of Wagner's melodic structure takes the form of statements and varied counterstatements of a salient motive, announced two, three, four, five, or even more times. Moreover, motives recur frequently. Such recurrences help us get our bearings within this vast sea of movement that seems to have no shore. Thus, at the climax of the entire Prelude, we hear the opening motive thrust forward by the horns, closing the circle, as it were, but with a much more powerful emotional impact than at the beginning.

Wagner did not invent the notion of a motive, figure, or passage which could be assigned to a character or situation. We saw how Mozart gave the Commandant in *Don Giovanni* a special dramatic value through "ombra" figures. Berlioz, in his *Symphonie fantastique,* refers again and again to the theme which represents the hero's beloved. It follows the hero everywhere, in his dreams, in his retreat to the country, up the steps of the scaffold, and in the nightmare of the Witches' Sabbath. Thus, it is called the *idée fixe.*

EXAMPLE 7·22 Berlioz: *Symphonie fantastique, idée fixe*

Verdi frequently quotes significant material to highlight a dramatic situation or to recall a previous one. In *Aida,* the motives associated with Aida (a slow, lyric, chromatic figure) and Amneris (a rapid, agitated, menacing figure) are recalled at critical points in the drama. These figures are called *remembrance* motives; they are used only occasionally, in contrast to Wagner's intensive use of leitmotifs. All three types bind the form through melodic recall.

Thematic Transformation

Perhaps the most important contribution that romantic music made to form grows from its preoccupation with important thematic material. Liszt's sonata exemplifies this approach. Earlier, we mentioned its styles and manners, its many different moods which succeed each other in such bewildering variety that the thread of continuity seems to disappear at times. Liszt endeavors to compensate by drawing most of his melodic material from four salient themes, which he transforms in many ways throughout the piece. These themes are changed drastically to conform to the various manners we have described above, yet at no time is it difficult to recognize them. The process of *thematic transformation* at the same time heightens interest and creates points of structural reference that help to hold the piece together for the listener. Here are some examples of Liszt's procedures:

EXAMPLE 7·23 Liszt: Sonata in B minor. Thematic transformations

a. Theme I—brooding, introspective: descending scale

Transformation—brilliant passage-work

b. Theme II—bold, impassioned, e'ectrifying: angular contour

Transformation—lyric, fanciful

c. Theme III—active, percussive: repeated tones

Transformation—songlike

To give the entire work some definite contour, Liszt has taken elements from the sonata form. He sets the bold theme against the lyric theme, with the usual contrast of key areas. In the center of the work, he builds a broad area of development, and the sonata winds up with a recapitulation of the two principal themes. This we can recognize as the outline of a sonata form, but, from phrase to phrase and section to section, we frequently lose that sense of purposeful arrival and clearly directed movement which gave rise to the classic sonata form. As we said before, the episodes are so different from each other, and frequently so loosely connected, that they would need little to make them independent pieces.

Liszt turns this particular fact to advantage; the contrast in style between the first and second sections is so great that they take on the roles of an opening and a slow movement respectively. The development is still another movement, a grand fantasy, while the recapitulation acts as a broad epilogue. Liszt took the cue from Beethoven in this respect; a number of the later works of Beethoven display multisectional form. A very familiar orchestral version of this multisectional form, with serious, lyric, stormy, and grandiose episodes, based on the transformation of two important themes, is Liszt's symphonic poem *Les Préludes.* The introspective, metaphysical idea of the title, that life is but a series of preludes, again demonstrates romanticism's preoccupation with destiny and the meaning of life. Liszt wrote the following about the piece, drawing his ideas from Lamartine's *Méditations poétiques:*

What is our life but a series of Preludes to that unknown song, the first solemn note of which is sounded by Death? The enchanted dawn of every existence is heralded by Love, yet in whose Destiny are not the first throbs of happiness interrupted by storms whose violent blasts dissipate his fond illusions, consuming his altar with fatal fire? And where is to be found the cruelly bruised soul, that having become the sport of one of these tempests does not seek oblivion in the sweet quiet of rural life? Nevertheless, man seldom resigns himself to the beneficent calm which at first chained him to Nature's bosom. No sooner does the trumpet sound the alarm, than he runs to the post of danger, be the war what it may that summons him to its ranks. For there he will find again in the struggle complete self-realization and the full possession of his forces.

The multisectional form, held together by thematic relationships, is probably the most characteristic of large-scale romantic formal types. It certainly accommodates itself to romantic modes of expression; indeed, it came into being through the necessities of structure created by these modes of expression. The binding action of important themes, which can establish a long-range statement and counterstatement relationship within a musical form, has been used by many composers since the end of the eighteenth century. Wagner developed a motive intensively, as a rule, whenever he introduced it or reintroduced it. He might vary it somewhat in harmony or rhythm, but he rarely changed its basic character or mood. Liszt and Strauss often made drastic changes in the style of a given theme or motive, so that the theme was truly transformed. (See Strauss's *Till Eulenspiegel* for an example of thematic transformation.)

Greater concern with thematic values as the central point in musical composition went along with the subordination of harmony as a form-building factor. Finally, in some styles this led to the complete elimination of harmonic elements as a means of organization. The final step, when all musical material is drawn from a basic and generating melodic pattern, comes with *tone-row* music and will be a subject for our next chapter.

To conclude this survey of romantic structure we return once again to the Prelude to *Tristan*. This time we shall see that there is a carefully planned structure for the constant flow of the music. Also, we shall look a bit more closely at the way in which Wagner builds his motivic continuity.

If we locate the dynamic curves and the stronger cadential gestures in the piece, the pattern is as follows:

EXAMPLE 7·24 Structural outline of the Prelude to *Tristan*

Peaks of the dynamic curve	17,	24,	44,	62,	74,	83	
Cadences	17,	24,	44,		74,		94
Key	A	A	C♯		A		A

Except at measure 24, where there is an authentic cadence, each of the cadences is deceptive; that is, the dominant harmony resolves, not to the tonic, but to VI, a chord which can represent the tonic, yet which does not complete the rhetorical sense of the harmony. The cadential plan, as you can see, begins in the area of A, reinforces it at measure 24, moves over to C♯ at measure 44, and returns to A at measure 74; A is again reinforced at measure 94. In respect to both key arrangement and proportion of length this plan has some resemblance to the key area plan of the classic sonata form.

Charting the motive layout also reveals a consistent and controlled plan. It is possible to make out eight or nine distinct figures. The first two are presented and developed in the opening section, to measure 17 (see Example 7·21). Another group occupies the large central section of the piece to measure 79, joined at measure 66 by the opening motive to reinforce the climax. From that point, figures from both groups are intermingled. Motivically, the entire Prelude is built as a chain of interlocking figures, organized in the free sequential structure illustrated in Example 7·21. The motives themselves show a consistency of formation and often a close similarity.

EXAMPLE 7·25 Consistency and similarity of motives from Wagner's Prelude to *Tristan*

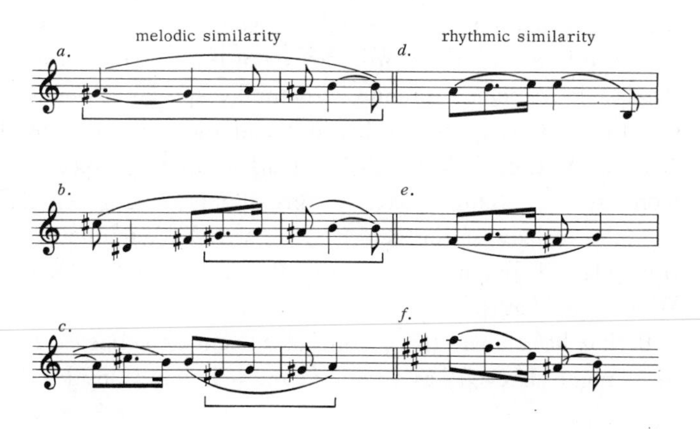

Because of the trailing effect and lack of strong punctuation that characterize the motive endings, Wagner is able to run motives together very smoothly, to mingle and vary them, and to achieve the so-called "endless melody" which is such a striking feature of his style. Note the similarities between motives *a, b,* and *c,* as well as between *d, e,* and *f.* See also measures 17–36 in the score. The distances between the successive climaxes grow shorter as the piece progresses; this contributes to the unbroken upward surge of intensity.

Putting together the comments on this piece, we can summarize as follows:

1. The first premise is the quality of sound–rich, unstable harmony; colorful, rather dense scoring.
2. Motion carries forward without sharp punctuation, in waves of increasing intensity; cadences articulate these waves but do not arrest motion.
3. The motives are fashioned to contribute to the forward movement–with upbeats, trailing afterbeats, and a general family resemblance that permits free manipulation without strong interruption or contrast.
4. Harmonically and motivically we can make out a three-part arrangement; the harmony departs from A and returns, while motives are treated in two groups: AB; B + A.

The precise technique which Wagner evolved in his music is epitomized in this piece; only by using this technique was he able to maintain and augment a compelling, even hypnotic effect over great periods of time. Like Beethoven, Wagner commands his own broadened time scale in this work.

As a final word on the subject of form in romantic music, one particularly brilliant and distinctive solution to the problem of structure should be mentioned. We have heard Berlioz's *Symphonie fantastique* in connection with a number of topics discussed in this chapter. The first four movements each conform to a standard structural type. The first is in *sonata form;* the second is a *waltz with trio;* the third is again in *sonata form;* and the fourth movement is a *march,* also *with trio.* But the last movement is unique, structurally speaking. For a clue to its structure, let us glance at Berlioz's scenario, appended to the score: ". . . a Witches' Sabbath . . . a fearful crowd of spectres, sorcerers, monsters . . . strange noises, groans, shouts of laughter, distant cries . . . the melody of the beloved . . . trivial, grotesque . . . the *Dies Irae* [Day of Judgment] . . . the *Ronde du Sabbat* [Rounds of the Witches' Sabbath].

Berlioz has framed this picture of ancient and timeless evil exulting in its night of revelry as a *fantasia* and a *fugue!* Consider the fantasia-like procedure of the first half of the movement, the short, weird episodes, often interrupted by violent contrasts. The effect is one of a monstrous improvisation. The devilish company is gathering. When all have arrived, the dancing begins; the dance is a fugue. Here Berlioz regards the fugal procedure, the imitations, as a means of building an excitement he might not have created with homophonic means. In this movement an archaic form, the fantasia and fugue, turns out to be the ideal vehicle for the scenario of the piece and the type of expression contained therein. Berlioz's forms generally are worked out with keen insight and a sense for the justness of the relation of structure and expressive content.

Form in romantic music may be summarized as follows:

I. Dynamic curve: large expressive contour
II. Weakening of cadences: idea of "open" structure
III. Short piece
  A. For piano, or voice and piano
  B. Generally one expressive value
  C. Preference for two-reprise or other period forms
  D. Larger works built up by grouping relatively independent short sections
  E. Strophic (repeated) and through-composed structure of songs
IV. Extended piece
  A. Sonata form
    1. Emphasis on thematic material
      a. "Masculine" first theme
      b. "Feminine" second theme
    2. Marked separation of sections as against classic integration of sections
  B. Thematic role in romantic form
    1. Leitmotif, idée fixe: musical signal
    2. Remembrance motive: recall of previous situation
    3. Thematic transformation: change in character of theme while retaining its original shape
  C. Symphonic poem (tone poem), based in many instances upon thematic transformation; multisectional form

In the preceding survey of romantic style, expression, and form, most of the material was drawn from three genres: orchestral music, keyboard music, and song literature. To complete our study of this period we shall look into two other media that were prominent in nineteenth-century music: opera and choral music.

Opera

Of all musical forms, opera lends itself best to the expression of the emotional and pictorial values especially cherished by romantic composers. These values—terror, tragedy, triumph, transfiguration, ecstasy, magnificent scenes of pageant, the mysterious solemnity of the cloister, the weirdness of the supernatural, and many others—hinted at or suggested in instrumental music, could be projected with tremendous impact by the combination of plot, scene, and music.

Opera, like instrumental music, was not one, but many things in the nineteenth century. We know romantic opera best in two different types: the opera of Wagner and the opera of Verdi. In order to point up the special expressive qualities of each composer, we shall consider them in comparison and contrast, using excerpts from Wagner's *Tristan* and Verdi's *Aida* as models.

As we listen to an excerpt or section from either work, it is not difficult to recognize which opera we are hearing. In general, the qualities of sound which each composer preferred are sharply different. Verdi's sound, as a rule, is thinner, more transparent, less richly mixed, higher in its center, and lighter than Wagner's. We hear the voice as the principal carrier of musical interest in Verdi, no matter what is going on. In Wagner, the voice is often but a single part in a complex web of intertwining lines; often the greater musical responsibility seems to be carried by the orchestra. Verdi's voices sing songlike material that is idiomatically suited for them. Wagner's melodic lines contain difficult intervals and imbalanced rhythmic patterns (see Example 7·5). Verdi's harmony is less unstable and searching than Wagner's; he stays in one key longer, makes cadences frequently, and is a master at creating striking contrasts of harmonic color.

Movement in each of these works tells us much about the expressive values. Verdi almost always manages to create a strong sense of pulse or beat. His movement has a physical energy and strength. Each impulse creates fresh momentum. Together with his lightness of texture, Verdi's active beat creates a buoyant sense of movement. The bass instruments often punctuate the flow, establishing points of rhythmic arrival. They do not fill in the lower ranges of the harmony to create the typical thickness of Wagner's sound and the heaviness of his movement.

Verdi's emphatic quality of movement, linked to a feeling for action, tends to coalesce into well-marked phrases and periods. Thus movement reaches arrival points with strong cadential effect. Wagner's phases of movement, characterized by a much less accented pulse, lack the clean-cut points of arrival we hear in Verdi. The phrases often trail off; elsewhere, the expectation for arrival is thwarted by deceptive cadences. Because of his well-defined phrase structure, Verdi can project contrast with maximum effectiveness and thus give fresh momentum to his music at critical points. Wagner does not deal with the element of contrast in so sharp or clear a manner. As we have seen, his music tends to accumulate intensity and strength by the expansion of one particular idea over a long period of time.

These qualities of sound, movement, and arrival arise from essentially different expressive aims in Verdi and Wagner. Verdi was concerned with the bold projection and the sharp contrast of specific emotions and the striking impact of dramatic incident. Wagner constantly tried to overwhelm the listener with the power, extent, and mass of a general emotional drive. Verdi's dramatic values are electric; Wagner's are hypnotic. The sense of time becomes more urgent in Verdi; in Wagner, we lose the sense of ordinary time passing.

The emotional content of *Aida* deals with love, patriotism, jealousy, power, and revenge—emotions that strike us with a strong sense of reality. We have felt them ourselves. The emotional content of *Tristan* deals with an obscure hate that is magically turned into love by a mysterious potion. This love reaches a state of blind ecstasy and comes to fulfillment in death. These are emotional experiences far beyond the realm of ordinary human joy and suffering. Verdi's plot is a complex set of interwoven motives and events, all pointing to the final tragedy. Wagner's plot is relatively much simpler and has fewer events. Therefore, Verdi's music is dedicated much of the time to developing *action;* Wagner's music, on the other hand, is devoted principally to developing emotional *moods.*

By way of illustration, we shall look at an excerpt from each opera. From *Aida,* we take Aida's soliloquy and prayer from Act I, beginning with the words *Ritorna vincitor* (Return victorious). From *Tristan,* we shall examine Isolde's recital of the curing of Tristan's wound. This is also from Act I and begins with the words *Wie lenkt' er sicher den Kiel* (How surely he guides the boat); it extends to the outcry *Tod uns Beiden* (Death for us both).

The two scenes have a certain parallelism. Each comes early in the opera. Each sets up an intense conflict of emotion that bears upon the plot. At the end both Aida and Isolde invoke a power that is beyond human understanding as the only answer to their inner conflicts. These similarities, however, serve only to make the essential contrasts more vivid.

First, there is a fundamental emotional difference between the two scenes. Aida's motives are clear; her feeling for Rhadames and her love for her father and her country, although they conflict, are both strong and genuine. Isolde's motives are shadowy and mixed; she, like Aida, is a captive; she hates her captor, not for his triumph, but for his unworthy role in acting for another in the question of love. Somehow, we sense that Isolde is already in love with Tristan. Her scene is charged with subtle psychological complexities and symbolisms. For Isolde the only answer is death; for Aida the answer must come from the gods, from whom she asks pity.

Each scene embodies its particular expressive qualities in form and movement. Wagner builds with ebb and flow, expanding the range of movement and intensifying the emotional effect until the tremendous outburst is reached at the very end and Isolde collapses. Regardless of the quickening or slowing of pace, there is a constant flow of movement, maintained by Wagner's typical unstable harmony, his shifting, imbalanced rhythms, the active development of motives, and the constant crescendos and decrescendos. The dynamic curve, which dominated the form of the Prelude, is here used to carry Isolde's emotional outburst to the point of frenzy. Whatever gestures or motives may be used are swept up by the current. Example 7·26 gives an approximate outline of this scene:

EXAMPLE 7·26 Diagram of Isolde's scene

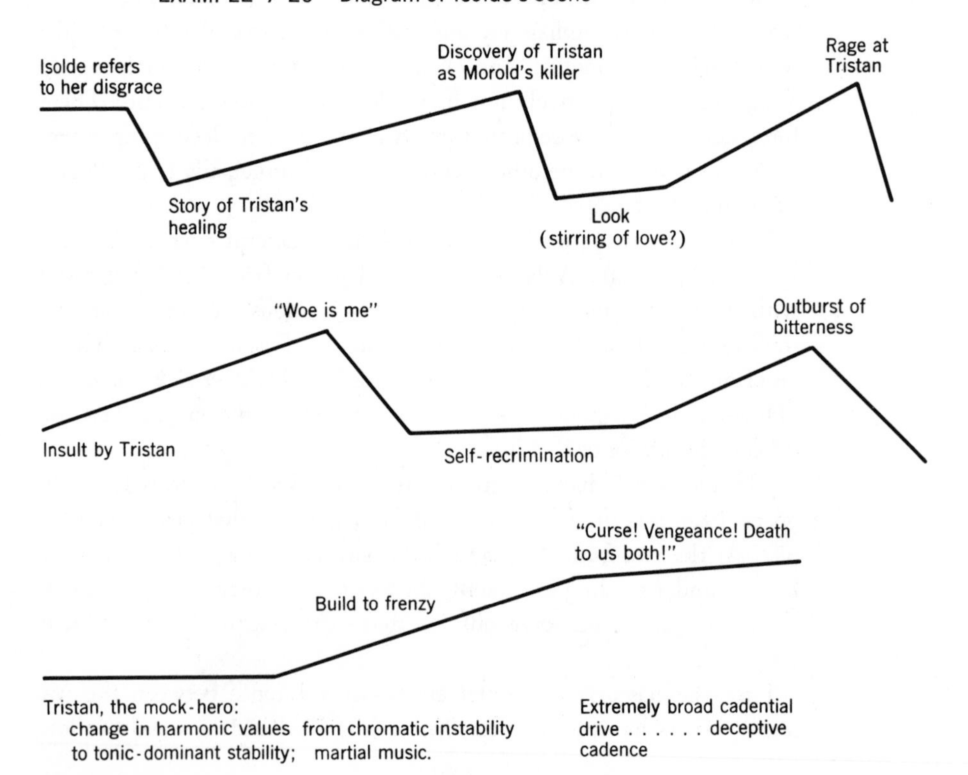

In contrast to the continuous flow of Isolde's scene, Aida's music shows sharp changes in pace and in intensity of movement. Moods change kaleidoscopically as Aida considers first one, then another of her conflicting desires and emotions. At the very beginning of the scene, the music underscores the emotional pull from two sides. Aida repeats the phrase she has just been singing with the chorus, *Ritorna vincitor.* Listen to the orchestra's chord on her last syllable: the upper instruments play a brilliant major chord, suggesting victory, while the bass adds an unstable tone which undermines the position of the harmony and suggests Aida's misgivings. The following example illustrates this penetrating bit of musicodramatic insight:

EXAMPLE 7·27 Verdi: *Aida*

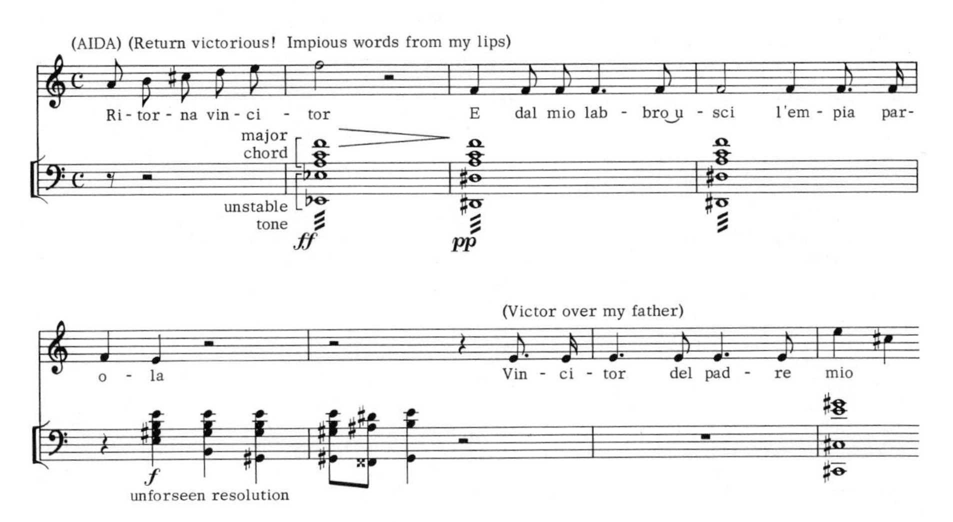

In the first recitative, the harmonic shifts are addressed to Aida's grave problem. Her feeling of loyalty rises to supplant, for the moment, her love for Rhadames. After this recitative, Aida decides, momentarily, to remain with her father. This decision is set in a short but perfectly balanced two-reprise form that moves in a swift and agitated manner. Here the regular form and the crystallization of feeling complement each other. At the end of this song, indecision returns and the moment of uncertainty is emphasized by a deceptive cadence. Again a recitative, rather songlike, in which Aida reflects on her love for Rhadames, follows; this is succeeded by a second aria, in which the decision is to place love above duty.

This second aria is set in a remote minor key, to suggest the impending tragedy that the decision will call forth. Finally, Aida, despairing to find the answer within herself, turns to the gods in prayer. Verdi has set this final section again as a song, with rounded and balanced phrases. The texture in this section, high, remote, shimmering, transparent, and vibrant, captures the spirit of mysterious invocation and stands in contrast to all four preceding sections, each of which had its own characteristic texture. The last section, in its gentleness of movement and steady continuity of sound, acts musically as an area of arrival for the entire scene; thus, it corresponds with the sense of dramatic resolution in the prayer. Verdi, as in his other music, plays contrasts effectively and theatrically against each other with an eye to the final reconciliation.

EXAMPLE 7·28 Diagram of Aida's scene

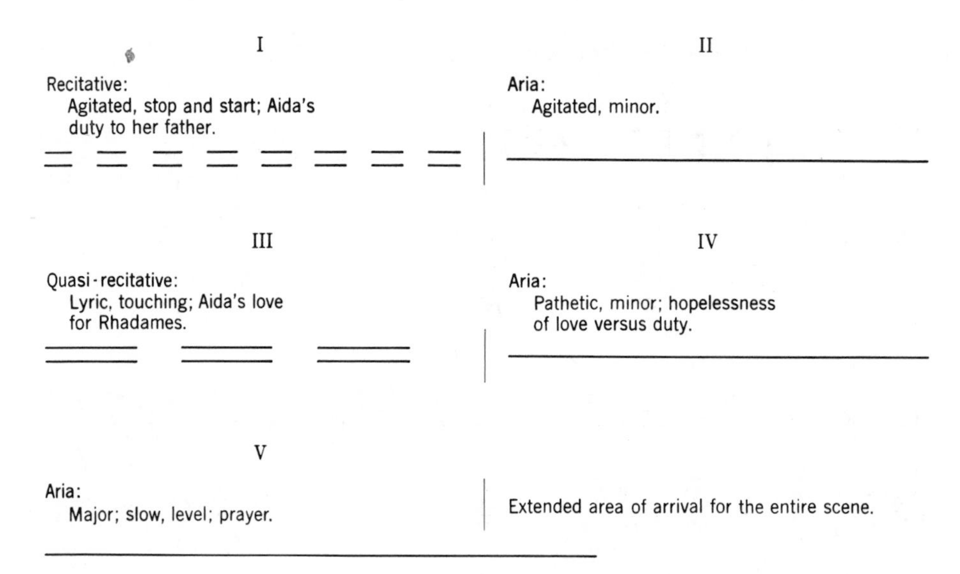

These two scenes show Verdi and Wagner in their typical mature style. Of the two, Wagner represents romanticism much more intensely than Verdi. The continuously expanding flow of Wagner's music is much more in the spirit of the romantic age than Verdi's well-defined articulations of movement. Verdi becomes romantic in his use of lyricism, in certain uses of chromaticism and harmonic instability, and in his exploration of color values, as in Aida's final song. Wagner shows a debt to classicism in his development of motives, harking back to Beethoven. Wagner's music drama, however, is entirely a creation of the nineteenth century. Verdi's opera is the nineteenth-century version of Italian opera, a genre with a long history and established traditions.

After Wagner and Verdi, the styles they represent continue to live in somewhat altered guise. Richard Strauss used many of the techniques of Wagner, his orchestration, his rich harmony, and the leitmotif, but departed from the grand metaphysical area of expression. Rather,

Strauss's operas tend to deal with personal issues, often with morbid psychological connotations, as in *Salome* and *Elektra.*

Giacomo Puccini is the chief heir of the Verdi tradition; also, he is the principal representative of the manner called *verismo,* which sought its subject matter in the realism of nineteenth-century city life. In this respect, Puccini is the counterpart of Zola, De Maupassant, and Flaubert in literature, and of Daumier in art. *La Bohème* of Puccini is one of the best-known operas in the entire repertory. It must be said, however, that Puccini does not use a *realistic* musical technique; rather, his music offers a very sweet, colorful, and ingratiating manner, sentimental instead of brutal.

Opera in the nineteenth century was written in styles other than those of Verdi and Wagner. In the 1820s and 1830s the most spectacular form was French grand opera; this was an elaborate type of production involving vast resources of chorus, ballet, and scenery, as well as the usual apparatus of orchestra and soloists. Grand opera centered upon subjects of historical interest and was directed principally toward the politically élite society of Paris under the rule of Louis Philippe, the "citizen king." Grand opera, whose chief exponent was Giacomo Meyerbeer, adopted in part the Italian musical style of composition, the ingratiating, nicely shaped style of Gioacchino Rossini. But the appeal of such works as Meyerbeer's *The Prophet* and *The Huguenots,* and Jacques Halévy's *The Jewess* was in their extremely effective combination of spectacle, popular plot, and assimilable music. Verdi, much later in the century, was to employ the spectacle of grand opera in his *Aida.*

Comic opera also had a vigorous life in the nineteenth century. Many of the tunes from this genre are familiar to us today, such as the Barcarolle from Jacques Offenbach's *Tales of Hoffmann,* Figaro's *Largo al factotum* and Rosina's *Una voce poco fa* from Rossini's *Barber of Seville,* and the waltzes from Johann Strauss's *Gypsy Baron* and *Die Fledermaus,* as well as a whole bouquet of tunes from Gilbert and Sullivan's *The Mikado, The Pirates of Penzance,* and other amusing and familiar favorites.

One important opera of the nineteenth century, Moussorgsky's *Boris Godunov,* was written in a manner entirely different from Italian, French, or German opera. Moussorgsky's work epitomizes the new Eastern European nationalism that developed in the later nineteenth century. In line with this tendency, Moussorgsky gave a central dramatic position to the chorus, which represents the Russian people. He turned his back on the sophisticated musical language of Western Europe, the language of Wagner or Verdi; instead he used the idioms, sounds, rhythms, and expressive qualities that would suggest the native culture of Russia. Here are two examples which illustrate two important aspects of Moussorgsky's style: (1) his sense for color and immediate impression, as represented in the bell sounds of the coronation scene; (2) his preference for simple, straightforward, down-to-earth music, as represented in an excerpt from Varlaam's song from Act I.

EXAMPLE 7·29 Moussorgsky: *Boris Godunov*

a. Coronation scene

b. Varlaam's song, Act I

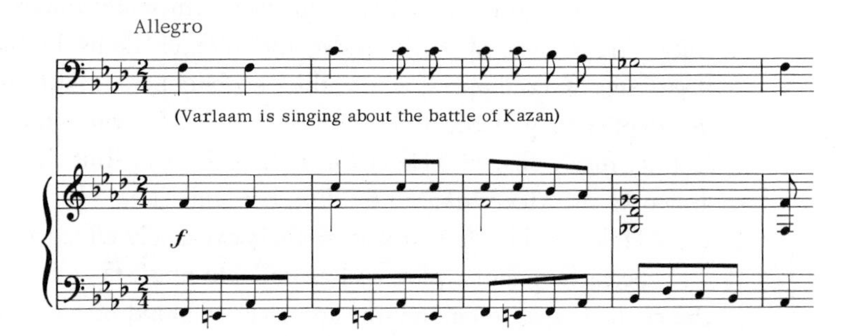

Moussorgsky disliked the academic development procedures of Western symphonic and operatic composition. Instead he preferred to create fresh effects, to spin out his material in a somewhat improvisatory manner, ringing the changes upon a few very simple motives. Tone color and rhythmic drive are central points in his style. Thus, Moussorgsky has influenced both the impressionists and the folkloric composers of the early twentieth century.

Other characteristic examples of nineteenth-century opera follow:

Verdi: *Rigoletto,* Act I to the end of the court scene. *Rigoletto* has some interesting points of comparison with Mozart's *Don Giovanni.* In both we have a licentious nobleman, a seduced daughter, an avenging father, and a fool. In *Don Giovanni* the father and the fool are separate characters, representing two extremes. In *Rigoletto* they are combined to create one of the most complex characters in all opera. At the end of *Don Giovanni,* the Commandant, as the agent of an authority higher than man, punishes Don Giovanni by dragging him to Hell and thus, in the eighteenth-century view, puts matters to rights. This arrival or cadential effect is reinforced by the final buffalike ensemble. No such balance exists in *Rigoletto.* The avenging father becomes the butt of a grisly joke when he discovers that his attempt to murder the Duke has misfired and that it is his daughter who has become the victim. The opera ends in this mood; there is no resolution, only a fantastic shock that carries far beyond the fall of the curtain. This is a typical romantic treatment of structure—an unanswered question. Evil, not good, triumphs, and Rigoletto, who tried to rise beyond his level, is forced even further down by clever and competent viciousness.

The comparison between the two operas is quite striking in the opening scene. The orchestral introduction has the same ominous tone in each; then the brilliant galanterie which follows in both works presents a similar contrast in the plot motives of the two operas, that is, the gay life as set against the motives of betrayal and revenge. The opening scene of *Rigoletto* is filled with bright tunes —the opening march, the Duke's *Questa o quella* (This woman or that) cast in a popular Italian song style, the minuet, the perigourdine (a French giguelike dance). Against this background, brilliantly scored, the melodramatic elements of the plot are superimposed and interspersed. The scene builds up to a tremendous climax with a curse and a premonition of horror. The final measures illustrate the kind of immense crescendo (an amplification of the eighteenth-century operatic and orchestral crescendo) with which so many scenes in Italian opera reach their climax and final arrival; the entire scene shows nineteenth-century grand opera at its best, a mélange of spectacle, melodrama, tunefulness—all moving in a powerful theatrical sweep.

Donizetti: *Lucia di Lammermoor,* the Mad Scene, Act III. This is one of the most famous scenes in Italian opera, a great tour de force for coloratura soprano. Lucy's madness comes on as a result of her murder of Arthur, the man she was tricked into marrying, her true love being Edgar of Ravenswood. The scene is shaped broadly into four sections, the first and third being cast as recitative and arioso, the second and fourth as formal arias. Lucy's derangement is pictured by means of visions, terror, and recollection in shifting moods. Throughout, the extravagant quality is delineated by elaborate coloratura ornamentations of familiar, slowly moving cadential harmonies and sharply etched, ingratiating melodic material. This scene represents early romantic expansion of classic Italian opera procedures.

Bizet: *Carmen,* Act I through the Habanera. In both its subject matter and its musical idioms, *Carmen* represents a more popular, realistic style than was usual in nineteenth-century opera. Bizet makes much use of local color; the music has a strong Spanish flavor, as in the Habanera (whose tune was not composed by Bizet himself, but by Yradier), the Seguidilla, and the gypsy music. In the opening scene we have a montage of colors, types, and characters; musically, this could be the counterpart of an early impressionistic painting with its brightness and prismatic effects that place separate elements into complementary juxtaposition. The Prelude itself is a set of episodes—toreador march, toreador song, once again the march, and then the music of fate. The opening scene is a colorful square in Seville; there is much movement as characters come and go. Soldiers, children, citizens, cigarette girls, Micaela, Morales, Don José, Zuniga, and finally Carmen—each moves into focus and out again. The music has a decided flavor of the dance, set off by the fanfares and marches of the soldiers. Bizet here sets a mood; relatively little takes place to carry the plot forward. For this we must wait until the end of the scene, when Carmen is arrested by Don José, who in turn finds himself captivated by his prisoner.

Romantic opera may be summarized as follows:

1. German
   a. Nationalistic, much local color (Weber)
   b. Use of leitmotif, Sprechgesang; avoidance of set numbers; use of rich harmony, heavy scoring; development of introspective and subjective moods (Wagner)
2. Italian
   a. Continuation of eighteenth-century traditions
   b. Set numbers, emphasis on broad melodic appeal, lighter scoring than in German, development of plot and character conflict
3. Realism and local color in important Russian and French operas of the late nineteenth century
4. Grand opera: spectacle, massive effects, popular appeal
5. Comic and light opera: carry-over of buffa tradition and procedure

Choral Music

Choral music in the nineteenth century mirrors many of the stylistic elements that characterize the romantic period in general. Grandeur and intimacy are both to be found, the former in such works as Mahler's

Symphonies Nos. 2 and 8 and the Requiem of Berlioz, and the latter in many brief part songs by Schumann, Brahms, and others. Another aspect comes into the picture—revival of the musical past (Mendelssohn's rediscovery of Bach, for example). Moreover, during the nineteenth century the discipline of musicology, that is, historical studies in music, began to take on considerable importance; this was part of the general interest in history and the past that characterizes the nineteenth century. One of the first areas of interest for music historians was the Renaissance. Much vocal music was transcribed and made available in modern editions, which in turn influenced romantic composers to emulate the style of Palestrina. One of the examples to be discussed below represents this antiquarian trend (Bruckner: Mass in E minor).

Another typically romantic trend is the addition of voices to the orchestra to achieve a more telling and powerful effect upon the listener. This combination of voices and orchestra, once used for concertato procedure, now becomes a means for expansion of musical expression. Beethoven, in his Symphony No. 9, established the precedent, which was carried on notably by Mahler, as well as Berlioz and Liszt.

Three examples of choral music in the nineteenth-century repertory have been selected to illustrate the antiquarian style, the grandiose style, and the sentimental, intimate part song:

Bruckner: Mass in E minor, Kyrie. The close similarity of the style of this piece to that of Palestrina is immediately sensed. The quasi-imitative entries, the slow, even tempo, the long notes, the conjunct part writing, and the closely spaced, full harmony—all these indicate a conscious effort to capture the spirit of Renaissance music of worship. The principal difference, of course, is in the far richer harmonic palette. We hear many seventh and some ninth chords; dissonance is treated more freely, and the piece is clear in its commitment to *key*, with strong cadences heard often. There is a remarkably close affinity between nineteenth-century chordal texture and its counterpart of the sixteenth century. Both are concerned with sound as a basis for expression; both maintain motion through a continuation of rich sound color.

Berlioz: Requiem: *Dies irae*. This section of the Requiem, the Mass for the Dead, comprises two sections: the *Dies irae* (Day of Judgment) itself and the *Tuba mirum* (Behold, the Trumpet Sounds). In the *Dies irae*, Berlioz recaptures the spirit of the original, the old medieval rhymed sequence, which foretells the Last Judgment. The style recalls that of plainsong and organum; we hear first the principal figure in unison, later elaborated with counterpoint. The archaic effect is enhanced by some elements of modal harmony.

Carrying out the antiquarian idea, Berlioz sets this section somewhat as medieval sequences were written, i.e., strophically, although each stanza is pitched higher to create a dynamic curve and to build to the climax that introduces the *Tuba mirum.* (Compare this treatment of the *Dies irae* with Berlioz's caricature of the traditional tune in the finale of his *Symphonie fantastique.*)

The *Tuba mirum* is a spectacular pictorialization of the trumpets of the Last Judgment. Berlioz's instructions call for four small bands of brass instruments to be placed at the four corners of the theater. They call back and forth to each other with fanfares, sometimes mingling with the full orchestra and chorus. The style is set by these fanfares; the voices themselves declaim in bold and impressive phrases. Structurally, we can hear a two-section form, much like the two-reprise form of earlier times, with a grand cadence to the dominant in the middle, balanced by a dramatically quiet cadence to the tonic at the end. This is genuine concertato music; Berlioz seeks space here, rather than overwhelming mass. The echoes and reverberations recall the early baroque (Gabrieli's *In ecclesiis,* for example). To make its full impact, this piece must be heard in concert, so that we can experience the magnificent expansion of sustained and reinforced major harmonies.

Brahms: *Liebeslieder Waltzes,* Op. 52. This is a set of eighteen short waltzes, set for two pianos and quartet of four mixed voices (soprano, alto, tenor, and bass). The waltzes are often performed without voices, inasmuch as the pianos contain all the essential musical material; the voices take up the principal melodies and accessory parts. Their main function is to add the personal quality, the singing manner to these very ingratiating miniatures. This is an excellent example of what is called *Gesellschaftsmusik,* music for companionship, full of the quality *Gemütlichkeit,* which may be translated as warm sentimentality. Part songs of a simple popular nature had long been a German tradition; in the nineteenth century the tradition experienced a great upsurge. In these works Brahms's skill in composition is discovered in many deft touches, richness of harmonic color, imaginative figuration, and superb melodies. Further, these works exemplify a characteristic aspect of nineteenth century music, the love of the waltz. We know the waltzes of Johann Strauss, Jr., but perhaps it is not as well known that many composers of the nineteenth century turned to the waltz at some time. Weber, Schubert, Chopin, Liszt, Berlioz, Mahler, Richard Strauss, and many others wrote music that typified the expansive, whirling motion of this dance that so strongly represents the centrifugal spirit of the romantic age.

Nineteenth-century choral music may be summarized as follows:

1. Grandiose manner
2. Expansion of scoring techniques; voices added to orchestra
3. Antiquarian and historical interest (Renaissance style, Bach)
4. Intimate, popular style

We have presented the romantic era in music as being motivated toward expansion; it reaches outward in many directions, propelled, it would seem, by a centrifugal impulse. Considering the enormous variety of styles, forms, and procedures wherein each composer seems to strike out for himself in an unexplored direction, it follows that romanticism is a time of individualism, not a time of common practice. Growing in different directions, two composers, each truly romantic in spirit, can be utterly opposed to each other in specific features of style and aesthetics; Mendelssohn and Wagner may be cited as examples of this aspect of romanticism.

All the special characteristics of romantic music, those which set it apart from its predecessors, are gradually exploited more and more as the nineteenth century moves to its close. The process of separation, by which elements found in classic music were taken out of context and highlighted, continues, so that by the beginning of the twentieth century a number of special techniques and styles were developed. There are refinements of certain qualities of romanticism, appearing under such names as *expressionism, impressionism, folkloric music,* and *neoromanticism,* which we shall examine in our next chaper.

As a final word on romanticism, we might speculate that it represents a phase of development in the growth of musical self-consciousness. Rationalism and authority might embody a sort of *supra*-consciousness, reflected by the concern with large-scale problems that found their solution in a classic balance. Romanticism represents nineteenth-century *self*-consciousness, the individual regarding himself as the principal focus of interest and importance. We might carry the analogy further and point to the concern with the *sub*-conscious which marks so much of twentieth-century art, philosophy, and psychology. Here, indeed, is the process of separation at work over centuries of thought and expression. Rejecting the answers of the eighteenth century, self-contained but incomplete, the romantic artist sought solutions in his own imagination, feeling, and mystic ethic. His inability or his unwillingness to reach a convincing resolution eventually engendered disillusionment and a strong counterwave to the expressive ideas so cherished in the nineteenth century. We are still living in an age in which romanticism is somewhat suspect; but we are learning to accept romantic expression, not for what it claims to do, but for what it *is*, a fascinating, distinctive, colorful tour of the human spirit.

The criteria for listening to romantic music may be adapted from those given in Chapters 5 and 6. Special attention should be given to (1) treatment of melody, in reference both to melodic style and to the organizing power of melody; (2) form, in reference to traditional (classic) or newly evolved (symphonic poem, dynamic curve) forms; (3) texture and orchestration.

Romantic musical style may be summarized as follows:

1. ***Sound:*** New and striking instrumental sonorities (Berlioz); exploitation of piano sonorities (Chopin, Schumann, Liszt); continuous play upon a special sonority (Schubert, Chopin, Mendelssohn); richness and fullness of sound (Brahms, Wagner)
2. ***Movement:*** Gentle, steady movement (Schubert, Mendelssohn); impulsive, explosive movement (Schumann, Liszt, Berlioz); continuously intensifying movement (Wagner); rhythmic imbalances (Brahms, Tchaikovsky, Dvorak, Liszt)
3. ***Arrival:*** Obscured cadences (Wagner); weakened or rhythmically shifted cadences (Schubert, Schumann); plagal cadences (Wagner, Brahms)
4. ***Movement and arrival:*** Retention of periodic symmetry (Schubert, Chopin, Mendelssohn); overlapping and telescoping of phrases and periods (Wagner); irregular phrase structure (Berlioz, Liszt); powerful movement toward arrival (Brahms)
5. ***Melody:*** Broadly singing style (Brahms, Schubert, Mendelssohn, Verdi, Donizetti); "angular" style, declamatory vocal writing (Wagner, Liszt, Strauss); leitmotif, *idée fixe,* thematic transformation (Wagner, Berlioz, Liszt, Strauss); reliance upon melody as organizing element
6. ***Rhythm:*** Steady, continuous, easy movement (Schubert, Mendelssohn); rhythmic imbalances (Wagner, Liszt, Berlioz, Brahms); less interaction between rhythmic instability and stability than in classic style
7. ***Harmony:*** Unstable, tritone-saturated harmonies (Wagner); exploitation of chord color and figuration (Schubert, Chopin, Schumann); deceptive cadences, half cadences in place of authentic cadences (Wagner); rapid modulations or shifts of tonal center (general trend)
8. ***Texture*** (see Sound): Greater emphasis on solo, virtuoso, and highly skilled ensemble performance due to greater difficulty of music
9. ***Forms:*** Short characteristic pieces (Schumann, Schubert, Chopin, Mendelssohn); standard classic forms (Weber, Schumann, Schubert, Mendelssohn, Brahms, Tchaikovsky, Verdi); forms based on leading motives: symphonic poem in a single movement (Liszt); leading-motive technique (Wagner)
10. ***Expressive aims and subjects:*** Intense, immediate emotional impact (many composers); interest in the faraway, the long-ago, nature, the homeland (Moussorgsky, Weber); pictorialism (Mendelssohn)

Genres and Compositions Discussed in This Chapter

Chamber music

Brahms: Quintet in F minor; *Mendelssohn:* Octet in E♭ major; *Schubert:* Quintet in C major; *Schumann:* Quintet in E♭ major

Choral music

Berlioz: Requiem Mass; *Brahms: Liebeslieder* Waltzes; *Bruckner:* Mass in E minor

Concerto

Brahms: Concerto in D major for Violin and Orchestra; *Paganini:* Concerto No. 1 in D major for Violin and Orchestra

Opera

Bizet: Carmen; Borodin: Prince Igor; Donizetti: Lucia di Lammermoor; Moussorgsky: Boris Godunov; Offenbach: Tales of Hoffmann; Puccini: La Bohème; Strauss, Richard: *Elektra; Salome; Verdi: Aida; Rigoletto; Wagner: Parsifal; Ring of the Nibelung; Das Rheingold; Die Walküre; Tannhäuser; Tristan und Isolde; Weber: Der Freischütz*

Orchestral music

OVERTURE:

Berlioz: Roman Carnival; Mendelssohn: Hebrides; Rimsky-Korsakov: La Grande Pâque russe (Russian Easter); *Schumann: Manfred; Smetana: The Bartered Bride; Weber: Oberon*

SYMPHONY:

Beethoven: Symphony No. 6 in F major (*Pastoral*); *Berlioz: Romeo and Juliet,* a dramatic symphony; *Symphonie fantastique; Brahms:* Symphony No. 1 in C minor; Symphony No. 4 in E minor; *Liszt:* A *Faust* Symphony; *Mahler:* Symphony No. 1 in D major; Symphony No. 2 in C minor; *Schumann:* Symphony No. 1 in B♭ major; *Strauss,* Richard: *Sinfonia domestica; Tchaikovsky:* Symphony No. 6 in B minor

ORCHESTRAL MUSIC OTHER THAN OVERTURE OR SYMPHONY

Liszt: Les Préludes (symphonic poem); *Brahms:* Variations on a Theme by Haydn; *Chabrier: España* (rhapsody); *Dvorák:* Slavonic Dances, Op. 46, 72; *Moussorgsky: St. John's Night on the Bare Mountain; Rimsky-Korsakov: Capriccio Espagnol; Strauss,* Richard: *Don Juan* (tone poem); *Till Eulenspiegel's Merry Pranks* (tone poem); *Tchaikovsky: Capriccio Italien*

Piano music

Brahms: Hungarian Dances; *Chopin:* Preludes for Piano, Op. 24; *Liszt:* Sonata in B minor; *Mephisto* Waltz; *Totentanz; Mendelssohn: Songs without Words; Schumann: Carnaval*

Song

Mahler: Das Lied von der Erde (The Song of the Earth) (songs with orchestra); *Schubert: Der Doppelgänger* (The Phantom Double); *Der Erlkönig* (The Erlking); *Die Stadt* (The City); *Thränenregen* (Teardrops); *Wohin* (Whither); *Ungeduld* (Impatience); *Schumann: Wenn ich in deine Augen seh'* (When I Look into Your Eyes)

Suggested Listening Projects

1. **Schubert, *Der Lindenbaum* (The Linden-tree)**

   Listen for: Folksong quality; exquisite but simple shaping of the melody; basically strophic structure of song; changes which Schubert made to integrate the structure, such as fluctuation between major and minor mode, variation in piano accompaniment for successive stanzas, changes in pace (hurrying forward and holding back) in piano accompaniment; picturesque touches such as chromatic figures at "wind"; use of horn figures to suggest rural setting.

2. **Chopin, Scherzo in B♭ minor**

   Listen for: Intensely dramatic contrasts; wide range; fluctuation between broadly singing melodic lines and extremely brilliant virtuoso figuration; use of one key at the beginning and another at the end; variations in quality of movement although the pace remains relatively constant.

3. **Mendelssohn, Symphony No. 3 in A minor, first movement**

   Listen for: Elegance of melodic material; songlike nature of themes; chorale style of introduction; emphasis on minor harmonies, suggesting a melancholy, nostalgic quality; neat balance of phrases; luminous orchestration; easy, swinging pace of Allegro.

4. **Moussorgsky, *St. John's Night on the Bare Mountain***

   Listen for: Short, colorful, pointillistic effects; modal harmony; tunes suggesting folk dances; tendency to repeat most phrases at least once; sectional structure.

chapter eight

Modern Music

Music in the twentieth century continues to exhibit the trends which were so characteristic of romantic music, the search for new and striking techniques of composition, the development of personal styles. To a person trying to obtain a perspective of modern music, the heterogeneity of styles is far more evident than any underlying unity which may exist. To point up this individuality of styles, few contrasts would be more striking than those offered by the Second Symphonies of Roger Sessions and Walter Piston. These two works, show completely different ideas of musical expression. In each work, the style is epitomized by the first few moments of the opening movement.

Piston's work begins with a broad, sweeping melody that has a distinctly romantic flavor and contour in its rather somber and reflective manner and its undulating rise and fall. Rhythmically, the Piston work has a regular, deliberate quality of movement, and at the beginning the phases of movement are projected broadly. Texturally, the sound seems to have a solid *core,* to be anchored to a strong base, giving a sense of fullness and richness. Harmonically, we have no difficulty sensing a tonal center. The tone on which the opening melody begins, the lowermost note of a minor triad, announces itself as the tonic; the harmony itself has a modal flavor, because of a raised sixth degree. You can hear this tone very clearly, since it stands just below the climax, the uppermost tone of the melody. Stylistically, this phrase in Piston's music suggests the serious, thoughtful manner of late nineteenth-century symphonists; the music of Brahms and Franck comes to mind.

FIGURE 15. The New York Philharmonic Symphony Orchestra, Leonard Bernstein, Musical Director. (Courtesy of *Black Star*.)

We are not able to orient ourselves so successfully at first in Roger Sessions' symphony. There, instead of a broad melody, motives and fragments are hurled at us with explosive force. Immediately there is a sense of development, of working-over; we are plunged directly into the middle of a profound struggle. Although we may feel subconsciously that a pulse is present underneath the furious give-and-take, it certainly is entirely different from the stable and steady meter of Piston's music. The texture contributes its share to the feeling of tension and instability. There is less of a core of sound; contrapuntal activity, a layering of component parts seems to be Sessions' idea of texture. On the other hand, the energetic propulsion of the motivic fragments requires less contact with the "earth" of a solid foundation of sound. Harmonically, Sessions has taken his cue from the post-Wagner trend; his music is saturated with the elements of instability and tension we have already described, *minus* the chordal matrix from which these elements originally had sprung. In this work Sessions' musical lineage appears to stem from various sources, from Beethoven in his serious manner, from Berlioz, possibly, in the technique of orchestration, from Wagner, in the harmonic procedures. Nevertheless, once we adjust ourselves to the somewhat forbidding facade of this music, we can feel the impact of a strong and, in its way, eloquent style; moreover, as we listen, it becomes evident that Sessions has a convincingly dramatic way of carrying his music forward.

The contrast between Piston and Sessions is even more striking when we realize that these two composers have had very similar backgrounds, that they are of about the same age, and that these two works were written within a few years of each other.

Other works from the modern period that illustrate the great range of stylistic variety are listed below:

Hindemith: Symphony, *Mathis der Maler*. This is a three-movement work built from instrumental sections of Hindemith's opera of the same name. In phrase structure, texture, and melodic outline this piece hardly differs from the traditional symphonic language of Beethoven and Brahms. We can hear, on the other hand, a marked difference in the harmonic language, which mixes familiar chord types with less familiar tone combinations and, most significant, tends to avoid the traditional grammar of cadential harmony. This piece was written in 1934.

Stravinsky: *Les Noces*. Arresting sounds of percussion instruments contrasted with the lyricism of the human voice, pungent ornamental dissonances, simple, childlike melodic figures handled in a very sophisticated rhythmic and textural manner—these are some of the qualities of this very unusual work written in 1923.

Prokofiev: *Classical* Symphony. A conscious parody of the eighteenth-century style. Obvious key feeling is juggled in a very skillful and elusive way, and well-formed themes and clear-cut phrase structure receive the same "off-center" treatment. This piece was composed in 1918.

In addition to these you might listen to Arthur Honegger's *Pacific 231* (1924), Bartók's Sonata (1926), Arnold Schönberg's String Trio (1946), and Aaron Copland's *Appalachian Spring* (1943–1944), each of which represents a characteristic stylistic facet of twentieth-century music.

Beyond the aesthetic and philosophical motivations that led composers in the nineteenth century to strike out for themselves, stylistically speaking, several additional stimuli arose in the twentieth century that gave added impetus to the search for different modes of musical expression:

1. Circulation of modern music through performance, radio, recording, and publication has made it possible for a composer to acquaint himself with virtually any current mode of musical expression.
2. Research in music history by modern musicologists has made musical values of past eras available to the composer of today.
3. Modern technology, particularly electronics, has opened new areas of exploration in the field of creating sound itself.

In today's musical Tower of Babel, the composer, critic, and listener are faced with a sticky problem at the very outset. They must define, in each musical composition, the very premises upon which its values and meanings are based. Today's music has no basic grammar upon which all agree, as in the eighteenth century with its sense of key and period structure. As a result we must first concern ourselves with the anatomy and physiognomy of modern music. This is as it should be. In music, as in any other mode of communication, we must have a pretty good idea of what is being said before we make up our minds whether or not we agree with the content of the expression or accept the manner in which it is being uttered.

Stylistically, today's music is not entirely uncoordinated. Since the end of the nineteenth century, certain lines of development have had significant strength, direction, and continuity. We shall describe these principal trends, considering their expressive values and feeling for movement, their techniques, their solution to the problem of form, their historical antecedents, and, where relevant, their association with other aspects of culture.

It was in the period directly following Richard Wagner that modern trends of musical composition began to crystallize. From this era, the saturation point of musical romanticism, two very different musical styles evolved. These were *impressionism,* developed principally by the French composers Claude Debussy and Maurice Ravel, and *expressionism,* cultivated by Austrian and German composers, such as Arnold Schönberg, Anton von Webern, and Alban Berg.

Impressionism

EXPRESSIVE VALUES

Impressionism represented a reaction against the philosophic and aesthetic ideas of Richard Wagner. It rejected his grandiose idealism, overdrawn heroic manner, and mysticism. Impressionist composers wished to project vague and evanescent moods; they avoided strong or violent emotional values. They created instead a feeling of subtle, subdued restlessness that did not seek resolution or arrival but gave the impression of movement being poised in mid-air.

Subject matter in impressionism centered around fantastic, faraway, nostalgic, and pastoral ideas. The music depicted the play of water, wind, and sea, the drifting of clouds, or the moods of colorful and exotic scenes. The titles of compositions are strongly evocative, such as *Delphic Dancers, Ondine* (The Water-Nymph), *What the West Wind Saw, The Engulfed Cathedral,* and *Footsteps in the Snow.* At all times, the object was to give a personal impression of some aspect of the external world in a form whose outlines were blurred and whose colors tended toward the pastel. Musical impressionism flourished in the last years of the nineteenth and the early years of the twentieth century.

TECHNIQUES

Impressionism used any musical device that had the power to evoke such moods and values. Particularly in the field of harmony new, strange, and colorful effects were developed. Impressionist composers were unsympathetic to the Wagnerian conception of artistic expression; nevertheless, they found much in Wagner's harmonic language that could be used for their own purposes. As we know, Wagner used tone combinations that give an effect of instability, of need for fulfillment and resolution. The opening of Wagner's *Tristan und Isolde* symbolizes romanticism's hopeless yearning, its sense of deep tragic emotion. This mood is established by the harmonic tension of the richly dissonant chords (see Examples 8·1 and 8·2).

Impressionism seized upon this quality of harmonic color and instability, but used it in an entirely different musical situation. Ravel's *Ondine* begins with a combination of tones quite similar to that which begins *Tristan.* But, as we can see, both the texture and the quality of movement are quite different. Ravel, in contrast to Wagner's profound metaphysical introspection, created a vague, fairylike atmosphere.

EXAMPLE 8·1. (Note the tones marked by squares)

a. Wagner: *Tristan und Isolde,* opening

b. Ravel: *Ondine* from *Gaspard de la nuit,** opening

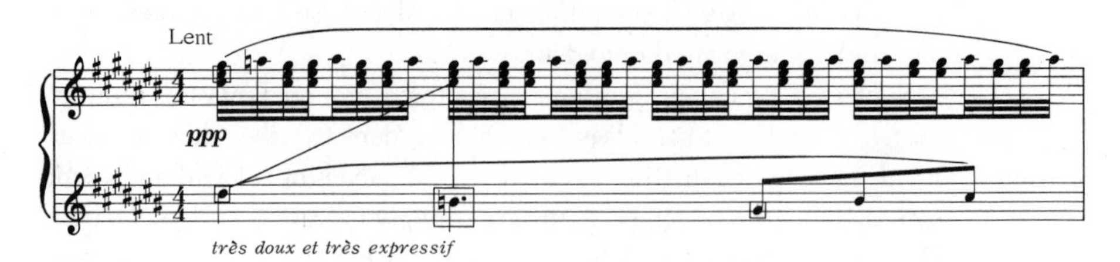

Wagner used many chords that were borrowed by the impressionists solely for the sake of color. Example 8·2 shows a series of these chords.

EXAMPLE 8·2 Debussy: Prelude, *Footsteps in the Snow**

It is remarkable that Debussy was able to use such rich harmonic effects in a short piece meant to portray the plaintive and melancholy mood of winter. The harmony actually contributes to the mood; each harmonic effect becomes a separate phase of movement; there is no building up of tension by piling on of momentum.

The impressionists not only picked and chose from late nineteenth-century harmony. They were alert to utilize any harmonic resource available. Frequently they turned to the musical systems of the Middle Ages, of folk music, or of exotic countries.

Each of these had possibilities for color that were entirely absent from the traditional harmonic system of Western music. In fact, the cadential formula of eighteenth- and nineteenth-century music was the one type of harmonic effect that impressionist composers generally avoided. They tried also to circumvent the major scale, the best representative of a key sense. As we have seen, the major scale represents the last word in clear harmonic definition. This potential for clear harmonic definition is closely associated with well-defined points of arrival in the structure of a piece. But such clear articulation was not sympathetic to the expressive ideals of impressionism. Moreover, scales other than the major had a

* Permission for reprint granted by Durand et Cie, Paris, France, copyright owners. Elkan-Vogel Co., Inc., Philadelphia, Pa., agents.

strangeness, an intriguing quality that attracted the impressionists. Their color effects were suitable for the palette of musical impressionism. Here are some examples. The excerpt is given and below it, in each case, the scale upon which the excerpt is based.

EXAMPLE 8·3 Ravel: Quartet in F, first movement *

Example 8·3 is a graceful, floating melody that takes advantage of the plaintive quality of the Phrygian scale upon which it is based. The Phrygian scale has a half step between the first and second degrees as well as between the fifth and sixth degrees. These half steps, being low in the scale, tend to suggest a resigned, rather than an energetic effect.

EXAMPLE 8·4 Debussy: Prelude, *Footsteps* *

This halting, broken melody also uses a scale which has the half steps placed low. This is the Aeolian scale, with half steps between 2 and 3, 5 and 6. Again the color of the scale sets up the mood.

The pentatonic scale, a gamut of five tones, is used in Example 8·5. Notice that it skips two notes on its way upward. It is a primitive kind of scale and has been used in folk music in many parts of the world.

*Permission for reprint granted by Durand et Cie, Paris, France, copyright owners. Elkan-Vogel Co., Inc., Philadelphia, Pa., agents.

EXAMPLE 8·5 Debussy: Prelude, *The Hills of Anacapri**

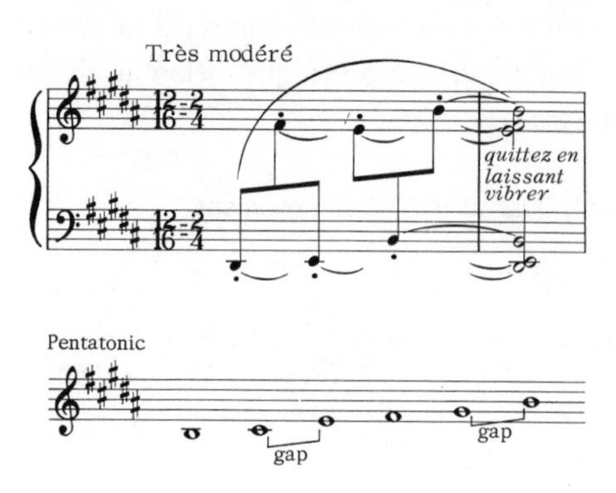

Debussy employs it here possibly to suggest the echoing reverberation of bells or shepherd's horn through the hills.

When a scale has intervals of different size, like those we have examined, it retains some power to establish points of reference. The special intervals are melodic landmarks. In the whole-tone scale, on the other hand, all the intervals are equal to each other, being whole steps. Therefore, this scale cannot establish a point of melodic reference. This vagueness is admirably suited to the aims of musical impressionism; hence, it has been intimately linked with this style, but its actual use has been somewhat less than its reputation would lead us to believe. Sometimes, as in Debussy's Prelude *Sails,* it forms the basis for a large section of a piece; at other times it appears fragmentarily. In *Sails* the whole-tone effect helps create the impression of a slowly swaying passive motion, the easy, indolent mood of a sailboat upon the sea.

EXAMPLE 8·6 Debussy: Prelude, *Sails**

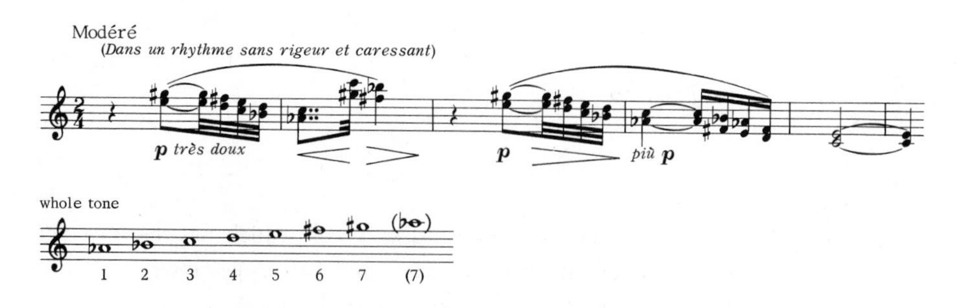

It is interesting to note that Debussy introduced a striking effect of contrast in the middle section of this piece by using the pentatonic scale.

Impressionist composers worked out many special effects of harmony that were new to music at that time. We have looked at a few of these, enough to realize that harmony in this style cannot be separated from texture and color. In impressionism, the chord is a resource for sonority effect, not a carrier of a dynamic quality of movement.

Indeed, texture was one of the principal concerns of the impressionist composer. Whatever he used in the way of instrumentation, wherever he placed his sounds, he was careful to create a transparent, luminous, self-sufficient quality of tone with a distinctive color value. Ravel and Debussy were especially fond of exploiting the pedal resources of the piano, which allow tones to reverberate long after the tone has been struck and give the effect of music floating in the air. The excerpt from *The Hills of Anacapri* (Example 8·5) shows how Debussy used this device.

FORM IN MUSICAL IMPRESSIONISM

It is rather apparent that such techniques of harmony and sonority would not be dedicated to building up extended or highly organized forms. On the contrary, the forms tend to be rather simple. The principal technique of structure was to string out a series of minute and relatively separate effects; at the same time, a consistency of texture was maintained as well as smooth connection between chords. Small and gentle phases of movement were repeated and varied but they did not develop any emotional intensity.

Many pieces in this style consisted of a series of episodes, sometimes in ABA form, sometimes in rondo form. Sonata form was rarely used. Impressionism found no use for the harmonic, rhythmic, and motivic contrasts and development which gave rise to sonata form. The effect of contrast between episodes was created by changes in texture, pace, or harmonic quality. Thus, in *Sails,* Debussy managed to project a striking contrast by using the pentatonic scale for the middle part and the whole-tone scale for the first and last parts.

One form-defining procedure was taken over from the romantic technique of building up to tremendous climaxes. This was the *dynamic curve,* in which a steady increase or decrease in the volume or intensity of sound provided a method for organizing small musical fragments into a larger line; the dynamic curve thus gave some overall shape to a section of considerable extent. The dynamic curve, however, *did not serve an emotional purpose in impressionism,* as it did in romantic music. Rather, it controlled the rise or fall in the intensity of an impression. Its function was pictorial, descriptive. As such, it made an effective framework for

Lever du jour (Daybreak), the first number in Ravel's *Daphnis et Chloé* Suite No. 2. Daybreak, the rising of the sun, and increasing action of the shepherds and shepherdesses—all describe a rising dynamic curve. Ravel begins the piece with the slightest murmur of sound, created by gliding harps and winds and muted, sustained strings, a perfect example of impressionism's pastel tone painting.

After some measures which expand this quality somewhat, a melody takes shape in the lower strings, crystallizing, as it were, out of the amorphous fragments heard at the very beginning. This melody, built principally from one-measure figures, grows by linking its motives together in a general upward direction. The broad dynamic curve of the entire piece is given point and focus by the wide sweep of this melody, which always begins low and rises gradually. Several climaxes are reached, attaining successively higher peaks, and the last, of course, is the highest. In its general contour, this piece resembles the Prelude to *Tristan,* but the details and nuances of style bring about a totally different result. Note in this piece how steady and even the rhythm seems, how stable and placid the general harmonic effect is, and how calmly the bass instruments support the texture. In these respects, Ravel's piece is diametrically opposed to *Tristan.*

Other examples of use of the dynamic curve may be heard in Debussy's *Fêtes* from his Nocturnes for Orchestra, which pictures an approaching and departing group of dancers and merrymakers, and in Ravel's *Bolero* and *La Valse,* which build up an impression of increasing physical excitement.

HISTORICAL ANTECEDENTS

Impressionism was only in part a reaction against Wagner. Throughout the nineteenth century many pieces written in a pictorial vein to evoke certain moods forecast the impressionism to come. For example Beethoven's Symphony No. 6, the *Pastoral,* is a series of five impressions of various aspects of rural life.

In Mendelssohn's *Hebrides* Overture, constant repetition of a short but graceful motive suggests the play of water, a typical impressionistic subject. Chopin was a valuable source book for the impressionists with his treatment of the piano pedal for sonority and his incredibly imaginative and delicate keyboard figuration. Wagner himself created the impression of water flowing when he spun out rolling motives at the beginning of *Das Rheingold.* These examples are but a few of the pictorial pieces that abound in nineteenth-century music. They serve to show how impressionism grew out of one aspect of romanticism.

IMPRESSIONIST PAINTING AND SYMBOLIST POETRY

Impressionism in music was closely allied with other activities in the creative arts that were taking place in Paris just before the turn of the century. Actually, musical impressionism acquired its name from painting, from the school of Monet, Pissarro, Sisley, and Renoir. These painters achieved the same blurred outlines, the same misty luminous effects that the composers worked out in their music. *Pointillism* was the painter's technique, a method of combining separate tiny bits of color suggesting the prismatic effects of light broken up into its constituent colors. Pointillism created much the same effect in painting that specific small moments of texture and sonority did in music. Both in painting and in music the quality of movement was floating, gentle, disembodied. Whistler's *Nocturne* has the characteristic shadings of impressionist art (see Fig. 16).

FIGURE 16. James McNeill Whistler: *Nocturnè*. Note the impressionistic play of light and shade in the representation of water, land, and sky. (Courtesy of the Metropolitan Museum of Art, Dick Fund, 1917.)

Symbolist poets and writers furnished much material for impressionist vocal music. Verlaine, Mallarmé, Maeterlinck, and others cultivated a style characterized by nuance, half-formed ideas, suggestion, and exotic and fantastic atmosphere. This manner of the symbolist writers found a strong response among impressionist composers. The trailing word image could be enhanced by the trailing musical phrase. Frequently symbolist poets tried to develop a purely decorative or musical quality in their texts, a play on sonorities without special reference to meaning. Consider the mellifluous quality of the following excerpt from *Apparition* by Stephen Mallarmé:

La lune s'attristait. Des séraphins en pleurs
Rêvant, l'archet aux doigts, dans le calme des fleurs
Vaporeuses, tiraient de mourantes violes
De blancs sanglots glissant sur l'azur des corolles.

Debussy's *Prelude to the Afternoon of a Faun* was inspired by Mallarmé's poem of the same name; his opera *Pelléas et Mélisande* is based upon Maeterlinck's drama; and he wrote songs to poems of Paul Verlaine.

Ravel wrote much that was impressionist in flavor, such as *Gaspard de la nuit, Daphnis et Chloé,* and *Rapsodie espagnole,* yet in all his works there was a sense for the long line not entirely compatible with the pointillistic techniques of impressionism. This linear aspect of Ravel's music led him to write works in traditional forms, particularly the sonata form, and to write much music that had no pictorial or special mood values. Frederick Delius in England, Alexander Scriabin in Russia, Charles Loeffler in America, Manuel de Falla in Spain, all wrote music in the impressionist style. Today impressionism has long died out as an active school. Indeed, toward the end of his life Debussy himself veered away from the pure impressionist style. Yet much of the harmonic vocabulary of today's music was first defined by the impressionists, and here and there in music written much later, atmospheric touches recall this style.

OPERA IN IMPRESSIONISM: DEBUSSY'S *PELLÉAS ET MÉLISANDE*

We have seen that Wagner's tone color and chord vocabulary influenced impressionism significantly. Early in his musical life, Claude Debussy was fascinated by the music of the German master. While he later renounced the aesthetic doctrines of Wagner and his Germanic predecessors, Debussy nevertheless was influenced in a rather curious way by Wagner when he wrote his opera *Pelléas et Mélisande*. As we listen to this work, we cannot avoid some striking reminders of *Tristan,* some direct and others which seem to be a specific reversal of attitude. Basically, the two stories are similar—there are two lovers and a betrayed husband-king; there is discovery and the death of the lover. Each opera uses a type of declamation suited to the language of its libretto. *Tristan*'s vocal lines pick up the extreme highs and lows of the strongly inflected German language; Pelléas mirrors the relatively narrow pitch range and the subtle quantitative rhythms of French. Both operas use leitmotifs and build long periods through restatement of these motives upon the dynamic curve. As we said before, there are similarities in the harmonic language, but as a rule *Tristan* tends to explode into violent expressions of emotion, while *Pelléas* tends to an understatement of feeling as in the beginning of Act II, when the lovers are alone. Still, we have a true Wagnerian climax in *Pelléas* at the end of Act IV, when Pelléas is killed by Golaud just at the moment of embrace. Throughout *Pelléas,* the techniques of impressionism are used to create and sustain the mysterious, elusive mood that characterizes this work. The interludes that separate the scenes of the opera serve as musical stage settings, bringing to our attention the forest that frames the action of the opera. The very opening measures epitomize Debussy's musical style: the first four measures give us an impression of archaic, remote, and mysterious elements by means of the low-pitched modal harmonies in deliberate, regular motion; the next three measures are built upon a characteristic rich and unstable harmony, carried forward in a rather uncertain wavering motion.

Following are additional examples of impressionism in music:

Delius: *On Hearing the First Cuckoo in Spring.* A pastoral mood pervades this piece. Among its characteristic features we hear rich, unstable harmonies that seem to melt into each other smoothly and gently; a singsong melody and a regular rhythm; a varied palette of orchestral colors, projecting the gentle, dreamy mood of the piece; a strong element of major and minor harmony, often colored by tones that add piquancy to the basic chord. The dynamic curve is in evidence, but, in line with the expressive quality of the piece, its profile is neither steep nor wide.

De Falla: *Nights in the Gardens of Spain: In the Generalife.* Many short episodes are joined in this piece, each with its play upon a quality of sound, a melodic figure, and a simple dancelike or songlike rhythm. The contrast is not extreme; there seems to be a deliberate and quiet progression from one episode to another. The orchestration often points up the color of individual instruments, such as the horns. The solo piano is handled in the typical style of the later nineteenth century, as an element of color and figuration. Note the sideslipping of harmonies which suggests the Oriental quality also seen in the flamenco.

Debussy: *Sirènes* from Nocturnes for Orchestra. Women's voices in four parts are added here to enrich the color that characterizes Debussy's orchestration. While they are assigned melodic fragments from time to time, the voices are principally concerned with adding their vibrant quality to the sound of the orchestra and with creating brief vocal arabesques that mesh with the decorative figures of the instruments. The harmony has a strong sense of major, often with added tones for color. Movement is gentle and singsong. The entire piece embodies once again the impressionist composer's preoccupation with the play of natural elements, this time the element being the sea.

Debussy: *Clair de lune* from the song cycle *Fêtes galantes* (poem by Paul Verlaine). The elusive imagery of this poem is suggested in the first few lines, paraphrased as follows: "Your soul is a rare landscape, in which charming masqueraders move, playing the lute and dancing, as if they were sad beneath their fantastic disguises." This text is set with an elegant melodic line that scans the syllables rather than reflects the sense of the words. The piano maintains a steady background motion against which it introduces fragments in a pointillistic pattern, although without marked contrast save in harmony. Debussy's harmony (the piece has a strong flavor of Dorian mode) and his figuration represent impressionistic techniques in this work.

Expressionism; Tone-row Music

EXPRESSIVE VALUES

Musical expressionism represented the most complete contrast possible to impressionism. Its object was to suggest the innermost world of feeling, not the external world of picture and mood. Expressionism tried to give an idea of the struggles, tensions, and contradictions working within the subconscious. This inner world has strange qualities of meaning; its drives are often perverse and destructive; disparate concepts are linked in an obscure manner. Expressionism deals with strange shapes, odd juxtapositions, disembodied fragments; there is no central core of substance, little contact with familiar realities. There is a striking parallel between the emergence of expressionism and the development of psychological techniques to explore the subconscious. Freud and expressionism are both aspects of man's concern with his inner psychic states. Naturally, the qualities of movement in expressionism would not be clear, direct, and smooth; rather, they are capricious, unpredictable, shifting, angular, irregular, brief, and incomplete.

Although Richard Strauss and Gustav Mahler did not go as far in this direction as later composers did, they dealt with subject matter that showed a strong tendency to portray distorted states of mind and escape from reality. Strauss's *Elektra* deals with matricide and insanity; *Salomé* centers on sadistic lust; *Till Eulenspiegel* upsets the whole world; *Don Juan* allows himself to be killed out of disappointment after surfeit; *Don Quixote* yearns for a lost world and tilts at windmills. Mahler's *Lied von der Erde* (Song of the Earth) combines late Viennese romanticism with some artificial *chinoiserie* in a work whose mood shifts from deep despair at the futility of life to momentary solace in toy scenes. In all this music there is little to suggest regeneration, of good struggling with evil and winning out, perhaps in a better world. The object is to report as strikingly and effectively as possible the nature of the problem, the state of mind; the resolution is not given.

TECHNIQUES

Expressionism was drawn to Wagner's dissonances, to his melodies that gave an effect of distortion through wide jumps and jagged outlines, and to his rhythmic patterns that conveyed a sense of conflict and restlessness. These were all techniques that created a feeling of instability. Expressionism wished to avoid well-defined points of arrival. Through constant use of arbitrary dissonant combinations it avoided giving any sense of tonal center. This was called *atonality*. Melodies that flowed evenly and rhythms that were regular also came under the ban since they can easily create a sense of stability. Yet the most important factor of all in creating expressionism's spidery, grotesque effects was its texture. There was no longer a substantial central core of sound, a merging of voices that gave body to the texture in music of earlier periods. Rather, there was a use of ornamental melodic voices generally placed at great distances in range from each other. Contrapuntal activity of great intensity was supposed to create musical interest and to compensate for the removal of the musical *terra firma*.

If impressionism borrowed a specific idea of tone quality from Wagner, expressionism developed his melodic, rhythmic, and harmonic techniques. The richness of sound that appealed to impressionism was exactly the value that expressionism eliminated. The diagram below shows the relative historical positions of impressionism and expressionism with reference to Wagner.

EXAMPLE 8·7 Historical positions of impressionism and expressionism

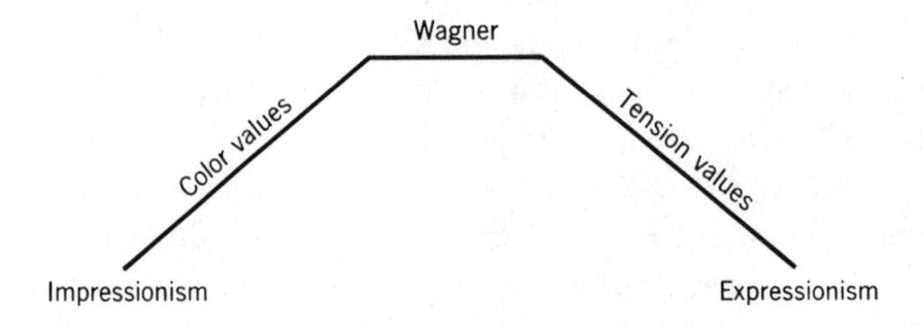

Arnold Schönberg was the leader in the school of musical expressionism. Probably the most celebrated work of this school is his *Pierrot lunaire,* a set of twenty-one melodramas for voice and five instruments. The subject matter of the poems deals with the nocturnal adventures of Pierrot of the Moon, a fantastic spirit. The imagery is vivid, but the meanings are elusive and dreamlike. Many of the poems have grotesque ideas, but at the same time they invoke an almost painfully nostalgic mood. The voice half sings and half speaks; this technique, developed from Wagner's declamatory recitative style, is called *Sprechstimme.*

Number 5 from *Pierrot lunaire,* Valse de Chopin, illustrates the compositional techniques of expressionism.

EXAMPLE 8·8 Schönberg: Valse de Chopin from *Pierrot lunaire,* No. 5 *

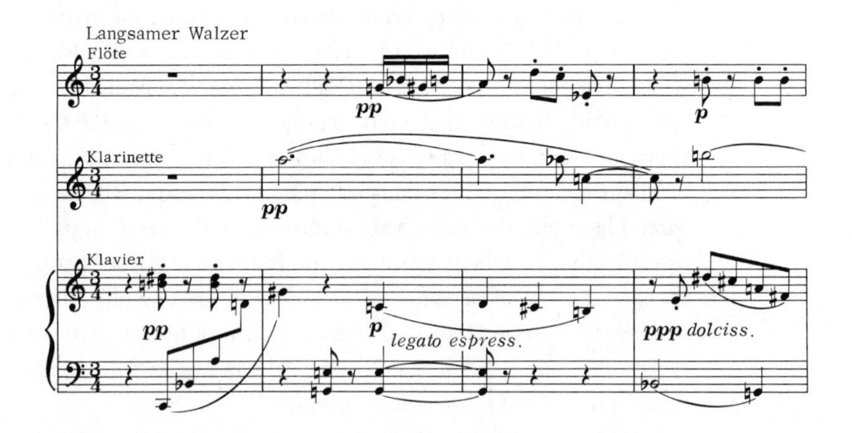

* Copyright by Mrs. Gertrud Schoenberg, Belmont Music Publishers. Used by permission.

Notice in this example the disembodied texture, the fragmentary bits of melody, the lack of a strong point of reference, and the constant tension. Schönberg here composed a nightmare parody of a waltz. The tiny melodic and rhythmic fragments of this piece could well fit into a romantic waltz if they were set together in a clear relationship of statement and counterstatement and if they were supported by a vigorous rhythmic and harmonic accompaniment. The nostalgia of this work and its debt to romanticism emerge most clearly in the final piece, No. 21, *O Alter Duft.*

EXAMPLE 8·9 Schönberg: *O Alter Duft* from *Pierrot lunaire,* No. 21*

The harmonic progression in this excerpt is a cadence, but the distortion of the lines disguises the sense of arrival and retains for the piece something of characteristic expressionist tension.

The values established by expressionism strongly pervade the styles of the present era. More than any other single factor, expressionism is responsible for the complexity of idiom that characterizes much modern music, as we heard in Roger Sessions' Symphony No. 2.

FORM IN MUSICAL EXPRESSIONISM

With regard to form, expressionist composers faced a difficult problem. They eliminated all the factors that made for clearly perceived stability and for creating a well-defined structural contour. Unpredictable, often contradictory qualities of movement prevented the music from reaching strong points of arrival. Relationships between statement and counterstatement were not easily projected. Large form was not the answer to the problem of structure in expressionism. On the contrary, expressionist music suggested that much was happening in a very short time. Every note and figure seemed an outward symbol of profound inner states of mind and experiences. Hence, a significant musical message could be hinted at in a very short piece. All twenty-one numbers of *Pierrot lunaire* are short; so are the Six Little Piano Pieces of Schönberg, dating from this period. Laconic manner and compressed form were the most characteristic aspects of expressionist structure. Some works with expressionist qualities, however, retained an expansive late romantic manner and were cast in broad forms, such as Mahler's *Das Lied von der Erde* and Richard Strauss's opera *Elektra.*

Within a given movement we find that the form takes shape by repetition and variation of distinctive melodic figures or by contrasts in texture or manner. The form is no longer outlined by harmonic or rhythmic strong points. For example, consider how Schönberg organized the first nine measures of No. 1 of *Pierrot.*

A	Measure 1	Statement of motive
A′	Measures 2–6	Counterstatements of first motive
B	Measure 7	New motive, textural contrast
A″	Measure 8	Repetition and variation of first motive
C	Measure 9	New motive, textural contrast

Motive A, a tinkling little arabesque figure that suggests the liquid quality of moonlight, returns throughout the piece as a refrain. We could say, then, that No. 1 of *Pierrot lunaire* is a rondo.

Expressionist music frequently relied upon a text to give some overall contour to its forms. More than half the works of Schönberg's early period involve a text. The highly charged emotional quality of this style was certainly effective as a setting for words with remote and elusive connotations.

As expressionism developed, certain tendencies became more and more manifest. Habitually a literal repetition of any kind was avoided, since it would create a static effect and break the tension. At the same time, a distinctive melodic figure was used in many varied ways throughout a piece as a means of obtaining some underlying unity. Eventually this led to a systematization known as the *tone-row technique* or the *method of composing with twelve mutually interrelated tones.*

The basic idea of tone-row technique is quite easy to grasp. Suppose we limit ourselves to a row of three notes, for purposes of explanation. In Example 8·10 *a* we have the three tones; in *b* we create a pattern or basic figure which reads 1 3 2. In *c* we use the pattern to create melodic figures of various kinds, taking care that no tone is repeated before the others have been heard; in *d* we make a chord of the pattern. Actually, this process has much in common with mathematical combinations and permutations. Provided that the relationships between the notes themselves remain fixed, the row can begin on any tone, can be played backward or upside down—or can undergo various combinations of these shifts of position. Change of pitch is called *transposition,* playing the row backward is called *retrograde motion,* playing it upside down is called *inversion,* and combining the last two, upside down and backward, is called *retrograde inversion.*

EXAMPLE 8·10 Tone-row construction

a. Three tones. E, G, D

b. Row: E, D, G

c. Melodic line built from row

d. Chords built from row

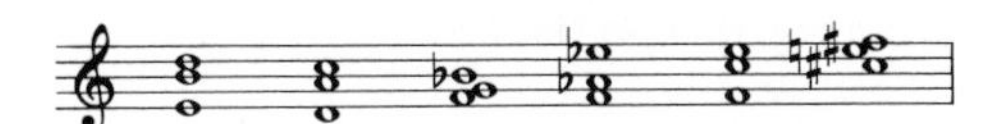

Now, if we should increase the number of tones in our row to twelve, to include all the tones of the chromatic scale, we are at the point of departure for composition in the tone-row technique. Later, some illustrations of the uses of a twelve-tone row from Schönberg's Quartet No. 4 will be given. Tone-row technique was codified by Schönberg in 1924 after he had realized that for many years he had been moving intuitively in this direction in his own style; his melodies, textures, and rhythms tended to avoid repetition and to grow through being varied. The technique was first applied consistently in Schönberg's Serenade, Op. 24, composed in 1923.

Each of the three composers who formed the early tone-row school, Arnold Schönberg, Alban Berg, and Anton von Webern, had his own personal style. Schönberg retained his romantic connections; works like his String Quartet No. 4 and his Piano Concerto show a strong flavor of

Brahms. Berg affected a more spectacular and often more immediately assimilable style. His opera *Wozzeck,* which uses tone-row procedures at various points, suggests the expressionism of Richard Strauss. This work, one of the great musicodramatic achievements of the twentieth century, is quite comprehensive in its range of style and expression. For example, Berg occasionally uses a simple, affecting melodic style, as in Marie's lullaby *Ei-o-po-peia.* Here and there, one hears the sound of a major or minor triad, strategically placed for expressive nuance; also, fragments of marchlike rhythms (Wozzeck is a soldier) crop up now and then. Moreover, Berg's idea of sound leans rather to the rich side than to the spare, open manner of other composers in the expressionistic school. In his *Lyric Suite* for String Quartet, Berg has created atmospheric effects not unlike musical impressionism.

Anton von Webern continued in the terse manner of expressionism, along the lines of the procedure exemplified in *Pierrot lunaire.* He represents the antiromantic wing of the tone-row school, and his influence is perhaps the strongest among younger tone-row composers. Webern's technique of writing very short pieces with very few notes has been particularly attractive to younger tone-row composers; they have progressively rarified the musical atmosphere of their compositions until the individual tones have become virtually disengaged from each other in pitch and texture.

For illustration of tone-row techniques of composition, we shall examine some excerpts from Schönberg's Quartet No. 4.

EXAMPLE 8·11 Schönberg: Quartet No. 4 *

a. The basic row

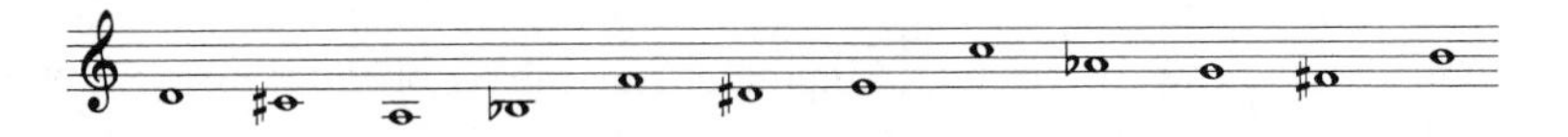

b. The opening theme of the first movement, in a vigorous, square-cut style

c. A transitional passage in the first movement, in a capricious, arabesque-like improvisation

* By permission. From Arnold Schönberg's Fourth String Quartet, G. Schirmer, Inc., New York. Copyright 1939.

d. A waltz, from the second movement

Tone-row composers have used traditional forms of eighteenth-century music, such as sonata form, rondo, fugue, and variation, in an effort to reconcile themselves with music of the past. These traditional forms were originally based upon clear harmonic orientation and sharply demarcated rhythmic groupings; yet these were the very values the tone-row composers rejected. Whether or not a successful merger of traditional forms and the perpetual variation procedure of tone-row music has been effected is a matter to be decided in each individual case. Common structural practice in the tone-row technique, as yet, is in the process of codification.

The number of composers using the tone-row at present is considerable, in both the older and the younger genèrations of modern music. Ernst Křenek, Luigi Dallapiccola, Wallingford Riegger, and many others have devoted themselves to composition based on the premises of the tone-row. We can discover an even more interesting phenomenon in the partial use of tone-row techniques by composers such as Bartók, Samuel Barber, and Stravinsky. This indicates a recognition of the organizational and expressive potentialities of the tone-row procedures.

HISTORICAL ANTECEDENTS

Expressionism and the tone-row school are the direct descendants of the metaphysical tendencies of the nineteenth century and their attendant chromaticism and dissonance. From the Sensibility and the Storm and Stress down through Beethoven, Liszt, Wagner, and Mahler runs a current of supercharged emotional values. Romantic preoccupation with the dark and sinister aspects of human imagination—witches, unholy talismans, the Devil himself—leads directly to the fantastic world of expressionism.

In retrospect we can see that certain musical techniques point the way from romanticism to expressionism. Prominent among these was an increasing reliance upon thematic values to organize the form of a composition (see Examples 7·20, 7·22, and 7·23). Harmony became involved and complex; it could not give as clear an outline of the form as it did in classic music. Themes became more distinctive and important; they were made points of reference, *leading motives.* In some works, such as Liszt's Sonata in B minor and Strauss's *Till Eulenspiegel,* themes were constantly being varied or transformed. Thus the opening theme of Liszt's Sonata has at different times a brooding, a demonic, a plaintive, a masterful, and an apocalyptic quality. This is not far from the perpetual variation of tone-row music.

Beethoven's last string quartets influenced the expressionist composers profundly. They were impressed by the deeply introspective quality, the tightness of structure, and the rich elaboration of motives that these works exhibited. For example, Beethoven's Grosse Fuge, Op. 133, which takes about fifteen or sixteen minutes to play, is built up entirely of two subjects which are developed and varied in an incredibly imaginative way. One of these subjects shows incipient tone-row features.

EXAMPLE 8·12 Beethoven: Grosse Fuge, Op. 133

Compare the first four notes of this subject with the beginning of Schönberg's row for his Quartet No. 4 (Example 8·11). Note that they are varied inversions of each other.

RELATIONSHIPS WITH ART AND LITERATURE

Musical expressionism was part of a general reaction against late romanticism and impressionism, a reaction that took place as well in literature and art. The term *expressionism* was taken from the German school of painting led by Paul Klee and Vassily Kandinsky. As in music, expressionist painters sought to convey intense and subjective qualities, characterized by strange shapes, odd relationships, and elusive meanings. An analogy between surrealist painting and expressionist music might be drawn considering the ways in which each mode of expression places familiar items into bizarre and unfamiliar contexts, removing them from their ordinary frames of reference.

In literature the dreamlike quality and the hidden meanings of symbolist poetry attracted expressionist composers. Stefan George provided the texts for a number of compositions by Schönberg and his colleagues. We can also see a parallel between expressionism's flow of compact yet obscure associations and the *stream-of-consciousness* technique being developed by James Joyce at that time in his *Ulysses* and other works.

Additional examples of tone-row music follow:

Berg: Violin Concerto. The basic row in this piece has been contrived to give a strong feeling of tonality. Note that the opening notes are arranged according to the tuning of the violin, in fifths, and that the more tense and colorful intervals follow. As first heard, the line is a broadly soaring arch, in the romantic vein; it establishes the rich lyricism and intense pathos which govern the expressive content of this work. The scoring is full and varied, the phrase structure is clear and has a broad sweep, the rhythms often have dancelike values.

Webern: Symphony, Op. 21. At the opposite pole from the style of Berg we find the extremely rarefied language of this work, which is actually a relatively short piece for chamber orchestra. In place of the richly declamatory manner of both Schönberg and Berg, we have an emphasis on "stark" design, lined out in the most economical fashion by single tonal points, each of which creates a taut counterstatement to the previous tone through changes in color, register, and duration. Perhaps this is the most idiomatic way in which a row can be used—a pointillistic play among the notes themselves with no direct reference to the rhetoric of earlier styles. The similarity in attitude of this music to certain types of abstract painting and literature is striking.

Folkloric Music

EXPRESSIVE VALUES

At the time that expressionism was coming into full stature, another significant trend was making itself felt strongly in European music. This was the folkloric style. You have heard music from the expressionist school; now listen to the Dance of the Adolescents from Igor Stravinsky's *Le Sacre du printemps*. There could scarcely be two kinds of music farther apart than expressionism and the folkloric style, as represented by the excerpt from *Le Sacre*. Here is a dance; but it is no dance such as we have encountered before in our study. This is no graceful court dance, nor even a jolly village whirl. It is primitive, tribal, pagan; it suggests a purpose far more serious than the dances which have traditionally provided entertainment in Western culture. The purpose is religious. We are told, in the scenario of the ballet for which *Le Sacre* was composed, that this is a dance of spring. Homage is paid to the earth in the hope of reaping good crops.

Certainly the most salient feature is the emphatic, percussive beat that carries the sound along. All the profound reflections and personal manner of romanticism are cast aside, and the aboriginal values of music,

FIGURE 17. Vassily Kandinsky: *Composition III. 1914.* (From the Collection of the Museum of Modern Art, Mrs. Simon Guggenheim Fund.)

the play of quantities and durations of sound are substituted in the evocation of a raw sense of activity. The beat is in charge.

As a contrast to this expressive quality, we hear, from time to time in *Le Sacre,* a simple folksong manner, often improvisatory in style. Thus, the two aspects of a folk music, dance and song, provide the raw material for a work that is highly stylized, strikingly imaginative, a work that created one of the most celebrated "scandals" in the history of music when it was first presented in Paris in 1913.

TECHNIQUES

Principal among all the technical features of this style is the beat and its treatment. We can hear quite easily that the distinctive rhythmic manner arises from two factors: (1) the ways in which beats are organized, and (2) the ways in which beats are performed.

In earlier styles we heard characteristic ways of treating the beat. Medieval and Renaissance music tended to generate an easy, steady flow of gentle beats. Baroque music also set up such a flow, but with considerably more emphasis. Dance music and music of the classic style organized beats in groups of two, three, four, or six, with regularly spaced periodic accents. Romantic music often displayed irregularities and uncertainties in the flow of beats. But folkloric music, as represented in our excerpt, developed its own distinctive way of organizing rhythmic groups.

In order to demonstrate the effect of handling rhythmic groups in the distinctive folkloric manner, try the following experiment:

1. First, count out a series of four-beat measures, making a stroke at each strong beat, as in Example 8·13.

EXAMPLE 8·13

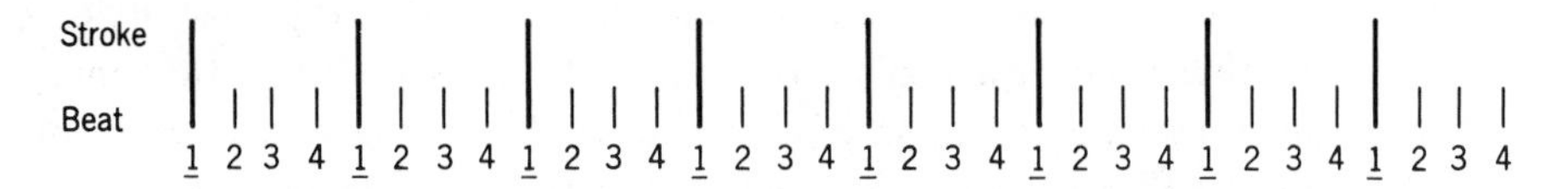

As you continue, notice that the beats, the accented strong beats, and the general quality of movement remain regular, smooth, and virtually automatic. You lose awareness of the rhythm as an immediate or challenging element.

2. Now try the same flow of beats, but after the first two groups of four, introduce a strongly accented beat after three, two, five, three, and four beats, as in Example 8·14.

EXAMPLE 8·14

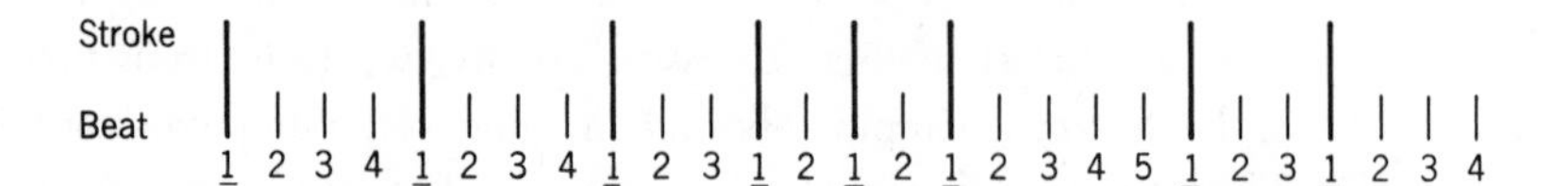

What a world of difference there is in the whole rhythmic concept! Instead of becoming dormant, the accent develops a life of its own, asserts itself in an electrifying way. The periodicity is broken and the impact of an unanticipated accent gives new energy and momentum to the musical flow.

Example 8·15 from the Dance of the Adolescents of *Le Sacre* illustrates this kind of rhythmic organization.

EXAMPLE 8·15 Stravinsky: *Le Sacre du printemps,* Dance of the Adolescents *

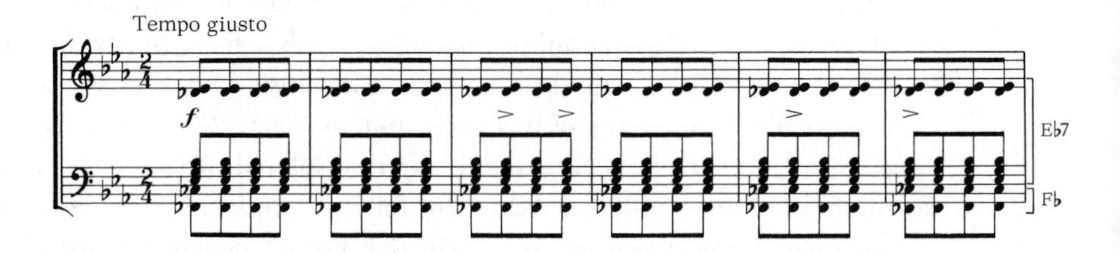

In order to secure and emphasize this rhythmic quality, the entire orchestra must participate. The usual custodians of the underlying beat, the percussion, are not sufficient to give the kind of weight, body, and color to the rhythmic strokes of this music. Thus, in Example 8·15 the burden is carried by the strings; they become quasipercussion instruments, and in the mass that they constitute in the grand symphony orchestra, they carry off the effect brilliantly.

Colorful scoring is closely associated with this rhythmic style. A rhythmic gesture not only involves a stroke; it has arresting, often unique qualities of sonority. As you listen to *Le Sacre,* you hear at every moment strikingly evocative sounds, tone colors splashed on brilliantly and barbarically, yet with subtle insight for the justness of the effect.

In contrast to the rhythmic violence and the flashing colors, the melodic material often has a simple folksong flavor. Melodies tend to be short in phrase; their range is small. They gain length by spinning out; fragments are often repeated with small melodic or rhythmic variations. These melodies tend to center around a single tone or to move back and forth between a few tones. The melodies frequently use the modal scales described in the section on impressionism. The total effect is rather singsong, as in Example 8·16.

EXAMPLE 8·16 Stravinsky: *Le Sacre du printemps,* The Games of the Rival Cities *

The harmonic language of this style frequently sounds opaque and crashingly dissonant. Yet if we pull all the pieces apart we find that the harmony is made up of simple, familiar, diatonic units, such as triads, open fifths and fourths, and scales which are put together in layers on top of each other or succeed each other in odd ways to create a dissonant effect. In other words, the harmonic values of folksong represent the starting point for the complex chord structures of the folkloric style. Example 8·14 illustrates the use of two chords from different keys sounded together but kept distinct by well-defined layering. This device is known as *polytonality*. Example 8·17 is an illustration of *pandiatonism,* a harmonic device in which notes from a diatonic scale are combined in nontraditional ways. Both polytonality and pandiatonism represent efforts to retain some of the stability and orientation value of triads and homogeneous scales while introducing special and piquant harmonic effects.

EXAMPLE 8·17 Stravinsky: *Le Sacre du printemps,* Rounds of Spring *

FORM IN FOLKLORIC MUSIC

Listening for the definition of form in folkloric music, we discover, as probably the most apparent feature, *contrasts* in texture and mood. The form takes shape in well-demarcated episodes. Within an episode the principal structural unit is a phrase or period whose length is determined by the composer's feeling that a certain effect has been sufficiently exploited. The phrases themselves take shape by varied repetition of figures and harmonies. A sense of movement within the phrase is projected by the permutations of rhythm, melody, and texture which we have described above. A natural concomitant of such structure is the dynamic curve, built by the accumulation of intensity, volume of sound, and increase of pace, at times. Points of arrival in phrases and in episodes are rarely familiar cadences; rather, arrival is signaled by some sort of climax in the dynamic curve, or by the beginning of a new effect, texture, or harmonic procedure. In this music, statement and counterstatement show a simple, down-to-earth relationship.

It was no accident that this style, with its colorful associations of primitive culture, its dominating dance rhythms, and its episodic forms based on sharp contrast, should have been developed in connection with modern ballet and stage arts. Most of Stravinsky's early music was stage music; his connection with the great choreographer Diaghilev is one of the celebrated associations in the history of music and dance.

By way of illustration, let us have a look at the way the first few episodes of *Le Sacre* are fitted together.

The very opening sounds presage the strange and exotic music to come. The improvisation of the bassoon in its highest, most tortured register, the interjected fragments by the clarinets in their lowest, most somber register, the curious pointillism of structure—all these create a world of musical imagery far removed from Western experience. Bit by bit the fragments coalesce, new motives dart in and out; an excitement is growing. The texture, transparent at first, becomes increasingly clouded and heavy. Suddenly the rising dynamic curve breaks off, and the bassoon, alone again, recalls for a moment its speculative thought of the beginning. In schematic terms, the form thus displays an ABA plan. The final A, while it may act for arrival, still has a tentative quality that enables it to serve as a transition to the next large episode, the Dance of the Adolescents. This dance is dominated by the rhythmic figure we first hear plucked by the strings. Around this rhythmic motive, above and below, melodic fragments are superimposed; these figures possess a tremendous rhythmic vitality. When they are combined with the driving rhythmic ostinato, the impact is explosive. As we might expect, the overall form of this episode turns out to be a dynamic curve; the dance works itself up to the point of frenzy and rushes directly into the next episode, The Play of Abduction, at which point the tempo becomes headlong. Indeed, this quickening of pace was perhaps the only effective way the music could move ahead from the climax of the previous dance. The remainder of this work should also be evaluated structurally by its gestures, textures, and rhythmic effects, rather than by harmonic or melodic analysis, at least by the layman.

HISTORICAL POSITION OF FOLKLORIC MUSIC

As we mentioned above, the first impetus toward the use of folk idioms came from composers in the nineteenth century. The composer who made the sharpest break with Western music was Moussorgsky. His phrase structure, percussive rhythms, and folklike melodic style had much influence on Stravinsky. Another representative of Russian nationalism, Rimsky-Korsakov, taught Stravinsky much in the way of orchestration. It was only when Stravinsky abandoned the folkloric manner for neoclassicism that he turned aside from Rimsky-Korsakov's conception of scoring.

The heyday of the folkloric style was during the second decade of the twentieth century. In addition to Stravinsky, Béla Bartók, who did a monumental study of Eastern European folk music, was the other principal figure in the folkloric trend. In both its techniques and its attitudes,

FIGURE 18. Thomas Hart Benton: *Homestead*. 1934. (From the Collection of the Museum of Modern Art, Gift of Marshall Field.)

this style has been tremendously influential upon later music. The free play of small, well-defined rhythmic groups is a strikingly characteristic manner among contemporary American composers. Nowhere do we find this better illustrated than in Aaron Copland's *El Salón México,* in which an exuberant offbeat rhythmic manner is combined with brilliant orchestration and a winning melodic content. Walter Piston frequently uses this calculated rhythmic imbalance, as we can hear in the last movement of his Symphony No. 2.

The simple song and dance values in folkloric music have been taken up by American, British, Russian, French, and Spanish composers, with or without percussive underpinning. Thus, Virgil Thomson, in his suite taken from music he wrote for the documentary film *The Plow That Broke the Plains,* uses the traditional hymn tune *Old Hundred* in one movement and the Western song *Montana* in another. Pioneer and rural American life has provided a rich source of material for contemporary American composers, ranging upward from the writer of hillbilly songs to the composer of serious and ambitious symphonies. Folksongs and dances make strong and immediate impressions upon the listener; he does not have to search long and perhaps painfully to grasp the portent of the music.

Here are additional comments on folkloric pieces in twentieth-century music:

Copland: *El Salón México.* This is one of the most popular and effective works composed by an American. Its lively shifting dance rhythms, its frank tunefulness, its brilliant and transparent scoring, the harmony that never strays far from the major mode in spite of many incidental dissonances, and its clear structural layout—all contribute to the delight of the listener. This piece exemplifies the picturesque type of folklorism, the kind that deals with local color. In this way, it carries on the tradition of such works as Rimsky-Korsakov's *Capriccio Espagnol* and Tchaikovsky's *Capriccio Italien.*

Bartók: Sonata for Piano. In this work the percussive beat and the irregular rhythm of twentieth-centry folklorism are used. The piano is made to act both as a percussion instrument and in its normal capacity as an instrument of figuration. There is a tremendous drive, often built up by the reiteration of a single note or a cluster of tones, especially in the first movement. The repetition of such tones or chords provides the listener with a sense of tonal center. There are very few figures that would qualify as melodies; most of the motives consist of two to eight tones; continuity is built up by varying and contrasting these motives (all of them very sharply characterized) in statements and counterstatements of irregular lengths. The final movement gives us material that has greater tunefulness than any of the preceding movements.

Jazz

Jazz is a world unto itself. It is only upon occasion that the concert tradition we have been tracing and jazz have come together. This is probably because the very business of jazz, its procedures and objectives, is quite different from that of music written for a listening audience. There are many kinds of jazz and many definitions and descriptions of this modern musical art. Several characteristics seem to be decisive for the style:

1. The underlying meter is regular, generally a rather emphatic two-four or four-four measure.
2. Above this there is a great deal of play against the beat, both in terms of syncopation and in slight anticipations or holding back that cannot actually be measured. The latter is what gives jazz its characteristic "pronunciation," causing us to recognize it immediately when we hear it.
3. Reflecting its popular and folkloric origins, jazz tends to build its periods in regular phrases, four measures in length. Marches, songs sung at work, and popular dances of the late nineteenth and early twentieth centuries, such as the cakewalk and ragtime, form one part of the ancestry of jazz. Melodic and rhythmic elements from West Africa also figure in the genealogy of jazz.
4. Melodically, much the same type of pronunciation is found as that which characterizes the rhythm of jazz. Often, tones are slightly inflected; the more prominent of these are known as "blue" notes; these represent a scale (African) that is slightly different from our present-day major and minor scales. When blue notes are sung or played on a variable-pitch instrument (saxophone, clarinet, string, trumpet, or trombone) we get the true "blue" effect. The piano, unfortunately, must play the blue note as a tone in the minor scale, and thus the piano cannot produce the special inflection that gives such an elusive charm to an expertly sung blues.
5. Much jazz is composed on the spot, as it is played. This improvisation is actually the basic rule of the game and is the feature which has led to an impressive body of musical practice in which there are recognized virtuosi who have polished and refined this art in its many facets. This is where jazz differs from other art music of today. It has a common

language, spoken by all, but mastered for purposes of expression only by a few. The analogy with the music of the eighteenth century is very close; at that time, dances and marches were also the common idiom, but only a few masters were able to discover fresh and distinctive ways of reaffirming the familiar patterns.

Jazz embraces many different styles of composition and performance. Such terms as Dixieland, New Orleans, Chicago, New York, swing, bop, and cool have been used at different times to designate a local or current jazz idiom. There is also a wide range of expression, from the exuberant Dixieland and boogie-woogie styles to the melancholy blues and the intricate and somewhat cryptic rhetoric of the master improvisers. The listener can appreciate individual traits in the strength and frequency of the beat, the clarity or ornamention of the melody, the richness of the harmony, the play of cross-rhythms, and the fullness, clarity, and balance of the instrumentation, as well as the texture.

The crossover between jazz and traditional concert music can be observed, from the jazz side, in the application of modern techniques of harmony, texture, and manner borrowed largely from twentieth-century French music; in this connection, Darius Milhaud has been very influential. His pupil Dave Brubeck derived much of his highly sophisticated style from his studies with Milhaud. On the serious side, we find that the early types of jazz, ragtime, and blues have fascinated modern composers. Hindemith, Bartók, Křenek, Milhaud, Stravinsky, Honegger,

EXAMPLE 8·18 Milhaud: *La Création du Monde* *

Tendre et doux

p

* Copyright 1929 by Editions Max Eschig, Paris; used by permission of Associated Music Publishers, Inc., New York.

Debussy, Copland, and Ravel—all these composers have borrowed rhythmic patterns, instrumentation effects, melodic formulas, and blue harmonies from jazz. Milhaud's very entertaining music to the ballet *La Création du Monde* takes off on jazz; throughout the piece we hear the characteristic harmonies and sonorities as well as the steady rhythms that mean jazz to us. We hear, especially, the plaintive tones of the saxophones dominating the orchestral sound. Example 8·18, taken from this work, illustrates blue harmony.

Gershwin's music, such as *Rhapsody in Blue* and the Concerto in F, represents probably the most successful effort to employ jazz idioms in an extended form.

FIGURE 19. Gino Severini: *Dynamic Hieroglyphic of the Bal Tabarin.* 1912. (From the Collection of the Museum of Modern Art, Acquired through the Lillie P. Bliss Bequest.)

Some of the phases and styles of jazz are listed below, along with a sampling of performers associated with these styles:

Dixieland (New Orleans): Kid Ory, King Oliver, later Louis Armstrong, Lu Watters
Swing: Benny Goodman, Count Basie, the Dorsey brothers (Tommy and Jimmy)
Boogie-Woogie: Albert Ammons, Pete Johnson, Meade Lux Lewis
Chicago jazz (New Orleans): Paul Whiteman, Louis Armstrong, Bix Beiderbecke
Bop: Dizzy Gillespie, Charlie Parker, Thelonious Monk
Cool jazz: Gerry Mulligan, Miles Davis, Dave Brubeck

Parody and Satire

Antiromanticism in the early twentieth century gave rise to many compositions that parodied or satirized romantic ideas or procedures, as well as those of still earlier periods. The idealism of the nineteenth century was replaced by a clever cynicism that took relish in making familiar musical ideas seem ludicrous or grotesque. One of the favorite subjects for parody was the waltz, the grandiose dance of the nineteenth century, the symbol of imperial elegance. Ravel's *La Valse* and his *Valses nobles et sentimentales* give the waltz a bittersweet distorted aspect; Schönberg's waltzes in *Pierrot lunaire,* Nos. 2 and 5, carry the process of distortion much farther. We have already mentioned the subject matter of Richard Strauss's music, which has an element of bitter satire.

Stravinsky's *L'Histoire du soldat* is perhaps the best example of a parodistic treatment of subject matter. In this piece, Stravinsky parodies the theme of Faust and the Devil, a favorite romantic topic; he also pokes fun at the rags-to-riches idea, which itself is a parody of the redemption wish of romanticism. Folk magic, such as we find in *Der Freischütz* (magic bullets) and *Das Rheingold* (the gold and the Tarnhelm) is treated in a satirical manner in the episodes dealing with the soldier and his violin. Musically, dances current in the early twentieth century are paraphrased, such as ragtime, tango, and waltz. The chorale style of Bach is satirized; also the French cancan (in the Royal March) and the baroque instrumental concerto. At the end, the Devil wins out; nothing is left but the percussion beating away, insistent and inarticulate, the victory of the new primitive world over the old decadent civilization.

Neoromanticism

Although the first quarter of the twentieth century saw a violent reaction against romanticism, it did not by any means cause the romantic idea in music to disappear. In many composers we find a direct continuation of romantic modes of expression. Latter-day romanticism uses the rich textures, the grandly serious manner, and the eloquent declamation of nineteenth-century orchestral music, but carefully adds musical techniques that have been evolved in the twentieth century. The long line and the big design are structural objectives in this style. Jean Sibelius, Sergei Rachmaninov, Howard Hanson, Ernest Bloch, Gustav Holst, and Ralph Vaughan Williams have written consistently in a romantic vein.

Bloch's *Schelomo,* Hebrew Rhapsody for Violoncello Solo and Orchestra, illustrates this trend in a very distinctive and personal manner. This piece encompasses a wide range of kaleidoscopic moods, deep introspection, intensely emotional declamation, wild abandon, exaltation, prophetic fervor. The solo cello becomes a hero, just as the soloist in the romantic concerto does. The grandeur of the conception, the fullness and richness of the scoring, and the demands made upon both the soloist and orchestra are in line with nineteenth-century traditions. Structurally, this piece also looks to music of the romantic era; it is in sonata form with well-marked thematic contrasts.

Schelomo cannot be mistaken, however, for a purely romantic composition. We find its harmony, with its biting dissonances, its exotic colors and scales, its strange progressions, often far removed from the world of romantic harmony. Moreover, the debt Bloch owes to the music of impressionism is frequently manifest. The chords that support the solo cello at the beginning of the piece bear witness to Bloch's impressionism; and the frequent use of the celesta in prominent places provides additional testimony.

Following are additional examples of romantic influence in twentieth-century music:

Bartók: Concerto for Violin and Orchestra. This is a broad, eloquent work that treats the violin as a melodic and ornamental instrument par excellence. The beginning of the first movement establishes the romantic mood immediately, as it sets the steady, pulsating accompaniment against the broad sweep of the violin solo. The harmony is clearly set in B minor, represented by its tonic triad at the onset. The violin line has an expansive melody, very much in the vein of the great violin concertos of the nineteenth century, such as those of Brahms and Tchaikovsky.

Britten: *Peter Grimes.* This opera appears to be modeled to a considerable extent upon the grand opera of the nineteenth century. It has a fairly large cast; the chorus has a very important role; there are arias, concerted numbers, and recitatives. The story itself has a relationship to the topics which romantic composers preferred. Peter Grimes is set against the villagers in a plot that symbolizes the struggle of the individual against the mass, a struggle which he is bound to lose. One number, a recitative at the end of the Prologue, illustrates how Britten used a modern technique, polytonality, to achieve a typically romantic pathos. Peter and his sweetheart Ellen are singing together; he is discouraged, she is reassuring. Britten set Grimes's music in F minor and Ellen's music in E major. The tonic harmonies of these two keys share the third, F minor's third being A♭, which is in pitch equivalent to E major's third G♯. The two lines imitate each other pivoting around the common note. Grimes's version carries an effect of bitterness; Ellen's, of hope. At the end, symbolizing the positive view, Grimes joins Ellen in her E major.

Neoclassicism

By the middle of the 1920s, preoccupation with romanticism, either for or against, seemed to have passed its most intense phase. Also, by this time, the era of exploration of specific new musical techniques was drawing to a close. Harmonically, any combination of notes seemed to be usable; melodically, there were few restrictions of contour or range; rhythmically, a whole new field had opened up; texturally, a tremendous catalogue of new sounds had been made available. Structurally, however, the new music had raised perplexing new problems. The minutiae of the early twentieth century, which were striking and distinctive gestures in their own right, did not submit easily to being organized into coherent forms. Neoclassicism represents an effort to achieve clarity and the big structural design.

EXPRESSIVE VALUES

In the strict sense, neoclassicism refers to the trend that appeared in the middle 1920s to use features of the music of the eighteenth century and earlier periods. Balance and clarity were sought in reaction against the one-sided exaggerations of impressionism, expressionism, and folkloric

FIGURE 20. Pablo Picasso: *Pierrot and Harlequin, Seated.* 1918–1919. (From the Collection of the Museum of Modern Art, Lillie P. Bliss Collection.)

music. Neoclassicism is characterized by an economy of means; very often a chamber music texture is used. Specific emotional connotations and pictorial values are avoided. There is a sense of purpose, of well-controlled movement directed solidly to a logical point of arrival. We find strong coherence in the melodic lines and the interplay of motives. Neoclassicism is not preoccupied with the easy drift of impressionism, the tortured spasms of expressionism, or the brutal stamp of folkloric music. Hindemith's String Quartet No. 3 and Stravinsky's Octet exemplify the neoclassicism of the 1920s.

Neoclassicism might also describe the aims of many composers writing after 1920 to reconcile traditional and contemporary musical values. Serious efforts have been made to codify musical practice in order to establish some areas of common usage. Whatever expressive objectives the composer might have, whatever special effects he may wish to employ, whatever his harmonic language, he has felt the need to place these factors in balance within a form of some scope. We cannot speak of a neoclassic harmonic style. Indeed, works that are clearly neoclassic can have diametrically opposed harmonic procedures. The harmony may be strikingly dissonant, as in the fugato which opens Hindemith's Quartet No. 3; or, it might be suavely consonant and give a clear sense of tonal center, as in the first movement of Randall Thompson's Quartet in D minor. We can speak of a neoclassic feeling for synthesis and the shaping of form. Neoclassicism is an attitude toward all musical materials; it is not a specific gesture, effect, or sonority value.

TECHNIQUES

In their techniques neoclassic composers have borrowed much from eighteenth-century music. Structural units are comparable to phrases and periods; harmonic effects of cadence are made, although not with traditional formulas. There is a lively give-and-take with distinctive, easily handled motives and much use of counterpoint. Contrapuntal lines tend to run smoothly, to rise and fall deliberately, and to spin out like the lines of Bach's music. The scoring is economical and transparent; interest has diminished in sound for sound's sake. Example 8·19, from Hindemith's Quartet No. 3, illustrates a typical neoclassic passage. Notice that the bass acts like a basso continuo supporting two solo parts, a typical baroque layout. The interest lies in the steady, controlled, yet free sense of movement that the winding lines create as they work against each other.

EXAMPLE 8·19 Hindemith: String Quartet No. 3, Op. 22, first movement *

* Copyright 1923 by B. Schott's Soehne, Mainz; used by permission of Associated Music Publishers, Inc., New York.

In the third movement of this quartet Hindemith coordinated a polarity of texture recalling baroque style with a twentieth-century technique, polytonality, to achieve a very sharply etched contrast between a melody and its accompaniment. The accompaniment, in the lower instruments, strums the chord of A major. The melody, played by the second violin, is very clearly in C major, being anchored on the first and fifth degrees of that key. The contrast is made even more vivid by the rhythmic differences in the two textural elements and by the fact that the accompaniment is plucked while the solo is played with the bow in a very legato style.

Polytonality is often used in neoclassic composition, since it tends to separate the component lines of a texture beyond the degree that pitch itself can accomplish. Bartók frequently uses polytonality, the *Diary of a Fly* from his *Mikrokosmos,* Book VI, being a clear-cut example in which the entire effect is dependent upon simple motives being set against each other in different keys. Milhaud also employs polytonality as a basic technique.

One of the most significant aspects of the neoclassic attitude is the publication of explanatory and didactic works dealing with contemporary techniques. We have already mentioned the systematization of expressionism by means of the tone-row. Strikingly enough, this took place just at the time that neoclassicism was making its first appearance in a definite manner. Two other outstanding composers of the present era have concerned themselves with codification: Béla Bartók and Paul Hindemith, both of them neoclassicists. Bartók, in his *Mikrokosmos,* has written a graded series of piano pieces using many contemporary devices for harmony and rhythm. These pieces are intended for the purposes of teaching piano. Hindemith, in his theoretical work *The Craft of Musical Composition* has made a notable contribution toward a harmonic system in which traditional and contemporary values can be reconciled and evaluated in relation to each other. In his idea of the *two-voice framework* he has proposed a norm for texture; in his idea of *harmonic fluctuation* he has provided a harmonic scheme for organizing basic structural units.

FORM IN NEOCLASSIC MUSIC

As we might expect, neoclassic music uses the forms of earlier periods, the sonata form, the rondo, the concerto grosso, the fugue, the chorale, the variation, the motet, etc. Moreover, some composers have been led to synthesize and coordinate various styles within a given piece, much as the Viennese classic composers did with the many styles available to them in the eighteenth century. Combining different styles in a composition has its pitfalls; if it is not done with skillful timing, the work may sound stylistically inconsistent and the composer will be open to the charge of eclecticism. Yet the values to be achieved by a wide range of expression are very rich; they can give contour and strength to the form.

One of the most successful works along these lines of synthesis, and one which has had a tremendously strong popular appeal is Bartók's Music for String Instruments, Percussion, and Celesta. We shall look at the structure of this piece in order to see how a neoclassic solution to the problem of form has been achieved.

1. The *first movement* is a fugue, worked out very tightly. The plan of the form is one of the most impressive solutions of the problem in all of modern music. It has no counterpart among the standard forms, yet it is thoroughly logical, and it is typical of Bartók's sense for structure. The diagram below shows the outline of the form:

EXAMPLE 8·20 Bartók: Music for Strings, Percussion, and Celesta; diagram: first movement

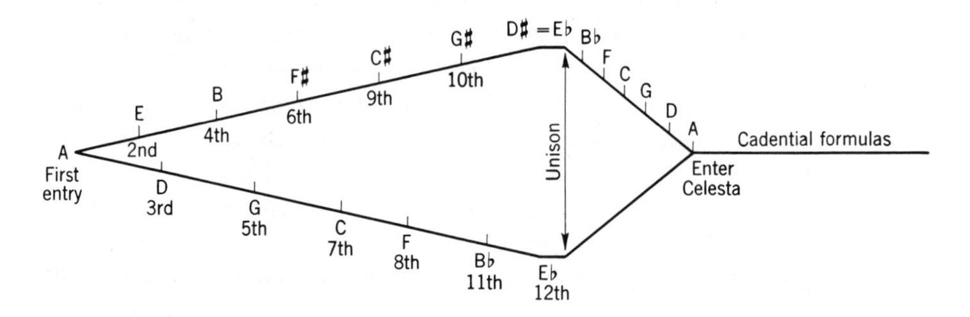

The most remarkable feature of this movement is the effectiveness with which Bartók has succeeded in directing movement forward to strong points of arrival. Notwithstanding the thoroughly dissonant harmony, a sense of progressing tonal centers is present. The entries of the subject explore systematically all the tonal centers of the chromatic scale. When the two streams of harmonic movement reach the point farthest away from the original tonal center, A, they have described a full circle and converge upon the tonal center, D♯–E♭. At this point the polyphonic texture disappears and an intensely powerful unison hammers out the E♭, the tone of arrival and the climax of the form. Reversing the build-up, the music returns to the original tonal center, A, in more relaxed fashion. Upon reaching the tonic, the final area of arrival in the movement, the music undergoes a striking change in texture. A curtain of sound created by the celesta, heard for the first time, and by shimmering strings introduces an element of textural stability not yet heard in the piece. The entries now begin and end on the tonic, giving the effect of being cadential formulas. There is a striking combination of styles in this movement: the neoclassic aspect is represented by the fugal manner and the tightly knit form; the chromaticism of the late nineteenth and early twentieth centuries saturates the harmonic idiom; at the return to A, the curtain of celesta and strings is frankly impressionistic.

Bartók's characteristic use of "wedge" shapes is manifest in this movement. In a wedge plan there is a point of departure that represents stability; this is generally the tonal center. The music progresses by stages away from this center and then returns. The diagram of the form given above shows a typical wedge formation. The subject of the fugue and the cadential formulas at the end of the movement represent this configuration melodically. Notice in Example 8·21*b* that the two lines moving together create a tone-row.

EXAMPLE 8·21 Bartók: Music for Strings, Percussion, and Celesta, first movement *

2. The *second movement* represents an electrifying contrast to the first. It is principally a dance, based on short, vigorous motives. The harmony, in contrast to the complete chromaticism of the first movement, is basically diatonic, with polytonal elaborations. Much is made of the percussive rhythms of folkloric music. The form is a clearly defined sonata form, as is shown in the following outline.

First key area	C	1–19	
Transition		20–68	
Second key area	G	69–185	(Note the broad cadences
Development		187–372	in G, 180–185)
Recapitulation Material of second key area at measure 412		373–520	

The key definition in the form is obvious; repetitions and cadences involving the tonal centers leave no doubt about harmonic points of reference. The principal expressive value is the dance quality. As such, then, this movement is quite in the spirit of a Beethoven or a Haydn sonata form. Moreover, the texture and part writing show the active manipulation of motives and the energetic contrasts that characterize Viennese classic style.

3. In the *third movement* again we have a tremendous contrast. The sound of the xylophone tapping away by itself at the beginning of this movement is one of the most unexpected and weird effects in all music, particularly as it follows the "down-to-earth" style of the second movement. A bit later the disembodied texture, created by totally different figures in viola, timpani, and xylophone, suggests expressionism, although the improvisatory style of the viola has folkloric associations. The entire movement is concerned with curious effects of sonority, and therefore recalls impressionism. The form, like the first movement, is a "wedge," this time worked out like a palindrome or mirror structure.

A. Improvisation	1–19
B. Lyric melody, first presented, then treated contrapuntally	20–44
C. Bell-like motive, treated percussively in many variations of texture	45–62
B. Return of lyric melody	63–75
A. Return of improvisation	76–83

Bartók, in this movement, has managed to keep the cadential sense very clear. This helps to bind the highly contrasted episodes into a smoothly continuous form. Each succeeding episode seems to come as a point of arrival, a cadential resolution to the movement of the preceding section.

4. The *finale* is a folk dance, an exhilarating summing up of the entire piece. The syncopations and cross-rhythms of folk music permeate the entire piece. The form is episodic, with rondolike refrains; contrasts are sharp; the melodic material is well defined, as dance tunes should be.

An interesting and amusing detail of style occurs in measures 262–270, where Bartók slips into a typical jazz break by giving a fresh nuance to the syncopations of his refrain theme. Throughout this last movement the sense of tonal center is more clear than in any previous movement. One might say that it is the harmonic area of arrival, then, for the whole composition, a relationship quite proper for a neoclassic concept.

The four movements of this work exhibit relationships between themselves that act to give the entire composition a special unity. We hear the subject of the opening movement in each of the succeeding movements: briefly and varied in the second movement; restated and developed at length in the B sections of the third movement; altered harmonically in the fourth movement to create a bolder, more diatonic effect, in keeping with the more open and assertive manner of the entire movement. Further, the four movements of the work show a pairing with respect to form: the first and third, with their qualities of instability assume the wedge form, while the second and fourth, with their powerful rhythmic drives, are organized respectively as sonata form and rondo. It is only in the last movement that the tonal center A, indicated in the first movement, is vigorously embodied with a strong flavor of the major mode. In this way, the final movement acts as an area of arrival for the entire work.

Some additional examples of neoclassic style in twentieth-century music follow:

Piston: String Quartet No. 3, first movement. Lean, transparent texture in this sonata-form movement accommodates the play of a vigorous figure grouped in irregular meters. (The measure count for the first twelve measures is: 7 7 6 6 5 6 6 6 8 6 5 6.) There is a sense of constant development, clear differentiation of material between the first and second key areas (in F and C, respectively) and a final confirmation of the home key at the end.

Stravinsky: *Symphony of Psalms.* This work shows a strong influence of baroque style. The first movement is set as a chorale with ornamental accompaniment; the second movement is a double fugue, one subject being assigned to the orchestra, the other to the chorus; the final movement is a choral fantasia in a number of episodes, arranged in something of a mirror order, as in the third movement in Bartók's Music for String Instruments, Percussion, and Celesta. The sense of key is very strong in this piece, with much conflict and wavering between major and minor, and especially between the tones E flat and E natural. Stravinsky's harmony, always sonorous, but not always set up in triads, governs his handling of the chorus. In chordal sections we hear a full, often edgy sound, spaced in the traditional distribution of choral music to achieve a balance of texture; occasionally, the chorus is used to declaim in unison or octaves; in the second movement, it engages in the active counterpoint of its fugue. Frequently, chords contain no third, so that the openness of fifths, fourths, and octaves governs the color. In this case, there seems to be a reference to music of the Ars antiqua and Ars nova periods.

Hindemith: *Das Marienleben* (The Life of Mary). Out of this cycle of fifteen songs set to poems by Rainer Maria Rilke, we have chosen the ninth, *The Marriage at Cana,* to illustrate a modern classicistic treatment of lyric material. This song is the climax of the cycle. The change from water to wine at the feast and its tragic implications are expressed by Hindemith in a monumental variation ricercar, recalling the contrapuntal techniques and structural layouts of the early Baroque era. To suggest the increasing gravity of the sense of the text, Hindemith composes the variations of the subject in augmentation, thus slowing the movement, until at the very end the subject appears in fragments. (See Beethoven, Symphony No. 3, second movement, for a similar effect.) Actually the sound fades to a single sustained tone by the voice, a typically romantic ending quite in keeping with the cryptic and grammatically involuted poetry of Rilke.

Ravel: *L'Heure espagnole.* This is a short opera that recalls the opera buffa of the eighteenth century in more ways than one. The story is typically buffa: among the suitors for the favors of Concepción, the wife of Torquemada the watchmaker, the winner is Ramiro, the muleteer, while the well-to-do bachelor Gonsalve and the banker Don Inigo both fail. Ravel has set this piece principally as a series of ensembles and short solo sections. The motive of the clocks gives Ravel the opportunity to compose many sections which have the regular repetitive structure one associates with the ticking and ringing of clocks. The total effect is a curious blend of eighteenth-century sophisticated comedy and tunefulness with Spanish local color and impressionistic techniques of composition.

See also the discussions of Hindemith's *Mathis der Maler* and Prokofiev's *Classical* Symphony at the beginning of this chapter.

New Systems in Twentieth-Century Music

During the twentieth century some composers have explored new ways of building scales and using instruments, ways which are different from the traditional usages of Western music. Impressionism, with its concern for fresh and evocative sonorities, gave a strong impetus to this trend, as did the knowledge of exotic musical cultures, such as Javanese, Indian, and Chinese. The striking effects of microtones—tones which are smaller than a half step—found in some folk music also stirred the imagination of modern composers. Below we have listed some of the representative experiments along these lines.

MICROTONES

An entire school, led by Alois Hába, was built up around the use of quarter tones by all types of performing media. Pianos with two full keyboards, tuned a quarter tone apart, were constructed to play this music. Other composers, such as Bartók and Bloch, have used microtones for incidental effects in music based otherwise upon the traditional chromatic scale.

NEW INSTRUMENTS AND NEW USES OF TRADITIONAL INSTRUMENTS

Among these may be mentioned Harry Partch's creation of an entire orchestra of new instruments, based largely on variations of older types, such as marimba, plucked string instruments, and percussion instruments. Some of these are tuned to a 43-tone scale. Also there are John Cage's prepared piano and Henry Cowell's manner of playing the strings of a piano as though they were a harp.

ELECTRONIC MUSICAL INSTRUMENTS

Since the development of radio and electronics many new instruments have been created that use electronic principles. Most of these have been modifications of the traditional instruments, such as keyboard, string, or wind, and have been intended principally for amplification of tone. The Theremin, an instrument which the performer plays by moving his hands through space near a control rod, is based upon a radio-wave principle. Interesting experiments have been made in which the possibilities of the tape recorder for altering and combining sounds were explored.

TOTAL ORGANIZATION

Twelve-tone music crystallized a technique in which all the tones of the chromatic scale were rigidly ordered in a series determined by the composer. This process, called *serialization,* has been applied in recent years to other aspects of musical composition such as duration of tones, strength of tones, and color. In such music, the composer uses his pre-established formula, his musical "genetic code," as a control for all action. Presumably, the listener will sense subconsciously that a special order is being projected, even though the immediate effect may seem very complex and the terms of the order or system may be scaled to very minute dimensions. Pierre Boulez in France and Karlheinz Stockhausen in Germany have been the leaders in this direction. Both are relatively young men, and it has been only in the past decade that their reputations and the spread of this school have grown to significant stature. Stockhausen has commented that only a study of his scores will bring about understanding of his music, that only a study of the performance will indicate adequate realization of the score, and that the listener need only hear, not understand. This means that the listener should use the general criteria of sound, movement, arrival, and expression to arrive at his own personal acceptance or rejection of the music, since the traditional embodiment of these criteria does not exist, as a rule, in music that represents this kind of total organization.

INDETERMINATE OR CHANCE MUSIC

Another kind of music making has been developing in the period since World War II. This involves certain fixed elements or procedures which are combined in performance with elements of improvisation or chance. Much depends upon the nature and relationship of these various elements. From the earliest days of music the art has grown through the interaction of preestablished material with freshly added ornamental material. Jazz is based upon this method, as well as much music before 1800. If the predetermined aspect is represented by a harmonic progression and by traditional musical instruments, then the chance element will most likely take shape in relatively familiar terms, as figures that emerge from the imagination of the performer based upon his own listening experiences. Lukas Foss's improvisation ensemble has proceeded along these lines. On the other hand, if the fixed elements are in themselves bizarre, perhaps involving sound sources not usually employed in musical composition, e.g., radios, tin cans, paper bags, or whatever may occur to the participants, then the random element itself will have a much greater impact of the unexpected and unusual; often the effects are intriguing, even unique. John Cage at the present time is a leader in this trend, which enjoys a great vogue throughout the musical world, especially among younger composers. Both for the total organization approach and for the indeterminate, traditional musical notation is inadequate; hence many variations and innovations in notation have been created to express instructions necessary for performance of these "studies."

For the listener, direction and purpose in this kind of music is not usually apparent; many of these experiments are directed to one of the fundamental appeals of music, *the power of sound to be evocative*. Thus, while they may appear intangible, they lie close to the wellsprings of musical experience. In each case, it is the inventiveness and warmth of the composer that make the work of art.

An early "experimental" work that has become something of a twentieth-century classic is Edgard Varèse's *Ionization*. This is written for a number of percussion instruments and other sound sources, such as bells, sirens, and automobile horns. Once we become accustomed to the startling effect of the sounds themselves, we can sense very clearly the phrase structure, statement and counterstatement, movement, arrival, climax, contrast, and continuity—all projected in sustained musical periods shaped by dynamic curves. Varèse's music has obviously grown idiomatically from the materials he has selected for his sound sources, and his judgment in disposing them results in an eloquent and unique work.

Summary

In retrospect, the modern period of music exhibits three phases: (1) continuation and intensification of tendencies already well developed in romantic music; (2) evaluation and codification of musical procedures; (3) exploration of new sounds and methods of organization. The first period extends to about 1920, the second period to about 1945–1950; the third phase, always present, became greatly expanded after World War II. It is notable that we find tremendous preoccupation with technique throughout the entire twentieth century. The romantic idea of self-expression, which was largely responsible for the development of individual styles, is no longer the basic motivating force in today's stylistic heterogeneity. Very often, the impression is given that a *modus operandi* is being sought, rather than a *modus vivendi*.

Briefly, we shall close with a summary of the principal features of the styles we have discussed:

1. **Impressionism**
   - *a. Quality of sound:* Interest in special effects of color, pervasive sonorities, exotic values
   - *b. Quality of movement:* Steady, moderate, level, without strong drive
   - *c. Expressive values:* Pictorialism, mood projection, prismatic effects, impressions of nature
   - *d. Technical resources:* Chromatic chords, modal scales, special effects of sonority

2. **Expressionism**
   a. *Quality of sound:* Hard, edgy, nonblended, frequently without core
   b. *Quality of movement:* Irregular, angular, explosive, highly tense
   c. *Expressive values:* Suggestive of inner states of tension, crises in the subconscious mind; subject matter sometimes turning to night, darkness, nightmares, unreality; parody
   d. *Technical resources:* Atonality, avoidance of traditional harmonic formulas; continuous spinning out; eventually tone-row technique
3. **Folkloric music**
   a. *Quality of sound:* Brilliant, striking colors, often harsh in effect, making strong immediate impact
   b. *Quality of movement:* Percussive, motoric; underlying regular beat grouped into varying measures; alternating at times with singsong lyric style
   c. *Expressive values:* Concern with the play of sounds and colors, based on a direct sensory appeal, but addressing itself to the analytic sense by subtle variations and imbalances; violence and lyricism contrasted
   d. *Technical resources:* Rhythms and figures based on folk-music patterns; the sounds of folk music; the melodic materials and scales of folk music; modality, polytonality, atonality; pandiatonism; massive effects of orchestration, often to create a percussive quality
4. **Parody**

   Parody, in its distortions, has some affinity with musical expressionism. It is less a style than an attitude. Hence, its resources, its qualities of sound and movement, and its expressive values will depend upon the object being parodied.
5. **Neoromanticism**

   The sound, movement, expression, and technical resources of neoromanticism resemble very closely those of the late romantic period, particularly the music of Brahms, Mahler, and Bruckner. The harmony makes use of greater dissonance, atonal or polytonal resources at times, and the scoring is more brilliant or exotic now and then. But the fundamental expressive aim is not materially different from that of sixty or seventy years past.
6. **Neoclassicism**
   a. *Qualities of sound:* Tendency toward transparency without loss of core; clarity without special search for brilliance; wide range of harmonic usage, from well-defined minor-major sounds to modality, polytonality, and atonality
   b. *Qualities of movement:* Inclined to be steady, purposeful, with indications of drive to rhythmic and harmonic points of arrival; sense of phrase and period structure quite clear, often with strongly maintained relation of statement and counterstatement
   c. *Expressive values:* Play of sounds, figures, gestures against each other without special emotional or picturesque connotations; feeling for self-contained, clearly projected design; desire for balance, codification, reconciliation within a large framework

d. *Technical resources:* Forms, styles, manners of preceding style periods, handled harmonically with resources developed in the twentieth century; considerable reliance upon contrapuntal procedures; development and working over of motives in the manner of baroque and classic music.

Genres and Compositions Discussed in This Chapter

Orchestral music

Bartók: Music for String Instruments, Percussion, and Celesta Concerto for Violin and Orchestra; *Berg:* Concerto for Violin and Orchestra; *Bloch: Schelomo,* Rhapsody for Violoncello and Orchestra; *Copland: Appalachian Spring; El Salón México; Debussy: Fêtes* from Nocturnes for Orchestra; *De Falla: In the Generalife* from *Nights in the Gardens of Spain; Delius: On Hearing the First Cuckoo in Spring; Hindemith:* Symphony, *Mathis der Maler; Honegger: Pacific 231; Milhaud: La Création du Monde; Piston:* Symphony No. 2; *Prokofiev: Classical* Symphony; *Ravel: Bolero; Lever du jour* from *Daphnis et Chloé* Suite No. 2; *La Valse; Sessions:* Symphony No. 2; *Strauss, Richard: Don Juan; Don Quixote; Till Eulenspeigel's Merry Pranks; Stravinsky: Le Sacre du printemps; Thomson: The Plow That Broke the Plains; Varèse: Ionization; Webern:* Symphony, Op. 21

Chamber music

Hindemith: String Quartet No. 3; *Piston:* String Quartet No. 3; *Ravel:* String Quartet in F; *Riegger:* String Quartet No. 1; *Schönberg: Pierrot lunaire;* Serenade, Op. 24; String Quartet No. 4; String Trio; *Stravinsky: L'Histoire du soldat;* Octet; *Thompson:* String Quartet in D minor

Piano music

Bartók: Diary of a Fly from *Mikrokosmos* Sonata; *Debussy: Préludes* for Piano; *Ravel: Ondine* from *Gaspard de la Nuit; Valses Nobles et Sentimentales; Schönberg:* Six Little Piano Pieces

Opera

Britten: Peter Grimes; Berg: Wozzeck; Debussy: Pelléas et Mélisande; Ravel: L'Heure espagnole; Strauss, Richard: Elektra; Salomé

Choral music

Debussy: Sirènes from Nocturnes for Orchestra; *Stravinsky: Les Noces; Symphony of Psalms*

Song

Debussy: Clair de lune from *Fêtes galantes; Hindemith: Von der Hochzeit zu Kana* from *Das Marienleben; Schönberg: Pierrot lunaire*

Suggestions for Critical Listening

1. *Sound*
   a. Range: middle or extreme registers; degree of fluctuation
   b. Amount: number of parts; constant or varied
   c. Strength: degree of strength; constant or varied
   d. Timbre: traditional or nontraditional; special effects
2. *Movement*
   a. Pace: speed; regularity
   b. Articulation: degree of separation between tones
   c. Intensity: vigorous, gentle, degree of fluctuation
   d. Meter: duple, triple, shifting, indeterminate
   e. Delineation of phrases
3. *Arrival*
   a. Cadential effects: how achieved
   b. Distinctness of arrival effect: clear, doubtful
4. *Melody*
   a. Types and size of intervals prominent in melody
   b. Performance of melodic line: one voice, several voices sharing
   c. Degree of melodic clarity or shape: well defined or not
5. *Texture*
   a. Traditional textures used or not used
   b. Degree of density or sparseness of texture
6. *Harmony*
   a. System used: Traditional triads, sevenths, etc.; whole-tone; modal; polytonal; pandiatonic; chromatic; atonal; tone-row; microtones; indeterminate pitch sounds; intervals other than twelve chromatic tones
   b. Tonal center: key; prominence; as point of arrival; clearly discernible, not clearly discernible
   c. Degree of consonance and dissonance
7. *Structure*
   a. Clarity of punctuation of phrases
   b. Relationship of statement and counterstatement: reception; variation; contrast
   c. Degree of sectionalization
   d. Return of previously heard material
8. *Stylistic qualities* (*see summary*)

Suggested Listening Projects

1. **Bartók, Quartet No. 5, first movement.**

Listen for: Percussive treatment of strings, contrasting with a liquid flow of short motives; intensive development of all material; tendency to return to basic thematic material again and again in a very clear manner;

clear effects of arrival, often signaled by the unison passage heard first at the beginning; setting of a tonal center by repetition of opening tone; use of the dynamic curve; dancelike material.

2. **Hindemith, *Mathis der Maler* (Matthias the Painter), first movement.**

   Listen for: Traditional handling of textures and phrase structure; well-defined tonal centers, without use of traditional dominant-tonic cadences; clear organization of sonata form by key shifts and thematic contrast; easily grasped development of motives; frequent use of unusual, dissonant harmonic combinations and angular melodic progressions to lend a contemporary flavor; rather long melodic lines.

3. **Berg, *Wozzeck*, Act I, scene 3, Military music and Marie's Lullaby.**

   Listen for: Mixture of highly dissonant, unstable harmony with many touches of traditional triad harmony; richness of sonorities; touches of impressionistic color; focus given to the unstable harmony by the military rhythms and figures; *Sprechstimme* contrasted with very graceful vocal lines in Marie's lullaby; balanced, clearly articulated phrase structure in the lullaby; Wagnerian touches in the use of rising sequences and the dynamic curve; the generally direct, vigorous emotional impact of the music.

4. **Copland, Symphony No. 3, second movement.**

   Listen for: Characteristic antiphonal, concertato treatment of instruments and groups of instruments; diatonic style of the themes; brevity of the motive, making it suitable for development; layering of textures rather than blending; contrasts of color between brass, wind, and strings, often emphasized by unison passages or brilliant registers; dancelike character of piece, contrasted with songlike manner of trio.

APPENDIX I

Musical Notation

Notation of Pitch

Music is notated upon a staff of five lines and four spaces; notes appearing above or below the staff are written on *leger lines:*

EXAMPLE 1 The musical staff and leger lines

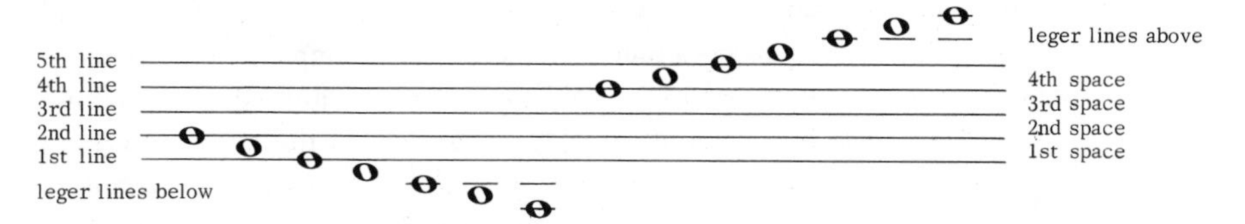

The pitch of tones upon the staff is located by *clefs.* A clef is a sign that represents a tone of a given pitch. Other notes are reckoned upward or downward from the clef tone. In Example 2 a section of the piano keyboard is pictured and the positions of the three clefs, *F, C,* and *G,* are given:

EXAMPLE 2 Clefs and their positions on the piano keyboard

a. Section of piano keyboard

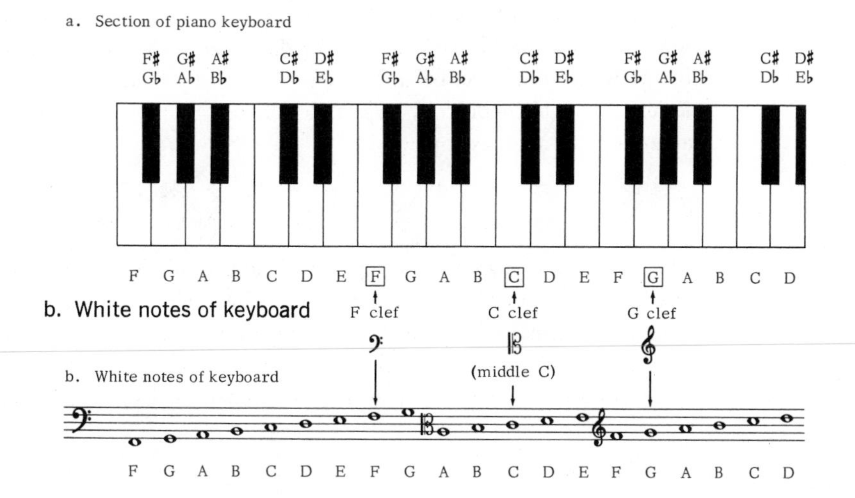

b. White notes of keyboard

In the clef notation of Example 2, F below middle C is fixed on the fourth line; middle C is fixed on the third line; G above middle C is fixed on the second line. The F clef on the fourth line is often referred to as the *bass* clef; the C clef on the middle line is called the *alto* clef; and the G clef on the second line is designated as the *treble* clef. These names refer to the voices that have required these clefs for a proper notation of music in their performing ranges. It is possible to use F, C, and G clefs to fix their respective tones on other lines, but this has rarely been done in music of the last two centuries. Most music employs the F and G clefs exclusively.

The tones written in Example 2*b* all represent the *white* notes of the keyboard. Among the white notes we find, in any octave, two half steps: between E and F and between B and C. All the other steps are whole steps. The white keys of the piano will give us a major scale starting on C.

Black keys are placed between two keys that form a whole step. The black keys divide the interval into two half steps, so that if we should play all the keys in order, we would hear a scale composed entirely of half steps, a chromatic scale. To represent the tones of the black keys in notation, *signs of alteration* are used: (1) a *sharp* (♯), which raises a tone a half step, and (2) a *flat* (♭), which lowers a tone a half step (see Example 2*a* for chromatic tones). A previously raised or lowered tone may be returned to its natural (white key) form by a *natural sign* (♮). Note that on the keyboard certain raised tones will sound the same as certain lowered tones. For example a sharped D (D♯) is the same as a flatted E (E♭). The choice among these depends upon the signature of the key in which the music is written.

In order to notate music that uses scales other than C major, we must incorporate alterations into the notation. For example, if we wish to write in a major key using E♭ as the key note or tonic, we shall have to alter three tones in order to arrange the scale in the following way:

1 1 ½ 1 1 1 ½
E♭ F G A♭ B♭ C D E♭

E♭, A♭, and B♭ are the tones altered from the natural series. These are gathered, for convenience, at the left-hand side of the staff, just after the clef. They constitute a *key signature,* in this case of three flats. If we should start on F, we would need one flat for the major scale, i.e., B♭. Starting on B♭, we would need two, B♭ and E♭, etc. The same procedure applies to minor scales, although the order of steps and half steps is different. The scale of C minor is given as an example:

1 ½ 1 1 ½ 1½(1) (1)½
C D E♭ F G A♭ B(♭) C

The numbers in parentheses represent the *natural* minor scale; the other numbers represent the *harmonic* minor scale, which borrows its leading tone from the major scale on the same beginning note, in this case C major. The natural or the sharp for the leading tone is always written in when it occurs, and it is not included in the key signature. Example 3 gives major and minor scales up to four sharps and flats. The alterations in the parentheses (♯) and (♭) are carried over into the signature. In the signature each alteration covers all octaves of the altered tone. Thus, the F♯ in G major means that all F's are to be sharped.

EXAMPLE 3 Major and minor scales and their key signatures

a. Major scales

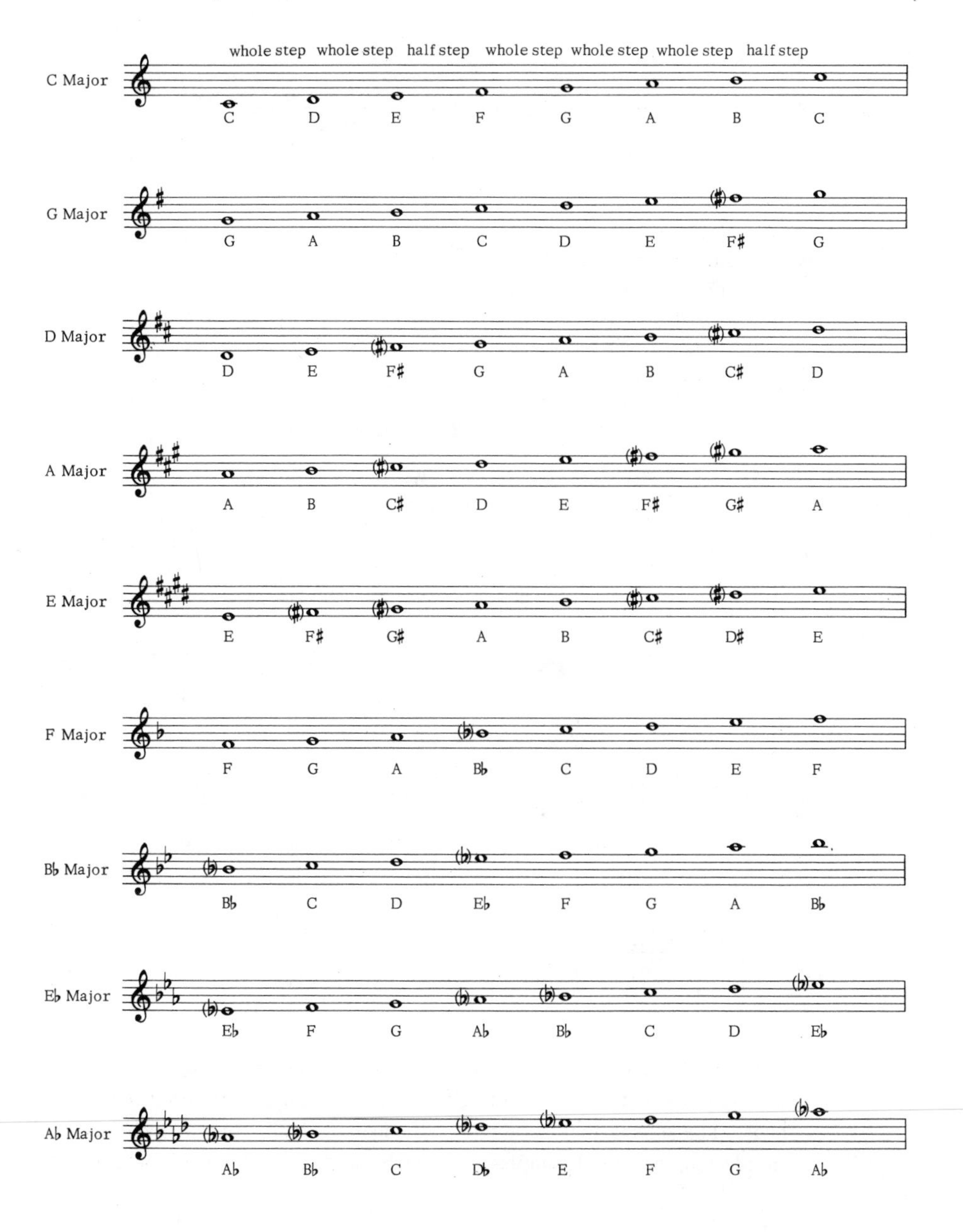

b. Minor scales (harmonic)

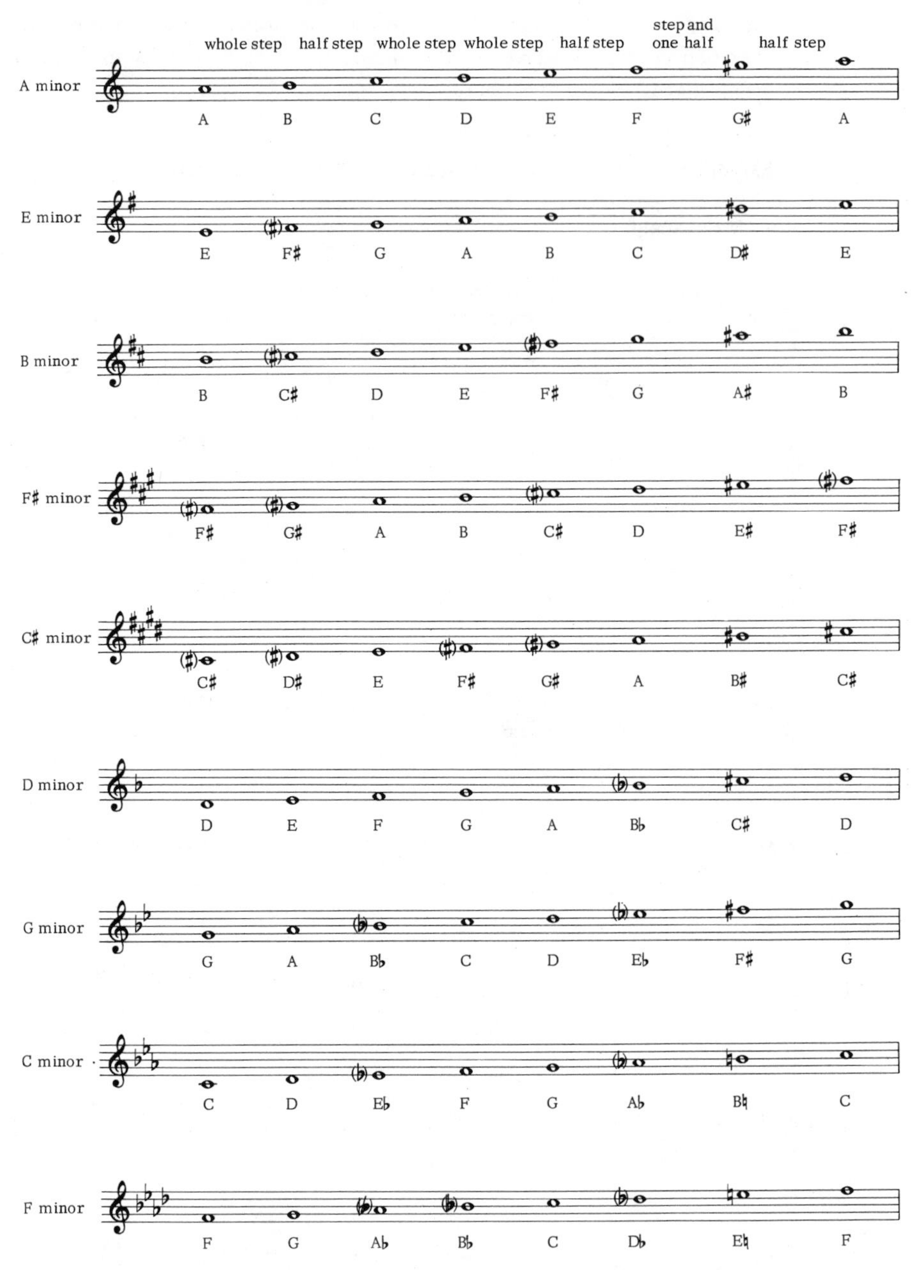

Using the keyboard chart and the clefs, a beginner in music reading will find it possible to test for himself certain musical effects discussed in this book. The effects include ranges of voices, melodic contours, chords, and simple progressions. Examples that can be studied in this way include:

Chapter 2, Examples 2·1, 2·16, 2·19, 2·36 to 2·45, 2·47
Chapter 3, Example 3·2
Chapter 4, Examples 4·1 to 4·4
Chapter 5, Examples 5·11, 5·13 to 5·15
Chapter 7, Examples 7·2, 7·4
Chapter 8, Examples 8·10*a*, 8·11

Notation of Time

Musical tones are written in various ways to indicate their duration. Our notation is basically arranged in a duple order, as follows:

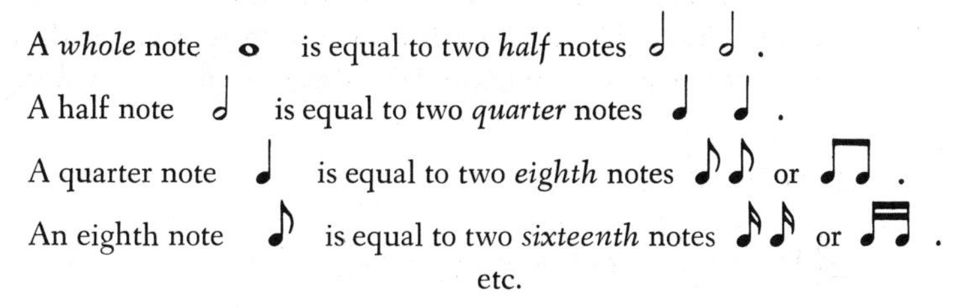

In performance, a time value is established for one type of note, according to *tempo* instructions (see page 32) given by the composer. The other values are then played in length as multiples or dividends of that tone. For example, if a half note is supposed to be two seconds in length, a whole note will require four seconds, a quarter note one second, and an eighth note one-half second. The following example illustrates the relative lengths of the notes, based upon a half note of two seconds in duration:

EXAMPLE 4 Relative duration of tones

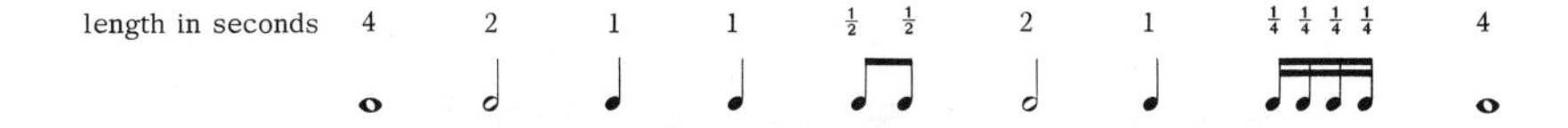

The time notation described above is based upon a division of length by 2. In order to express triple division, we add a dot to a tone. The dot denotes that the tone will have one-half of its original length added to it. Thus a dotted quarter note will be one and a half times as long as a nondotted quarter and three times as long as a nondotted eighth. Dotted tones are notated as follows:

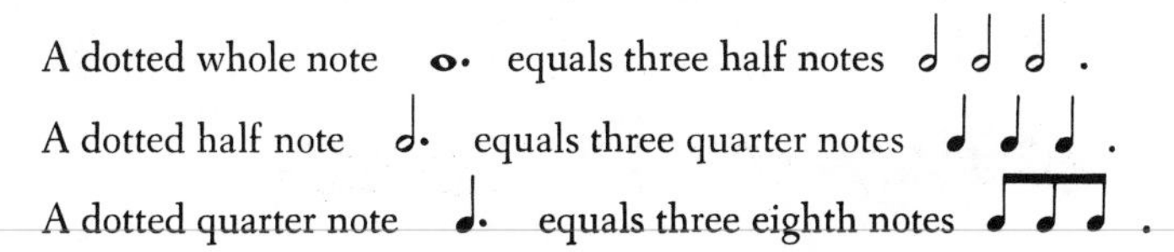

Example 5 illustrates the relative lengths of dotted and nondotted tones.

EXAMPLE 5 Lengths of dotted and nondotted tones

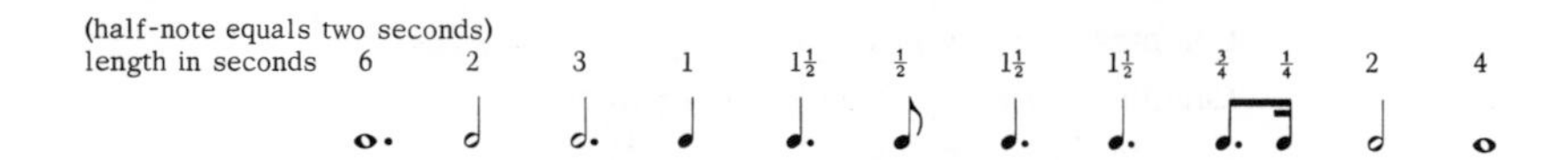

At the beginning of a piece or a movement of a larger composition, on the first staff, we find a numerical figure just to the right of the key signature. From time to time, within a piece, there may be other such figures. These figures ($\frac{4}{4}$, $\frac{6}{8}$, etc.) designate the kind of *measure* from which the piece or section is built. The measure is a short span of time, marked off by a *bar line* | ; the figures mentioned above designate the internal structure of the

EXAMPLE 6 Measures

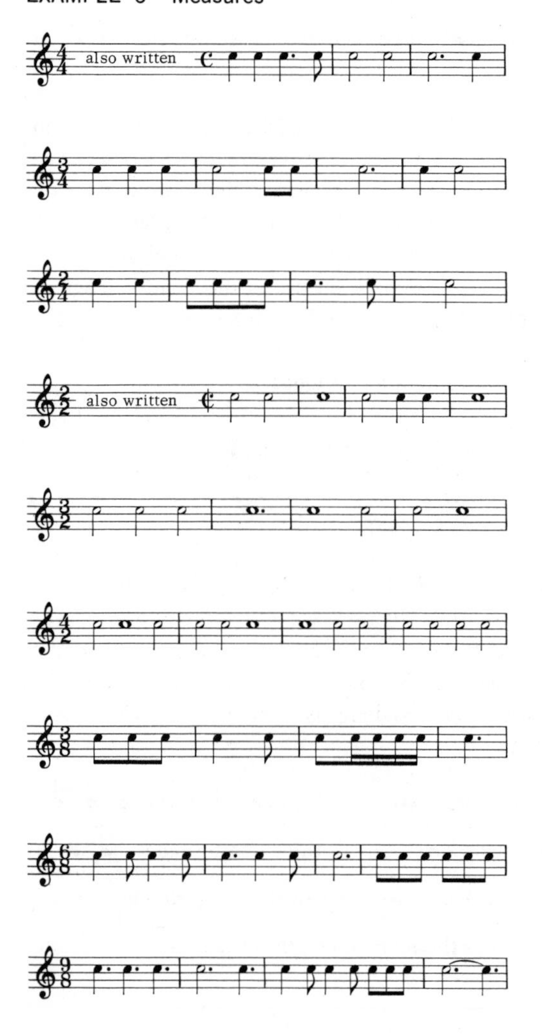

measure. The lower figure tells us which kind of note is to be used as the unit of counting; half notes are designated as 2, quarter notes as 4, and eighth notes as 8. The upper figure tells us how many of such notes are to be included in a single measure: 2, 3, 4, 6, 8, etc. Example 6 illustrates a number of different measures. The numerical figure that designates a measure is called a *time signature.*

The basic principles of musical notation explained above should be helpful to the beginning music reader in working out some of the simpler illustrations in this book. Musical notation is a very complex process. It has changed a great deal throughout the centuries. Each system of musical notation, each change or elaboration, has been developed in order to allow musicians to communicate effectively with one other. Musical notation is a set of signs by which the composer can give an approximate idea of how he would like to have his music sound. In some cases, the instructions are laid down as accurately and as minutely as possible. This is especially so in music of the nineteenth and twentieth centuries. Earlier, notation was often a kind of shorthand, a blueprint, as it were, which the performer would use only as a general guide to procedure and expression; he was free to add a considerable amount of his own invention to the notated music, as is done today upon the lead sheet of a jazz score. Such notation required not only skill in reading and performance, but an intimate knowledge of the style and considerable ability to compose and improvise.

No matter how precise the notation may be, it can give only an approximation of what is to be said musically. A performer may play a score as accurately as he can, in pitch and in time; yet there will always be minor variations and nuances that give special character to a performance. That explains why two performances of the same work, both reasonably faithful to what is written down, will sound quite different in spirit.

APPENDIX II

Ranges of Orchestral Instruments

(Notated as Sounded)

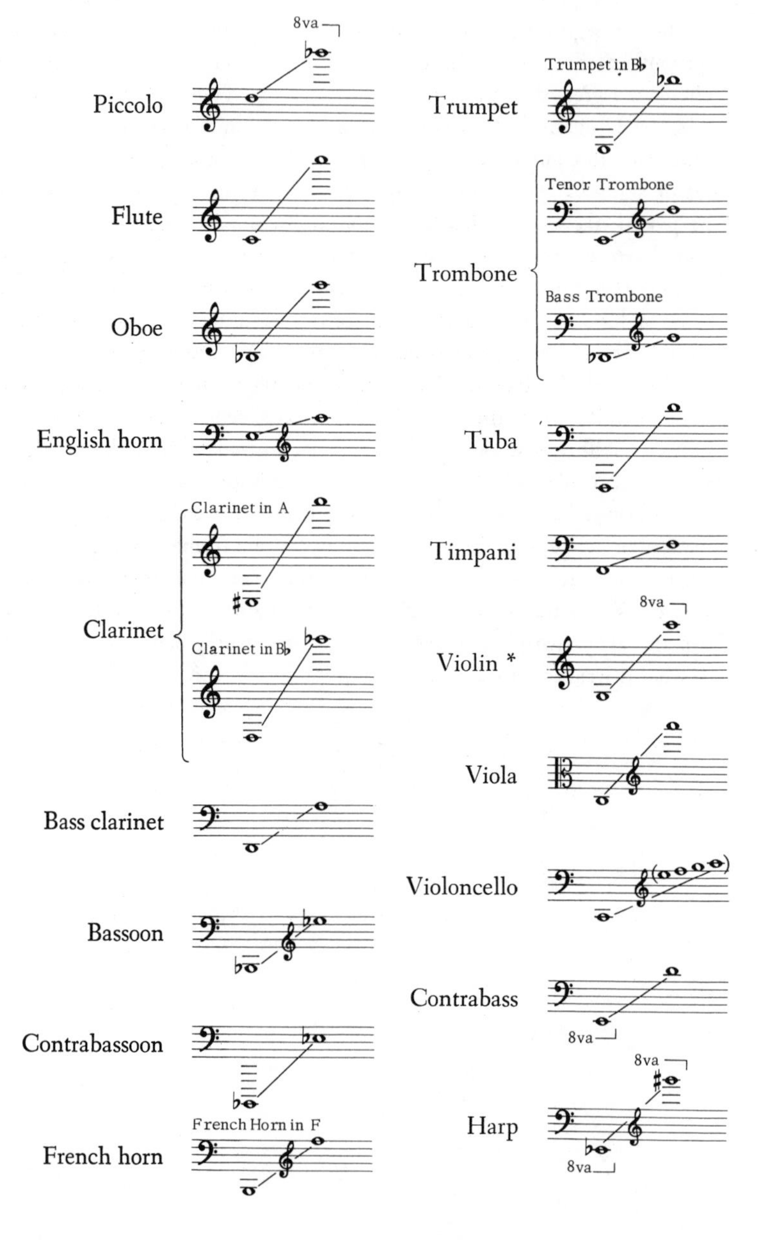

* There is no fixed upper range for the violin family, i.e., violin, viola, violoncello, contrabass.

General Glossary of Terms

In addition to terms in common use, this glossary defines historical terms and special words employed in this book. (Glossary terms are not included in the Index.)

a cappella: Literally, "for the chapel"; hence without accompaniment. Applied to choral singing without instruments.

accelerando: Becoming faster in tempo.

accidental: A prefixed sign which alters the pitch of a tone. (*See* natural, sharp, flat.)

ad libitum: "At will." Indicates a style of performance in which strict metric regularity is abandoned for a freer quality of movement. Applies also to a voice or part which may be included or omitted at will.

Alberti bass: A simple accompaniment for the left hand of a keyboard instrument, consisting of chord figurations in a narrow range. The Alberti bass was named after Domenico Alberti, an Italian keyboard composer of the mid-eighteenth century. This kind of accompaniment accommodates a simple style of music, especially the singing-allegro much preferred by amateurs in the early classic period and later.

alleluia: A melismatic passage, expressing jubilation and praise.

allemande: A dance of moderate pace, rather heavy quality of movement, duple meter; German in origin.

alto: Voices of upper middle register are called *alto voices*. This applies to singers, violas, horns, clarinets, and other instruments.

anthem: Originally, a sacred choral composition with English words from the scriptures; now applied to sacred or solemn compositions for chorus.

antiphon: A type of plainsong, derived originally from antiphonal or alternating manner of performance (solo versus group).

arco: Literally, "arch" or "bow"; applied, in string performance, to playing with the bow.

aria: A composition for solo singer and accompaniment, generally of considerable length with much melodic elaboration; also applied to instrumental music using the style of the aria. Either an independent piece or part of a larger work.

aria da capo: The standard form for the Italian opera aria of the late Baroque era; it consisted of a principal section, a contrasting middle section, and a return to the principal section, often with elaborations. *Da capo* means "to the head" (beginning) once more.

armonia perfetta: In later Renaissance and Baroque times, the major triad.

Ars antiqua: The polyphonic style of the twelfth and thirteenth centuries, characterized by use of the rhythmic modes.

Ars nova: The polyphonic style of the fourteenth century, characterized by the use of duple and triple meter and by complex relationships of rhythm that broke down the system of rhythmic modes.

a tempo: An indication for the performer to resume the original pace after slowing down or speeding up.

atonal: Pertaining to or characterized by harmony that gives no indication of tonal center or avoids procedures that tend to define tonal centers.

augmented triad: A three-note chord consisting of an augmented fifth and a major third above the lowermost note.

authentic cadence: The strongest harmonic effect of arrival. It involves dominant with 5 in bass moving to tonic, and usually 7 moving to 8 or 2 to 1 in uppermost voice.

authentic mode: A mode in which the final occurs as the highest or lowest note of the range or scale.

bagpipe: A style which imitates the effect of the bagpipe, consisting of a drone or sustained tone in the bass, above which the melody plays the characteristic flourishes. Also called musette.

ballad opera: English comic opera of the eighteenth century.

band: A large instrumental ensemble using no strings (except occasionally double-bass).

bass: Usually designates the lowermost voice of an ensemble if the range of that voice lies in the bass (F) clef; applied also to human voices and to the lowermost representatives of instrumental families: cello, string bass, bassoon (and double bassoon), bass trombone, and tuba. Sometimes the very lowest voices are designated as *contrabass*.

basso continuo: *See* continuo.

beat: A pulse or stroke which, in a series, helps establish the quality of movement, involving pace and accent.

binary form: *See* two-reprise form.

blues: Originally an important type of early American folksong and folk music, now a jazz style; characterized by certain tones in the melody or harmony that do not correspond to Western diatonic scales, i.e., the *blue* notes, which are obtained by lowering or flatting a given note.

boogie-woogie: A type of fast blues characterized by a driving beat in duple time, over an ostinato bass that moves regularly through tonic, subdominant, and dominant harmonies.

bop: A form of jazz composition developed in the late 1940s; characterized by rather complex harmonies and rhythms, and striking scoring.

bourrée: A popular dance of the Baroque era, in quick duple time, with a short upbeat.

brass instruments: A family of instruments, constructed of metal, producing their tones by lip vibration against a metal mouthpiece. The family includes cornets, trumpets, French horns, trombones, and tubas. The bugle is also a brass instrument.

caccia: Literally "hunt." A canonic piece of the fourteenth century, whose text describes a hunt, a pastoral scene, a market place, or some other aspect of picturesque life. The music often has touches of realistic imitation of the text.

cadence: A pause or stopping point, usually applied to a harmonic progression.

cadential formula: A harmonic phrase which proceeds through the cycle of departure-movement-arrival, as represented by:

1 Tonic harmony — 2 subdominant harmony
3 Leading-tone harmony — 4 tonic

cadenza: A section in improvisatory style, which allows the performer freedom to elaborate while the accompaniment pauses; in solo music a section resembling a cadenza in style.

caesura: A point of arrival; a resting point. Variable in its action, comparable to the comma, semicolon, or period of a sentence.

canon: A strict or literal imitation by one voice of a preceding voice, at a prescribed interval of pitch and time.

cantata: Literally, a "sung piece." A composition, sacred or secular, for soloists and/or chorus and instruments, containing a number of individual pieces—chorus, solos, recitatives, chorales, sinfonias—at the discretion of the composer.

cantus firmus: Literally, "fixed song." The melody used as a framework upon which a composition was built.

canzona francese: An instrumental paraphrase of the French chanson; the ancestor of many of the instrumental forms of the seventeenth and eighteenth centuries.

cembalo: German and Italian name for the harpsichord.

chaconne: A dance in moderately slow triple time, used characteristically as a pattern for a series of variations. The element might be a melodic line, a harmonic progression, or a recurrent bass line. Similar to the passacaglia.

chanson: French secular vocal composition.

chorale: Hymn tune of the German Protestant church; also, composition using a chorale as a cantus firmus.

chorale prelude: An organ piece based upon a chorale tune and performed as a prelude or introduction to the singing of the chorale tune itself by a Lutheran congregation. An important vehicle for variation and elaboration in the baroque music of Germany.

chords: A vertical combination of tones; also refers to figurations made up of familiar combinations, such as triads and seventh chords.

chord of tension: Generally, a chord which contains some element of instability, such as a tritone, second, seventh, augmented sixth, or ninth. These intervals all call for resolution.

chromatic: Referring to the presence of alterations in the harmony or melody. (*See* natural, sharp, flat, chromatic scale.)

chromatic scale: The scale which uses all twelve chromatic tones, as, for example, from D to C♯.

clavecin: French word for harpsichord.

clavier: Any keyboard instrument.

clef: A sign placed upon a staff to locate the position of tones. Originally these signs were letters: G above middle C, middle C, and F below middle C. The clefs presently in use are treble (G on second line), alto (C on middle line), tenor (C on fourth line), bass (F on fourth line).

clockwork: Refers to mechanical instruments whose music is programmed on a rotating wheel or similar device. Also may be applied to music which imitates the simple precise manner of a clockwork instrument. The eighteenth century produced many elaborate clockwork devices, including musical instruments.

coda: Literally, "tailpiece." A section at the end of a movement, intended to provide a satisfactory summing up and conclusion.

color: The special quality or qualities inherent in tones produced by various instruments and voices, singly or together; qualified by such terms as *brilliant, rich, muffled, dark, reedy, transparent, edgy.*

commedia dell'arte: Italian improvised comedy of the Renaissance, of which opera buffa was an offshoot. Built on stereotyped plots and characters.

concertante: The principal or solo instruments in an ensemble.

concertato: A style in which the participating voices and instruments "compete" with each other in an active give-and-take; first applied to early seventeenth-century vocal music with instruments.

concertino: The solo group in a concerto grosso.

concerto: An extended composition for solo instrument or instruments and orchestra, usually in three movements.

concerto grosso: A concerto in which the "grosso" signifies the tutti, and the concertino is a small group of soloists.

conjunct interval: A melodic interval that gives the impression of moving by step. The largest conjunct interval is the major second; anything smaller—minor second, microtone—gives a conjunct impression. Anything larger—minor third or more—gives the impression of movement by leap.

consonant: A relative term, generally equated with harmonic stability or euphony: applied to harmonic intervals. Standards of consonance have varied during the history of Western music.

continuo: The bass part in a baroque composition, usually played by a keyboard instrument (or lute) which provides the chords indicated in a figured bass, reinforced by a cello or viola da gamba.

contrast: The effect achieved when two musical elements are placed in a bold or significant juxtaposition with each other. Contrast may be direct and immediate, as between two different melodic motives, or it may be long-range, as between two important keys or two different movements. The tension and the effects of contrast contribute importantly to musical structure.

contredanse: A quick dance in duple time, often used in finales.

cool jazz: An outgrowth of bop that carried forward the experimental and inventive trend.

counterpoint: The placing of distinctive musical lines against each other simultaneously.

coup d'archet: Stroke of the bow. Powerful unison passage sometimes used to begin a large orchestral work.

courante: A moderately quick dance in triple time, employing momentary shifts in accent; French in origin.

crescendo: Increase in strength or loudness of sound.

dances: See pages 39, 132, 169–170.

decelerando: Becoming slower in tempo.

deceptive cadence: A cadence in which the expected chord of resolution is displaced by some other harmony, leaving the ear not quite satisfied, requiring further cadential action.

decrescendo: Decrease in strength or loudness of sound, also *diminuendo.*

detaché: Performed so that the successive tones are separated clearly from each other but not markedly so. (*See* legato, staccato.)

development: Working over of melodic material by (1) breaking it up into its motives, (2) re-forming motives into new phrases, (3) changing the shape of motives, (4) directing the harmony into shifting key patterns. These procedures are usually found in the section following the exposition of a sonata form, but they are constantly used in almost any large composition. Specifically, the X section of a sonata form.

diatonic scale: A scale of seven different tones, containing five whole steps and two half steps arranged so that the half steps are placed a fourth or fifth apart. The effect of a diatonic scale is one of evenness and balance.

diminished triad: A three-note chord consisting of a diminished fifth and a minor third above the lowermost note.

diminuendo: *See* decrescendo.

diminution: Presentation of a subject in shortened note values.

disjunct interval: A melodic interval larger than a second.

dissonance: A relative term, generally equated with harmonic instability, or sometimes with *disagreeable* or *unpleasant* sound; applied to harmonic intervals. Standards of dissonance have varied during the history of Western music. (*See also* consonant.)

divertimento: *See* serenade.

Dixieland jazz: *See* New Orleans jazz.

doctrine of the affections: An aesthetic theory of the seventeenth and eighteenth centuries in which certain musical figures were considered apt for various expressive and rhetorical purposes; one affection was maintained throughout a given movement.

dominant: The fifth degree of a scale or key; the triad, seventh, or ninth chord built upon the dominant degree.

downbeat: An accented tone, usually found at the beginning of a measure or upon a normally stressed beat.

duet, duo: A composition for two performers.

duplum: A part above the tenor in Ars antiqua music.

dynamic curve: A means of organizing a large section of music by constant growth in tension, generally leading to a significant climax, or, conversely, by constant decrease to a point of minimum action.

dynamics: The strength of sound. Dynamic signs include:

pp	pianissimo	very soft
p	piano	soft
mp	mezzo piano	moderately soft
mf	mezzo forte	moderately loud
f	forte	loud
ff	fortissimo	very loud
sf	sforzando	sudden, short, strong accent

echo: Repetition of a figure, with a sharp drop in strength of sound.

electronic music: Music produced by means of electronic sound media, which permit a greater range of sound control and experimentation than is possible with traditional instruments.

Empfindsamkeit: *See* Sensibility.

endless melody: A term applied to Wagner's style in which motives are linked together so that a clear sense of punctuation is avoided, thus creating a very broad phase of melodic movement.

enharmonic: refers to the notation of a tone in two possible ways, for example, as G♯ or A♭. At the piano, enharmonic tones have the same pitch.

episode: In rondo form, a section contrasting with the principal theme or refrain.

estampie: An important dance and song form of later medieval times. It is built structurally in a series of repeated phrases or sections.

étude: Literally, a "study." A short piece, developing one particular type of figuration, designed for pedagogical purposes. In the nineteenth century études were sometimes written for concert performance.

exposition: In sonata form, Part I, comprising key areas I and II.

expressionism: An early twentieth-century school of composition concerned with expression of strongly subjective feelings, often reflecting subconscious imagery; characterized by freely treated dissonances, angular melodic lines, irregular rhythms, and sparse texture.

familiar style: Refers to choral music composed so that the poetic and musical meter coincide, one tone to a syllable, and the voices carry out a single-action isometric pattern.

fandango: A Spanish dance in moderately quick triple time.

fanfare: A flourish upon the notes of the major triad, usually performed by brass instruments, with occasional accompaniment of drums. Frequently imitated by other instruments in music of the classic style.

fantasia: A work of improvisatory character, usually for keyboard (harpsichord, organ); brilliant virtuoso passages, harmonic explorations, irregular qualities of movement.

fauxbourdon: A technique of early fifteenth-century music in which the upper voices move parallel to the lowermost voice at intervals of thirds and sixths; an early stage of the triad system of harmony.

feet: Metric units applied to poetry and taken over in medieval times by music. (*See* Chapter 2.)

figured bass: A bass line in which the chords to be provided above were indicated by numbers that specified certain intervals.

final: The tonic of a mode.

finale: Last movement of a sonata, symphony, quartet, or other multimovement work; also applied to the final section of an operatic act.

flamenco: Spanish gypsy music, a prominent feature of which is a progression of chords that "slide" up and down a scale, reflecting the fingering technique of the guitar; highly improvisatory and colorful.

flat: A sign (♭) which lowers by a semitone any note before which it is placed.

folkloric music: Music in a style that took shape during the latter part of the nineteenth century, particularly in Eastern European countries; characterized by simple melodic material, vigorous rhythms, and striking and brilliant textures and colors.

free imitation: Imitation in which each entering voice moves freely after presenting the subject, which itself may be varied.

free organum: Organum in which the added voices move in different directions from the cantus firmus, retaining much the same rhythmic pattern.

French overture: The instrumental number which preceded operas and ballets in French baroque theater performances; a slow ceremonious opening section, using dotted rhythms, followed by a quick imitative section, in the manner of a canzona.

frottola: Popular rather than courtly Italian vocal composition of the late fifteenth and early sixteenth centuries; a predecessor of the madrigal.

fugue: Literally, "flight"; hence, a composition in which voices follow or chase each other. Strictly speaking, fugue is a process in which a theme or subject is presented and worked over in contrapuntal imitation by two or more parts. This process lent its name to pieces so composed. Fugal imitation is not as thorough, nor as exact, as canonic imitation.

galant style: The light, popular, elegant style that dominated musical taste in the later eighteenth century. It was characterized by light, simple textures, ingratiating melodies, song and dance idioms, contrasts, and mixing of affective values. It was opposed to the learned style and to the unity of affective value of the Baroque era. It was also called the *free* style as opposed to the *strict*.

gavotte: A French dance in moderately quick duple time; a typical feature is its beginning in the middle of a measure, with an upbeat of two quarter notes; well-marked divisions in the phrasing to reflect the steps of the dance itself.

Gesamtkunstwerk: Term used by Wagner to designate the merging of music, language, staging, and pantomime to create a comprehensive work of art.

gigue: A quick dance in six-eight or nine-eight, often treated imitatively. English in origin.

give-and-take: A texture that is basically homophonic, but which shows many aspects of contrapuntal treatment; the melodies are shared between the component voices; incidental imitations enter and disappear; the accompaniment figures have distinct melodic interest. This type of texture is one of the important features of the classic style.

grace note: A short note, ornamenting a principal note which follows it. Grace notes are not counted in the metrical notation of a measure.

ground bass: A melody given to the bass, repeated many times, over which the treble instruments play variations.

half cadence: A harmonic pause upon the dominant, equivalent to a comma or semicolon in language.

harmonic series: When a tone is sounded, the vibrating body (string, reed, pipe, membrane) vibrates, in addition to its full length, in successively smaller fractions. Each of these fractions produces a faint tone auxiliary to the principal or fundamental tone. The combination of all these tones is called the *harmonic series*. For example, C has the following series:

C c g c e g
1 ½ ⅓ ¼ ⅕ ⅙ etc.

The tones above the fundamental are called *overtones*. The prominence of certain overtones has much to do with the specific tone color of a voice or instrument.

harmonic tension: Instability in harmony, especially when a resolution is forthcoming or implied.

harmony: The element of music which deals with the relationships tones can form with each other to give a sense of position, stability and instability, and specific sonority value, aside from melodic, rhythmic, or textural considerations.

harpsichord: An important keyboard instrument of the Renaissance and Baroque eras, producing its tone through the plucking of strings by quills. Constructed in many sizes and types.

homophonic: Pertaining to music in which one principal melodic idea is stated at a given time.

hunt: A quick march or dance idiom, using gigue or contredanse patterns, characterized by the use of fanfares.

idée fixe: A term (applied to Berlioz's *Symphonie fantastique*) which refers to a distinctive melody heard in each movement; this melody represents the "fixation" of the poet-hero upon the idea of his beloved; it interrupts or is part of various episodes in his life. (*See also* leitmotif; thematic transformation.)

imitation: The taking up of the subject or melody by successive voices in turn; said of polyphonic music.

impressionism: A musical style in which subtle textures and colors were used to convey impressions of the physical world, such as the play of light, air, or water; also to suggest exotic, nostalgic, and sentimental subjects.

incidental music: Music intended for performance during the course of a play or other dramatic presentation. Such music may accompany dramatic action, be performed for dances or songs, or it may signal entrances and exits.

instability: A quality in rhythm and harmony which indicates movement, imbalance, action, dissonance. (*See* stability.)

integrated arrangement: Phrase and period structure in which many of the points of punctuation are disguised in order to create a somewhat less symmetrical form and to extend the work. Used in the larger compositions of the classic style. (*See* sectional arrangement.)

intermezzo: An interlude piece; name also given to certain pieces of light or lyric character; also light entertainments given between the acts of serious Renaissance and baroque theatrical performances.

interval: Distance between two tones. Intervals are named according to the staff degrees they encompass. Thus a second covers two degrees; a third, three; etc. Intervals are further qualified according to their exact size. Their dimensions are as follows:

minor second	½ step
major second	1 step
augmented second	1½ steps
diminished third	2 half steps
minor third	1½ steps
major third	2 steps
diminished fourth	1 step, 2 half steps
perfect fourth	2½ steps
augmented fourth	3 steps
diminished fifth	2 steps, 2 half steps
perfect fifth	3½ steps
augmented fifth	4 steps
minor sixth	3 steps, 2 half steps
major sixth	4½ steps
diminished seventh	3 steps, 3 half steps
minor seventh	4 steps, 2 half steps
major seventh	5½ steps
octave	5 steps, 2 half steps

intonation: In Renaissance music, an instrumental piece used as a prelude to liturgical singing; called intonation because it sets the tone (tonic of the mode) of the song to follow. Generally, tuning of a voice or instrument with regard to accuracy of pitch.

introduction: An opening section preceding the body of a movement, usually in slower tempo than the main part. Often employs the French overture idiom, possibly the aria style, or the Storm and Stress. In classic works, the introduction builds a strong cadential drive to prepare for the advent of the allegro.

inversion: In harmony, placing the root, or root *and* third, of a chord in the upper voices and thereby causing the third or fifth of a chord to become the lowermost tone. Also, the reversal in direction of the intervals of a melody.

jazz: A style evolved in the early twentieth century, based upon march and dance patterns elaborated by syncopation, melodic nuances, characteristic scoring, and much improvisation upon a basic melody or progression.

jota: A Spanish dance in quick triple time, characterized by shifts between groups of two beats and three beats: *1* 2 3 *1* 2 3 versus *1* 2 3 *1* 2 3.

key: A tonal center, generally one defined by cadential (leading-tone) action; the system of tones governed by a given tonal center, such as C major, F minor. The key sense in Western music is said to have become fully developed in the late seventeenth century when cadential formulas were first used in great strength and numbers, saturating the harmony.

key area: A section of a composition centering upon one key.

key area form: A form based upon the opposition of key areas; especially applied to the harmonic plan of sonata form, I-V; X-I.

ländler: A German dance in triple meter, similar to the waltz, but with some elements of the minuet.

leading tone: Ordinarily, the seventh degree of the major scale or the seventh degree (raised) of the minor scale. A leading tone, being part of the tension element of a cadential formula, *leads* to its tonic. The term is also applied to any tone which has a leading function in harmony.

learned style: In later eighteenth century, contrapuntal composition; also the strict style, with more rigorous control of dissonance than is found in the galant style.

legato: performed in a smooth manner, without noticeable break in sound. (*See* detaché, staccato.)

leger line: Line added below or above a staff in order to notate tones lying outside the staff.

leitmotif: A significant motive, which may have a distinctive melodic, rhythmic, or harmonic quality and which is assigned to some idea, person, or situation; it is introduced in the musical composition to signal or to develop the idea to which it is attached.

libretto: The text or book of an opera or oratorio.

lied: German for song.

liturgical: Pertaining to Church rites and services.

liturgical drama: Representation of a Biblical story in dramatic form, using plainsong, original music.

local color: The use of folksong and dance idioms or special themes associated with a given region or country.

madrigal: A secular vocal composition of the Renaissance, cultivated first in Italy, then taken up toward the end of the sixteenth century in England.

major scale: A scale in which the order of whole steps and half steps is: 1 1 ½ 1 1 1 ½.

marcato: Literally, "marked": said of a vigorous style of performance.

march: A piece in duple time and of steady meter, using incisive (dotted) rhythmic patterns, regular period structure. Tempo varies according to occasion (quick for military, moderate for ceremonial, slow for funeral).

mass: The most important service of the Catholic Church, commemorating the sacrifice of Christ on the cross.

mastersinger: The fifteenth- and sixteenth-century continuation of the minnesingers. In contrast to their aristocratic forebears, mastersingers were middle-class townsmen and artisans. (German: *Meistersinger.*)

mazurka: Polish dance in quick triple time, with strong accent on beat 2 or 3.

measure: A group of beats marked off on a musical score by a vertical line.

measured organum: Organum in which the upper voice or voices, and sometimes the cantus firmus, move in the measured system of the rhythmic modes, using patterns of long and short tones.

melismatic style: In plainsong, the style of a melody that has melodic elaborations upon one syllable.

melismatic organum: Organum in which the added voice is in melismatic style, while the cantus firmus moves in long notes.

melodic interval: The distance between two tones sounded successively.

melodic motive: A melodic fragment, two notes in length or longer, which gives a distinct impression of manner or style.

melody: A series of tones which moves forward to delineate and complete a meaningful musical shape.

mensural notation: A system of notation expressing specific relative value for tones, comparable to our present notation. Evolved in Ars nova music as an elaboration of modal (long-short) notation.

menuet: A dance of French origin, in triple meter, with a moderately quick yet elegant and graceful quality of movement.

meter: Grouping of beats into small, recurrent units. *Simple duple* meter involves two beats; *simple triple* involves three beats; *compound duple* involves four or six beats subdivided into two subgroups of two or three each; *compound triple* involves triple division, the subgroups containing two or three beats each.

microtones: Intervals smaller than the half step of traditional Western music, used sometimes for ornamentation of a basically diatonic or chromatic harmony, sometimes as constituent elements of the harmony itself.

middle C: The note C at the midpoint of the piano keyboard.

Minnelied: Minnesinger's song.

minnesinger: German counterpart of the troubadour.

minor scale: Scale characterized by the minor third between 1 and 3. The *natural minor scale* has the following order of steps and half steps: 1 ½ 1 1 ½ 1 1. In order to make the minor scale effective cadentially, the seventh degree was made a leading tone with the following order: 1 ½ 1 1 ½ 1½ ½. This *harmonic minor scale* had to be adjusted to eliminate the awkward melodic interval between 6 and 7. Therefore, in the *melodic minor scale* the order is as follows: 1 ½ 1 1 1 1 ½.

minor triad: A three-note chord, consisting of a perfect fifth and a minor third above the lowermost tone.

modes, medieval and Renaissance: Scales used to codify melodies, according to finals, ranges, and distribution of whole and half steps.

modulation: A formal shift of tonal center, usually confirmed by an authentic cadence in the new key. Also, a change of key.

monody: In the early baroque style, the music for solo singer and chordal accompaniment in recitative style developed around 1600 as a reaction to the highly developed polyphony of the Renaissance. Generally, music for one voice.

motet: A composition based upon measured organum in which one or more of the upper voices has words (*mots*); also an important Ars nova form; a category of Renaissance music.

motto: A figure devised from syllables used for singing; employed as a cantus firmus.

musette: *See* bagpipe.

music drama: Term used to distinguish the works of Wagner from other nineteenth-century operas and to emphasize his particular conception of opera.

nationalism: The trend toward the cultivation of national ideas and idioms in the later nineteenth century. Principal among the national schools were the Russian, Bohemian, and Scandinavian. Nationalism was a countermovement to the international idioms of Germany, France, and Italy.

natural sign: A sign (♮) which cancels the raising or lowering effect of a previous sharp or flat.

neoclassicism: The tendency in the twentieth century to organize music along the lines of eighteenth-century principles of construction, using contrapuntal layouts, well-defined phrase structure, transparent texture, often strongly emphasized cadences and keys.

neoromanticism: The retention, in twentieth-century music, of certain broadly expressive attitudes of romanticism, together with its rich texture and harmony.

neumatic style: In plainsong, the style of a melody in which several notes are sung to one syllable.

New Orleans jazz: The early style of jazz, characterized by performance by three or more wind instruments, supported by other instruments which perform a rhythmic function (piano, banjo, percussion, bass); rather free simultaneous improvisation in what is basically a popular kind of march style. *See also* jazz.

obbligato: Literally, "obliged." A part or voice necessary to the full realization of the composition. (*See* ad libitum.) At present, the term has just the opposite meaning, indicating an ornamental part accompanying the principal melody (as a violin or flute supporting a singer).

octave: An interval consisting of five whole steps and two half steps. The most consonant interval in music, since the two notes sound as upper and lower duplicates of each other.

office: In Catholic Church liturgy, the services held at specific hours of the day.

opera: A drama, performed with scenery and action, sung throughout, and accompanied by some instrumental group. Some eighteenth- and nineteenth-century comic operas have occasional spoken dialogue.

opera buffa: Comic opera, derived from commedia dell'arte episodes interpolated into serious theater performances in the seventeenth century; great variety of styles and forms, ensemble numbers.

opéra comique: French comic opera of the eighteenth century.

opera seria: Principal operatic type of the later Baroque period; elaborate arias interspersed with recitatives; subject matter drawn from Greco-Roman history or mythology, involving persons of noble birth.

opus: Literally, "work." A composition or group of compositions designated usually with numbers, thus giving the chronological position of the work within the output of a single composer.

oratorio: A dramatic representation of a religious or thoughtful subject, using many of the techniques of opera.

orchestra: A large group of instrumental performers, including string instruments.

organal voice: A voice added to the cantus firmus in organum.

organum: The earliest polyphony, consisting of a plainsong cantus firmus and organal voices.

ornamentation: The art of adding figures to a given musical text, a process which was already in operation during plainsong times and which is still in use today.

ostinato: A ground bass.

outer voices: In seventeenth-, eighteenth-, and nineteenth-century music, the outer voices are usually the most important in the entire texture. They provide a framework for the sound, and they control the forward progress of the music.

overture: The instrumental piece, usually in sonata form, which serves as a prelude to an opera. Also applied to the symphony in eighteenth-century concerts, indicating derivation of the symphony from the operatic overture.

pace: The speed at which music moves.

pandiatonism: In twentieth-century music the use of tones from a diatonic scale in chords that do not represent traditional triads and seventh chords.

parallel organum: Organum in which the added voice or voices move parallel to the cantus firmus at the interval of a fourth, fifth, or octave.

parlando: A style of singing in quick, separate, even notes, with a syllable to each note; "patter" singing, featured in opera buffa.

parody: In Renaissance music, the elaboration of a smaller polyphonic composition into a larger one, as, for example, a Mass elaborated from a motet, madrigal, or chanson. In the earlier twentieth century, the use of familiar styles and types of music in a rather grotesquely distorted manner; the waltz is a favorite subject for parody.

passacaglia: *See* chaconne.

passepied: A French dance in quick triple time.

passion: An oratorio dealing with the sacrifice of Christ.

pedal: A foot-operated mechanism; the pedal keyboard of the organ; *pedal-point* refers to a sustained tone held while other voices move, the passage generally extending for several measures.

pentatonic scale: A scale that has five tones, corresponding to 1 2 3 5 6 of the major scale, or 1 2 4 5 7 of the minor scale; its lack of half tones gives it a special character and a flexibility of use but imposes a very tight limitation on progression in the scale; used as a coloristic device in impressionism.

percussion instruments: Instruments whose tone is produced by striking a membrane, wood block, or bar of metal. Percussion instruments include the kettledrum, snare drum, bass drum, xylophone, chimes, tambourine, and cymbals.

perfect fifth: An interval encompassing five scale degrees, containing three whole steps and one half step. The perfect fifth is one of the strongest embodiments of harmonic stability.

period: A section of music, generally consisting of two or more phrases, ending with a full or conclusive point of arrival and containing a rather fully expressed musical idea.

phase of movement: A musical statement whose progress forward is marked off and controlled by points of departure and arrival. Phases of musical movement are variable in length.

phrase: A fairly short section of music with a well-defined point of arrival, containing clearly formed ideas, yet lacking something in form or sense to be complete.

pictorialism: The linking of distinctive musical ideas to specific pictorial or literary effects; the musical idea suggests by its design the nonmusical concept.

pitch: The level of musical sound, based on the number of vibrations given out by any specified tone.

pizzicato: An indication for string performers to pluck the strings with the fingers.

plagal cadence: A cadence in which the subdominant precedes the tonic. This is a very restful sort of cadence and is heard in the amen phrase at the end of many sacred compositions.

plagal mode: A mode in which the final occurs in the middle of the range or scale.

plainsong: Medieval church song; also referred to as Gregorian chant.

point of arrival: The point at which a phase of movement reaches an end or is marked off from the succeeding phase. This may be a caesura or a cadence; it may arrest movement partially or completely.

point of departure: A statement, gesture, idea, or impulse which provides the opening momentum for a phase of musical movement. This may be a sound quality, a rhythm, a motive, or a general expressive quality.

point of imitation: A section of a piece using imitation.

polka: A Bohemian dance, quick, in duple time, very popular in the nineteenth century.

polonaise: A Polish dance, much favored in the seventeenth and eighteenth centuries; quick triple time, accent on second beat.

polychoral: A performance group divided into two or more sections that are opposed to each other in the give-and-take of musical material; applied especially to Venetian music performed in St. Mark's Cathedral during the late Renaissance and the Baroque periods.

polyphonic: Pertaining to music which employs counterpoint.

polytonality: The simultaneous performance of passages in two or more keys; also refers to chords built with tones from more than one key.

prelude: An introductory piece, generally for keyboard; a piece in an improvisatory style.

prima prattica: The polyphonic style of the Renaissance; *see* seconda prattica.

program music: Music written to a story or scenario; the allusions are more specific than in eighteenth-century musical pictorialism and more fully carried out.

psalm tone: A melody, characterized by many repeated tones, used in plainsong to recite the Psalms.

quartet: A group of four performers; a composition for four performers.

quintet: A group of five performers; a composition for five performers.

recapitulation: In sonata form, the section following the X, in which the material of the exposition is presented in the home key to resolve the harmonic contrast first established. It acts as a rhyme to the exposition.

recitative: Musical declamation, in no set meter or rhythm; echoes the inflections of speech.

recitative accompagnato: A vocal declamation accompanied by distinctive short figures in the orchestra; employs some of the expressive songlike manner of the aria; no standard key or phrase plan.

recitative secco: Vocal declamation over the sustained or punctuating chords of a keyboard instrument. Less expressive than accompagnato, generally quicker, employing the rhythmic patterns of ordinary speech.

refrain: The principal theme of a rondo. More generally, a section that returns periodically in a song, dance, or larger work.

register: Section of the range of an instrument or voice with a characteristic color. In organ performance, a set of pipes governed by one stop.

remembrance motive: A distinctive motive or passage associated with some situation in an opera and recalled when reference is made again to the situation. Less intensively employed than leitmotif.

repetition: Restatement of any musical effect, melody, rhythm, harmony, texture, phrase, period, etc. Repetition may be literal or varied. In any case, repetition may be taken as counterstatement.

resolution: In counterpoint and harmony, the settling of dissonance or tension by conducting the dissonant tones to tones which are consonant.

retrograde: Reversal of order in the tones of a subject.

rhapsody: An improvisatory piece, along the lines of a fantasia; structurally, often written as a series of episodes.

rhythm: The element which generates, measures, organizes, and controls musical time.

rhythmic modes: Rhythmic patterns used in measured organum; based on poetic meter (long and short syllables).

ricercar: In Renaissance music, the instrumental counterpart or paraphrase of a motet; also, an improvisatory piece much like a toccata or intonation.

ripieno: Literally, "filling up"; the full orchestra in a concerto.

ritardando: Becoming slower in tempo.

ritornello: The orchestral section of an aria, heard at the beginning and end, and sometimes within the body of the aria. Also the tutti section of a concerto.

rococo: An eighteenth-century style, applied to art as well as music, designating a highly ornate type of embellishment.

rondo: A piece built by alternations of refrains and episodes, as in ABACADA.

root position: A chord position in which the lowermost note is the fundamental root or generator. (*See* harmonic series.) In practice this works out so that the root is the lower note of the perfect fifth of the triad. In chords which have no perfect fifth, the root is considered to be the bottom note when the chord is arranged in thirds.

round: A simple type of imitation, in which a number of voices, beginning at different times, sing the same melody over and over again.

1 2 3 4 1 2 3 4
4 **1** 2 3 4 1 2 3
3 4 **1** 2 3 4 1 2
2 3 4 **1** 2 3 4 1

All voices begin with **1**.

rubato: Literally, "robbed." A manner of performance in which time values are stolen from some tones in order to give greater stress or expressive accent to others.

sarabande: Rather slow dance in triple time, with an accent of length generally upon the second beat of the measure; Spanish in origin.

satire (and parody): In the late nineteenth and early twentieth centuries, the distortion and ridiculing of familiar or traditional ideas and musical idioms. This was often done with a strong flavor of bitterness or irony.

scale: A stepwise series of tones, usually denoting a rising line. Scales are qualified according to the arrangement of whole steps and half steps. (*See* major scale, minor scale, mode, whole-tone scale, chromatic scale, diatonic scale.)

scherzo: Italian for "jest." A quick, dancelike movement, which all but supplanted the minuet in the nineteenth-century symphony.

seconda prattica: The new, bold treatment of dissonance for expressive purposes, and generally the heightening of expressive values, in early baroque music.

sectional arrangement: Phrase or period structure in which the punctuation is well marked and a strong sense of symmetry arises from the relatively equal length of sections.

semitone: A half step; the smallest interval commonly used in Western music.

Sensibility: A style of performance and composition concerned with intimate, capricious, sentimental expression; closely allied to lyric poetry of the later eighteenth century.

sequence: Restatement of a motive or phrase upon several successively higher or lower levels; a way of giving a larger contour to a group of motives or phrases.

serenade: Music for evening, generally light and entertaining in character; especially applied to sets of instrumental pieces often performed outdoors, consisting of marches, dances, variations, and songlike movements, as well as one or more longer movements in sonata or rondo form. Sometimes included virtuoso passages for solo violin or winds. Term used interchangeably with divertimento.

serialism: The organization of musical events through a pattern in which each element has a fixed position in relation to the others; such a pattern is called a series; it governs the order of tones, rhythms, or scoring in a piece.

sextet: A group of six performers; a composition for six performers.

sharp: A sign (♯) which raises by a semitone any note before which it is placed.

signature: The group of sharps or flats and the meter indication of a composition; both are found at the beginning of the piece; the key signature (sharps or flats) is placed at the left of each staff system throughout the piece.

sinfonia: Orchestral introduction to Italian opera; also applied to instrumental episodes in concertato or dramatic works.

singing-allegro: Quick, songlike melodic style with Alberti bass accompaniment or simple rhythmic support, favored in Italian-style compositions of the classic era.

Singspiel: German comic opera of the eighteenth century.

solo: A single instrument or voice; a passage performed by a single instrument or voice.

soloistic: Term applied to virtuoso figurations in classic music derived from the baroque concerto.

sonata: From *canzona da sonar*. An important instrumental form of the Baroque period, consisting of three or more movements in alternating slow-fast tempo; performed as a solo or as a piece for a few instruments.

sonata da camera: Sonata performed as chamber music.

sonata da chiesa: Sonata performed as church music.

sonata form: The most important form of the classic era; basically, a long-range harmonic plan (*see* key area form) in which each key area has distinctive thematic material. *See* exposition, development, recapitulation, coda.

soprano: Literally, "above." The highest women's voice; also the highest instrument of a family, such as the soprano saxophone.

sostenuto: Sustained.

Sprechgesang: A type of singing evolved by Wagner to mirror the accents and expressive nuances of his dramatic texts.

Sprechstimme: Vocal performance in which the music is half sung, half spoken; no fixed pitches, only relative rise and fall suggesting the inflection of speech.

stability: In rhythm and harmony, rest, balance, arrival, consonance. Stability is a quality which is not absolute but is relative to what is taking place. For instance, one might say that a certain chord is somewhat unstable but acts as a point of arrival for the preceding very unstable chord; therefore, the second chord seems relatively stable.

staccato: Performed in a markedly detached manner. (*See* detaché, legato.)

staff: The system of five lines upon which music is notated.

stile brisé: Highly ornamented French style, derived from lute music.

stile rappresentativo: *See* monody, recitative, seconda prattica.

Storm and Stress: Applied to a late eighteenth-century manner concerned with impetuous, agitated, violent expression; influenced by the *Sturm und Drang*, the early stage of German romantic drama and literature.

string instruments: A family of instruments constructed of a sounding box over which strings are stretched. The tone is produced by drawing a bow across the strings or by plucking. The modern orchestral strings are violins, violas, cellos, string basses.

strophic: Characterized by the use of the same music for the stanzas of a poem.

subject: A distinctive melodic statement, generally in a large composition, which will be developed in some fashion after it has been presented.

superius: The soprano, treble, or uppermost voice in a polyphonic setting.

suspension: An effect achieved when one or more voices are held over as one chord moves to another. These voices are *suspended* and create dissonances, which are then directed or resolved into the proper tones of the second chord.

syllabic style: A style in vocal music in which each syllable of the text has a single note. This applies particularly to one style of plainsong.

sympathetic resonance: The vibration caused in a resonating body (string, pipe) when a nearby body of the same length is sounded.

symphonic poem: A one-movement orchestral work with a number of episodes, suitable for epic, heroic, dramatic program music; established by Franz Liszt.

symphony: The most important orchestral form of the late eighteenth and nineteenth centuries. A three- or four-movement work, of which the first movement is always in sonata form.

syncopation: Shift of accent or length from the normal position occupied by a point of arrival; it creates imbalance and intensifies movement.

tactus: The unit of time in Renaissance music.

tarantella: A quick Italian dance in six-eight time, giguelike.

tastar de corde: The technique of the improvisatory ricercar.

temperament: The act of modifying or tempering: applied to the tuning of instruments (especially keyboard) to adjust for minor discrepancies which arise when the ratios of the harmonic series are used.

tempo: Synonym for *pace*. (*See* Chapter 2 for various tempo designations.)

tenor: The voice that sings the cantus firmus in medieval polyphony; the voice which "holds," often in long notes. Generally, a low middle range of voice or instrument, such as a male tenor voice, cello, bassoon, or tenor trombone.

terrace dynamics: The change in strength of sound achieved sharply by alternations of tutti and solo in a concertolike texture.

tessitura: The general working range of a vocal part in a song or aria.

texture: The composite action of the component voices or parts performing at any given time; includes monophonic, unison, single action (isometric), melody and accompaniment, imitative and nonimitative polyphony, and give-and-take.

thematic transformation: The technique of altering the character of a theme without destroying its basic shape or identity; frequently used in romantic music to establish structural unity.

theme: A distinctive melodic statement, usually part of a long movement.

three-part structure: Ternary form (ABA), the important feature of which is some sort of contrasting episode setting off two statements of the principal idea, phrase, period, or larger section.

through-composed: Characterized by modification of the music for various stanzas in the musical setting of a poem (*see* strophic) or by little or no repetition of sections.

toccata: Literally, "touched"; applied to a study for keyboard or possibly string instrument in the manner of a fantasia or prelude.

tonal center: A tone which is given prominence in a phrase, period, or larger section acting as a point of reference, arrival, or stability. This prominence can be given by melodic, rhythmic, or, most strongly, harmonic means.

tone-row: A distinctive pattern using all twelve tones of the chromatic scale without repetition; this pattern acts as the source material for an entire movement or composition. *See also* serialism.

tonic: The tonal center, the principal note of a key or mode.

total organization: Serialism in which all events in a composition are controlled, including pitch, rhythm, scoring, and dynamics.

treble: A voice or instrument performing in a high range, such as a treble viol. The high range itself, as applied particularly to choral composition.

tremolo: In strings, the rapid repetition of the same note. The term has also been used to designate a rapid alternation between two notes.

triad: A chord of three tones, reducible to a fifth divided by a third.

trill: An ornamental figure consisting of the rapid alternation of a principal note with the note directly above.

trio: A composition for three instruments. Also applied to the second part of a minuet movement, the B of the ABA form. Typically, this second dance featured a group of solo instruments, often three; hence the name, trio.

trio sonata: A texture involving two solo instruments and continuo; a composition using this texture; actually, four performers are required (*see* continuo).

tritone: The augmented fourth, involving three whole steps, as F to B. The term is also applied to inversion of the augumented fourth, i.e., the diminished fifth, since both have a similar function of creating harmonic tension to indicate a tonal center.

trope: An addition to an authorized liturgical text.

troubadours: Poet-musicians of the Middle Ages in southern France.

trouvères: The counterpart of troubadours in northern France.

two-part structure (binary form): A form consisting of two complementary sections. The cadence or the point of arrival of the first part usually gives an impression of being incomplete or of requiring further action; the point of arrival or cadence of the second part acts as a completion of the form.

two-reprise form: A dance-derived form consisting of two sections or periods; the first ends with an open or inconclusive cadence, the second with a conclusive or closed cadence; material in the two sections tends to be similar.

tutti: The full ensemble in a baroque instrumental work.

unison: A combination which is created when two or more voices sound the same tone.

upbeat: A note or group of notes preceding an accented tone. The upbeat usually is found immediately preceding the measure line (or bar line).

variation: The alteration or elaboration of one or more features of a subject or theme. Also compositions in which the procedure of variation is the principal means of carrying the structure forward.

verismo: The operatic style that corresponds to literary and artistic realism in the late nineteenth century.

vers mesuré: A type of French sixteenth-century secular vocal music in which the time values of the tones reflect the scansion of the poetic text employed; sung in familiar style.

vibrato: A rapid and very small change of pitch in string-instrument and in vocal performance. Properly handled, in moderation, vibrato can add richness and expressive nuance to given tones.

viola da gamba: The bass of the viol family (six-string instruments), used widely in baroque music to complete the continuo.

whole-tone scale: A scale that uses whole steps exclusively, such as C D E F♯ G♯ B♭; characterized by a vagueness of harmonic focus and a special richness of color.

woodwind instruments: A family of instruments, constructed of a keyed tube of wood (or metal) and producing sound by the vibration of a reed (or double-reed) in the mouthpiece (with the exception of the flute). In addition to flutes, the family includes clarinets, oboes, bassoons.

List of Composers

Bach, Johann Christian, 1735–1782, b. Leipzig: The youngest son of Johann Sebastian Bach. Composer of orchestral works, chamber music, operas. Very successful in London. He influenced Mozart greatly, particularly with reference to the use of the Italian galant style.

Bach, Johann Sebastian, 1685–1750, b. Eisenach: Greatest master of the late Baroque period. Bach's music represents the final culmination of the baroque style and a synthesis of many different idioms. He wrote in many media and forms, and though he wrote no opera, he employed operatic techniques in his cantatas, passions, and other choral works. Served at Weimar, Cöthen, and Leipzig. Among his important works are the Mass in B minor, the *Well-Tempered Clavier, The Art of the Fugue,* and the six *Brandenburg* Concertos.

Bach, Karl Philipp Emanuel, 1714–1788, b. Weimar: Son of Johann Sebastian Bach. Identified with the *Empfindsamkeit* manner. A brilliant keyboard performer at the court of Frederick the Great. Exerted considerable influence upon Mozart and Haydn. Solo works for keyboard, concertos, orchestral works.

Barber, Samuel, 1910– , b. West Chester: American composer of orchestral and chamber music. His works, based largely upon traditional forms and harmonic procedures, are frequently performed in America and Europe.

Bartók, Béla, 1881–1945, b. Nagyszentmiklós: Hungarian composer in the forefront of the folkloric trend of the twentieth century. Bartók, moreover, had an extremely eloquent and distinctive personal style which influenced many composers. Important works include six string quartets, Concerto for Orchestra, operas, orchestral works, teaching pieces (*Mikrokosmos*).

Beethoven, Ludwig van, 1770–1827, b. Bonn: German composer whose music represents the culmination of the classic style as well as an important link to nineteenth-century romanticism. He exerted a profound influence upon ideas of musical construction and expression, establishing the concept of the "monumental" symphony, and intensifying expression much beyond the scope of his predecessors. He wrote nine symphonies, of which the Third, the *Eroica,* is a landmark in the history of music. Seventeen string quartets, thirty-two piano sonatas, opera *Fidelio,* five piano concertos, much other chamber music.

Bellini, Vincenzo, 1801–1835, b. Catania, Sicily: Opera composer noted especially for the attractiveness of his melodic style. Chief works are *Norma, I Puritani, La Sonnambula.*

Berg, Alban, 1885–1935, b. Vienna: Together with Von Webern and Schönberg, Berg represents the grand triumvirate of twelve-tone music in the first half of the twentieth century. Pupil of Schönberg. His music tends to be more directly grasped and more openly dramatic than that of his two colleagues. His opera *Wozzeck* is one of the monuments of the modern lyric stage.

Berlioz, Louis Hector, 1803–1869, b. near Grenoble: French composer whose treatment of the orchestra was highly original and imaginative; his textures and phrase structure foreshadowed modern techniques of orchestration and composition. Important works include the *Symphonie fantastique,* the symphony, *Harold in Italy,* the operas *Benvenuto Cellini* and *The Trojans,* a Requiem Mass, the dramatic symphony *Romeo and Juliet,* and the secular oratorio *The Damnation of Faust.*

Bizet, Georges, 1838–1875, b. Paris: Opera composer whose work *Carmen* is one of the most popular of the entire operatic repertoire. *Carmen* represents the new realistic lyric drama, with emphasis upon sharp dramatic impact, fresh and striking color, and winning melody.

Bloch, Ernest, 1880–1959, b. Geneva: Bloch's music combines various aspects of impressionism, folkloric style, and romanticism, held together by a firm neoclassic command of structure and of polyphonic procedures. Important works include *Schelomo* (rhapsody for violoncello and orchestra), a Violin Concerto, Quintet for Piano and Strings, two concerti grossi, a Sacred Service, chamber music of various types.

Borodin, Aleksandr, 1833–1887, b. St. Petersburg: A member of the group that worked for the establishment of a Russian national school. His music uses many materials based on folk idioms; some compositions are descriptive of Russian or Asiatic scenes, such as the opera *Prince Igor* and the symphonic sketch *On the Steppes of Central Asia.* The Symphony No. 2 in B minor is a well-known concert item.

Boulez, Pierre, 1925–   , b. Montbrison: French composer. Leader in the post-Webern serialist trend, applying total organization to serial techniques. Best-known work is *Le Marteau sans maître,* a suite for contralto and six instruments.

Brahms, Johannes, 1833–1897, b. Hamburg: Principal representative of the classic tradition in nineteenth-century music. Brahms's music, particularly his symphonies, concertos, chamber music, and choral works, has the grand manner and the broad scope associated with great music of the classic era. His songs and small keyboard pieces reflect romantic moods very characteristically. Brahms's style, particularly his rhythms, textures, and broad melodies, was frequently imitated by later composers.

Britten, Benjamin, 1913–   , b. Lowestoft, Suffolk: English composer noted especially for his operas, which include *Peter Grimes, Albert Herring, The Rape of Lucrece, Gloriana, The Turn of the Screw.* Britten has developed a very direct, easily grasped style, drawn from many traditional sources and eminently suited for dramatic purposes.

Bruckner, Anton, 1824–1896, b. Upper Austria: Austrian composer noted especially for his nine symphonies and for sacred music. Bruckner transferred the techniques and the manner of Wagner to orchestral music.

Buxtehude, Dietrich, 1637–1707, b. Hälsingborg: Composer of the North German school, and organist who contributed to the evolution of the suite, the fugue, and German sacred music. Strong influence on Johann Sebastian Bach.

Byrd, William, 1540–1623: Important Tudor composer, versatile in all forms of English Renaissance music. Works include Masses, motets, anthems, madrigals, chamber music, and keyboard music.

Caccini, Giulio, c. 1546–1618, b. Rome: Italian composer who was one of the principal exponents of the new monodic style, in which he wrote madrigals and operas. His *Euridice* is the first opera presented in a public theater. He also wrote a book of madrigals called *Nuove musiche,* in which new techniques of vocal performance are described.

Carissimi, Giacomo, 1605–1674, b. near Rome: Roman composer noted chiefly for his oratorios. An exponent of the stile rappresentativo. His oratorios include *Jephthe, The Judgment of Solomon, Jonah, Balthazar.*

Carter, Elliott, 1908– , b. New York City: American composer, whose music is stylistically related to that of Stravinsky and Bartók. He has developed a concept of *metric modulation,* which controls changes of pace according to proportional formulas.

Cherubini, Luigi, 1760–1842, b. Florence: Italian composer of operas and instrumental music. Cherubini was admired by Beethoven, upon whom he had considerable influence. He was also an important musical theorist and, as his music shows, a skillful contrapuntalist.

Chopin, Frédéric, 1810–1849, b. near Warsaw: Polish composer; one of the most important figures of the early romantic period. Almost exclusively a composer for piano, Chopin worked out an individual style which explored the sonority resources of his instrument. Works include two concertos for piano, four scherzi, fantasies, ballades, preludes, études, valses, polonaises, mazurkas, etc.

Copland, Aaron, 1900– , b. Brooklyn: One of the most widely performed American composers. Copland has developed a highly distinctive personal style, based in part upon folk-dance rhythms and American folk melodies. His music turns to subjects of popular interest, such as the orchestral works *El Salón México* and *An Outdoor Overture,* and the ballets *Appalachian Spring* and *Billy the Kid.*

Corelli, Arcangelo, 1653–1713, b. near Imola: Italian composer and violinist. Important in the development of late baroque chamber and orchestral music. Sonatas and concertos comprise his chief works. Teacher of many eighteenth-century violinists.

Couperin, François, 1668–1733, b. Paris: French composer at the court of Louis XIV. Brilliant clavecinist, evolving a distinctive manner of ornamentation. Compositions for organ, clavecin, choral works, chamber music, orchestral works. His keyboard style, explained in his *L'Art de toucher le clavecin,* influenced Johann Sebastian Bach.

Cowell, Henry, 1897–1965, b. Menlo Park: American composer notable for experiments in sonority and for works in many forms, including symphonies, chamber music, choral music, stage music. Cowell has been interested also in Oriental musical systems and has introduced Oriental elements into his concert music. He has written books on music and much musical criticism.

Dallapiccola, Luigi, 1904– , b. Pisino: Italian composer; works include the opera *Il Prigionero,* chamber music, and orchestral works. Writes in the twelve-tone system, adapting it to Italianate style.

Debussy, Claude, 1862–1918, b. St. Germain-en-Laye: French composer; the principal figure in musical impressionism. Important works include the opera *Pelléas et Mélisande,* which, in its subtle nuances and calculated understatement, represented a strong reaction against Wagner's emphasis and violence. Debussy wrote many songs, preludes and other works for piano, orchestral works including the nocturnes *La Mer* and *Iberia,* and some chamber music.

Delius, Frederick, 1862–1934, b. Bradford: English composer; one of the foremost exponents of impressionism. Important works include the opera *A Village Romeo and Juliet,* orchestral rhapsody *Brigg Fair,* the orchestral variations with chorus, *Appalachia,* many descriptive works for orchestra, operas, concertos, and choral works.

Deprès, Josquin, c. 1450–1521, b. Hainaut: Represents the first complete embodiment of Renaissance style, and very likely the finest. His music combines mastery of Netherlands counterpoint (imitation, canon) with a clarity of structure and sureness of harmonic procedure (feeling for cadential action) derived probably from Italian music. He wrote Masses, motets, chansons, some instrumental works.

Donizetti, Gaetano, 1797–1848, b. Bergamo: Italian opera composer. Wrote over sixty operas, including *Don Pasquale, The Daughter of the Regiment, The Elixir of Love, Lucrezia Borgia,* and one of the greatest favorites in the entire operatic repertoire, *Lucia di Lammermoor.* Donizetti's music is distinguished by an extremely elegant, ingratiating melodic style.

Dowland, John, 1562–1626: English composer and lutenist. Works include lute songs, lute solos, and instrumental ensemble pieces.

Dufay, Guillaume, c. 1400–1474: Netherlandish composer, representing the period during which the Renaissance style was evolved. Strong influence upon the generation which followed him. Sacred and secular works which show the tendency toward triadic sonorities.

Dukas, Paul, 1865–1935, b. Paris: French composer of orchestral works, ballets, and an important opera, *Ariane et Barbe-Bleu.* His most noted work, the orchestral scherzo *L'Apprenti-Sorcier* embodies both traditional structural and impressionistic color devices, a combination characteristic of his general style.

Dunstable, John, c. 1370–1453, b. Bedfordshire: English composer; one of the most important figures in the change of style from Ars nova to Renaissance. Spent a number of years in France.

Dvorák, Anton, 1841–1904, b. Muhlhausen: Bohemian composer, whose strong interest in folk subjects is shown in such works as his *From the New World* Symphony, the Slavonic Dances, the American Quartet. Brilliant orchestrator with a vivacious imaginative style of composition. His Second Symphony, little known, is one of the finest works of its kind after Beethoven.

Elgar, Sir Edward, 1857–1934, b. Broadheath: English composer; Master of the King's Musick. One of the principal representatives of English romanticism, largely influenced by Brahms. Works include oratorios, cantatas, symphonies, chamber music. His *Enigma Variations* for orchestra and the oratorio *The Dream of Gerontius* are among his most celebrated works.

Falla, Manuel de, 1876–1949, b. Cadiz: Spanish composer, particularly important for his use of Spanish idioms and subjects. Works include the ballets *Love, the Magician, The Three-Cornered Hat, Nights in the Gardens of Spain.*

Fauré, Gabriel, 1845–1924, b. Pamiers: French composer, notable for his retention of classic structural and developmental principles, within which he evolved many striking harmonic, melodic, and expressive nuances. He was a teacher and had strong influence upon the present generation of French composers. Operas, ballets, orchestral works, chamber music, choral works, of which the Requiem is perhaps best known. Director of the Conservatoire de Musique in Paris.

Franck, César, 1822–1890, b. Liége: Belgian composer and organist. Symbolized reaction against operatic domination of French music; strong influence on later composers, such as D'Indy, Chausson, Ropartz. Works include the famous Symphony in D minor and chamber, organ, and choral music. Franck was constantly trying to reconcile the rich harmonic language of the late nineteenth century with traditional principles of structure.

Frescobaldi, Girolamo, 1583–1643, b. Ferrara: Italian organist and composer who was important in the evolution of a distinctive seventeenth-century keyboard style. Organist of St. Peter's in Rome. Fantasias, ricercare, toccatas, canzone, capriccios, and other types of keyboard music.

Froberger, Johann Jakob, 1616–1667, b. Stuttgart: German composer and organist. Important in the early history of the baroque suite.

Gabrieli, Andrea, c. 1510–1586, b. Venice: Composer and organist, especially important in the evolution of an idiomatic instrumental style in the sixteenth century. Many works in various media.

Gabrieli, Giovanni, 1557–1612, b. Venice: Nephew of Andrea Gabrieli. One of the foremost figures in the evolution of the concertato style, and hence of modern instrumental music. A forerunner of baroque music; teacher of Schütz. Works for divided chorus and for combinations of voices and instruments, including *Sacrae Symphoniae.*

Gershwin, George, 1898–1937, b. Brooklyn: Foremost American representative of the popular style, equally successful in straight song and dance forms or in larger forms which develop and extend jazz material. Works include opera *Porgy and Bess, Rhapsody in Blue,* Concerto in F for piano, *An American* *in Paris,* and numerous highly successful and long-popular musical comedies, such as *Strike Up the Band, Lady, Be Good, Let 'em Eat Cake.*

Gesualdo, Carlo, c. 1560–1613, b. Naples: Composer of madrigals, distinctive for their unusual chromatic style and highly affective manner of expression, marked by strong contrasts.

Glinka, Michail Ivanovitch, 1804–1857, b. Novosspaskoe: Russian composer who pioneered the nationalist movement in his native country. He wrote in a wide range of genres, the most important works being the operas *A Life for the Tsar* and *Russlan and Ludmilla.*

Gluck, Christoph Willibald von, 1714–1787, b. Erasbach: German composer noted especially for his "reform" of opera, in which he substituted a simpler style for the more ornate Italian manner, giving more immediate and direct expression to the dramatic content. His "reform" operas include *Orfeo ed Euridice, Paris and Helen, Iphigenia in Tauris, Iphigenia in Aulis, Armide,* and *Alceste.* Gluck also wrote operas in the Italian style.

Gounod, Charles François, 1818–1893, b. Paris: French composer whose opera *Faust* is one of the most frequently performed works in the operatic repertoire. In addition to other operas, Gounod wrote many sacred works.

Gregory I (Pope from 590–604): The Pope supposedly responsible for the coordination and systematization of plainsong. His role has not been fully established historically; there is evidence pro and con.

Grieg, Edvard, 1843–1907, b. Bergen: Norwegian composer, influential in the establishment of a national school. In his harmonic innovations, his handling of sonority and color, Grieg foreshadows some of the techniques of impressionism. Works include incidental music for Ibsen's drama *Peer Gynt,* Concerto for Piano in A minor, chamber music, and many songs and small works in lyric vein.

Griffes, Charles T., 1884–1920, b. Elmira: American composer, with leanings toward the impressionist style. Works include *Roman Sketches* for piano (including the well-known sketch *The White Peacock*), the symphonic poem *The Pleasure Dome of Kubla Khan,* songs, chamber music. His music shows some Oriental influences.

Handel, Georg Frideric, 1685–1759, b. Halle: German composer who represents, with Johann Sebastian Bach, the culmination of the late Baroque period. Much of his life was spent in England, where he wrote many operas, oratorios (*The Messiah*), concertos, chamber music. His style has unexcelled rhythmic vigor and a bold melodic manner.

Hanson, Howard, 1896– , b. Wahoo, Nebraska: American composer. Director of the Eastman School of Music. Principally known for symphonic works and the opera *Merry Mount.*

Harris, Roy, 1898– , b. Lincoln, Oklahoma: American composer whose works have drawn often from American folk culture and history for subject matter and style. Many orchestral works and compositions in various media.

Haydn, Franz Joseph, 1732–1809, b. Rohrau: Austrian composer; the oldest of the Viennese classic group (*see* Mozart and Beethoven). More than any other, Haydn was responsible for the structural and technical principles underlying the mature classic forms. Wrote 104 symphonies, 88 quartets, oratorios, including *The Seasons* and *The Creation,* keyboard music, choral music, operas. Many years in service with the Esterházy house; later, in London, Haydn composed some of his greatest works.

Hindemith, Paul, 1895–1963, b. near Frankfurt: German composer noted for his classic tendencies, as exemplified in the use of traditional forms, consistent contrapuntal texture, key-controlled structure. Works in many media and forms; his symphony *Mathis der Maler* (from the opera of the same name) is a classic of the modern period. An exponent of "music for practical use," written to accommodate the limitations of amateur performers. Very influential on younger composers.

Hoffmann, E. T. A., 1776–1822, b. Königsberg: German writer and musician noted for his enthusiastic support of the romantic movement.

Holst, Gustav, 1874–1934, b. Cheltenham: English composer of orchestral, dramatic, chamber, and choral music. His orchestral suite *The Planets* is his most noted work.

Honegger, Arthur, 1892–1955, b. Le Havre: Swiss composer, generally linked with the postimpressionist French composers. Wide range of style in his music, from the futuristic sketch *Pacific 231* (impression of a locomotive) to *Pastorale d'été* (a delicate nature study). Very successful with stage and dramatic music, especially his oratorio *King David* and his music for Claudel's mystery play *Joan of Arc at the Stake.*

Ibert, Jacques, 1890–   , b. Paris: Contemporary French composer of operas (including *Angélique, The King of Ivetot*), attractive instrumental works, and considerable music for the motion pictures.

Indy, Vincent d', 1851–1931, b. Paris: Noted French composer and music educator. Cofounder of the Schola Cantorum. His music is oriented toward the past, using traditional forms and styles of expression. D'Indy, an important theorist, wrote *Cours de composition musicale.*

Isaak, Heinrich, c. 1450–1517: Netherlands composer who held posts in Florence, Vienna, and Rome, thus helping to disseminate the Flemish polyphonic style of composition. Many masses and motets, chorales, and secular works; also instrumental works. *Choralis Constantinus* is a cycle of motets written for the liturgical year for the cathedral of Constance, Switzerland.

Ives, Charles, 1874–1954, b. Danbury: One of the most individual figures of the twentieth century. Within a style basically romantic, Ives experimented with harmonies, textures, sonorities, rhythms, anticipating many of the procedures of modern music. Orchestral works and chamber, keyboard, and theater music.

Jacobi, Frederick, 1891–1952, b. San Francisco: American composer of chamber and orchestral works. His music leans to romantic idioms exhibiting a fresh melodic manner. Works include *Hagiographa* for piano and string quartet; concertos for violin, for piano, and for cello; *A Sabbath Evening Service;* and the opera *The Prodigal Son.*

Jannequin, Clément, c. 1485–?: French composer; the first important representative of sixteenth-century French music; writer of many chansons, some of them extended pictorial representations of scenes or events; also motets and other sacred music.

Kodály, Zoltán, 1882– , b. Kecskemét: With Bartók. Kodály represents best the modern Hungarian school. His interest in Hungarian folk music is profound and has influenced his style. His work covers many media; the *Háry János* suite for orchestra, from the opera of the same name, is well known. His style, in addition to folk-music elements, exhibits features of impressionism, romanticism, and contemporary harmonic practices of atonality and polytonality.

Křenek, Ernst, 1900– , b. Vienna: One of the more noted representatives of twelve-tone music, of the generation following Schönberg. Also interested in jazz as a stylistic resource, as well as other contemporary techniques. His opera *Jonny spielt auf* displays jazz elements; his opera *Karl V* is in the tone-row technique. Křenek has also written small pieces to demonstrate the applicability of tone-row techniques to simple lyric expression.

Landino, Francesco, 1325–1397, b. Florence: The principal representative of Italian Ars nova music. Known for his secular music, madrigals, cacce, ballate. Organist of the Church of Lorenzo. In contrast to the French Ars nova, with its rhythmic complexities, Landino's music displays typical Italian cantilena qualities.

Lassus, Orlandus, c. 1532–1594, b. Hainaut: One of the greatest composers of the late Renaissance, a Netherlandish composer who represents, with Palestrina, the culmination of the Roman sacred style. Lassus also wrote in the style of French chansons, German songs, and Italian madrigals. He thus epitomizes the ideal of the cosmopolitan culture of the Renaissance.

Leoninus (twelfth century): The earlier of the two composers (*see* Perotinus) who represent the Notre Dame school of composition. He was important in establishing the use of rhythmic modes in melismatic organum.

Liszt, Franz, 1811–1886, b. near Ödenburg: Hungarian composer and pianist who was a prototype of the transcendental virtuoso of the romantic period. His brilliant declamatory style of composition and performance, his harmonic innovations, his flamboyant expression had a profound effect upon musical style during his life and afterward. He established a single-movement form with many episodes, called the *symphonic poem,* which suited the many changes of mood and feeling in his music. The most famous of these is *Les Préludes.* Also wrote *Hungarian Rhapsodies,* brilliant piano works, *Faust* Symphony. Influenced Richard Wagner and Richard Strauss.

Lully, Jean Baptiste, 1632–1687, b. Florence: Italian composer who became the virtual dictator of French music at the court of Louis XIV. Established a style of opera, including recitative, and a style of orchestral performance that prevailed in France for almost a century. Lully was responsible also for the establishment of the French overture as an important instrumental form.

MacDowell, Edward, 1861–1908, b. New York City: One of the earliest American composers to receive international recognition. His music includes large-scale compositions modeled after European patterns, such as his concertos for piano. He has also written charming characteristic smaller pieces, such as the *Indian Suite* for orchestra and *Woodland Sketches* for piano.

Machaut, Guillaume de, c. 1300–1377, b. Machaut: The most noted representative of French fourteenth-century music. Composer of secular songs, motets, and the first polyphonic setting of the Mass by a single composer.

Mahler, Gustav, 1860–1911, b. Kalisz: Bohemian composer noted chiefly for his broadly scaled symphonies and for songs with orchestral accompaniment. Conductor of the Metropolitan Opera and New York Philharmonic Society. His style has many facets, a grandiose manner recalling Beethoven and Wagner, a poignant lyricism (perhaps his most convincing vein) in the manner of the Viennese song composers, and a starkness, expressed in clashing dissonances and strange textures, foreshadowing expressionism. Both the lyricism and the expressionist tendencies are manifest in one of his last works, *The Song of the Earth,* a song cycle with orchestra.

Marenzio, Luca, 1553–1599, b. Coccaglio: Italian madrigalist, one of the finest composers in the genre. His works show the tendencies toward chromaticism that foreshadow baroque harmonic and expressive style.

Mason, Daniel Gregory, 1873–1953, b. Brookline: American composer, educator, and writer on music. Works include symphonies and chamber music.

Massenet, Jules, 1842–1912, b. Montaud: French composer of operas, the best known being *Manon* and *Hérodiade.* His music is characterized by an ingratiating melodic style. Professor at the Conservatoire.

Mendelssohn-Bartholdy, Felix, 1809–1847, b. Hamburg: German composer whose elegant style, crystal-clear structural layouts, easy manner, and exquisite melodies have made his music a concert favorite. Well-known works include the *Scotch* and *Italian* Symphonies (Nos. 3 and 4), the violin concerto, music for Shakespeare's *A Midsummer Night's Dream, Hebrides* Overture, *Songs Without Words* for piano. Mendelssohn was largely responsible for the revival of interest in Bach during the nineteenth century.

Menotti, Gian-Carlo, 1911– , b. Cadigliano: Highly successful composer of operas including *The Medium, The Telephone, The Old Maid and the Thief, Amahl and the Night Visitors, The Consul,* etc.

Meyerbeer, Giacomo, 1791–1864, b. Berlin: Opera composer born in Germany but noted as the founder of French grand opera in Paris in the 1830s. His works include *Robert the Devil, The Huguenots, The Prophet,* and *The African.*

Milhaud, Darius, 1892– , b. Aix-en-Provence: French composer, a member of the post-Debussy group known as *The Six.* A prolific writer in a wide variety of forms and idioms, from dissonant polytonality to traditional major-minor and modal harmony. His work is characterized by clarity of design and elegance of melodic manner. Works include much chamber music, theater music, operas *David, Medea, Christopher Columbus,* and orchestral music.

Monteverdi, Claudio, 1567–1643, b. Cremona: Italian composer; one of the first and among the greatest composers of the Baroque era. Established opera on a firm footing after the experiments of the Camerata. Pioneer and extremely successful exponent of the new use of dissonance for expressive purposes. Works include operas *Orfeo, The Return of Ulysses, The Coronation of Poppea,* many madrigals, and sacred works.

Moore, Douglas, 1893– , b. Cutchogue, N. Y.: American composer of operas, symphonic works, and chamber music. His works include the operas *White Wings, The Devil and Daniel Webster, The Ballad of Baby Doe.* Orchestral music includes *The Pageant of P. T. Barnum, Village Music, A Farm Journal.* Moore's style is clear and straightforward, with strong emphasis upon frank, appealing melody; idioms of traditional American songs and dances appear frequently in his music.

Morley, Thomas 1557–1602: Important Elizabethan composer of madrigals and keyboard music. Organist at St. Paul's Cathedral. Author of the first theoretical treatise on music published in England, *A Plaine and Easie Introduction to Practicall Musicke.*

Moussorgsky, Modest, 1839–1881, b. Pskov: One of the foremost representatives of the Russian nationalist movement. Rejecting Western techniques of building form, he used characteristic folk rhythms and melodies, combining them with a sense of brilliant color and dramatic effect. The opera *Boris Godunov* is his masterpiece. *Pictures at an Exhibition* for piano, later orchestrated by Ravel, is a piquant group of sketches. He had strong influence upon the impressionists.

Mozart, Wolfgang Amadeus, 1756–1791, b. Salzburg: One of the great triumvirate of the Viennese classic era (with Haydn and Beethoven). One of the most astonishing geniuses in the history of music. He represents the full flowering of the eighteenth century in music. He combined dramatic, popular, and learned styles, contributed to the broadening of classic structure, established the modern piano concerto, coordinated buffa and seria styles in opera, expanded the expressive role of harmony in all media. His style is based upon an Italianate, operatic melodic manner strengthened and expanded by a sure sense for counterpoint and harmonic action. Operas *Don Giovanni, The Magic Flute, The Marriage of Figaro, Così fan tutte,* etc., symphonies, concertos, chamber music, choral music, etc.

Offenbach, Jacques, 1819–1880, b. Cologne: Famous French composer of burlesque opera and *opéra comique. Tales of Hoffmann* is his masterpiece; also wrote *Orpheus in the Underworld, La Belle Hélène, The Grand Duchess of Gerolstein,* etc. His music is characterized by vivacious dance rhythms, captivating melodies, and a general effervescence of manner.

Okeghem, Jean d', c. 1430–1495, b. Flanders: Netherlandish composer, spanning the generation between Dufay and Deprès. Important in establishing imitative counterpoint as a basic technical feature of Renaissance music. Sacred style characterized by long, weaving melodic lines, retaining something of the mystic quality of medieval Gothic music. This is in contrast to the "rational," clearly organized treatment of short motives by Okeghem's pupil Deprès. Sacred and secular works, some instrumental music. Master of the Chapel Royal in France.

Paganini, Niccoló, 1782–1840, b. Genoa: Supposedly the greatest violin virtuoso in music history. The counterpart of Franz Liszt, with whom he is responsible for establishing the idea of the superhuman performer. His violin compositions, concertos, and studies make fantastic demands upon the technique of the performer.

Palestrina, Giovanni Pierluigi da, 1524–1594, b. Palestrina: The epitome of the Roman sacred school of polyphony. Palestrina's music has served as model for contrapuntal composition for more than three hundred years. Style characterized by smoothness of movement, gently rounded melodic contours, carefully used dissonances, richness and sweetness of sonority. Masses, motets, psalms, hymns, and other sacred music, some madrigals in a quasi-sacred style.

Pergolesi, Giovanni Battista, 1710–1736, b. Jesi: Italian composer chiefly famous for his opera buffa, *La Serva padrona,* which took Europe by storm in the mid-eighteenth century and which served as a model for succeeding composers in that genre. Also wrote chamber music, serious operas, choral music.

Peri, Jacopo, 1561–1633, b. Florence: A member of the Florentine Camerata and composer of the first opera (*Dafne*) set in the *stile rappresentativo.*

Perotinus (twelfth and thirteenth centuries): The later of the two important composers of the Notre Dame school (*see* Leoninus). Noted for the full realization of modal rhythmic procedure (in all voices) and for some organa in four parts.

Piston, Walter, 1894– , b. Rockland, Me.: American composer of orchestral and chamber music. Style combines contemporary scoring, rhythmic patterns, and harmonic devices with a classic clarity of structure and purpose. Piston has also written a number of books on music.

Poulenc, Francis, 1899–1963, b. Paris: French composer of the postimpressionist era. His music is attractive and witty.

Prokofiev, Sergei, 1891–1953, b. Sonzovka: Outstanding modern Russian composer, with works in many different media. Operas (*Love of Three Oranges* frequently performed), symphonies, concertos, chamber music, choral music, including *Alexander Nevsky,* a cantata, *Peter and the Wolf,* an immensely successful fairytale for narrator and orchestra. His style has much melodic appeal; his music addresses itself directly to the audience.

Puccini, Giacomo, 1858–1924, b. Lucca: Principal representative of the Italian verismo school of opera. *La Bohème, Tosca, Madame Butterfly* are standard items in the repertoires of most opera houses. Style distinguished by broad, somewhat sentimental melodies, rich orchestration, with a colorful harmonic support that has many unusual touches. Has influenced much present-day music, including semipopular and theater music.

Purcell, Henry, c. 1659–1695, b. London: The principal representative of English baroque music. His opera *Dido and Aeneas* is one of the masterpieces of dramatic composition. Chamber music, choral music, incidental music for the stage.

Rachmaninov, Sergei, 1873–1943, b. Onega: Russian composer and pianist. Concertos, symphonies, orchestral music, piano works, operas. His music continues the romantic tradition represented earlier by Tchaikovsky.

Rameau, Jean Philippe, 1683–1764, b. Dijon: Important French composer and theorist. Wrote operas in the tradition of Lully, extending harmonic and melodic scope, also orchestration. Author of epoch-making treatises on harmony, the foundation of harmonic theory to the present day.

Ravel, Maurice, 1875–1937, b. Ciboure: French composer. With Debussy, the principal representative of French impressionism. In addition, Ravel displays a neoclassic vein with emphasis upon well-developed melodic lines. Works include the orchestral works *Boléro, La Valse, Rapsodie espagnole, Daphnis et Chloé, Ma mère l'oye* Suite, the opera *L'Heure espagnole,* and many chamber, kéyboard, vocal works.

Rimsky-Korsakov, Nicholas, 1844–1908, b. Tichvin: Russian composer noted for his skill in orchestration and for his brilliant colorful style of composition. Works include the orchestral pieces *Scheherazade, Capriccio espagnol, Russian Easter* Overture, symphonies, operas, chamber music. He turned frequently to Oriental subjects and idioms for his material. Strong influence on the young Stravinsky. Professor at the St. Petersburg Conservatory.

Rossini, Gioacchino, 1792–1868, b. Pesaro: Italian opera composer, noted especially for *The Barber of Seville,* the last great work in the eighteenth-century opera-buffa tradition. Other operas include the grand opera *William Tell, Semiramide, Cinderella, Tancred,* etc. Overtures to Rossini's operas are popular concert items although most of the operas have rarely been performed recently.

Saint-Saëns, Charles Camille, 1835–1921, b. Paris: Eminent French composer, pianist, and conductor. His opera *Samson and Delilah,* symphonic poems *Danse macabre, The Spinning Wheel of Omphale,* and his concertos for violin, piano, and cello are frequently heard.

Scarlatti, Alessandro, 1660–1725, b. Palermo: One of the pioneers of the Neapolitan opera; important in the evolution of the da capo aria, the accompanied recitative, and the sinfonia preceding the opera. Composer of much chamber and choral music. Maestro of the royal chapel at Naples.

Scarlatti, Domenico, 1685–1757, b. Naples: Son of Alessandro Scarlatti. Important as a harpsichordist and composer. Wrote hundreds of pieces for his instrument, working out many innovations of figuration, sonority, and harmony, leading to the modern keyboard style. Preferred the galant manner, although he wrote a considerable amount of contrapuntal music.

Schönberg, Arnold, 1874–1951, b. Vienna: Leading figure of the twelve-tone school, which he established in the 1920s. Works show an evolution from Wagnerian and Brahmsian romanticism through expressionism, to a wide range of form and expression in the twelve-tone technique. Began his career in Vienna; in 1936 became professor of music at the University of California at Los Angeles. Works include *Pierrot lunaire,* a chamber work for voice and instruments, the sextet *Transfigured Night,* four string quartets, opera *Moses and Aaron,* many chamber and keyboard works.

Schubert, Franz, 1797–1828, b. Lichtenthal: Austrian composer; one of the leading figures of early romanticism. His lyric style was embodied in hundreds of exquisite songs and was also evident in his orchestral and chamber music. Regarded as the founder of the German *lied* style. Eight symphonies, of which the great C major ranks among the finest in symphonic literature; considerable chamber music, including *Death and the Maiden* string quartet, *Trout,* quintet, choral music.

Schumann, Robert, 1810–1856, b. Zwickau: Important German romantic composer, pianist, and writer on music. Best in smaller forms, songs and short piano pieces such as *Carnaval, Kreisleriana, Scenes from Childhood.* Four symphonies, concertos for piano, violin, cello, chamber music. Schumann's style contains a wealth of harmonic detail and innovation, interesting rhythmic imbalances within regular period structure. Editor and co-founder of *Neue Zeitschrift für Musik.*

Schütz, Heinrich, 1585–1672, b. Köstritz: German composer; the link between the earliest Italian baroque style of Giovanni Gabrieli and the late German baroque. Responsible for much of the systematization of procedures in German sacred music of the seventeenth century. Many sacred and secular works. Music director to the Elector of Saxony.

Scriabin, Alexander, 1872–1915, b. Moscow: Russian composer notable for his efforts to create a new chordal basis for harmony, constructing chords by fourths instead of thirds. This procedure is exemplified in his symphonic poem *Prometheus.* He also tried to coordinate color and sound in performance, prescribing colors to be projected on a screen while music was being performed. In general, his works have a late romantic flavor, his keyboard music showing the influence of Chopin.

Sessions, Roger, 1896– , b. Brooklyn: Influential American composer, linked stylistically to advanced trends. His manner is serious and introspective. Symphonies, operas, chamber music.

Shostakovitch, Dmitri, 1906– , b. St. Petersburg: Russian composer, one of the leading symphonic composers of the present day. Uses traditional forms and manners of expression with freshness and imagination. Symphonies, operas, chamber music.

Sibelius, Jean, 1865–1957, b. Tavastehus: Finnish composer; one of the leading symphonic composers of the early modern period. Rather conservative and traditional in his procedures; works are conceived on a grand scale and in serious vein. Principal works are for orchestra, including seven symphonies, many tone poems, and smaller works. Some chamber and vocal music.

Smetana, Friedrich, 1824–1884, b. Leitomischl: Important as a figure in the Bohemian national school. His opera *The Bartered Bride* is his most notable work. He is known also for the set of six orchestral pieces entitled *My Country,* of which *The Moldau* (descriptive of the river Moldau) is familiar to concert audiences everywhere. Smetana's music has a strong flavor of Slavonic song and dance.

Stamitz, Johann, 1717–1757, b. Deutsch-Brod: Bohemian composer who became the leader of the Mannheim orchestra and in this position exerted a profound influence upon the growth of the modern orchestral style.

Strauss, Johann, Jr., 1825–1899, b. Vienna: The Waltz King. Strauss epitomizes the musical spirit of nineteenth-century Vienna with his incomparable waltz melodies, the brilliant scoring of his music, and his rhythmic élan. Among his world-famous waltzes are *The Beautiful Blue Danube, Tales from the Vienna Woods, Roses from the South, The Artist's Life, Wine, Women, and Song,* and many others. His operetta *Die Fledermaus* is a masterpiece of its kind.

Strauss, Richard, 1864–1949, b. Munich: German composer of the late romantic and early modern period, noted first for his tone poems, including *Don Juan, Till Eulenspiegel, Death and Transfiguration;* later for his operas, including *Elektra, Salome, Der Rosenkavalier.* Also wrote many songs, some chamber music. Strauss followed the path laid out by Wagner and Liszt, adding melodic and harmonic elements distinctly Italian in flavor.

Stravinsky, Igor, 1882– , b. Oranienbaum: Russian composer; one of the most important figures of the contemporary era. Early works in folkloric style, such as the ballets *Petrouchka, The Firebird, The Rite of Spring,* the cantata *The Wedding;* later works in neoclassic vein, such as the Symphony of Psalms, Octet, opera *The Rake's Progress.* Works in many media. Stravinsky's rhythmic and textural innovations represent a major contribution to twentieth-century musical techniques.

Sullivan, Sir Arthur, 1842–1900, b. London: The musical half of the English team, Gilbert and Sullivan, which produced the comic operas *Trial by Jury, Iolanthe, The Mikado, The Yeomen of the Guard, H.M.S. Pinafore,* etc. Notable for their fine melodies and delightful patter songs.

Tchaikovsky, Pëtr Ilich, 1840–1893, b. Kamsko-Votinsk: Russian composer whose works are among the most popular and frequently performed in all concert literature. Although his works are a little loose in structure, the brilliance of his orchestration, the excellence of his melodies, his sureness of effect, and his vivid imagination have made his music a favorite everywhere. He is unexcelled as a composer for ballet, e.g., *Sleeping Beauty, Swan Lake, Nutcracker.* Of six symphonies, the last three are well known, also his concertos for violin and for piano, the opera *Pique Dame,* the overture-fantasy *Romeo and Juliet.*

Thompson, Randall, 1899– , b. New York: American composer of choral, symphonic, and chamber music. Professor of music and chairman of the department at Harvard University.

Thomson, Virgil, 1896– , b. Kansas City: American composer and former music critic of the *New York Herald Tribune.* Noted for his opera *Four Saints in Three Acts* (texts by Gertrude Stein). Music for motion pictures (*Plow That Broke the Plains,* etc.). Thomson's style has a strong flavor of traditional American songs and dances.

Varèse, Edgard, 1885–1965, b. Paris: Composer noted for his successful exploration of nontraditional musical techniques, especially in the realm of sonority. His most familiar work is *Ionization* for thirty-five different instruments, mainly percussion.

Vaughan Williams, Ralph, 1872–1958, b. Gloucestershire: One of the most distinguished modern English composers. Symphonies, operas, chamber music, choral music. Strong interest in English folk song, the style of which appears frequently in his music.

Verdi, Giuseppe, 1813–1901, b. Le Roncole: The master of nineteenth-century Italian opera; continued and developed the tradition of eighteen-century opera. The dramatic power, the stageworthiness, the keen psychological insight, the well-delineated melody, and the effective scoring of Verdi's operas mark him as supreme in the genre. His last works, *Otello* and *Falstaff,* show a modification of the set number plan toward a more continuous flow of music and action. *La Traviata, Il Trovatore, Rigoletto,* and *Aida* are probably his most popular works.

Villa-Lobos, Heitor, 1881–1959, b. Rio de Janeiro: Prolific Brazilian composer. Over 1300 works. Strong element of Brazilian folk music in his style.

Vivaldi, Antonio, c. 1675–1741, b. Venice: Important late baroque composer, notable for his brilliant concertos, of which there are hundreds extant. His works served as models for the concertos of Johann Sebastian Bach. (Bach transcribed a number of Vivaldi's concertos.)

Wagner, Richard, 1813–1883, b. Leipzig: Tremendously influential and important German composer; creator of the music drama, an operatic form different in many respects from the other opera types of Wagner's era. Wagner established stylistic trends in harmony, scoring, and expressive content that have had their repercussions to the present day. Works include *Lohengrin, Tannhäuser, The Flying Dutchman, Tristan und Isolde,* the *Ring* Cycle, *Parsifal, The Mastersingers of Nurenberg.* Wrote his own librettos; evolved his own theories of art. Subject of countless books, studies, articles.

Walton, William, 1902– , b. Oldham: English composer of opera (*Troilus and Cressida*), symphonic works (*Portsmouth Point* Overture), choral works (*Belshazzar's Feast*).

Weber, Karl Maria von, 1786–1826, b. Oldenburg: Early romantic German composer; wrote the first German opera, *Der Freischütz,* distinguished by folk elements such as pastoral locale, German folk music, traditional story. Other works include operas (*Oberon, Euryanthe*), concertos, chamber music, *Invitation to the Dance.* Weber's style is brilliant, facile, with a boldness and dramatic impact suggestive of Beethoven's music.

Webern, Anton von, 1883–1945, b. Vienna: The most advanced of the three Viennese tone-row masters (*see* Berg, Schönberg). Webern wrote in a highly condensed, cryptic style, with sparing use of sonority resources. Orchestral, vocal, chamber music. Webern's manner has found many adherents among younger tone-row composers.

Weelkes, Thomas, d. 1623: English madrigal composer, one of the most accomplished in the genre.

Wolf, Hugo, 1860–1903, b. Windischgräz: Austrian composer, noted chiefly for his superb songs, many of which were set to the poems of Edward Mörike.

Recommended Readings

Abraham, Gerald, *A Hundred Years of Music,* Gerald Duckworth & Co., London, 1949.

A survey of romantic and early modern music. Many valuable observations on style and aesthetics.

Apel, Willi, *Harvard Dictionary of Music,* Harvard University Press, Cambridge, Mass., 1944.

Compact one-volume dictionary giving information on musical terms and music history. Good bibliographies. No biographical material.

Bekker, Paul, *The Story of the Orchestra,* W. W. Norton & Company, Inc., New York, 1936.

The history of the modern orchestra from the eighteenth century to the twentieth.

Bukofzer, Manfred, *Music in the Baroque Era,* W. W. Norton & Company, Inc., New York, 1947.

An excellent history of music from 1600 to 1750. Styles, forms, aesthetics, and sociology are linked together in an informative and interesting manner.

Chase, Gilbert, *America's Music,* McGraw-Hill Book Company, New York, 1955.

A comprehensive study of American music to the present day. A valuable reference.

Einstein, Alfred, *Mozart, His Character, His Work,* W. W. Norton & Company, Inc., New York, 1945.

Although a biography, the best work in the English language dealing with eighteenth-century classic music. The eighteenth-century scene is set forth in rather full detail.

Einstein, Alfred, *Music in the Romantic Era,* W. W. Norton & Company, Inc., New York, 1947.

Survey of the principal trends and concepts of nineteenth-century music. Much speculation on style and aesthetics.

Forsyth, Cecil, *Orchestration,* The Macmillan Company, New York, 1936 (rev. ed.).

A comprehensive study of orchestral instruments, both past and present. Valuable reference.

Grout, Donald, *A History of Western Music,* W. W. Norton & Company, Inc., New York, 1960.

A comprehensive history of Western music in one volume. Well documented.

Grove's Dictionary of Music and Musicians, St. Martin's Press, Inc., New York, 1955.

The most comprehensive dictionary of music in the English language. Extended treatment of most topics, both technical and biographical.

Hansen, Peter, *An Introduction to Twentieth Century Music,* Allyn and Bacon, Inc., Boston, 1961.

A compact, well-organized survey of the principal style trends of the modern era.

Lang, Paul Henry, *Music in Western Civilization,* W. W. Norton & Company, Inc., New York, 1941.

A monumental work, encompassing the relation of music to art, philosophy, literature, religion, and politics from Greek times to the end of the nineteenth century. Well written, full of challenging ideas.

Ratner, Leonard G., *Harmony: Structure and Style,* McGraw-Hill Book Company, New York, 1962.

A companion book to *Music: The Listener's Art,* explaining music theory on the basis of the criteria of sound, movement, and arrival; the relation of these criteria to harmonic progression, structure, and style.

Reese, Gustave, *Music in the Middle Ages,* 1940, and *Music in the Renaissance,* 1954, W. W. Norton & Company, Inc., New York.

Two comprehensive studies of music covering the period from Greek music to 1600. A great deal of specific information. Recommended for students engaged in research in these periods.

Slonimsky, Nicolas (ed.), *Baker's Biographical Dictionary of Musicians,* 5th ed. G. Schirmer, Inc., New York, 1958.

Compact one-volume dictionary providing biographical material. Complement to the Apel dictionary. Good bibliographical references.

Thompson, Oscar (ed.), *International Cyclopedia of Music and Musicians,* 9th ed., ed. Robert Sabin, Dodd, Mead & Company, Inc., New York, 1964.

Good popular reference with a number of extensive articles.

Tovey, Donald Francis, *Essays in Musical Analysis,* Oxford University Press, London, 1935–1939; and musical articles from the *Encyclopaedia Britannica,* Oxford University Press, London, 1944.

Beautifully written articles on specific compositions and musical topics, containing many original and fresh insights on musical style and form. Tovey was one of the soundest musical analysts of our century.

Composers on music

Hindemith, Paul, *A Composer's World,* Harvard University Press, Cambridge, Mass., 1952.

Schönberg, Arnold, *Style and Idea,* Philosophical Library, New York, 1950.

Sessions, Roger, *The Musical Experience of Composer, Performer, and Listener,* Princeton University Press, Princeton, N.J., 1950.

Stravinsky, Igor, *Poetics of Music,* Harvard University Press, Cambridge, Mass., 1947.

Biographies (arranged chronologically by composer)

Schrade, Leo, *Monteverdi, Creator of Modern Music,* W. W. Norton & Company, Inc., New York, 1950.

Westrup, J. A., *Purcell,* J. M. Dent & Sons, Ltd., London, 1938.

David, H. T., and A. J. Mendel, *The Bach Reader,* W. W. Norton & Company, Inc., New York, 1945.

Spitta, P., *Johann Sebastian Bach,* Novello, London, 1899 (the monumental work on Bach).

Flower, Newman, *George Frideric Handel,* Charles Scribner's Sons, New York, 1948.

Kirkpatrick, Ralph. *Domenico Scarlatti,* Princeton University Press, Princeton, N.J., 1953.

Einstein, Alfred, *Gluck,* E. P. Dutton & Co., Inc., New York, 1936.

Geiringer, Karl, *Haydn, a Creative Life in Music,* W. W. Norton & Company, Inc., New York, 1946.

Einstein, Alfred, *Mozart, His Character, His Work,* W. W. Norton & Company, Inc., New York, 1945.

Thayer, Alexander, *Beethoven,* The Beethoven Association, New York, 1921 (a monumental work on Beethoven's life).

Burk, John, *The Life and Work of Beethoven,* Random House, Inc., New York, 1943.

Tovey, Donald F., *Beethoven,* Oxford University Press, London, 1945.

Brown, Maurice J. E., *Schubert: a Critical Biography,* St. Martin's Press, Inc., New York, 1958.

Barzun, Jacques, *Berlioz and the Romantic Century,* Little, Brown & Company, Boston, 1950.

Weinstock, Herbert, *Chopin, the Man and His Music,* Alfred A. Knopf, Inc., New York, 1949.

Chissell, Joan, *Schumann,* J. M. Dent & Sons, Ltd., London, 1948.

Newman, Ernest, *The Man Liszt,* Charles Scribner's Sons, New York, 1935.

Newman, Ernest, *Wagner as a Man and Artist,* Alfred A. Knopf, Inc., New York, 1924.

Toye, F., *Giuseppe Verdi: His Life and Works,* William Heinemann, Ltd., London, 1931.

Geiringer, Karl, *Brahms, His Life and Work,* Houghton Mifflin Company, Boston, 1936.

Calvocoressi, M. D., *Musorgsky,* J. M. Dent & Sons, Ltd., London, 1946.

Vallas, L., *Claude Debussy: His Life and Works,* Oxford University Press, London, 1933.

Demuth, N., *Ravel,* J. M. Dent & Sons, Ltd., London, 1947.

Stevens, H., *The Life and Music of Béla Bartók,* Oxford University Press, New York, 1953.

Vlad, Roman, *Stravinsky,* Oxford University Press, London, 1960.

Index

EVOLUTION OF VOCAL MUSIC

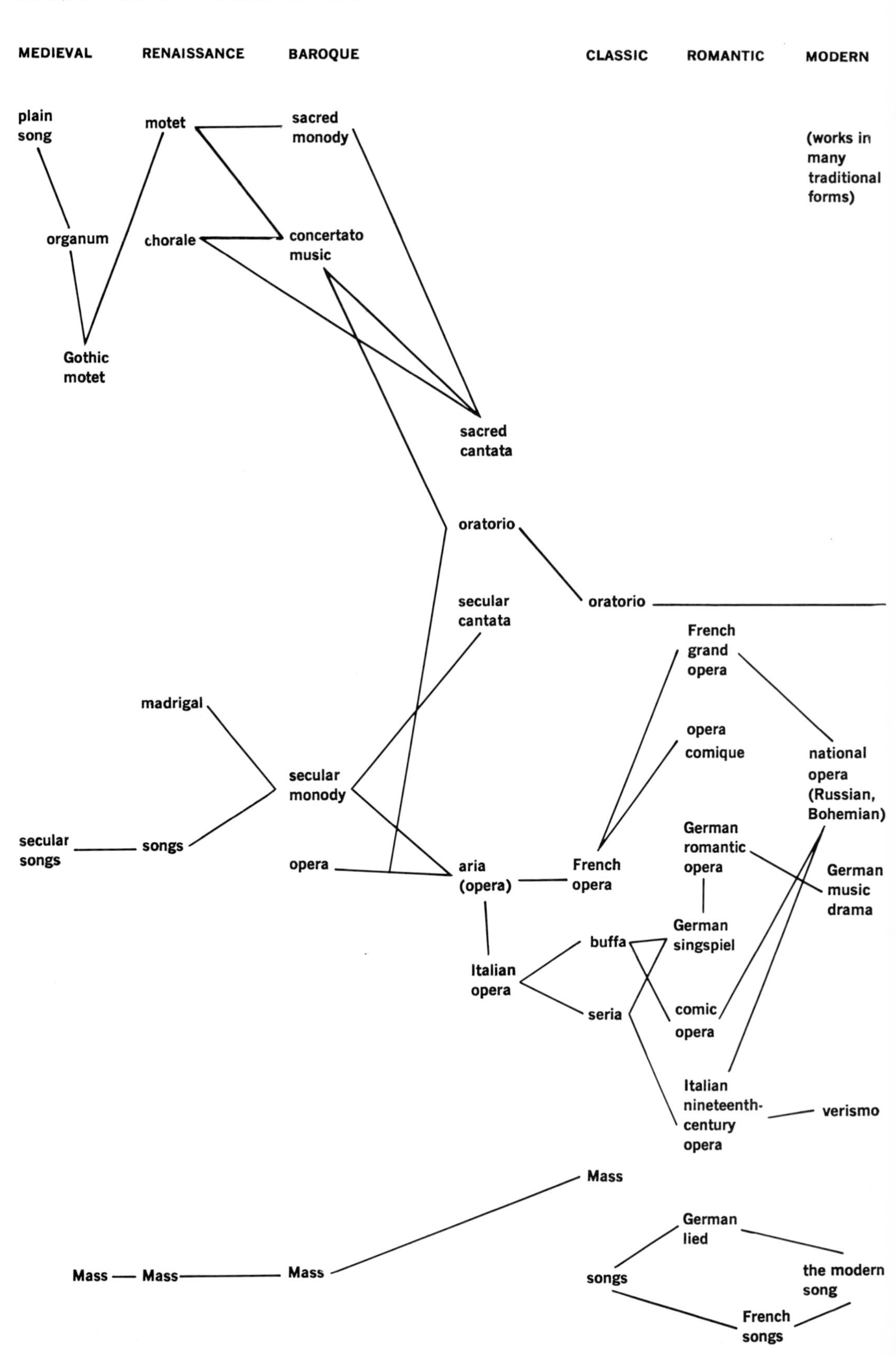